# The Name High Over All

**A Commentary on Hebrews**

Richard Brooks

**EP BOOKS**
1st Floor Venture House, 6 Silver Court, Watchmead,
Welwyn Garden City, UK, AL7 1TS

web: www.epbooks.org

e-mail: sales@epbooks.org

EP Books are distributed in the USA by:
JPL Distribution
3741 Linden Avenue Southeast
Grand Rapids, MI 49548
E-mail: orders@jpldistribution.com
Tel: 877.683.6935

**British Library Cataloguing in Publication Data available**

ISBN: 978-1-78397-161-9

# Contents

# Introduction

Who wrote Hebrews? We are not told. *When was it written?* It is not stated. *Where was it written from?* We do not know. *Who was it written to?* It does not say. Not a very encouraging start, you may feel, for a commentary from which you are hoping to find some help in understanding this portion of New Testament Scripture. So we had better revisit these questions and seek to say a little more.

Before we do that, however, there is a further question—one which is actually the most important question of all. So this is the one which should really be asked first. And this time the answer is immediately to hand. *What is Hebrews all about?* Or, to rephrase the question straightaway, *Who is Hebrews all about?* Of this, there is no doubt whatsoever.

## Who is Hebrews all about?

Hebrews is chiefly, pre-eminently, gloriously about the Lord Jesus

Christ. This is made clear right from the off, in the magnificent opening verses.

> Long ago, at many times and in many ways, God spoke to our fathers by the prophets, but in these last days he has spoken to us by his Son, whom he appointed the heir of all things, through whom also he created the world. He is the radiance of the glory of God and the exact imprint of his nature, and he upholds the universe by the word of his power. After making purification for sins, he sat down at the right hand of the Majesty on high, having become as much superior to angels as the name he has inherited is more excellent than theirs (1:1–4).

His, and his alone, is the name high over all. The entire book (as is the case for the entire Bible) is concerned to set forth the Second Person of the Godhead, in the fullness of his glory and majesty, his grace and his tenderness. In the course of the first chapter, Jesus is stated unequivocally as divine (for example, 'Your throne, O God, is forever and ever', 1:8, quoting Psalm 45:6). Equally, as Hebrews unfolds, there are many verses which declare his humanity (for example, 'Since therefore the children share in flesh and blood, he himself likewise partook of the same things', 2:14). So there is a clear focus upon both Jesus' deity and his humanity, the great mystery of his two complete, perfect and distinct natures in his one person.

In Hebrews as a whole, many names and titles are ascribed to the Lord Jesus. He is 'a merciful and faithful high priest in the service of God' (2:17), 'the apostle and high priest of our confession' (3:1), 'faithful over God's house as a son' (3:6), 'Jesus, the Son of God' (4:14), 'a priest forever, after the order of Melchizedek' (5:6, quoting Psalm 110:4), 'a forerunner on our behalf' (6:20), 'the guarantor of a better covenant' (7:22), 'a minister in the holy places' (8:2), 'a high priest of the good things that have come' (9:11), 'the mediator of a new covenant' (9:15), 'the founder and perfecter of our faith' (12:2), 'Jesus Christ … the same yesterday, today and forever' (13:8), 'the great shepherd of the sheep' (13:20), and (while, as we shall see in commenting upon the verse, the reference here in context may more likely be to God the Father, yet the truth expressed is absolutely true of God the Son) 'to whom be glory forever, and ever. Amen' (13:21). What a marvellous array!

The whole of Hebrews, from its beginning (1:1) through to its end (13:25), is taken up with him. And this great and fundamental truth sheds light for us upon the other questions which we raised at the beginning. Let us return to them now, though in a different order, and adding another one as we go.

## To whom was Hebrews written?

The overwhelming sense given all the way through is that it was written to what we might call Jewish Christians—that is, those who had been converted to Christ from a background of Judaism, those who had been savingly united to the Lord Jesus by grace through faith and had thereby become Christians. This seems most likely. The title by which we tend to refer to the book—The Letter to the Hebrews— is not taken from the book itself, though it is attested as far back as early in the third century. It is certainly an appropriate shorthand title, as becomes clear from a reading of the book as a whole.

As for where they were located at the time of writing, we lack the necessary information. The mention of Italy in 13:24 does not require them to be resident there (any more than it requires the author to be there either, on which see below). Jerusalem has been suggested, largely on the basis of the mentions of all that went on in the temple. That is not conclusive, but is more likely than somewhere in Italy.

They are obviously very familiar with the Old Testament, as the many citations from that part of Scripture testify. In order of appearance, they come from Psalm 2:7, 2 Samuel 7:14, Deuteronomy 32:43, Psalm 104:4, Psalm 45:6–7, Psalm 102:25–27, Psalm 110:1, Psalm 8:4–6, Psalm 22:22, Isaiah 8:18, Psalm 95:7–11, Genesis 2:2, Exodus 25:40, Jeremiah 31:31–34, Psalm 40:6–8, Deuteronomy 32:36, Habakkuk 2:3–4, Genesis 21:12, Proverbs 3:11–12, Exodus 19:12–13, Haggai 2:6, Joshua 1:5, and Psalm 118:6. In addition, the whole argument and illustrations of chapter 11 require the readers' familiarity with these Scriptures. They have clearly been steeped in them.

## Why was Hebrews written?

It is an examination of this question which inclines us to the position
just stated that it was first addressed to Christian converts from
Judaism. The clue is found in the various danger signs visible to
the writer of Hebrews. The main cause for concern is that the
recipients seemed to be wearying of Jesus and the gospel, and were
casting longing eyes back to the Judaism from which they had come.
To be more precise, they looked to be ready (had some of them
done so already?) to abandon the once-for-all sufficient sacrifice
of the Lord Jesus Christ on the cross for sin and for sinners—the
salvation provided by God himself—and to return to the priests,
altars, sacrifices, offerings and ceremonies of Old Testament days.
Nothing could spell greater folly for them than that. Why, having
been brought out of the shadows and into the sunlight, think of
returning to the shadows again? When the Lord Jesus has done
everything that possibly needs to be done to reconcile sinners to the
offended holy God, what can be the sense in reverting to the things of
former times which were all pointing towards him and have now been
fulfilled in him?

Our writer is very much a pastor. We shall have cause to observe
this at various points in the commentary, especially when he speaks
to them as 'we', including himself, rather than exclusively as 'you'.
There is much of the 'you' here (as there needs to be in preaching, for
the preacher is the mouthpiece of God, declaring God's word in the
clearest possible terms). But there is also plenty of the 'we' and 'us'
here (as there needs to be, for the preacher is a pastor, a shepherd of
souls, who desires the Lord's very best for the flock, and is aware of his
own neediness in the process).

However stridently he has to address those to whom he writes
(as, for example, in 2:3, 'how shall we escape if we neglect such a
great salvation?'; 3:12, 'Take care, brothers, lest there be in any of you
an evil, unbelieving heart, leading you to fall away from the living
God'; and compare also 4:11, 13), he still holds out good hope for
them, that they will stand firm in the gospel and stay close to Jesus

(as, for example, in 6:9, 'Though we speak in this way, yet in your case, beloved, we feel sure of better things—things that belong to salvation'; 10:39, 'But we are not of those who shrink back and are destroyed, but of those who have faith and preserve their souls'; and compare also 12:1–2, 13:1 and 13:20–25).

No one is mentioned by name from among the recipients, but the writer seems well acquainted with them, and they with him. He calls them 'brothers' and 'beloved', and, at the end (13:24) sends his greetings to them all—'Greet all your leaders and all the saints'. Both they and he know, mutually, 'our brother Timothy' (13:23), and our writer expresses there the hope of visiting them, along with Timothy ('with whom I shall see you if he comes soon').

Putting this all together, it becomes clear that the great purpose of the writer in penning Hebrews is to magnify the Lord Jesus Christ in one aspect after another of his person and work, and in doing this to warn the readers of the dangers of wandering away from Jesus and the gospel, lest they end up committing apostasy and are lost after all. The classic sections 6:4–6 and 10:26–29 are absolutely key in this regard. He sets out to shake them to their very roots, in order to get them to examine exactly where they stand with the Saviour—are they his or are they not? As already observed, he does not lose good hope that they do belong to Jesus; and he takes every opportunity to encourage them—indeed, to exhort and beseech them—to persevere to the end and not drop out along the way between here and heaven.

## Who wrote Hebrews?

We have to admit that in terms of what we are actually told in the book, we simply do not know. Unlike some other New Testament books, it does not begin, 'Paul, an apostle of Christ Jesus by the will of God', 'James, a servant of God and of the Lord Jesus Christ', or 'Peter, an apostle of Jesus Christ'. In this sense, Hebrews is completely anonymous. My own position, in writing this commentary, is that it should remain so. Quite simply, if we had needed to know who it was (humanly speaking) who wrote it, we would have been told. That we have not been told, argues that we do not need to know. Nothing whatsoever hangs upon it for our understanding or appreciation of the book. What we do know, most certainly, is that whatever human hand did the writing, Hebrews (like all of Scripture) comes from God. It is 'breathed out by God and profitable' (2 Timothy 3:16); 'men spoke from God as they were carried along by the Holy Spirit' (2 Peter 1:21).

The traditional position on the authorship of Hebrews has been to ascribe it to the apostle Paul. Of course, that might be so, and there are reasonable grounds for it. There are also reasonable grounds against it. It is quite wrong, however, that Paul being the author becomes a virtual matter of orthodoxy, when it can be nothing of the kind. Other candidates who have been put forward by their various supporters have included Barnabas, Luke, Apollos, Clement and others, but it is all speculation. There is merit in the view that it was written by an apostle, because of it being accepted as Scripture by the church from its earliest days. If so, we cannot affirm with certainty which apostle. The whole question is taken up in detail in various commentaries.

For ourselves, in this commentary, we proceed upon the basis that we are not given the identity of the human author, so do not know who he is. We are just thankful to God for letting us have Hebrews in our Bibles, and would hate the very thought of being without it, so precious is it to us. Consequently, when we refer to the author we shall call him 'our writer', 'the author', or some such address. How can we call him by his name when we do not know what it is?

## Where was Hebrews written from?

Once again, we do not know because we are not informed. Because of 13:24 ('Those who come from Italy send you greetings'), it is held by some that Italy (Rome?) is where it originated. That is not the necessary inference of that statement, however.

## When was Hebrews written?

This, too, has to be a matter of some conjecture. A date before AD 95 is required, in that Clement of Rome made use of it in a letter he wrote to the Corinthians in AD 95/96. Working back, a date before AD 70 is also very likely. That was the year of the fall of Jerusalem and the destruction of the temple. No mention is made anywhere in Hebrews of these events having already happened. Rather, the impression can be gleaned from some parts of the letter that the temple sacrifices are still in operation. A date in the mid-to-late AD 60s is most likely.

## Approaching the commentary

Following this brief 'getting our bearings' introduction, there follows a synopsis of Hebrews, and then the commentary itself. No quotations are given from other writers on this portion of the New Testament, though I am, of course, indebted to many of them. It is always appropriate to remember the words of the apostle Paul, 'What do you have that you did not receive? If then you received it, why do you boast as if you did not receive it?' (1 Corinthians 4:7). The two fullest and most legendary commentaries on Hebrews are those by William Gouge and John Owen. John Calvin and John Brown have also written on the letter, as have Albert Barnes and Adolph Saphir. Among more recent offerings on Hebrews, the commentary of Philip Edgcumbe Hughes is of particular help. Also worthy of note is that of Peter T O'Brien, as well as the briefer work by Stuart Olyott. A W Pink must be mentioned for his substantial and very profitable exposition. Many others have written and preached on Hebrews, and their lack of mention here must not be taken in any wrong way.

It will soon be discovered that one of the features of the present commentary is that, more often than not, verses of Scripture are quoted in their own words, rather than by a reference. The purpose of this is not to extend the size of this volume, but for a very practical reason. Too often (I know myself all too well in this) lists of Bible references tend to get skipped, however important they may be to whatever is under discussion. Hopefully the manner adopted here will largely avoid this. The Bible version used for the commentary is the English Standard Version (ESV).

So it is time to set off together on a journey of discovery, the Holy Spirit of God being our teacher (John 16:13–15). Here awaiting us in Hebrews are 'the unsearchable riches of Christ' (Ephesians 3:8). Here set before us in richness and fullness is God's 'inexpressible gift' (2 Corinthians 9:15). Here to our delight is the one who 'is altogether desirable' (Song of Songs 5:16).

# Synopsis

Brotherly love (13:1)
Hospitality to strangers (13:2)
Compassion for the needy (13:3)
Marriage (13:4)
Contentment (13:5–6)
Imitation (13:7)
The unchanging Jesus (13:8)
Steadfastness (13:9)
Bearing reproach for Jesus (13:10–13)
Heavenly mindedness (13:14)
Praise (13:15)
Generosity (13:16)
Submission (13:17)
Prayerfulness (13:18–19)
The closing benediction (13:20–21)
Parting words and greetings (13:22–25)

# Chapter 1
# Jesus, prophets and angels

Without prologue of any sort (not even mention of his own name) the writer to the Hebrews sets straight off, pitches straight in, with full vigour and enthusiasm. There is no holding him back for a single moment from what he has to set forth concerning the Lord Jesus Christ. He is like the author of Psalm 45, who wrote in his opening verse: 'My heart overflows with a pleasing theme; I address my verses to the king; my tongue is like the pen of a ready scribe'. Our writer is so exercised lest any of his readers should follow through the tendency he observes in them to desert Jesus that he is determined to spare no effort and to leave no stone unturned in keeping them holding fast to the Saviour. He alone it is who has the highest claim upon them, for he is exalted above all. Throughout the epistle he meets them on their own ground, as it were, beginning here in chapter 1 with the prophets and the angels.

## Jesus and the prophets (1:1–2)

Our God is the God who speaks. He is the communicating God. The idols of the nations 'have mouths, but do not speak' (Psalm 115:5), while the true and living God, Jehovah, makes his voice heard. He is also the God of variety in the ways he does this. He *spoke to our fathers by the prophets'* and *'he has spoken to us by his Son'*. He has done this *'Long ago'* and he has done this *'in these last days'*. He has done this, moreover, *'at many times and in many ways'*.

Let us begin by unravelling this full and involved statement. *'God spoke to our fathers'* (all the generations which preceded us, but with a particular reference here to the people who lived throughout the Old Testament period). He did this *'by the prophets'*. They were all his mouthpieces, speaking what he gave them to utter, rather than giving expression to what they thought God might say or what their own ideas and opinions were. There is a reminder here of the great truth that 'All Scripture is breathed out by God' (2 Timothy 3:16). The encompassing word *'prophets'* covers in one sweep the so-called major ones, such as Isaiah and Jeremiah, and the so-called minor ones like Amos and Zephaniah; the well-known ones, such as Ezekiel and Daniel, and the lesser-known ones, including Nathan and Micaiah; the earlier ones, like Samuel and Elijah, and the later ones, such as Nahum and Zechariah.

Through these many prophets, God had so much to say. This was both *'at many times'*, or 'in many parts'—not all at once but spanning the whole of history up to and including Malachi (after whom the voice of prophecy was silent for some four hundred years until the appearance of John), and *'in many ways'* (by word of mouth, through angels, in dreams and visions, by miracles—in prediction, poetry, prose, proverb, figure, symbol, discourse, warning, exhortation, commandment and promise). He manifested his own character as the eternal, exalted, holy and merciful God; his righteous will and commandments, expressed most comprehensively and for all time in what we call the moral law (the ten commandments); and his gracious purposes for the salvation of sinners, by way of the countless messianic prophecies.

These latter are particularly rich and glorious, and deserve special notice in the context of this letter to the Hebrews, which is so centrally taken up with the Lord Jesus Christ. Jesus is, for example, 'a star (that) shall come out of Jacob, and a sceptre (that) shall rise out of Israel' (Numbers 24:17); he is the one whose 'name shall be called Wonderful Counsellor, Mighty God, Everlasting Father, Prince of Peace' (Isaiah 9:6), who 'was wounded for our transgressions' and 'crushed for our iniquities' (Isaiah 53:5); he is 'a righteous Branch' who 'shall reign as king and deal wisely, and shall execute justice and righteousness in the land' (Jeremiah 23:5); he it is who 'shall stand and shepherd his flock in the strength of the LORD, in the majesty of the name of his God' (Micah 5:4); he is 'the sun of righteousness (who) shall rise with healing in its wings' (Malachi 4:2).

Those to whom Hebrews was originally written were people who knew their Old Testaments. Indeed, so fond were they of those Scriptures that they were in danger of drifting away from the position they had been brought to in Christ through grace and returning from light to shadow. Yet these very Old Testament books are full of the Lord Jesus Christ himself—pointing to him, speaking of him, delighting in him, longing for him. He himself says so: 'it is they that bear witness about me' (John 5:39). All that God had spoken *'to our fathers by the prophets'* had, again and again, revolved around the Lord Jesus Christ. There is no getting away from Jesus in the Old Testament, and neither should they (or we) want there to be! So it is fundamental to our writer's approach in Hebrews.

Yet things were never intended to be complete with the Old Testament. For after speaking there *'at many times and in many ways'*, what has God now done? What was it all leading up to? What was it all in preparation for? The answer is crystal clear: *'but in these last days he has spoken to us by his Son'*. In each case it is God who has spoken, but there is the most significant of distinctions. We may bring this out more clearly by rendering God's 'speakings' as follows: 'God having spoken ... spoke'. There is both discontinuity and continuity.

The prophets were the prophets. Jesus is the Son. That could not be said about any of them. They were many. He is the one and only. Through him, the Father has *'spoken to us'*—the *'us'* covering both the Hebrews to whom this letter was written in the first place (along with all those of the New Testament age) and, down the centuries, we who are reading it now. All mankind, in every generation, is *'spoken to'* by God, and all are responsible for what they do with what they hear.

The *'last days'* is a regular biblical way of describing the whole period between the first and second comings of Jesus—his incarnation (which has happened) and his return (for which we still wait). Here in 1:2, as well as this broader reference, it has a tighter aspect to it of the days in which the writer and those to whom he wrote lived. The point he is making, right from his opening words here, is that now the Son himself has come—announced by angels, greeted and worshipped by shepherds and wise men, heralded by John. He has lived, died, been buried, risen again, ascended to heaven, and reigns in majesty.

The prophets had the grand privilege, as well as the solemn responsibility, of testifying to him before he came. In them, however, revelation was fragmentary and unfinished, while in Jesus it is perfect and complete. They declared the message; Jesus is the message. Now he has come. There is a very great difference between the will of God being revealed to and through the prophets, and that will being revealed in and through God's own incarnate Son—between God speaking though men, and God speaking through the God-Man. Jesus is, by definition, therefore, superior to the prophets. While they spoke of him, they were always subject to him: 'For the testimony of Jesus is the spirit of prophecy' (Revelation 19:10).

If God's people of old listened to the prophets, how much more should they (and we) listen to God's Son, 'for he was teaching them as one who had authority' (Matthew 7:29). Not to do so incurs special guilt. All that God has spoken to us by his Son should have the highest claim upon our attention in view of the exaltedness of this messenger. Yet how few paid attention to him during his lifetime, and (sad to say) how few do so today. Do you make priority and take trouble to read all that God has spoken? Do you listen carefully and follow obediently all that is preached to you from God's Word? And do you relish most of all from the Scriptures all that you read and hear concerning 'Christ Jesus (who) came into the world to save sinners' (1 Timothy 1:15), of whom we all are chief?

So, completely seamlessly, the writer moves from prophets to angels, yet without actually leaving the prophets behind. That is why these first four verses of Hebrews 1 are so intricately woven together.

## Jesus and the angels (1:2–14)

Everything spoken by God through his prophets (and, in particular, everything that he spoke through them of his Son, the Lord Jesus Christ) was a preparation, then, for his final and ultimate revelation actually in and through the Son himself. In order to demonstrate the panoramic sweep of this astounding revelation, we are treated to a mind-blowing and mouth-watering sequence of no less than seven glorious statements concerning the Lord Jesus Christ, followed immediately by seven glorious prophecies concerning him. The fact that there are seven of each is significant, for in the Bible seven is the number of perfection and completeness. The theme of this entire epistle—the pre-eminence of Christ—is immediately plunged into as a great sea.

### Seven glorious statements

These appear one after the other in verses 2 and 3. While these statements undoubtedly reinforce Jesus' superiority over the prophets, it is his superiority over the angels which quickly becomes the chief focus, not only throughout this first chapter, but all the way to the end of the second as well. Let us relish them closely, one by one. They follow their own natural order.

(1) *'whom he appointed heir of all things'*. As a result of him being *'his Son'* (his only Son, whom he loves) the Father has appointed Jesus to this great height. For the Father thus to appoint the Son does not imply any disunity within the persons of the Godhead, for although he is manifest in three persons (Father, Son, Holy Spirit), God is

one. 'The LORD our God, the Lord is one' (Deuteronomy 6:4). 'I and the Father are one', declares Jesus (John 10:30). Among men, an heir receives his estate or inheritance in succession to his father. In relation to the Son, however, the Father does not relinquish or give up anything. What the Father does, he does through the Son. What the Son does, he does for the Father.

The language of divine appointment makes plain that this is not an honour which Jesus takes upon himself (an argument which will be taken up in chapter 5 with respect to his priesthood (5:4–5)). It goes back to the eternal counsels of the Godhead, into which it is not ours to pry, and is not something which was decided upon in time and history. This very fact on its own secures the absolute security, certainty and unchangeableness of the Son's inheritance. It is guaranteed. It can never be lost. 'My counsel shall stand, and I will accomplish all my purpose', God declares (Isaiah 46:10).

This inheritance or heirship has special reference to Jesus' mediatorial work and reminds us of this classic statement: 'Ask of me, and I will make the nations your heritage, and the ends of the earth your possession' (Psalm 2:8). An heir has an inheritance. So while *all things* belong to Jesus since he is God (including the entire universe complete with the heavenly realms, the whole human race, the new heavens and earth yet to come, and even hell itself), what in particular is the inheritance to which he is heir? The answer is, his blood-purchased redeemed: 'the ransomed of the Lord', Isaiah 35:10; 'his people', Matthew 1:21; 'the church', Ephesians 5:25; 'a great multitude that no one could number, from every nation, from all tribes and peoples and languages', Revelation 7:9; 'his bride', Revelation 19:7.

When on earth, Jesus, the Son of Man, had nowhere to lay his head. Behold him now—*'the heir of all things'*. He is the possessor and lord of all things. Everything belongs to him. This is a title expressing lordship and dominion. The Father has appointed him who is his infinite love and delight. 'The Father loves the Son and has given all things into his hand' (John 3:35). Jesus himself states, 'All that the Father has is mine' (John 16:15). If it should occur to you to ask, 'are not we, who are Christians, also referred to in the New Testament as sons and heirs?' the answer is 'indeed so!'—we are 'heirs of God and fellow heirs with Christ' (Romans 8:17). This, though, is on the basis of our union with Christ, and not owing to anything whatsoever in ourselves. It is of us (us!) that Jesus is speaking when he addresses his Father (and ours) in these words: 'The glory that you have given me I have given to them, that they may be one even as we are one' (John 17:22).

Of which of the angels can this ever be said: *whom he appointed the heir of all things*?

(2) *'through whom also he created the world'*. We know from the opening verse of Scripture that, 'In the beginning, God created the heavens and the earth' (Genesis 1:1). Creation is the sovereign work of God alone (watch out for 11:3 later on where this very truth will be stated specifically). Yet in our present verse it is affirmed that it was through the Son that God created the world. Yet this should not surprise us—certainly not, in the light of such verses as John 1:1–3, 1 Corinthians 8:6, and Colossians 1:16 ('For by him all things were created, in heaven and on earth, visible and invisible, whether thrones or dominions or rulers or authorities—all things were created through him and for him').

Furthermore, this phrase in 1:2 supplies us with an unequivocal and crystal-clear assertion of Jesus' deity, he who became incarnate, the Word made flesh. He is the eternal Son of God, who 'was daily his delight, rejoicing before him always' (Proverbs 8:30). The Lord Jesus Christ is not 'part God'—he *is* God, and let there be no doubt upon the point. And as we shall discover in 1:10, in the quotation from Psalm 102, our writer (without hesitation or apology) applies to Jesus the words applied in the psalm to Jehovah concerning creation.

Given that Scripture teaches that creation is the work of the triune God, we must not only think of the Father, but of the Son and the Holy Spirit as well. 'In the beginning, God created the heavens and the earth' (Genesis 1:1) is a Trinitarian statement. As for *'the world'*, this is literally 'the ages', encompassing everything that is and will be, and not only what has been from the beginning—both the present and the future age, the present world and the world to come.

Of which of the angels can this ever be said: *'through whom also he created the world'*?

(3) *'He is the radiance of the glory of God'*. Once again, no inferiority of the Son to the Father is indicated. Our problem here (as so often) is the limitation of language to express the inexpressible.

This phrase takes us back to John 1:14: 'and we have seen his glory, glory as of the only Son from the Father, full of grace and truth'. The sense is of a 'reflection', along the lines of our saying 'like father, like son'. In the incarnate Lord Jesus Christ, *'the radiance'* (brightness, splendour, effulgence, excellence) of God is perfectly and gloriously manifested. What the apostle Paul refers to as 'the glory of God in the face of Jesus Christ' (2 Corinthians 4:6) is exactly that—the true glory of God, and never something less merely on account of it being manifested through Jesus' humanity. Recall what happened at Jesus' transfiguration, when 'his face shone like the sun, and his clothes became white as light' (Matthew 17:2).

However, remember this also. This is Jesus' own glory, as well as being the reflection of the Father's glory. It is the glory of God, and our writer is enforcing the truth continually that Jesus is God. 'And now, Father, glorify me in your own presence with the glory that I had with you before the world existed', Jesus prayed in John 17:5. This is the glory which blinded Saul on the Damascus road.

What a delightful representation this is for us of the Son of God— the very brightness of God's glory. It is supremely in Christ that God is truly revealed. Without this revelation we would be very much in the dark. So how thankful we should be for it. Just as the brightness of the sun cannot be separated from the sun itself, and all the glory of the sun is seen in its brightness, even so (if only we could grasp it) the glory of the Father is reflected and seen in the Son, without the Son being anything less than wholly divine himself. And this being so, he is essentially and divinely glorious.

Of which of the angels can this ever be said: *'He is the radiance of the glory of God'*?

(4) *'and the exact imprint of his nature'.* Special note needs to be taken of that little word *'and'.* As so often in Scripture, it is highly important, for it establishes a clear and direct link. These two connected statements, speaking of radiance and imprint, need to be held closely together, and when done so combine the companion 'twin' truths of the *oneness* and the *distinctness* of the Father and the Son.

The word for *'imprint'* makes here its only appearance in the New Testament. We might render it 'stamp'. The idea is of an engraved character or the impression made by a seal. Another illustration would be a branding iron used on an animal. The writer's point is that the Son (while being the Son) reveals the very person and nature of the Father. Jesus himself said so, of course, when he said to his disciples in the upper room, 'Whoever has seen me has seen the Father' (John 14:9). The apostle Paul makes a similar assertion: 'He is the image of the invisible God' (Colossians 1:15).

Thinking of the illustration here of the image of an original mould, say on clay or wax, nothing can be more like the original than the image. Even if you can never see the original, you know what it is like from the image on the wax. The one betrays the very form and features of the other. This is precisely what Jesus does with the Father. 'For in him the whole fullness of deity dwells bodily' (Colossians 2:9). The angels cannot do it, but he both can and does. 'No one has ever seen God; the only God, who is at the Father's side, he has made him known' (John 1:18).

We are confronted here with what Paul calls 'the mystery of godliness' (1 Timothy 3:16), God being manifest in the flesh. The invisible becomes visible in the Lord Jesus Christ. The eternal one is revealed in human form. In one attribute after another, as we contemplate Jesus in the gospel accounts, we behold the nature of God. Think it through. The Lord Jesus Christ manifested God's holiness and power, his grace and compassion, his righteousness and tenderness, and much more besides. See him healing the sick and raising the dead, calming the storm and cursing the fig tree, receiving sinners and exposing hypocrites, casting out demons and doing the work of the kingdom, preaching the truth and combating falsehood. Everything the Father is, and has and does, so the Son is, and has and does. All the divine perfections are beheld in Jesus. All of the divine glory shines forth in him.

Of which of the angels can this ever be said: *'and the exact imprint of his nature'*?

(5) *'and he upholds the universe by the word of his power'*. The creating one is the sustaining one! He who created all things and is heir of all things upholds all things, even the entire universe with no exceptions. Who could do this but one who is very God of very God? The verb 'uphold' speaks of carrying, bearing, supporting, taking things forward to their designed end, and all of this without any intermission or interruption. Think of all in which *'the universe'* consists, and realise that none of it could exist, act or continue for one moment without the eternal Son of God's upholding of it.

In the most vital sense, the fall recorded in Genesis 3 changed everything. Sin entered in, bringing separation from God for all mankind, death and judgment in its wake. The devil appeared to have scored a great victory. Man became a rebel, and creation itself was ravaged. None of this, however, can impede the rule and government of the Lord Jesus Christ over *'all things'* (translated here *'the universe'*). Indeed, but for his upholding of it, the entire universe would fall apart and come to nothing. Mountains and valleys, oceans and deserts, the heavenly bodies in their various orbits, the entire face of the earth—everything is in his hands. His work of creating was a great work, and so is his work of upholding. This is the magnificent truth of Colossians 1:17: 'And he is before all things, and in him all things hold together'.

The question arises: how does Jesus do this? The answer is that he does it *'by the word of his power'* (or, as we might translate it, 'by his powerful word'). The divine word is the expression of the divine power. This was so in creation, when (day by day) God spoke, and what he spoke then came to be. He said 'let there be'—and there was! Similarly, by his word, according to his will and purpose, by his strength and power, under his authority, the universe is upheld. It is not that God 'set things off' or 'got things going' and that creation now continues 'under its own steam'. Far from it! Every moment that things continue is an evident testimony to the upholding work of God, ascribed here specifically to the Lord Jesus Christ, appointed to the task. His will must be done. His kingdom cannot fail. And this *'word of his power'* is sometimes a word of grace, sometimes a word of judgment, and sometimes a mixture of the two.

'All authority in heaven and on earth has been given to me', declared Jesus after his resurrection (Matthew 28:18). That statement dovetails with this statement in 1:3. Christ's dominion is in view here. It was evident during his earthly life (for example, as we noted above, as he calmed the storm, healed the sick, raised the dead, cast out demons, and so on). Yet over all things (visible and invisible—past, present and future) this rule of the Lord Jesus Christ extends. All of providence is in his hands.

Of which of the angels can this ever be said: *'and he upholds the universe by the word of his power'?*

(6) *'After making purification for sins'*. There is a significant distinction here with what has preceded. The truths concerning the Lord Jesus Christ affirmed so far in verse 3 remain constantly true, while the present statement records something that he has done in the past, a once-for-all event, rather than something he is still doing. The tense of the verb (*'After making'*, having made, when he had made) makes this clear. This takes us back, of course, to Calvary, to the cross.

The cross, 'Christ crucified', Paul tells us, is 'a stumbling block to Jews and folly to Gentiles' (1 Corinthians 1:23), but this does not impede our writer from holding forth here. He parades the cross as among Jesus' highest glories. Rightly so! How great the work of creation was: all things, out of nothing, in six days. How great the work is of upholding all that has been made. Yet how much greater the work of salvation is! When the Lord Jesus Christ died upon the cross, it was as a sacrifice for sin (not his own, for he had and has none, but ours, who are sinners by nature and in practice). It was 'a fragrant offering and sacrifice to God' (Ephesians 5:1), pleasing and acceptable in his sight. All the sins of all who trust in Jesus for salvation in every age have been thoroughly purged away. We bring no offerings or sacrifices of our own, for none such could ever avail for us, any more than they did for Cain when he brought 'an offering of the fruit of the ground' (Genesis 4:3).

Great glory has been brought to the Godhead through the work of Christ, for 'Salvation belongs to the LORD!' (Jonah 2:9). And great blessing is brought to the redeemed, 'For Christ also suffered once for sins, the righteous for the unrighteous, that he might bring us to God' (1 Peter 3:18). As our writer will declare later, 'without the shedding of blood there is no forgiveness of sins' (9:22); and again, 'Christ, having been offered once to bear the sins of many' (9:28). So we come to God's throne of grace and plead the merits of that blood—'the blood of Jesus his Son (which) cleanses [the tense signifies 'goes on cleansing'] from all sin' (1 John 1:7).

This work of Christ is a finished work. It has been done, and done completely. No loose ends remain to tie up. Again, our writer will have much to say about this in the course of the letter—in particular when he is contrasting the many priests with their repeated sacrifices with the blood of bulls and goats, in the Old Testament, with Christ, the one priest with his one sacrifice of his own blood, in the New. Yet this is already here in brief seed: Jesus is priest, victim, sacrifice, offering, altar, everything, in himself. His glory shines forth from Calvary.

Of which of the angels can this ever be said: *'After making purification for sins'*?

(7) *'he sat down at the right hand of the Majesty on high'.* Throughout these statements, the writer has been mounting higher and higher, and now he reaches the summit. Let us tease out the rich teaching here in this way.

Who *'sat down'*? The one who has been described in the epistle thus far. The heir, the creator, the radiance, the imprint, the upholder, the one who made purification—he is the one who sat down.

When did he sit down? Observe here the crucial connection: *'After making purification for sins, he sat down'*. The one who made purification for sins then sat down. After he had done the one, he did the other, and in that precise order. After dying on the cross (and being laid in the tomb, and rising from the dead, and ascending into heaven), Jesus sat down. It was a formal act at that point. Only then; not before.

Why did he sit down? Sitting down indicates work completed (again, wait for our writer's own exposition of this in chapter 10), and this completion is thoroughly accepted and approved by the Father. It is striking that in the tabernacle furniture described in detail in the Old Testament, no chair is provided. There could be no sitting down because the sacrifices were always going on and the work was never finished. But everything is different now! Up until this point in his life and ministry the Lord Jesus has been continually active. Now he adopts the attitude of rest and repose (although—again as the letter will reveal later—this is not an inactive rest in which he now does nothing at all). He now continues his work arising from Calvary (ruling the world, head over the church, making intercession for his people, preparing heaven for us, and much more besides), but the Calvary work itself in terms of sacrifice and offering is over. Let the children of God rejoice!

Why at *'the right hand'*? This position speaks of supreme honour, affection and authority, all of which belong to the Lord Jesus. In the phrase that he is *'at the right hand of the Majesty'*, 'the Majesty' is God (compare Colossians 3:1, 'where Christ is, seated at the right hand of God'). This reminds us that Jesus is the beloved Son of the Father, while himself being God as the second person of the Trinity.

Why *'on high'*? Because of what the words signify: exaltation, sovereignty, rule, a throne not of this world (for while the thrones of this world are here today and gone tomorrow, his abides for ever).

The phrase *'on high'* may be rendered 'in high places' and carries the sense even of 'the highest height', the most exalted position of all ('Therefore God has highly exalted him', Philippians 2:9). It needs to be borne in mind, of course, that the great statement here is not to be taken literally, as if to limit or confine Jesus in any way. Rather, unlike the angels, he is absolutely and eternally over all, and cannot be hemmed in in any way. He is 'King of kings and Lord of lords' (Revelation 19:16). 'God exalted him at his right hand as Leader and Saviour' (Acts 5:31), 'so that at the name of Jesus every knee should bow, in heaven and on earth and under the earth, and every tongue confess that Jesus Christ is Lord, to the glory of God the Father' (Philippians 2:10–11).

Of which of the angels can this ever be said: 'he sat down at the right hand of the Majesty on high'?

So these seven glorious statements concerning the Lord Jesus Christ have been set forth. His glory has thereby been displayed. This, however, is not done so that we may merely read about him or admire him, but that we might bow down before him and give him the glory; love and adore him; and seek to speak of him and commend him in every way. Our writer is not content only to write theology (truth and doctrine). He writes, ultimately, to draw forth from us doxology (praise and worship).

In order to this end, he completes this immediate section of Chapter 1 with verse 4. As we have seen, everything so far has been designed to assert and prove Jesus' superiority over the angels. Now there is the addition of 'the name': *having become as much superior to angels as the name he has inherited is more excellent than theirs'.* The 'name' in Scripture so often speaks of the nature and character of a person. This is especially so regarding the Lord. It is a summary word which gathers up into one everything about him. A classic example of this is Proverbs 18:10: 'The name of the LORD is a strong tower; the righteous man runs into it and is safe'.

There is something more here, however. As the next verse(s) will celebrate from the Old Testament, the special thing here is that Jesus is the Son. True, 'for a little while (he) was made lower than the angels' (2:9), but things are very different now. The incarnate Son, who became thereby the humiliated and crucified Saviour, is now 'crowned with glory and honour because of the suffering of death' (2:9). He is the risen, ascended, glorified Son—something which (on its own!) sets him apart completely from any angel or from all the angels put together. As a result, both his name and his inheritance are *'more excellent than theirs'*.

We may wonder, since our writer is at such pains to demonstrate at length and in detail Jesus' superiority over the angels, whether those to whom he wrote were already espousing (or were in serious danger of holding) over-elevated views of angels (as folk have done at various times in history, and as the Christians in Colossae to whom Paul wrote appeared to be doing, Colossians 2:18). We cannot be sure, but if this is so, it could well have arisen out of their tendency anyway to be re-immersing themselves in Old Testament religion and ritual at the expense of a full-orbed view of Christ. Angels in themselves present no rival whatsoever to the pre-eminence and lordship of Jesus; but men, in their mistaken and unbalanced views of them, can end up by making them (or other people or objects) into such rivals.

Our writer does not leave things here in his treatment of Jesus and the angels, notwithstanding the magnificence of these seven glorious statements about the Lord Jesus Christ. There is more still to come, continuing now with:

## Seven glorious prophecies

He turns now directly to the Old Testament to establish further his case of Jesus' superiority over the angels. This is a most important section, and must not be either overlooked or hurried through. Along the way, it secures the key truth that the Old Testament is full of Jesus. He is to be found there on page after page. In particular, he appeals to the Psalms (2, 104, 45, 102 and 110), along with references from Deuteronomy and 2 Samuel. The opening words, *'For to which of the angels did God ever say'*, make clear what the writer is out to prove, selecting those texts which are most suitable and effective for carrying his argument persuasively.

(1) verse 5a: Psalm 2:7. This psalm is a strikingly messianic psalm (though are not all the psalms messianic to different degrees?—it's just that this one stands out from many of the rest in this regard). It speaks very richly of Jesus as the Lord's anointed and of his kingly reign, often opposed but never defeated. Jesus is 'King of kings and Lord of lords' (Revelation 19:16). The Father himself declares of him, his Son, 'As for me, I have set my King on Zion, my holy hill' (Psalm 2:6—the verse immediately preceding that quoted here in 1:5). Jesus' empire is universal.

To no angel did God ever say, '*You are my Son, today I have begotten you*', but only to Jesus. He is the divine Son, as was testified by the angel Gabriel to Mary: 'He will be great and will be called the Son of the Most High' (Luke 1:32); by the Father himself at Jesus' baptism and transfiguration: 'and behold, a voice from heaven said, "This is my beloved Son, with whom I am well pleased"' (Matthew 3:17; compare Matthew 17:5); and by the apostle Paul: 'and was declared to be the Son of God in power' (Romans 1:4). The fact drawn attention to of God saying this of the Son is itself highly significant. How, in particular, do we know that Jesus is the Son of God? We know, because God the Father himself has said it, he has revealed it.

The '*begotten*' refers to the begetting of the incarnate Son, in the holy manner of the virgin conception recorded in Luke 1:35: 'The Holy Spirit will come upon you, and the power of the Most High will overshadow you; therefore the child to be born will be called holy—the Son of God'. It can carry also the sense of 'constituted' or 'appointed'.

But what is the reference to '*today*'? Differing proposals have been advanced, including in eternity, in his incarnation or his baptism, or at his resurrection and exaltation. It may seem difficult to choose, and we might even be inclined to ask whether we need to choose. On balance, however, it will be best to associate it with his resurrection and all that followed it in terms of his exaltation and glorification—

in a word, his vindication. Preaching in Acts 13, Paul makes this association, relating the fulfilment of Psalm 2:7 directly to Jesus' resurrection (Acts 13:32–33). And in the Romans 1:4 text already quoted, Paul states that the time when Jesus 'was declared to be the Son of God in power' was 'according to the Spirit of holiness by his resurrection from the dead, Jesus Christ our Lord'.

Christ's Sonship is unique, and belongs neither to angels nor men. All are subordinate to him.

(2) verse 5b: 2 Samuel 7:14. The words quoted here by our writer were originally spoken to King David by the prophet Nathan, concerning Solomon. They comprise part of a rich promise given to David regarding the future of his line and kingdom, God promising that he would be a father to the son (seed, offspring) he would give to David to succeed him. 'And your house and your kingdom shall be made sure forever before me. Your throne shall be established forever' (2 Samuel 7:16). This came as a particular comfort to David when it was given, as the house that he desired to build for the Lord was to be built instead by his son Solomon.

That does not in any way exhaust those words which Nathan spoke, however, or the divine promise therein made. Solomon was far from perfect, and the ultimate fulfilment of this promise clearly could not be found in him. It reached much further into the future, as is seen in the way in which both the prophets of God and the people of God throughout the Old Testament years continually looked forward to the true fulfilment which would only come in God's Son, the 'Son of David' (as Jesus is called himself).

This quoted promise is part of the many divine promises which included the Messiah and, indeed, which terminated in him. As further proof (should such be needed) that Jesus is central to this promise of old and that he is the ultimate and chief focus of it, it may be observed that it is applied directly to him in Luke 1:32–33 ('He will be great and will be called the Son of the Most High. And the Lord God will give to him the throne of his father David, and he will reign over the house of Jacob forever, and of his kingdom there will be no end'), as well as in Peter's preaching at Pentecost (Acts 2:30) and Paul's preaching in Antioch of Pisidia (Acts 13:22–23). Jesus' kingdom would truly be an everlasting kingdom, established forever, and his house and kingdom indeed made sure forever. Isaiah takes this theme up very beautifully in chapter 9 (and elsewhere) of his prophecy: 'Of the increase of his government and of peace, there will be no end, on the throne of David and of his kingdom, to establish it and to uphold it with justice and with righteousness from this time forth and for evermore' (Isaiah 9:7).

*'I will be to him a father, and he shall be to me a son'* is supremely the word and promise of God the Father to God the Son. The Father acknowledged Jesus as his Son, while the Son delighted to obey him in all things. Never was anything like it ever uttered by God to any angel.

(3) verse 6: Deuteronomy 32:43. A word ought to be said straightaway, in case you look this verse up in your Old Testament and cannot find it. Our writer is taking his quotation here from the Septuagint (that is, the Greek translation of the Hebrew Old Testament), not from the translation of the OT that we have before us in our English versions. A similar wording is also found in the Septuagint of Psalm 96:7, which our author may also have had in mind.

To begin with, what is meant by *'when he brings the firstborn into the world'*? It is a reference to the incarnation, *'the world'* referring here to the habitable earth (though some disagree and see it rather as referring to Christ's second coming, and the angelic worship which will be rendered to him at that time). The 'firstborn' is Jesus (as in verses like Colossians 1:15, 'the firstborn of all creation'; Romans 8:29, 'the firstborn among many brothers'; and Revelation 1:5, 'the firstborn of the dead'), though 1:6 is the only New Testament verse where 'firstborn' appears on its own. This is very appropriate for it can be seen that this bolsters immediately our writer's argument that Jesus is much superior to the angels, for, once again, there is nothing at all in this present verse that God ever addressed to any angel. Jesus' uniqueness as *the* incarnate Son and as *the* incarnate Redeemer shines forth. Once more, it indicates pre-eminence, excellence, dignity and dominion. 'Firstborn' can also speak of those who are most beloved (in Jeremiah 31:9, Ephraim is described as the Lord's 'firstborn')—so how well suited a title for the Lord Jesus!

And what does the quote state? *'Let all God's angels worship him'.* Angels worship; Christ is worshipped. There is all the difference between the two! Worship is due to God alone, and the Lord Jesus Christ, as the second person of the Trinity, is God. Remember the apostle John's encounter with an angel in Revelation 19:10, where John himself—the beloved disciple—had to be reminded of this basic lesson. Indeed, in the Deuteronomy text the 'him' of *'worship him'* refers to Jehovah, while here in 1:6 where that text is quoted, it refers to Jesus. So the point cannot be missed, can it? The one whom angels are bidden to worship is the Lord Jesus Christ, God incarnate, the Word made flesh. How could they be bidden to worship anyone who is less? And how can we?

(4) verse 7: Psalm 104:4. Back with the psalms! This psalm is a magnificent celebration of God's greatness in the realms of creation and providence. How this should call forth his praise!

Early in its course, the psalm makes mention of the angels, when it declares of God that, *'He makes his angels winds, and his ministers a flame of fire'.* From this we learn that the angels are God's *'ministers',* his messengers, his servants, who do his bidding; that their response to his pleasure is swift and immediate (*'winds'*—the word may also be rendered 'spirits', though here 'winds' is preferable); and that they bear a holy character and brightness of appearance (*'a flame of fire',* or 'flaming fire'), even as the one who commands and sends them is holy and glorious. Fire also in Scripture speaks of judgment, and in Jesus' parable of the wheat and the weeds the angels appear as the agents of divine wrath (Matthew 13:41).

Their work is most honourable, yet most humble. They serve, they serve willingly, they serve fervently. Yet just as we noted earlier that while angels worship, Christ is worshipped, so now we may add this: first, angels are created, Christ is uncreated; second, angels serve, Christ is served. Once again, there is all the difference between the two! Our writer continues relentlessly to build his case of the superiority of the Lord Jesus Christ above the angels. This is enforced further straightaway.

(5) verses 8–9: Psalm 45:6–7. What a psalm of psalms Psalm 45 is. Well may it be described as the Song of Songs in miniature, dealing as that precious book of Scripture does with the beautiful relationship of Christ and his church (Christ and the Christian) in terms of husband and wife—Jesus, the heavenly bridegroom—the church, the purchased bride. It is absolutely exquisite! As with the Song of Songs, so with Psalm 45: it is not satisfactory to say that they are speaking largely of Solomon, for they are not. They are speaking first and foremost of the Lord Jesus Christ, for again and again the words are not applicable to Solomon.

The previous verse began, 'Of the angels he says', and what God says of the angels, as we saw, is very honourable. This present verse, however, begins, *'But of the Son he says'*, and the contrast between *'the angels'* and *'the Son'* could not be more strikingly stated. 1:7 puts the angels in *their* place (albeit, some place!), while 1:8 puts Jesus in *his* place (an altogether superior and exalted place).

There are several things of note here. Firstly, the Lord Jesus Christ is referred to unequivocally as God: *'Your throne, O God'*—another clear attestation of his full deity, being equal in power and glory with the Father and the Holy Spirit. This is nothing less than a direct address to the Messiah, calling him God. Here is very solid ground for the Christian's faith to rest upon without fear, for it assures us of Jesus' all-sufficiency, and that we have all things and abound in him.

No contradiction of these opening words of the psalm quotation is present in verse 9, where it is said of Jesus, *'therefore God, your God'*. The point is this: Jesus is God from all eternity, as the second person of the Trinity—yet *as* the second person of the Trinity, the incarnate Son, God the Father is his God. So we read in the Gospels of Jesus praying to the Father, speaking about doing the Father's will, and glorifying the Father. On the cross, taking the opening words of

Psalm 22 upon his lips, he 'cried out with a loud voice', the words, 'My God, my God, why have you forsaken me?', being at that time bereft for a season of the felt comforts of both the Father and the Holy Spirit (Matthew 27:46). In a different setting, in the course of the day when he had risen from the dead, he said to Mary Magdalene in the garden, 'Do not cling to me, for I have not yet ascended to the Father; but go to my brothers and say to them, 'I am ascending to my Father and your Father, to my God and your God', speaking so graciously of our union with himself (John 20:17).

Secondly, we find here some of the characteristics of the Messiah's kingship: it is perpetual (*forever and ever*'), royal (*'sceptre*', an emblem of authority and government as seen in Esther 5:2), righteous (*'uprightness ... You have loved righteousness and hated wickedness*'— loving righteousness and hating wickedness are inseparable), and glorious (*'therefore God, your God, has anointed you with the oil of gladness beyond your companions*'). How very different from the kingdoms and kingships of men! We may borrow the words of the Queen of Sheba when, after visiting Solomon, she was completely overwhelmed with what she saw. 'And behold, the half was not told me'. She then continued, drawing this conclusion (a conclusion which is even more appropriate when spoken of those who are Messiah's subjects): 'Happy are your men! Happy are your servants, who continually stand before you and hear your wisdom! Blessed be the LORD your God who has delighted in you ...' (1 Kings 4:7–9).

This last statement of 2:9 is particularly rich. The Hebrew word 'Messiah' and the Greek word 'Christ' both mean 'Anointed One'. The figure used here reminds us of God's ancient method of anointing the kings of Israel for their establishment in office (note, by way of example, 1 Samuel 10:1, for Saul; 2 Samuel 2:4, for David). It may also have a savour about it of the reference in Psalm 133:2 to the 'precious oil' which was poured on the head of the high priest, Aaron, and which ran down on the collar of his robes, speaking of the anointing of the Lord Jesus Christ, who is 'a priest on his throne' (Zechariah 6:13).

The reference to *the oil of gladness*' is a reference to the Holy Spirit (oil is often so), and the truth that Jesus has been anointed by God with the Holy Spirit *'beyond (his) companions'* takes us directly to John 3:34, where we read, 'For he whom God has sent utters the words of God, for he gives the Spirit without measure'. At the beginning of Isaiah 61, in a passage which Jesus refers to himself when preaching in the Nazareth synagogue in Luke 4, we read, 'The Spirit of the LORD God is upon me, because the Lord has anointed me …' (Isaiah 61:1, compare Luke 4:18). A reference to Jesus and the Spirit also appears in connection with Jesus' baptism ('the Spirit descending on him like a dove', Mark 1:10). Great rejoicing and blessing attends the priest-kingship of Jesus.

Thirdly, who are Jesus' *'companions'*? We are, if we have believed on his name and been saved—and what an amazing grace that is! When with his disciples in the upper room before his betrayal, trial and crucifixion, Jesus spoke of the Holy Spirit in these terms: 'I will send him to you. And when he comes …' (John 16:7–8). Just prior to his ascension into heaven Jesus instructed his disciples: 'But you will receive power when the Holy Spirit has come upon you, and you will be my witnesses …' (Acts 1:8). And well on in his preaching on the day of Pentecost, Peter declared: 'Being therefore exalted at the right hand of God, and having received from the Father the promise of the Holy Spirit, he has poured out this that you yourselves are seeing and hearing' (Acts 2:33). It is through the mysterious work of the Holy Spirit that a sinner is born again (John 3:5, 7). The Holy Spirit is our teacher ('the Spirit of truth', John 16:12) and our sanctifier ('the Spirit of holiness', Romans 1:4; 'sanctification by the Spirit' (2 Thessalonians 2:13)).

(6) verses 10–12: Psalm 102:25–27. It is thrilling to discover how, without any hesitation or fear of objection, the writer of Hebrews takes this selection of Old Testament texts and applies them, one by one, to the Lord Jesus Christ—something, perhaps, which we might not always dare to do, if he had not done it first! Yet the psalm applies so clearly and extensively to Jesus.

The present psalm from which a quotation is supplied, Psalm 102, begins with the anonymous psalmist seeking God in prayer in what he calls 'the day of my distress' (Psalm 102:1–2). It proceeds to include an impassioned plea for the Lord to 'arise and have pity on Zion; it is the time to favour her; the appointed time has come' (verse 13), and 'that a people yet to be created may praise the LORD' (verse 18). And it builds up, in conclusion, and to the church's great encouragement, to a contrast between the perishable nature of 'the earth, and the heavens' and the unchanging nature of Jehovah (from verse 26).

It is this last portion which appears now in Hebrews 1—and the words spoken of God in the psalm are applied directly here to Jesus. He, states our writer, *'laid the foundation of the earth in the beginning, and the heavens are the work of (his) hands'*. Although *'they will perish'*, yet Jesus will *'remain'*. While *'they will all wear out like a garment'* and *'like a robe (he) will roll them up'* and *'like a garment they will be changed'*, yet there will be no change where Jesus is concerned. Why? Because he is *'the same, and (his) years will have no end'*.

The world which Jesus created is not here to stay in its current state. 'For the present form of this world is passing away' (1 Corinthians 7:31). He who created the universe by a word can just as readily destroy it by a word. Yet while the creation fades, the Creator flourishes. He is completely undisturbed by all that transpires according to his direction. Even amidst a collapsing universe, with kingdoms rising and falling, one generation being succeeded by another, with wars and rumours of wars and cataclysmic happenings to creation, the Lord Jesus Christ reigns—unchanged, unchanging. In that sense, nothing affects him. The figures of a worn out garment and a rolled up robe indicate the ease with which this divine work will be accomplished—and, by implication from the verb *'changed'*, the comparable ease with which the creation of the new heavens and earth will also be accomplished. And he it is who promises his people, 'I will never leave you nor forsake you' (13:5). In him we may safely confide, and on him we may truly depend.

Looking again at the words of the psalm as here spoken of Jesus, the especially striking thing is the repeated 'you': *'You, Lord … your hands … you remain … you will roll them up …you are the same … your years will have no end'*. Our writer is certainly not shy in asserting to the full the absolute deity (and so the eternity and the omnipotence) of the Lord Jesus Christ, and neither should we be—against all comers who, whether through unbelief, deceit or the arrogance of ignorance, question or deny it. Ample emphasis in this epistle will be given, in due time, to the fullness of Jesus' humanity, and in this we rejoice beyond words. But, for now, it is his divinity which is in sharp focus, and how our hearts should sing! Immediately we are drawn to the great statement in the closing chapter of this letter, where we read most gloriously that 'Jesus Christ is the same yesterday and today and forever' (13:8). We call this his 'immutability'. Throughout all the endless ages of eternity his name will be praised. All of which here, it almost goes without saying, contributes very significantly to the writer's armoury in setting forth the superiority of Jesus to the angels. For how could these words from the psalm ever be spoken of them?

(7) verse 13: Psalm 110:1. So we come to the seventh, and final, Old Testament quotation in this sublime series. Psalm 110 is one of the major messianic psalms, frequently quoted or implied in the New Testament in connection with Jesus, the Son, in relation to the Father—including by Jesus with reference to himself (Matthew 22:43–44). The psalm's opening verse, quoted here, even appears some dozen times in Hebrews, and presents the words of the Father to the Son (for the preface in Psalm 110:1 to the part of the verse now before us is, 'The LORD says to my Lord'). In the course of the psalm as a whole, Jesus is set forth as Son, Lord, High Priest, Redeemer and Conqueror.

The reference to the *'right hand'* recalls to us 1:3, to which is now added *'until'*. This does not imply something merely temporary (still less, fragile or inadequate) about Jesus' kingship, glory or rule—far from it, for the verb 'sit' may itself be translated 'be sitting', implying a permanent position. Already 1:8 has asserted the eternal nature of his throne, while 1:12 has made clear his own eternal nature itself. Rather, it makes us aware that throughout the whole long period until Jesus' second coming, the final ushering in and establishing of the two final states (heaven and hell), and the creation of the 'new heavens and a new earth in which righteousness dwells' (2 Peter 3:13), there are many enemies and hostile forces arrayed against him, his gospel and his church. All of these, however, will most assuredly be overcome, every one of them, and brought into entire subjection to Jesus. The figure in the phrase *until I make your enemies a footstool for your feet'* is from the Old Testament, and recalls how victorious champions would place their feet upon the necks of their enemies, thus describing the subjection of the vanquished to the victor.

Our writer will take this up in the next chapter when touching on the 'not yet, but now' theme in 2:8–9 (how we see Jesus now, and how we shall see him, where subjection to him is concerned), and we shall consider that when we come to it. In passing, 1 Corinthians 15:24–28 also comes to mind, speaking as it does of the Son delivering 'the kingdom to God the Father after destroying every rule and every authority and power'. Note also in that same passage: 'For he must reign until he has put all his enemies under his feet'. Then, at last, the mediatorial work of Christ will be concluded and his final victory won. Can it come soon enough for us, as we wait and watch and long for him—the complete vindication of the Lord Jesus Christ, and that of his church with him?!

So these seven glorious statements and these seven glorious prophecies, all pertaining to our Lord and Saviour Jesus Christ, are now ended. In each of them individually, and in all of them together, Jesus' superiority over the angels has been established (although the theme will continue through chapter 2, with different arguments presented). So far as this first chapter of the letter is concerned, however, verse 14 still remains for comment. It poses an appropriate question in the light of all that has gone before it. 'Are they (the angels) not all ministering spirits sent out to serve for the sake of those who are to inherit salvation?'

Although not quoted as an eighth Old Testament text in the sequence here, Psalm 103:20–21 is brought to mind. 'Bless the LORD, O you his angels, you mighty ones who do his word, obeying the voice of his word! Bless the LORD, all his hosts, his ministers, who do his will!' Nothing in this first chapter of the epistle is intended to demean the angels. We have already stressed their most honourable position. Yet even the angels of the highest rank do not equate with the Lord Jesus. They are each and all totally subservient to him. He alone is the one before whom they (and we) bow in awe and adoration, giving him at all times the worship that is his due.

1:14 does, however, throw interesting light upon the angels and their function. They are *'ministering spirits'*—that is, they are employed to execute the will of God. Being *'spirits'*, they have no bodies, and are invisible and speedy. One thing they are not, however, is idle—hence the word *'ministering'*. The word indicates that they are servants, couriers, and under authority. They are not their own, but belong to the one by whom they are *'sent out'*, namely the Lord himself; they are his agents. For what purpose? A high one: *'to serve for the sake of those who are to inherit salvation'*. Indeed the word for *'ministering'* contains the sense of engaged in public service, rendering assistance, affording succour. They are on active service, 'because the king's business requires haste' (1 Samuel 21:8). And those whom they serve, in the Lord's name, are the people of God, the redeemed, the church. What a dignity this puts upon mankind—made in God's image, so marred by the fall, yet in Christ most gloriously redeemed. Royal and famous personages in the world are surrounded by armed guards and the like who are as vulnerable as they are themselves. Christians have angelic servants and an angelic guard.

In their ministering to us the angels are an example to us in several ways. To begin with, they serve the very best of Masters, and count it a privilege and pleasure to do so. In the second place, they remind us that it is a leading principle among those who belong to the Lord that we are to serve, assist, aid and encourage one another as best we can, and not live for ourselves or expect to have everything done for us. Finally, they present this challenge: we, in the Master's service, often have to be pressed, cajoled, asked more than once, and then be checked up on to see if we're getting on with the job. The angels do not have this problem. They are focused, wholehearted, and see things right the way through.

Scripture abounds in instances of angelic service in this way. It is invariably unseen, but very real. Little do any of us know how much we owe, under God, to the angels. Let just a few biblical examples suffice. We find them guiding Abraham's servant in the quest for a wife for Isaac (Genesis 24); acting in connection with the Lord's chastisements (2 Samuel 24); waiting upon Elijah, first in the matter of food and drink, then stirring him to be up and doing for the Lord, when he thought he was finished (1 Kings 19); protecting and supporting us (Psalm 91); rejoicing over repenting and returning sinners (Luke 15); involved in the healing of infirmities (John 5); delivering from danger and extremity (Acts 5); and conveying safely to heaven the souls of those who have died in the Lord (Luke 16). This last mentioned is of particular comfort for the people of God— for when shall we so need heaven-sent aid as when our soul leaves our body and is transported up to God? As for their future service, the angels will gather the elect from the ends of the earth when Christ returns (Matthew 24); they will 'separate the evil from the righteous' for the last judgment (Matthew 13); and they will be our companions in heaven, joining with all the redeemed in praising the Lord (Revelation 7). How about that! Dear believer: did you realise that angels, these glorious attendants on Christ's throne, are appointed to be your servants? Happy they are in the task, and blessed we are through their service—and all to the glory of God, and, in particular in the present context, to the praise and the pre-eminence of our Lord and Saviour Jesus Christ.

What magnificence this all adds up to. God has given us his word, first through his prophets and now through his Son. This blessed Son, having done all that is needful for our salvation, is now exalted in heavenly places, and directs his angels in serving our needs. May we be glad of their companionship, look forward to meeting them, and—most of all—desire the day when our 'eyes will behold the king in his beauty' and 'will see a land that stretches afar' [literally, 'a land of far distances' or 'far horizons'] (Isaiah 33:17).

## The offices of Jesus

Before leaving this first chapter and proceeding to the second, however, something of key importance remains to be relished. In earlier days than our own, much more used to be heard and preached concerning what we refer to as 'the offices of Christ' than is the case these days. Yet it is not possible to appreciate his person and work anything like adequately without this vital and precious aspect.

The Lord Jesus Christ has three 'offices': he is prophet (his teaching office), priest (his redeeming office) and king (his ruling office). All are testified to plainly in the course of Hebrews 1. Let us take a brief, though adoring, look at each one.

Firstly, *Jesus is our prophet*. In this role, he teaches and instructs us by his word and his Spirit all those things we need to know, and most especially concerning our salvation. This office is implicit in 1:1–2, where, God having spoken through the many prophets, now has spoken his final word to us through his own Son. They taught, and (not least) they taught about Jesus. He himself is 'the truth' (John 14:6), and is the supreme revelation of God and the supreme teacher of the things of God to us.

Secondly, *Jesus is our priest*. This is a major theme of this entire epistle, but has already been introduced in 1:3, with what is said there about Jesus 'making purification for sins'. His priestly work, as the name of this office implies, has to do with his sacrifice and offering of himself upon the cross at Calvary, satisfying divine justice and reconciling us to God. Alongside this 'finished' aspect to his priestly work ('It is finished', John 19:30), however, there is also a 'continuing' aspect to it. This is stated in 7:25, where it is declared that as our great high priest now in heaven, Jesus 'always lives to make intercession for them' ('them' being those just described in the same verse as 'those who draw near to God through him').

Thirdly, *Jesus is our king*. The royal nature of Jesus has been brought to the fore in references to him 'upholding the universe by the word of his power' (1:3), his position 'at the right hand of the Majesty on high' (1:3), the angels worshipping him (1:6), his throne and sceptre (1:8), his rolling up of the earth and the heavens (1:12), and all that is contained in the Psalm 110:1 quotation in 1:13. In this capacity, he is 'head over all things to the church' (Ephesians 1:22); he loves, cherishes, shepherds, guides and defends his flock; and he deals victoriously with all his (and so our) enemies. When Melchizedek makes his appearance later in the epistle, the combination of priest and king in Jesus will become all the more explicit.

# Chapter 2
# Solemn warnings and glorious blessings

There are many difficulties and dangers which beset the Christian's journey to heaven. Some come from outside us (the devil's assaults, worldly allurements, temptations to compromise, unhelpful company, and the like). Some come from within us (such as our often unbelieving heart, careless walk, inconstant progress, lukewarm devotion). One of the chief of these many difficulties and dangers (and one which can come from either outside or within us) is drifting.

Writing to a people who were showing serious signs of this very thing (in their case, especially drifting away from the pure gospel of grace in Christ Jesus, back into Old Testament ritual and shadows), our writer takes up this theme with serious intent. In so doing, this all serves his main concern throughout the epistle of setting forth the pre-eminence and superiority of Jesus. In the first chapter he demonstrated this with regard to the prophets and the angels. Now in the second chapter he continues with the angels, but not in a manner whereby he repeats himself. There is nothing at all in this chapter which is surplus to requirements. He has new material to present, new arguments to pursue, new exhortations to press.

The chapter has three natural divisions: verses 1–4, 5–13 and 14–18, although there are no jagged edges between them. The whole flows very smoothly.

## Great salvation (2:1-4)

He starts as he means to go on. *'Therefore we must pay much closer attention to what we have heard, lest we drift away from it'* (2:1). It is interesting to note that he includes himself in this exhortation. Not 'you must pay much closer attention to what you have heard'; rather, in each case he writes 'we', not 'you'. He does not set himself above them, anymore than any minister of the word and pastor of the flock should do. Certainly the 'you' manner of address is often very appropriate in preaching and writing, but so also, much of the time, is the 'we'. Pastor and people alike are all sinners saved by grace, with nothing either in or of ourselves in which to boast. All of us need to give more than casual or ordinary heed to the gospel of God. We face the ever-present danger of falling into carelessness with regard to paying proper and constant attention to all that God says to us in his unchanging word.

Before commenting closely on all of 2:1–4, however, it is worth going straight to verse 3, for this is where we find the key phrase in this first section of the chapter.

### The key phrase (2:3)

This key phrase is *'such a great salvation'*. They are in grave danger of drifting (2:1) and neglecting (2:3)—drifting from and neglecting something they know, have espoused, yet are now turning their backs upon. What is that? Nothing less than salvation itself—salvation in all its surpassing greatness and amazing wonder. The words *'such a great'* (or 'so great') imply that the ultimate greatness of salvation is beyond expression in words.

The question arises: in what ways is salvation great? The answer has several layers.

- *It comes from the great God.* When turning to God in repentance for his sins, David asks, 'Restore to me the joy of your salvation' (Psalm 51:12). We might have expected him to speak of 'my salvation', as it is David who had received it and possessed it. He speaks of it, however, as 'your salvation'—that is, God's salvation. And he does so for an obvious reason: it is the gift of God. 'Salvation belongs to the LORD!' (Jonah 3:9). Or, as the apostle Paul puts it, 'For by grace you have been saved through faith. And this is not your own doing; it is the gift of God' (Ephesians 2:8). Everything about salvation proceeds from God, from God triune. Hence it is customary to speak of salvation planned (by God the Father), salvation accomplished (by God the Son), and salvation applied (by God the Holy Spirit)—although this must not be so pressed as to miss the truth of the involvement of each of the three persons of the Godhead in the whole matter of the planning, accomplishing and applying of salvation.

- *It deals with great matters.* What could be more important than the salvation of eternal souls? What could be more serious than heaven or hell? The natural state of every human being, even from our mother's womb, is that of sin and alienation from the God of purity and glory. Again, the united testimony of David and Paul may be summoned. David acknowledges this in the psalm just quoted: 'Behold, I was brought forth in iniquity, and in sin did my mother conceive me' (Psalm 51:5). Paul, addressing the Christians at Ephesus and reminding them of how they were before their conversion, states: 'And you were dead in the trespasses and sins in which you once walked' (Ephesians 2:1–2). Since sin's wages is death (Romans 6:23), every sinner (which means everyone) is under God's judgment and condemnation, helpless and hopeless before him. Yet this appalling predicament is the very thing which God's salvation deals with!

- *It was purchased at great cost.* In order for even one sinner to be saved from sin and reconciled to God, let alone 'a great multitude that no one could number' (Revelation 7:9), the sacrifice of the Lord Jesus upon the cross was needful. Hebrews will be full of this, the further into the book we delve. Let these few examples suffice for the time being. 9:14 speaks of 'the blood of Christ, who through the eternal Spirit offered himself without blemish to God'. 10:12 asserts that 'when Christ had offered for all time a single sacrifice for sins, he sat down at the right hand of God'. 12:24 refers to 'Jesus, the mediator of a new covenant' and refers to his 'sprinkled blood'. Clearly it all has to do with his sacrifice and offering of himself upon the cross at Calvary, where he 'suffered once for sins, the righteous for the unrighteous, that he might bring us to God' (1 Peter 3:18). Nothing else and nothing less could suffice. The sinless one was made sin, 'so that in him we might become the righteousness of God' (2 Corinthians 5:21). Jesus' merits, blood and righteousness comprise the sinner's only plea before God, that he would show us mercy for Jesus' sake.

- *It provides great blessings.* The list of them is extensive, and includes sins completely and forever forgiven, the indwelling of the Holy Spirit, being adopted as God's children, made inheritors of all of God's 'precious and very great promises'(2 Peter 1:4), the assurance that God 'fulfils his purpose for (us)' (Psalm 57:2) and that 'for those who love God all things work together for good' (Romans 8:28), 'a pure heart and a good conscience and a sincere faith' (1 Timothy 1:5), deliverance from the fear of death and from hell itself, and an eternal inheritance in heaven, 'where Christ is' (Colossians 3:1). Some of the biggest 'gospel words' bear upon the blessings of salvation—words like justification, substitution, propitiation, sanctification and glorification.

- *It rescues from great perils.* Some of these have been touched upon above, but it is worth recalling what they include: deliverance from God's wrath in all its fury, from hell with its terrors and torments, from death with its sting and threatenings, and from a life of anxiety and foreboding.

All of this (plus, surely, a great deal more) should leave us in no doubt that salvation is indeed *'great'*—and not only 'great' declares our writer, but *'such a great salvation'*. It could not be greater. So what follows in the light of this?

## The key warnings (2:1–4)

These may be summarised in a fourfold way.

(1) *Don't drift from it.* The picture is clear and simple: a boat loosing its safe anchorage or moorings and either gliding away or being swept away. It can happen deliberately, but equally it can happen through sheer carelessness and inattention. It can be seen coming, or it can take us unawares. Sometimes we are careful, at other times careless. Sometimes we are interested, at other times indifferent. Sometimes we are profited, at other times not. Sometimes we are 'red hot', at other times 'stone cold'. There is never a moment when we can afford to sit back, take it easy, or just assume that because we have held fast so far we will automatically carry on doing so. Drifting is terrifyingly easy. The very best of Christians can do it (and have done). The verb *'drift away'* makes its only New Testament appearance here in 2:1. So many things can creep in (including 'the cares of the world', Matthew 13:22, or 'the desires of the flesh and the desires of the eyes and pride in possessions', 1 John 2:16), and, before you know it, the deed is done.

The writer speaks in verse 1 of *'what we have heard'*. This will have an immediate reference to the teaching contained in the first chapter (note the *'Therefore'* with which the sentence begins), every sliver of which needs to be dwelt upon; but is also of wider reference urging all who will receive the letter to recall and review all that they have ever learned about the glorious gospel of the grace of God. It is one thing to hear the truth, but always another thing to remember what we hear, hold fast to it, and put it into practice day by day to God's glory. Forgetting is the easiest thing to do. Yet the very enormity of the gospel, and the pre-eminence of Jesus in that gospel, demands that we never cease to *'pay much closer attention'* to it, that we give abundant and earnest heed to it. However much and however well we have been taught, we have not yet grasped the half of it. Hebrews is very much an epistle of admonition, as we shall discover time and again. Perseverance in the faith and with the faith is an abiding theme of the letter, one central to the author's intent in writing.

(2) *Don't compare it unfavourably.* The prophets are important. The angels are important. But it is the Lord Jesus Christ who is God's last word to mankind (remember 1:2), and he is not to be compared unfavourably with them for he outshines and excels them. There is none to compare with him, and there is no gospel but the gospel.

In particular in verse 2 there is a further mention of angels and *'the message declared by'* them. This message *'proved to be reliable'* and *'every transgression or disobedience* (that is, of it and to it) *received a just retribution'*. What is intended here? It seems most likely that this is a reference to God's giving of the law at Mount Sinai, the astounding event recorded in Exodus 19 and 20. Whilst the law was given through Moses (who is yet to be mentioned in Hebrews—his turn will come), he it is who mentions their presence at that time ('The Lord came from Sinai ... he came from the ten thousands of holy ones, with flaming fire at his right hand', Deuteronomy 33:2). Moreover, Stephen, when ministering for the last time before his martyrdom, speaks of 'the law as delivered by angels' (Acts 7:53); and Paul links the angels and Moses together when writing that the law 'was put in place through angels by an intermediary' (Galatians 3:19).

But why does our author mention this at all? Because he is in pursuit all the time of his single focus—the superiority of Jesus. Given that the law (the giving of which involved angels) was a valid and reliable message, and that every infringement of that law (*'every transgression or disobedience'*) brought punishment (*'received a just retribution'*), then how much more reliable, how much more noteworthy, how much more worthy of our closest attention is the word which God has spoken through his Son—the word of the gospel. In no way here is the law being disparaged. How could it be, for 'the law is holy, and the commandment is holy and righteous and good' (Romans 7:12)? The law must not be spurned—but neither must the gospel! The law brought death, while the gospel brings life. The law brought condemnation, while the gospel brings salvation. The law waits for Christ, it points to Christ, it leads to Christ. Then, when the sinner is saved through Christ alone, it is this very law (the moral law, the ten commandments) which becomes the rule of life for the believer as part and parcel of living a life pleasing to the Lord who has saved us by his grace. Law and gospel are not enemies, both being the gift of God and both setting forth his glory. The true believer loves God's law, for it is written upon his heart. Yet it is in the gospel that the grace and mercy of God is most fully set forth, and that the divine provision is made abundantly for sinners.

(3) *Don't neglect it.* For an unbeliever to *'neglect such a great salvation'*, as if it is of no relevance to him, has nothing to say, is not worth considering, or is out somehow to do him harm (as some unbelievers can appear to think), and to remain unbelieving, is serious beyond words. Sinner: only God's salvation can do you any good! But then for the professing believer to neglect it (the sense is of making light of it, putting it on one side, turning away from it, outgrowing it, walking out on it, abandoning it—and, ultimately, as the warnings coming in chapters 6 and 10 will show, committing apostasy) is foolish beyond words. Has not God done everything for you in the gospel? Do you lack anything at all in and from the Lord Jesus Christ? Are not your past, present and future all undertaken for? Yet you would now neglect this glorious, eternal, divine, gracious salvation? Come to your senses before it is too late! Remember the *'just retribution'* following a light attitude to the law (everything is always 'just' with God). Do not imagine that the taking of a similarly light view of the gospel will fare any better—no!—it will fare much worse. Neglect is enough on its own to bring ruin. Neglect of a garden will soon fill it with weeds—neglect of attending to business will soon hasten its end—neglect of taking the correct medication will soon make the condition worse—neglect of road safety will soon end in an accident. The conclusion is obvious: if we neglect God's salvation, how shall we escape?

(4) *Don't belittle it.* Our author still has more to say about this great
salvation, as he continues to warn and urge against any neglecting
of it. He reminds his readers (and that includes us) of these two
facts: *'It was declared at first by the Lord, and it was attested to us by
those who heard'* (2:3). He has already asserted that God spoke the
message of the law by the angels; now he affirms that God has
spoken the message of the gospel by his Son. Therein is the gospel's
peculiar excellence, and yet another salvo in his argument proving
Jesus' superiority over the angels. The mediation of the Son (through
him) is above the mediation of the angels (through them). It is not
surprising, in the light of this, that the writer employs a 'must' when
laying upon all his readers the most solemn duty and obligation to
give their fullest possible attention to God's declarations. Minds must
be applied to it. Hearts must be engaged with it. Consciences must be
aroused by it. Wills must be directed in it, that obedience may follow.

Both the writer and his readers have heard, received and can
vouch for this message (again he includes himself along with them
in the *'us'*—a detail here which would not seem to support Pauline
authorship, for Paul is at pains to stress in Galatians 1:1, 11 that he
received both his apostleship and his message not from men but
directly from the Lord).

2:4 emphasises further this warning not to belittle God's great
salvation, and so not to belittle the gospel itself: *'while God also bore
witness by signs and wonders and various miracles and by gifts of the
Holy Spirit distributed according to his will'.* God's own testimony to
his truth is the most important testimony of all. Where the gospel of
his grace, the good news of salvation, mediated through his Son, is
concerned his testimony is comprehensive and impressive. It involved
*'signs and wonders and various miracles'.* Both Old Testament Hebrew
and New Testament Greek have a way of speaking in triads—three
words linked together, all referring to similar things, yet each having
their own nuance. Examples include 'the testimonies, the statutes, and
the rules' (Deuteronomy 4:45), and 'psalms and hymns and spiritual
songs' (Colossians 3:16).

In the present instance, *'signs'* (a favourite word in John's Gospel) speaks of mighty works pointing to the doer of them—Jesus' miracles, for example, were never works done merely for their own sake, still less just to impress or gather an audience, but rather his works always revealed something of his person. The second of this triad, *'wonders'*, carries the sense of a divine work which calls forth wide-eyed wonderment and amazement from those who witness it with their own eyes. The third is *'various miracles'*, which might be translated 'powerful deeds', and is a reminder that God can perform whatever he wishes, however he wishes, and is not constricted to any one single way of working.

Additional mention is made of a further divine testimony, namely *'gifts of the Holy Spirit'*. This will refer to the significant occasions, especially in the book of Acts, where healings, tongues speaking (speaking in real foreign languages, though ones unknown to those speaking, as on the day of Pentecost) and other striking events took place. All of these things combined (the signs, the wonders, the miracles and the gifts) were *'distributed according to (God's) own will'*. God is sovereign in all that he does. He is not open to question or contradiction. He testifies to his own truth precisely as he chooses. 'Our God is in the heavens; he does all that he pleases' (Psalm 115:3). Is he not allowed to do what he chooses with what belongs to him (Matthew 20:15)? It goes without saying that all that he pleases is always that which most contributes to the setting forth of his glory— in particular, his glory as evidenced in his great salvation.

All of this assures us of the sure and immovable foundation upon which this great salvation rests. Consider this: the Lord himself has declared it, those who heard it confirmed it, and in addition (to help us in our weakness?) God authenticated it by the various acts of divine power mentioned in 2:4. And that's without mentioning the testimony of prophets and angels. It amounts to witness and testimony piled high!

## The key applications

They are twofold, and can be expressed succinctly. Drifting is *as much a danger* to us as it was to the first recipients of Hebrews. So what we have in 2:1–4 about that danger of drifting is *as necessary a warning* to us as to them. Don't do it!

## Jesus and us (2:5-13)

The writer of Hebrews has still not left the angels, but now adopts a different approach. In chapter 1, the Lord Jesus Christ is evidenced as superior to the angels on the basis of him being the Son of God. Here, as chapter 2 proceeds, his superiority rests upon him being the Son of Man. Putting it another way: in the first chapter Jesus' deity was to the fore, while now it is his humanity which becomes the focus. There is a clear and deliberate progression in our author's argument in these central verses of the chapter.

### He begins with angels (2:5)

Angels serve; they do not rule. *'Now it was not to angels that God subjected the world to come, of which we are speaking'*. The reference to *'the world to come'* speaks of the reign of the Messiah, the Lord Jesus Christ—future to the prophets when they spoke and wrote about it, present in the time Hebrews was written (the Messiah having come, in fulfilment of the many prophecies that he would), but still future in terms of its fullness and eternal consummation. So far as its present aspect is concerned, the various things mentioned in the previous verse (signs, wonders, miracles and gifts) are confirmation that the reign is very much underway. They were part and parcel of the preaching of the gospel, and each provided their own confirmation of it.

The great point our author is making through all this, of course, is his now well-established urging that these are things which are true only of Jesus and pertain only to him—not angels. Angels are not lords—Jesus alone is Lord! Angels do not rule—Jesus is the one who rules! Praise and honour, power and authority, belong to him, not to them. His name (remember 1:4) is superior to theirs. The apostle Peter proclaims this triumphantly when he speaks of 'Jesus Christ, who has gone into heaven and is at the right hand of God, with angels, authorities, and powers having been subjected to him' (1 Peter 3:21–22). There is no mistaking what he means.

## He proceeds to man (2:6–8)

In order to develop his argument further, the writer calls in support from another psalm, this time Psalm 8—support which refers to man, and not to angels. This is the psalm of David which begins famously with these words: 'O LORD, our LORD, how majestic is your name in all the earth! You have set your glory above the heavens'. It continues with the psalmist's expressions of adoring amazement at the wonders of God's creation (heavens, moon, stars) and then arrives at the point we have here in 2:6 concerning man. The insignificance of man (his feebleness and frailty) is presented here in stark contrast to the majesty of God, as if to say, 'we know something at least of how excellent and glorious God is, but in comparison, what is man? Really, nothing at all. The remarkable thing, surely, is that God should ever have made him at all in the first place or, having done so, ever be mindful of him, care for him, or take any notice of him at all!'

It is very striking that in introducing this psalm at this point, the writer does so with the words, *'It has been testified somewhere'* (perhaps even more literally, 'somewhere someone has solemnly testified'). These words do not for one moment imply that our author couldn't quite locate the quote he was after (are you familiar with that experience?), but rather that those to whom he wrote were so steeped in the Old Testament that they would be able to locate it immediately for themselves.

*'What is man, that you are mindful of him, or the son of man, that you care for him?'* What is there about man which singles him out as being a special candidate for God's special interest, concern and care? Why should man be thus favoured above all else? What is it about him alone in the whole of creation? How this is in glaring opposition to the contemporary view of man which would be inclined rather to reverse things altogether and come out with something along the lines of 'who is God that we should be mindful of him, bother about him, take any notice of him?' We live in days marked by man's need

for 'self esteem', which schools are urged to impress upon children from the earliest age—their worth, thinking well of themselves, being independent and self sufficient individuals.

Yet having said this, something more (of great importance) needs to be said by way of balance—and this, the chosen psalm does. Man himself is part of God's creation. Indeed, the Genesis 1 account leaves us in no doubt that man is the very crown of God's creation. This is implicit in the words involving the Trinity, 'Let us make man in our image, after our likeness ... So God created man in his own image, in the image of God he created him; male and female he created them. And God blessed them.' (Genesis 1:26–28). To him is given 'dominion' (Genesis 1:26). For all his feebleness and puniness, man has great dignity, having been created in God's image, thereby to have fellowship with God. Adam stood completely distinct from every other part of the created order in the Garden of Eden—and he stood in that way not only for himself as an individual but for the entire human race, for all mankind, as their (our) federal head.

Although man is *'made ... for a little while lower than the angels'* (man has become mortal, subject to death for a season, while angels retain their immortality throughout), yet God *'has crowned him with glory and honour'* (2:7). Man is not related to fish or monkeys—he is gloriously related to God. And while, with the fall of man into sin (Genesis 3), this glory and dignity has been lost so much and so tragically, yet traces of it remain—and by the gospel, in the new birth, more than the sinner lost in Adam is restored to us in Christ. This is what the apostle John is in such raptures about: 'To him who loves us and has freed us from our sins by his blood and made us a kingdom, priests to his God and Father, to him be glory and dominion forever and ever. Amen' (Revelation 1:5–6). One day, moreover, 'we are to judge angels' (1 Corinthians 6:3), and God shall put *'everything in subjection under (our) feet'* (2:8). The Lord's redeemed will be advanced to a position of unimaginable *'glory and honour'* and will be set in a most exalted situation in God's everlasting kingdom. Is this something of what the prophet Daniel is alluding to when he writes, 'But the saints of the Most High shall receive the kingdom and possess the kingdom forever, for ever and ever' (Daniel 7:18—notice verse 27 of that same chapter also)? Here, surely, is something to fire the Christian's spirit, however dull, difficult or discouraging present circumstances might be. Remember what is in store, focus upon the divine promises, seek a greater appreciation of what you already are in Christ—and what you yet shall be!

## He arrives at Jesus (2:7-9)

To leave things here, however, would be a great mistake—a mistake which would essentially miss altogether the point the writer to the Hebrews is making. For his purpose in citing these verses from Psalm 8 is not to set forth the biblical doctrine of man as *the end of his argument*, but as a vital and compelling *means to his true end*. Understand it like this: to whom does what is written in these psalm verses ultimately refer? To man? No. To whom, then? To the Lord Jesus Christ. Remember that the truth still being proved is Jesus' superiority to the angels. Man is superior to the angels (for even those bright and burning heavenly beings are not the object of God's grace and favour in salvation—indeed, they themselves 'long to look' into these very things (1 Peter 1:12)). What the psalm says in respect of the doctrine of man serves our author's ultimate perspective of drawing upon what the psalm says rather in respect of the doctrine of Christ.

In the New Testament this psalm occurs on a number of occasions with application to Christ, the perfect man. Of him, above all others, did David originally write, *'You made him for a little while lower than the angels; you have crowned him with glory and honour, putting everything in subjection under his feet'*. It is Jesus who, supremely, was made (by God the Father, though in entire and willing submission to the Father) *'for a little while lower than the angels'*. This took place with his incarnation and is described by Paul in the familiar and moving terms of Philippians 2:6–8. Jesus, 'though he was in the form of God, did not count equality with God a thing to be grasped, but made himself nothing, taking the form of a servant, being born in the likeness of men. And being found in human form, he humbled himself by becoming obedient to the point of death, even death on a cross'. It was all for God's glory in accomplishing our salvation.

The phrase *'for a little while'* indicates that what we speak of as Jesus' state of humiliation was only for a strictly limited period. It was followed—as both Psalm 8 and Philippians 2 testify—by his state of coronation (or exaltation, or glorification—or all three!). Now God has *'crowned him with glory and honour'*—which is exactly what Paul says when writing, 'Therefore God has highly exalted him and bestowed on him the name that is above every name' (Philippians 2:9)—how beautifully Scripture consistently interprets Scripture, testifying thereby to its internal unity and the absolute absence of any contradiction within it. In that magnificent coronation psalm (Psalm 24, in its latter part), we read that the gates have lifted up their heads, the ancient doors have been lifted up, and the King of glory has gone in—in where?—into heaven! The Lord Jesus Christ is now risen, ascended and glorified, and we his people are risen, ascended and glorified in him, even though we have not yet arrived in heaven. What awaits us ultimately in reality is already our possession in title.

The outcome of Jesus' coronation is described in the words *'putting everything in subjection under his feet'*. His humiliation is followed by his coronation, which state signifies his sovereignty. No single angel, nor the whole company of angels put together, have everything in subjection under their feet. Rather, they are among those who are themselves in subjection. The Lord Jesus Christ is King, Lord and Ruler of the universe, the nations and the church. It is all part of his pre-eminence. All of which is enforced with the words, *'Now in putting everything in subjection to him, he left nothing outside his control'*. The matter could not be stated more confidently or comprehensively than that.

Yet it may appear that this presents a potential problem—one which our writer acknowledges and does not dodge. It is one thing to speak of everything being in subjection under Jesus' feet, but (and here is the perceived problem), *'At present, we do not yet see everything in subjection to him'* (2:9). We might just mention, for fullness, that some interpreters are of the view that the writer of Hebrews is contrasting here man and Jesus—that is to say, although we do not see everything in subjection to man, what we do see is

Jesus who is crowned with glory and honour. We do not follow that view, however (although it is certainly true to observe that humanity has been honoured to an astounding degree in the Lord Jesus Christ actually becoming man, taking upon himself human nature). The writer, as already noted, while he proceeded to man from the angels, has now left man behind and has arrived at Jesus and is now taken up exclusively with him.

So then, what of this 'problem'? Is it a real or an imagined one? The tension is between *what we do not see* and *what we do see*. It is certainly true that as we look around it does not appear that everything is in subjection to Jesus. Still the nations rage and still the peoples plot in vain. Still the kings of the earth set themselves, and still the rulers take counsel together 'against the LORD and against his anointed, saying, "Let us burst their bonds apart and cast away their cords from us"' (Psalm 2:1–3). Still people oppose the truth (2 Timothy 3:8), still false prophets arise and lead many astray and still lawlessness is increased (Matthew 24:11–12), still much even of the true church is lukewarm (Revelation 3:16). Still 'all who desire to live a godly life in Christ Jesus (are) persecuted, while evil people and imposters (go) from bad to worse, deceiving and being deceived' (2 Timothy 3:12–13), and still 'the devil prowls around like a roaring lion' (1 Peter 5:8). And that's only for starters. From such a review as that of how things appear in the world and in the church, there seems much evidence to indicate that everything is in anything but subjection to Jesus.

That very apparentness, however, is where faith needs to come in, and to come in strongly. Yes, that may be what we see, but we see something else as well, and this 'something else' gives the lie completely to a pessimistic or hopeless set of conclusions about things. What is this 'something else'? The writer introduces it with the stark 'but' of contrast. *'But we see him who for a little while was made lower than the angels, namely Jesus, crowned with glory and honour'*. It is worth noting that although our writer has been speaking of Jesus in various ways right from the very beginning of the letter, this is the first mention of his name, *'Jesus'*. Our writer continues to apply to the Lord Jesus the verses from Psalm 8 that he has already quoted. And this is what provides the solution to the 'problem'. Faith is the clue. Faith looks not only around, but up; and what faith sees when it looks up (Jesus crowned with glory and honour) it must then apply rigorously and in hope to what it sees when it looks around (everything not yet in subjection to him). The verb *'crowned'* envisages the placing of a victor's crown upon the head. Recall here the words of Peter while preaching at Pentecost: 'Let all the house of Israel therefore know for certain that God has made him both Lord and Christ, this Jesus whom you crucified' (Acts 2:36).

It is precious to the eyes of faith to view Jesus' shame and humiliation, scorning and suffering, rejection and agony replaced by his glory and honour—that glory and honour which is his due. The former was *'for a little while'*, though a very deep and solemn while. For this season he *'was made lower than the angels'*, both in becoming incarnate and in being subject (as a real man) to dying. That season is now passed, however, and Jesus is exalted 'far above all rule and authority and power and dominion, and above every name that is named, not only in this age but also in the one to come' (Ephesians 1:21). The crown of thorns on earth is now replaced with a crown of glory in heaven. It is this coronation of Jesus written of in 2:9 which is the guarantee of his people's reigning with him, crowned with glory and honour as well. What a glorious inheritance in Christ awaits the redeemed of the Lord! 'Worthy is the Lamb who was slain to receive power and wealth and wisdom and might and honour and glory and blessing!' (Revelation 5:12).

At this point, the writer to the Hebrews becomes more personal, as once again he draws in both his original hearers and us. Jesus' suffering preceded his crowning. The purpose of his suffering, *'the suffering of death'*, was *'so that by the grace of God he might taste death for everyone'*. The import of *'taste'* is 'to experience to the full, to go right down into'. It speaks eloquently of the bitterness of the experience, the costliness of it, and the infinite fruit which issued from it. This was no ordinary death, and no ordinary tasting of it. It has even been described as a roasting with fire, as was prefigured by the Passover lamb. He drank to the full every last dregs of the cup. So much for those deniers of truth, who claim that Jesus never really died on the cross but merely went into a swoon; and that in consequence he never really rose again because he had not died in the first place. Away with such thoughts!

It was in order that sinners may truly live that Jesus truly died. He endured the agonies of death by crucifixion and entered the domain of the dead when laid in the garden tomb so that all who believe upon his name may be delivered from the condemnation sin brings and the eternal punishment that death ushers into. Jesus' own words, spoken shortly before Calvary and spoken of what was to take place at Calvary ('The hour has come for the Son of Man to be glorified', John 12:23), establish very strongly the solemn point that the way of suffering was the way of glory for him and blessing for his people.

The suffering and the death were unspeakable. Not for Jesus a calm and peaceful death with family and friends gathered around the bed, or with soft music playing in the background. His experience of death, rather, was in darkness, pain and loneliness—a death to satisfy all the clamouring demands of infinite divine holiness and justice—a cursed death, for 'Cursed is everyone who is hanged on a tree' (Galatians 3:13, quoting Deuteronomy 21:23)—a death in our (the sinner's) place and for our (the sinner's) sake, who could (and can) do nothing whatsoever to deal with our sins, save ourselves, or reconcile ourselves to God. We are helpless of ourselves, neither can angels help us. The Lord Jesus Christ has done everything. Our business is to avail ourselves of that 'everything'.

The *'everyone'* (as well as being a potent way for the writer to the Hebrews to remind his essentially Jewish recipients that the gospel is as much for Gentiles as for Jews, that Jesus died as much for the one as for the other) is a delightfully spacious word, full of grace, for while only those whom God has chosen to save will be saved, yet the gospel is to be offered freely (as a genuine offer) to all sinners, with the divinely given assurance that 'everyone who calls on the name of the Lord will be saved' (Romans 10:13). The *'for'* in the *'for everyone'* speaks the language of substitution—Jesus dying *'for'* sinners, in their place.

In the immediate context of Hebrews so far, *'everyone'* has a special reference to 'those who are to inherit salvation' (1:14), the 'many sons' (2:10), and the 'brothers' (2:11). Yet this free offer of Christ to sinners—imploring them, 'be reconciled to God' (2 Corinthians 5:20)—is not a tease but a truth. That is why we glory 'in the cross of our Lord Jesus Christ' (Galatians 6:14).

Full weight must be laid upon all of this being *'by the grace of God'*, for it could certainly never have been any other way. This is free favour indeed. If God had not been pleased to be gracious (to show grace, kindness, mercy, love, compassion freely and abundantly to poor and needy sinners—who not only do not deserve that grace but positively deserve the very opposite, his punishment and wrath), then there would be no salvation at all, whether 'such a great salvation' or any other sort. God is not obliged in any way to do anything for sinners. We are all wholly dependent upon God having been gracious, and the knowledge that, as he himself expresses his own heart towards us, 'As I live, declares the LORD God, I have no pleasure in the death of the wicked, but that the wicked turn from his way and live' (Ezekiel 33:11).

## He brings all these together (2:10–13)

So complete and so compelling is the writer's case in establishing beyond doubt or question the superiority of the Lord Jesus Christ to the angels, that they have almost dropped out of the picture altogether. They are still there in the background, however, for the case still has a little way to run. He still wishes to do some more unfolding, and uses the interesting word 'fitting'. *'For it was fitting that he* [God], *for whom and by whom all things exist, in bringing many sons* [us] *to glory, should make the founder of their salvation* [Jesus] *perfect through suffering'* (2:10). All that God ever does is *'fitting'*—appropriate, suitable, the right thing, the best thing, to fulfil his own designs, and (most importantly of all) in accord with his own character (such as his justice and righteousness, his wisdom and holiness, his patience and kindness, his mercy and love) and thereby for his own glory. Not least is this true in the matter of the plan of salvation, or, as it is also commonly referred to, the scheme of redemption. This plan, this scheme, wholly fitted God's wisdom, his holiness, his power and his grace. He was under no obligation whatsoever towards sinners in this matter, but he judged it *'fitting'*, pleasing and glorifying to himself, to act graciously towards us.

The statement concerning God, that he it is *'for whom and by whom all things exist'*, is richly glorifying to him. It speaks at once of his sovereign creation of all things and the total dependence of all things upon him. All that exists does so *'for'* him and *'by'* him. He is the reason for its existence and it is through his agency that things have their existence. This is wholly in tune with Paul's soundly-struck note, 'For from him and through him and to him are all things. To him be glory forever. Amen' (Romans 11:36). This God—this is the point here in Hebrews—so appointed that the way in which sinners should be saved (*'bringing many sons to glory'*) was through *'the suffering of death'* already noted in 2:9, and here further adverted to in Jesus, *'the founder of their salvation'* being made *'perfect through suffering'*.

There is much here. First, *concerning Jesus*. What is said of him here?

- He is *'the founder of'* (our, his people's) *salvation'*. The word *'founder'* also carries the varied meanings 'pioneer, captain, author, prince, leader'. It conveys the sense of the one who goes before, opens the way, guides into that way and then leads the entrants on. With regard to our salvation, having accomplished it on earth he now awaits us in heaven having (as our founder and captain) gone ahead of us and entered into heaven itself 'as a forerunner on our behalf' (6:20). He has led the way to heaven in which we now follow in his tracks. The title expresses dignity and eminence. It is used here very appropriately of Jesus. He is all of these shades of meaning in one. Jesus is every believer's 'all in all'. All things pertaining to our salvation rest upon him. Only he can convey us safely through the life and walk of faith in life below, and issue in the triumph of faith in glory above. We possess all things in him, but have nothing without him. How brimfull of encouragement this is to tried and weary souls.

- He was made *'perfect through suffering'*. This has sometimes puzzled readers of Hebrews, but it need not do so. Put aside immediately any thoughts of Jesus having to be made perfect because he was somehow imperfect. Such a thought cannot possibly be entertained for a moment. The word refers rather to Jesus' unique and complete perfection, fitness and suitability for undertaking the work necessary for our salvation, his utter consecration and dedication to that work, as well as instancing how everything that he underwent and experienced (including, and especially, all the suffering) contributed to that perfection, fitness and suitability, that supreme and unique qualification which belonged to no one else. It speaks of his completeness for the work he undertook for sinners.

The writer will expand on this later, very especially in two magnificent passages—later in this present chapter from verse 14, and then in the closing paragraph of chapter 4. For now, the suffering here in 2:10 contributed vitally to his fulfilment of the prophecies of the suffering Servant of the Lord (especially Isaiah 53); the way on the cross in which he 'disarmed the rulers and authorities and put them to open shame' (Colossians 2:15); his rich ability to sympathise with his people in their sufferings and temptations and to minister to them at such times; and his all-round identification with us, while himself always remaining without sin.

There is also something exceedingly significant said here *concerning believers*. What is said of them here?

- We are *'sons'*. The doctrine of adoption is integral to salvation, and one of the most precious privileges of it. The apostle John catches something of the breathtaking wonder of it in these words: 'See what kind of love the Father has given to us, that we should be called the children of God; and so we are' (1 John 3:1—and he continues in the same vein for the next couple of verses). The apostle Paul also is fully aware of the stupendous nature of this truth: 'So you are no longer a slave, but a son, and if a son, then an heir through God' (Galatians 4:7). It is a long way from being a slave to being a son, but this is part of the transformation which the grace of God works upon the sinner who believes upon the Lord Jesus Christ for salvation. This sonship—'and I will be a father to you, and you shall be sons and daughters to me, says the Lord Almighty' (2 Corinthians 6:18)—arises out of our being reconciled to God. We approach God now as our Father, and address him as such (Matthew 6:9; Romans 8:15). His ear is ever open to the prayers of his children—so open that he says to us, 'Before they call I will answer; while they are yet speaking I will hear' (Isaiah 65:24). Never was a son or a daughter more welcomed or loved in the family than the children of God are welcomed and loved by him.

- We are being brought *'to glory'*. Although while here on earth many of the congregations of God's children meet together, worship him and serve him as part of little (sometimes very little) flocks, yet the company of God's redeemed ones as a whole is not small at all. It comprises 'a great multitude that no one could number' (Revelation 7:9), drawn quite literally from every part of the globe. This illustrates the *'many'* of 2:10. All will be brought to glory and it will be Jesus' own glory that we share, the glory of the one who has gone before us in obedience, in suffering and in actual entrance into glory. In his great John 17 prayer, Jesus said to the Father, 'The glory that you have given me I have given to them, that they may be one even as we are one' (John 17:22). Not one will be missing on that glorious and blessed day when 'the ransomed of the LORD shall return and come to Zion with singing' (Isaiah 35:10). This is the whole divine intent from the very beginning—not for God to save a people for himself and then lose some of them along the way, nor for some to arrive safely in heaven while others fail to make it. And in order to ensure this *'bringing many sons to glory'*, Jesus utters for us this assuring promise: 'My sheep hear my voice, and I know them, and they follow me. I give them eternal life, and they will never perish, and no one will snatch them out of my hand' (John 10:27–28—note carefully also John 6:37–40). In title, of course, the children of God are already 'blessed …

in Christ with every spiritual blessing in the heavenly places' (Ephesians 1:3), on the basis of Christ's finished work and our union with him. It only remains for us to arrive there. We cannot bring ourselves, we need to be brought—and *'the founder of (our) salvation'* will see to that!

The oneness of Jesus and his own is further stated and developed in verses 11–13. *'For he who sanctifies and those who are sanctified all have one origin'* (2:11). There has been some discussion over who the *'he'* is in *'he who sanctifies'*, but the context would demand that it refers to the Lord Jesus Christ (even though, within the Trinity, the work of the sanctification of believers is the special preserve of the Holy Spirit). By insisting upon the reference here being to Jesus, the Christ/ believer union, already handled in depth in this chapter, remains focal to the writer's argument. This connection will continue in view later in the epistle, in verses like 10:10 ('And by that will we have been sanctified through the offering of the body of Jesus Christ once for all') and 10:14 ('For by a single offering he has perfected for all time those who being sanctified'), to quote but two. The blood of Jesus, shed sacrificially upon the cross, is sanctifying blood day by day, as well as pardoning blood. One of the things Christ Jesus is made to us, in the ample fullness of salvation, is 'sanctification' (1 Corinthians 1:30), and we 'are sanctified by faith in (him)' (Acts 26:18). The great work of sanctification, of course, is that whereby we are made more like Jesus, growing increasingly into his likeness, being day by day more consecrated and devoted to him, in preparation for that blessed day when 'we shall be like him, because we shall see him as he is' (1 John 3:2). It is a progressive work, but a certain one. It will not fail in its outcome.

What is the meaning of the phrase *'all have one origin'* (literally, 'are of one')? This also has caused considerable discussion. Attempts have been made to argue for it teaching that Christ and believers share a common spiritual origin (that is to say, he is the Son of God and believers are sons of God in him), or that Christ and believers share a common humanity in Adam (pointing to the genealogy of Jesus in Luke 3 which traces his human ancestry right back to Adam).

Neither of these interpretations is satisfactory, however. It is much more preferable, in view of the language of the whole of this verse, to treat it as expressive of the common human nature which Christ and Christians share. He is 'the Word (who) became flesh' (John 1:14). He was 'born in the likeness of men' (Philippians 2:7). Indeed, 2:14 will shortly itself declare that 'Since therefore the children [believers] share in flesh and blood, he himself [Jesus] likewise partook of the same things'. It always goes without saying (though always is well said) that Jesus remained and remains at all times 'without sin' (4:15)—without this cardinal truth detracting in any way from the reality of his own humanity and the equal reality of his sympathy with us in our own humanity. The union between Jesus and believers is intensely intimate.

As a result of this, Hebrews continues, *'That is why he is not ashamed to call them brothers'* (2:11). Jesus' identification with his own is such that he is not ashamed of us. This is quite startling, for knowing our own hearts we are all too well aware of countless reasons why he might be ashamed of us. But he is unequivocal on the matter. Not only are fellow Christians brethren one of another (a precious truth), but all Christians are Christ's own brethren (an even more precious truth); and that second truth precedes the first, for without the second the first would not exist. It has been described as a community of nature which is shared by both the sanctifier and the sanctified. Jesus used this language on the day of his resurrection when speaking to Mary ('my brothers', John 20:17). It exhibits amazing condescension, that he should ever think or speak so. He has come for us and he has come to us. He has given himself to us and taken us to himself. The language of the Song of Songs is necessary to capture the beauty of this, in the words 'My beloved is mine, and I am his' (2:16) and 'I am my beloved's, and his desire is for me' (7:10). Romans 8:29 describes Jesus as 'the firstborn among many brothers'. How the hearts of his people should rejoice.

There then follows a choice selection of three Old Testament quotations, each in its own way affirming what is being said. First up is Psalm 22:22—that magnificent messianic psalm which begins in the depths of Christ's dereliction upon the cross and ends upon the heights of his vindication and glory. There is much more in this psalm than the psalmist David's testimony—indeed there is much in the psalm that cannot very well be applied to David at all, while there is nothing in the psalm which cannot be applied to the Messiah. It is a psalm of the cross and a psalm of the crown, all in one. Continuing the sentence of 2:11, the writer proceeds: *saying, "I will tell of your name to my brothers; in the midst of the congregation I will sing your praise"*. At the point at which these words occur in the psalm, they are the outburst of great joy on the part of the Saviour as he addresses the Father, and open the section which leads eventually to the triumphant conclusion of the psalm. These words themselves speak of the Lord Jesus (*'I'*) proclaiming (*'will tell'*) the glory of God (*'your name'*) in and to his church (*'my brothers'*). This is that glory witnessed in particular in 'the goodness and loving kindness of God our Saviour' (Titus 3:4), the 'good news of a great joy' (Luke 2:10), 'the gospel of the grace of God' (Acts 20:24). This work of proclaiming, publishing, declaring God's *'name'* (who he is, what he is like, what he has done) is what Jesus came to earth to do. It is his office of 'prophet' which we touched on at the end of chapter 1, and accords with his own statement concerning himself in John 14:6, 'I am ... the truth'. Consider also his words in his great prayer: 'I have manifested your name to the people whom you gave me out of the world' (John 17:6). And he exercises this ministry *'in the midst of the congregation'*, that is to say, in his church—his golden lampstand in the midst of which he walks (Revelation 1:13, 2:1).

The two further quotations are both taken from the prophecy of Isaiah, beginning with Isaiah 8:17. *'And again, 'I will put my trust in him'* (2:13). This also appears in a messianic passage, where the Lord Jesus Christ is spoken of as 'a sanctuary and a stone of offence and a rock of stumbling to both houses of Israel, a trap and a snare to the inhabitants of Jerusalem' (Isaiah 8:14). But how does it help the present cause of the writer to the Hebrews? Why has he selected at this point a verse which has its original context in things pertaining to Isaiah and God's people in the prophet's day? It is, in fact, highly appropriate, and in Isaiah's prophecy itself the verse occurs in the midst of a number of prophecies and predictions relating to the Messiah. These words represent Jesus (from his own mouth) trusting the Father, thus proving once more his true (not bogus) humanity and his real (not imagined) identification with us. In all that he did— for us—Jesus was wholly confident and trusting in the Father. Never was his confidence in Jehovah shaken.

He lived his entire life on earth consciously before the Father (he whom he describes in John 20:17, speaking in that verse to Mary, as we noted earlier: 'my Father and your Father'). This is particularly and poignantly clear in the course of his agony in Gethsemane, when he uttered the memorable words, 'Father, if you are willing, remove this cup from me. Nevertheless, not my will, but yours, be done' (Luke 22:42). *'I will put my trust in him'* was the constant expression of his heart. Even his enemies acknowledged this of him—when he was upon the cross they shouted mockingly, 'He trusts in God' (Matthew 27:43—were they knowingly thinking of Psalm 22:8, even quoting it?). It is Jesus who is speaking, first and foremost, with the words, 'I have set the LORD always before me; because he is at my right hand, I shall not be shaken' (Psalm 16:8). It was in this very attitude that Jesus, 'for the joy that was set before him endured the cross, despising the shame' (12:2). Truly, he is one with us, and is supremely able 'to sympathize with our weaknesses' (4:15)—being one who was no stranger to offering 'up prayers and supplications, with loud cries and tears, to him who was able to save him from death' (5:7).

To round off the trio the writer quotes Isaiah 8:18. *'And again, "Behold, I and the children God has given me"'* (2:13). These words follow straight on in Isaiah 8 from the ones just considered, though comprise only part of Isaiah 8:18. The entire verse, in the Isaiah context, runs thus: 'Behold, I and the children whom the LORD has given me are signs and portents in Israel from the LORD of hosts, who dwells on Mount Zion'. The writer to the Hebrews feels no need to quote the verse right through to its end, for his point is made amply in the words he does quote. His recipients, being people steeped in Old Testament Scripture, would no doubt have been able to recite the remaining words for themselves.

The value for us of noting the complete Isaiah verse, however, is that this messianic portion of the prophecy was delivered in dark days in the nation and among God's people. Yet even (indeed, especially) at such a time the Saviour could speak without hesitation of those whom he would save, the Redeemer could rejoice assuredly of those whom he would redeem. We are his brothers of whom he is not ashamed (2:11), and we are his children given to him by the Father (2:13). Wondrously, how pleased he is to own us! Nothing could thwart the saving purposes of God. Nothing ever can, and nothing ever will. This applies, of course, just as much to our own dark days in the nation and among God's people.

There is a double movement here. The Father gives the children to the Son. The Son presents these children to the Father. The first movement took place in the eternal counsel of the Godhead, when God 'chose us in him [Jesus] before the foundation of the world' (Ephesians 1:4). 'Yours they were, and you gave them to me', says Jesus to the Father (John 17:6). Herein is our preciousness to the Saviour. The second took place in time and history as the result of Jesus' life, death and resurrection. So here he is, the 'one mediator between God and men, the man Christ Jesus' (1 Timothy 2:5), presenting his redeemed and purchased ones to the Father, having accomplished completely and successfully 'the work that you gave me to do' (his further words to the Father, in John 17:4). God has his people and he will not fail to secure them. Christ has his bride and he will not be in heaven without her.

Surely also there is in consequence a far horizon aspect to this choice of the Isaiah text at this point. Paul writes in Ephesians 5:27 that Jesus will 'present the church to himself in splendour, without spot or wrinkle or any such thing, that she might be holy and without blemish'—this being the ultimate reason for which he 'loved the church and gave himself up for her' (verse 25 of the same chapter). Incidentally, there is no confusion between Jesus presenting the church both to the Father and to himself—to the Father, as the one who gave the church to him in the first place, and to himself as his beloved bride, the desire of his heart. And Jude, in verse 24 of his letter, begins his closing doxology with the words, 'Now to him who is able to keep you from falling and to present you [the church] blameless before the presence of his glory with great joy'.

## The heart of Jesus (2:14–18)

There now follows what is without question one of the most precious paragraphs in the entire letter to the Hebrews. It is as if, from 1:1 until this point, the writer has been ascending a staircase, rising higher and higher, in his unwearied pursuit of demonstrating once and for all the total superiority of the Lord Jesus Christ to the angels. He now approaches the top rung of the staircase as he completes his argument.

His opening words in 2:14, *'Since therefore'*, have about them the sense of both a connection with what has gone before and an approaching conclusion. This whole section is exceedingly full and we need to study it closely, piece by piece. It has, however, one outstanding and overarching theme which must be kept continually in mind: the loving heart of Jesus. What is that heart like?

### It is condescending

*'Since therefore the children* [us] *share in flesh and blood, he himself* [Jesus] *likewise partook of the same things'* (2:14). In a most remarkable way, this statement takes us to the very heart of Jesus' incarnation. The word 'children' has just been in evidence in the last of the three Old Testament texts just employed and refers to those whom the Lord Jesus came to save and does save. They *'share in flesh and blood'* (actually 'blood and flesh' in the original)—a phrase which denotes human nature, the common bond of all humanity, wherever they come from, whenever they live, whoever they are. Men make many distinctions among themselves, not least in the attempt to make some superior to others or more worthy of attention, but 'flesh and blood' is a great leveller. It speaks of frailty and mortality, and indicates limitations.

Nothing unusual so far, but there soon is, when we are told that Jesus *'himself likewise'* (the two words, the second of which might be rendered 'in like manner', giving added weight and emphasis to the astonishing statement just coming) *'partook of the same things'*. There will be more of this in verse 17, but this is enough for now. Here the reality of the incarnation is made inescapable. It leaves no room for any suggestion that in 'being born in the likeness of men' (Philippians 2:7) there was something wanting in Jesus' manhood, or that it was anything less than absolutely real and genuine—flesh of our flesh and bone of our bones. He did not indulge in the mere appearance of humanity, but in its very reality. Moreover, he did this willingly—that is indicated in the word *'partook'*.

The necessary caveat, 'yet without sin', will come in due course at 4:15, both assuring us that his humanity was not poisoned or infected by all that belongs to our fallen humanity, and thereby guarding his own glory. Even that caveat, however, crucial though it is, does not and must not be allowed to detract from the reality that 'the Word [Jesus, the Son of God] became flesh and dwelt among us' (John 1:14). As we shall discover shortly in this present paragraph of chapter 2 (and even more so later on), this is intended to be of the utmost comfort and encouragement to believers, tossed as we so regularly are with life on the ocean waves of day by day experience—to know that a man there is, in truth a real man, who both knew what it is and still knows what it is to partake of our human nature. He sorrowed and he rejoiced. He knew vigour and he grew weary. He had friends (though not many) and he had enemies. He suffered and he triumphed.

Two different verbs are used, in different tenses from one another, to significant effect. Humans *'share'*, while Jesus *'partook'*. The first indicates a constant state; it is always the case that humans share human nature. The second indicates that when Jesus took our nature upon himself this was a once only unique event, when in his incarnation he became one with us. It bears the sense of 'to take hold of'. He looked upon us. He did not remain aloof from us. He took to himself something with which ordinarily he had nothing in common, that was not natural to him. He humbled himself for us. Was there ever such condescension? Is there anything to cause us such wonderment as this? For this is the one (don't forget all that we learned from the first chapter) who, among other things, is 'the heir of all things', 'the radiance of the glory of God' and who 'upholds the universe by the word of his power'.

We need not be surprised that the task of announcing this marvellous happening was entrusted to angels (for we have already been taught that they do God's bidding and are our servants). But it is no angel who has actually become incarnate. It will not surprise us that—at the time of this announcement to the shepherds on that memorable night—'the glory of the LORD shone around them' (Luke 2:9) as they made the heavenly proclamation. But they were only the vehicles of communication, not its subject. In order for his people to become one with him, it was necessary for Jesus to become one with his people. In order that believers 'may become partakers of the divine nature' (2 Peter 1:4), it was necessary for Jesus to partake of our human nature. Nothing less than this has happened in the incarnation.

## It is conquering

Leading out of what he has just stated, the writer to the Hebrews continues by giving the reason for this remarkable act of the Lord Jesus.

Why did he partake of our flesh and blood? It was *that through death he might destroy the one who has the power of death, that is, the devil*. The New Testament has different ways of putting into words why Jesus became incarnate. He did not come to flatter us, to make us feel good about being done a favour, or out of some sentimental or romantic intent. He was born in order that he would die—birth, of necessity being a fundamental requirement for death, and having to precede it. No life, no death. Paul writes famously, 'The saying is trustworthy and deserving of full acceptance, that Christ Jesus came into the world to save sinners' (1 Timothy 1:15). John declares, 'And we have seen and testify that the Father has sent his Son to be the Saviour of the world' (1 John 4:14). Peter speaks of 'the God of all grace, who has called you to his eternal glory in Christ' (1 Peter 5:10). It is another verse from John, though, which captures the perspective of where we are in Hebrews, in his assertion, 'The reason the Son of

God appeared was to destroy the works of the devil' (1 John 3:8). For high on the list of these 'works of the devil' is his wielding *the power of death* and his holding people in *fear of death* and *lifelong slavery* to it. The verb *destroy* here in 2:14 speaks of 'bringing to nothing' or 'rendering inoperative'. It does not signify literally 'putting out of existence', for the devil is still anything but out of existence; but it certainly carries the force of 'brought into subjection' and 'having its power crushed'.

To understand 2:14–15 a question needs to be asked. How can Jesus suffering death (*through death*) result in the overthrow of this merciless tyrant (*the one who has the power of death, that is, the devil*)? The key is to be clear that at Calvary, where the sinless and spotless Son of God and Son of Man laid down his life and died, a massive encounter took place. The devil, the 'strong man' of Luke 11:21, was taken on in person by the 'one stronger than he' of Luke 11:22, who overcame him in a fierce battle in the hours of darkness. There, continuing the picture in that latter verse, Jesus took 'away his armour in which he trusted' and divided 'his spoil'. Satan was overcome; his power was broken. Or, to use Paul's language in Colossians 2:15, already quoted in this commentary, 'He [God] disarmed the rulers and authorities and put them to open shame, by triumphing over them in him [Christ]/it [the cross]'.

The devil only holds the power of death in a secondary sense, rather than an ultimate one. Ultimately all the issues, both of life and death, are in divine hands and under divine control. Death is not some independent force, neither does the devil have the last word concerning it. Jesus, by his own death and resurrection, destroyed the destroyer. He leads captivity captive. He snatched victory completely from the devil, vanquishing the devil in the devil's own domain. No other's death would ever have sufficed. In consequence, that which might have had the appearance of an utter humiliation and failure for Jesus (the cross) was actually a glorious triumph and victory for him (over the devil). God and man's arch-enemy was utterly, convincingly and devastatingly routed by the incarnate Jesus. Jesus has stripped the devil of his powers, has punctured his boasts, and has shattered his intents.

This glorious victory won by the Lord Jesus Christ has a remarkable delivering effect. Of course, his death deals with our sin, satisfies God's justice, vindicates the holiness of the law, and turns aside God's wrath that we all deserve to bear. Yet there is more, and that 'more' is focused upon in 2:15. This particular effect is to *'deliver all those who through fear of death were subject to lifelong slavery'*. Many things can fill people with fear—fear of the dark, fear of flying in aeroplanes, fear of being in unknown places, are among them—but *'fear of death'* can have a terrifying and paralyzing effect. In one sense, this is not surprising. Indeed it is needful. For death is the result of sin, and this must be borne in mind here. The two go together. 'Therefore, just as sin came into the world through one man [Adam], and death through sin, and so death spread to all men because all sinned', writes Paul in Romans 5:12. Shortly after that he makes his famous statement, 'For the wages of sin is death' (Romans 6:23). Had there never been sin, there would never have been death. Death is the inevitable fruit of sin. So the sinner will, not surprisingly, be afraid of death, even if he will not admit it to others (or, sometimes, even to himself). It is the great unknown, and often the great taboo, not to be mentioned. It visits the palace and the hovel, strides all across the world, and recognises no barriers to its entrance when each person's appointed time arrives. Well has it been called 'the king of terrors'.

This very *'slavery'* can be like a stranglehold on all whom it grasps. It induces helplessness. Jesus, however, and only Jesus, can deliver from this *'fear of death'* and this being (quite literally) *'subject to lifelong slavery'*. True, the unknownness of death as an actual experience remains, as much for the Christian as for the unbeliever, for the simple and obvious reason that it only happens to us once, and doesn't happen until it happens. Yet all those who are trusting Christ as their Saviour from sin are trusting him also as their Conqueror over death. Hold the two together. When we know that the Lord Jesus 'has freed us from our sins by his blood' (Revelation 1:5), we are to know equally that he has freed us from the *fear of death*'—for it was our sin that was behind our fear and was the cause of it in the deepest sense, death being the divine judgment upon sin. Jesus has been there, into death, into the grave, even though as yet we have not. Moreover, he has been there as *'the founder/captain of (our) salvation'* as part and parcel of *'bringing many sons to glory'*, as we learned from 2:10. That, surely, is why Christians can now actually speak of death as their best friend, next to Jesus. Best friend next to Jesus? Yes, because it takes us to him, who is our very best friend of all. Let this be a mark of our genuineness as Christians (if that is what we are): that we view death through the Lord Jesus Christ, and not something on its own. Death is one of the things included in Paul's list at the end of Romans 8, not one of which any longer 'will be able to separate us from the love of God in Christ Jesus our Lord' (Romans 8:39). It has lost its sting (1 Corinthians 15:55). Not only has the fear of it been removed, but death itself can no longer do us any harm. The 'king of terrors' has been dealt with by the 'King of kings'.

## It is compassionate

This is the third feature here regarding the loving heart of Jesus. As well as being condescending and conquering, it is also compassionate. This truth is present immediately, as our writer continues. *'For surely it is not angels that he helps, but he helps the offspring of Abraham'* (2:16). The verb *'helps'* is a strong one and carries the sense of 'to lay or take hold of'. It appears in the Gospels in significant contexts—such as Jesus stretching out his hand and rescuing Peter from the waves as he began to sink, or taking the blind man by the hand prior to restoring his sight. It is a verb expressive of almighty power, the power of the one who is 'mighty to save' (Isaiah 63:1).

It has been proposed by many that this opening phrase of 2:16 means that Jesus did not come to the aid of angels, but rather came to the aid of mankind. This, on its own, would seem altogether too weak, however. We may ask, reverently, how would the angels need Jesus to come to their aid? More than this is required. That 'more' resides in the interpretation that relates this help to Jesus' incarnation. He has not taken to himself angelic nature and likeness but human nature and likeness. He has not come to save angels, even fallen ones (indeed, take a moment to ponder the most solemn truth of Jude 6), but to save sinners.

This truth of Jesus' humanity has been central to the author of Hebrews' exposition throughout this second chapter and remains so here. Though himself superior to the angels, he has willingly been made 'for a little while lower than the angels' (2:7) on behalf of *'the offspring* (seed, descendants) *of Abraham'*. And who are they? Just as we noted at an earlier point that in the Luke 3 genealogy of Jesus his human ancestry is traced back to Adam, so in that of Matthew 1 it is traced to Abraham. This is covenant language, for God established his covenant with Abraham and with his seed or offspring. This would ring particularly true to the ears of the Jewish recipients of this letter. All of the covenant promises find their fulfilment in Jesus, so *'the offspring of Abraham'* who are in view in the verse presently before us are God's covenant people—and so (once again) the very same as the 'many sons', 'brethren' and 'children' already mentioned in recent verses. This is confirmed by the words, 'And if you are Christ's, then you are Abraham's offspring, heirs according to promise' (Galatians 3:29).

*'Therefore he had to be made like his brothers in every respect' (2:17).* There is a necessity insisted upon here, indicated by the first word of the verse. In order for him to accomplish that just spoken of in 2:15, it was necessary (needful, of the essence) for Jesus *'to be made like his brothers'*. His partaking of our flesh and blood was an intimate thing, involving real feelings and emotions (we use that word carefully). This constitutes part of the *'in every respect'*. Nothing is lacking in him with regard to all that is needful for his oneness of association with us. It is blessed to know that we have a feeling, sympathising and compassionate Saviour, one whose heart is continually towards us. And this was necessary *'so that he might become a merciful and faithful high priest in the service of God'*. This is early days in the epistle to take up a close exposition of Jesus' priesthood, but the statement of it is in an important and suitable place here. It gives us another example of the 'if there isn't one thing, there isn't another' principle, this time being: if Jesus had not become incarnate, if he had not taken our

nature upon him, he could never have become for us '*a merciful and faithful high priest in the service of God*'. Yet the one thing being true, so is the other—and to our great blessing.

We need a 'high priest … to act on behalf of man in relation to God' (5:1). Why? Because God is holy and we are sinful; God is glorious and we are defiled; God is exalted and we are fallen. We need one to 'bring us to God' (1 Peter 3:18), and who, having done so, will represent us, undertake for us and intercede for us in heaven. Only the Lord Jesus Christ fulfils the brief, and in order to be in a position to do so became incarnate for us. The writer to the Hebrews will not let the point drop.

How is it that Jesus has become our high priest? He has done so through being '*merciful and faithful*' in making '*propitiation for the sins of the people*'. Mercy and faithfulness are among the most striking attributes of our God. He is 'rich in mercy' (Ephesians 2:4) and characterised by 'great mercy' (1 Peter 1:3). He is 'faithful, by whom (we) were called into the fellowship of his Son' (1 Corinthians 1:9) and 'faithful and just to forgive us our sins' (1 John 1:9). As our matchless and glorious Saviour, Jesus has acted mercifully and performed faithfully. Mercy involves grace, compassion and sympathy. Faithfulness speaks of trustworthiness, reliability and endurance. So without question mercy and faithfulness describe and are true of the Lord Jesus. He is merciful, he is faithful. He came in mercy, to show mercy. He came in faithfulness, to be faithful. Between them, mercy and faithfulness combine considerateness, understanding, fellow-feeling and dependableness in a most exquisite connection. His mercy issues in his faithfulness, while his faithfulness flows from his mercy. They cannot be separated. This makes him the very high priest that we require. All our hope and confidence rests in him.

And while this was '*in the service of God*', or 'in the things pertaining to, or in regard to, God' (doing the Father's will, obeying the Father's command, seeking the Father's glory), it was continually with his people in view. That being so, some have proposed that a distinction may be drawn between '*merciful and faithful*' along these lines: Jesus is merciful towards man and faithful towards God. This is not without truth, of course, but does not need to be pressed to the limits here, for it is true without question that Jesus is both *'merciful and faithful'* to his people.

With his people in view, to what end? This end: *'to make propitiation for the sins of the people'*. We are faced here with one of the massive gospel words in the New Testament, *'propitiation'*. It is not to be translated 'reconciliation', neither is it to be confused with 'expiation'. Expiation focuses upon Jesus' work of atonement through his sacrifice upon the cross (which issues in reconciliation), whereas propitiation speaks specifically of the turning aside of God's wrath away from us and upon our Saviour, and our consequent entering into his favour. This wrath has been described as his holiness stirred into activity against sin. God cannot abide sin. He can have no connection with it, nor give any approval to it. The prophet Habakkuk declares of him, 'You are of purer eyes than to see evil and cannot look at wrong' (Habakkuk 1:13). We all, being sinners, 'were by nature children of wrath' (Ephesians 2:3); and while that is a present condition yet it will be experienced in its fullest dimension, by those who are still in their sins, at the last judgment, when 'we must all appear before the judgment seat of Christ' (2 Corinthians 5:10). It is only 'Jesus who delivers us from the wrath to come' (1 Thessalonians 1:10). An important verse in this context from John's Gospel underscores the seriousness of this: 'Whoever believes in the Son has eternal life; whoever does not obey the Son shall not see life, but the wrath of God remains on him' (John 3:36).

To return to *'propitiation'* in 2:17, there is a great wonder here, a wonder of grace. Despite God's standing hatred of and opposition to sin, in all its shapes and forms, he still maintains an intense love to sinners. Indeed, Paul insists (to our great thankfulness and joy), 'God shows his love for us in that while we were still sinners, Christ died for us' (Romans 5:8). The innocent one took the place of the guilty. The righteous one stood as substitute for the unrighteous. The beloved one bore the sins of the enemies. The obedient one suffered for the rebellious. Putting it slightly differently, the head took responsibility for the members—for Christ and his people are one. Be sure to feel the full force of all of this! It is not that Jesus, by his suffering and death, somehow successfully persuaded the Father to be merciful to us after all, for the will of the Father and the will of the Son 'are one' (John 10:30). Rather, Jesus' offering of himself upon the cross as *'a merciful and faithful high priest'* is itself the permanent expression of the Father's love towards us and his eternal desires of salvation for us. Thereby God's holiness and justice are completely satisfied, and everything needful has been accomplished for God to declare to his people, 'I, I am he, who blots out your transgressions for my own sake, and I will not remember your sins' (Isaiah 43:25). What angel could have had any role in this?

In the Calvary sacrifice the psalmist's words are demonstrated: 'Steadfast love [or, mercy] and faithfulness meet; righteousness and peace kiss each other' (Psalm 85:10). There had to be the incarnation for there to be the propitiation, and there had to be the propitiation in order to secure pardon and forgiveness for *'the sins of his people'*. Jesus had to become one with his people (think back to verse 14) in order for our guilt to become his and our debts be paid by him. We cannot help going back in our minds to the words of 'an angel of the Lord' when he appeared to Joseph in a dream, announcing the conception of Jesus in Mary's womb, and giving this key instruction: 'and you shall call his name Jesus, for he will save his people from their sins' (Matthew 1:21). That is precisely what Jesus has fulfilled— Saviour in the name he bears and Saviour in the work he has done.

*'For because he himself has suffered when tempted, he is able to help those who are being tempted'* (2:18). The second chapter of Hebrews closes with this rich and encouraging truth. The sequence of thought in 2:14–18 brings things quite naturally to this point. Jesus 'partook of the same things [our flesh and blood]' (verse 14), he was 'made like his brothers in every respect', he became 'a merciful and faithful high priest in the service of God', he made 'propitiation for the sins of his people' (all these from verse 17), and now a vital conclusion is affirmed. It has to do with the way in which his humanity avails for us.

First, *a truth is stated*: *'he himself suffered when tempted'*. Temptation was a great trial to Jesus throughout his earthly life. He was not exempt from it. The truth here that Jesus *'suffered when tempted'* indicates the reality and heaviness of his experiences in this realm. They were very real, even though there was never any question or possibility of him yielding to them, neither was there ever any inclination of his heart to do so. Although Jesus *'suffered when tempted'*, never—not even once—did he ever sin when tempted.

The devil was forever at his heels, and even when he withdrew from Jesus it was only ever 'until an opportune time' (Luke 4:13). Satan sought to tempt Jesus into sin, into doubt concerning his calling, through putting enemies into his path, to turn aside from the way of the cross, or to look for some easier way of victory. The psalms are full of references to Jesus' trials and temptations, and he speaks very vividly to his disciples in Luke 22:28, saying to them, 'You are those who have stayed with me in my trials [or, temptations]'. His sufferings exceeded those of others in every way imaginable. In all of this, Jesus was victorious—not least in the great temptations and trials of Matthew 4/Luke 4 when he employed well-chosen Scriptures to see the devil off. Paul speaks in Philippians 3:10 of how we may 'share his sufferings', which is a deep matter. But here in 2:18 is a deeper matter still—Jesus sharing in our sufferings, being tempted with our temptations, assaulted with our assaults, being 'put to the proof' (a meaning behind both trials and temptations).

So, secondly, *a conclusion is drawn: 'he is able to help those who are being tempted'.* Putting this in the simplest way, Jesus has already been where we now have to go in the experience of temptation and trial. He has travelled this way before us. Stating it even more concisely: he has been there. And the fact that he was not overcome, he did not fall, he never succumbed either to the temptation or under the trial, strengthens our confidence in his all-sufficiency to come to our aid whenever we need him. We find in him a sympathizing heart, a strengthening hand, a sincere friend and a sensitive ear. The fact that *'he is able'* is a most cheering one for us, for it gathers into one Jesus' fitness, his willingness, and his readiness to do so. His help is continually at hand. Indeed, the verb *'help'* (or 'succour') indicates running to the cry of someone in need or danger and providing immediate and appropriate aid. The Lord Jesus Christ is ever ready to hasten to help us—with his care, his comforts, his power and his tenderness.

Yet, glorious though this is, a question is sometimes raised, a question which runs the risk of taking the edge off all this. It may be put like this: given that although Jesus *'suffered when tempted'*, and although his temptations were very strong and his sufferings thereby very real, how is it that without ever having had the actual experience of sin Jesus can thoroughly identify with us and help us when we (sadly, and repeatedly) do sin? To raise this highly pastoral question here at this point is, in one sense, to pre-empt 4:15, which we have yet to come to (and shall treat fully when we do come to it). Yet it does begin to be raised at 2:18, so at least some comment needs to be made straightaway.

So the best thing to say, for now, is that if Jesus in having *'suffered when tempted'* actually had committed sin, he would have become a fellow sinner with us, not different from us in that respect. The whole purpose of his incarnation would have been made void. We need a sinless one to be 'a merciful and faithful high priest' for us (remember, their sinfulness was no small part of the inadequacy of the endless succession of Old Testament priests with their equally endless succession of sacrifices 'which can never take away sins' (10:11)). If Jesus had even once fallen into sin, the entire basis of his priesthood would have vanished. So far from his sinlessness ('one who in every respect has been tempted as we are, yet without sin', 4:15) being some impediment or drawback where his helping us poor tempted ones is concerned, it is exactly the opposite—a great strength, a strong tower, a mighty fortress. In inviting us to himself for help, comfort and succour, we are led 'to the rock that is higher than' we ourselves are (Psalm 61:2). We discover most delightfully and with great relief and joy that, 'His left hand is under (our) head, and his right hand embraces (us)!' (Song 2:6).

Again, arising out of his sinlessness, Jesus, having been sorely tempted yet without falling, is set before us as an encouragement to victory over temptation in our own lives. We are not him, but we possess 'Christ in (us)' (Colossians 1:27), and we have the assurance (and, through grace, the experience) of being 'strengthened with power through (God's) Spirit in (our) inner being, so that Christ may dwell in (our) hearts through faith' (Ephesians 3:16–17). Do not ever discourage yourself (or others) with the entirely false thought that somehow, because Jesus did not actually sin, he knows less about temptation than we who are all too familiar with sinning. The truth is that he knows far more about temptation than we do and has been far more aggressively pressed with it than we have, so he is the only one who can effectively come to our aid. Furthermore, the more we need him and call upon him, the more we shall prove he is there, in all the reality of his humanity and in all the abundance of his Saviourhood. He will never leave us or forsake us (13:5).

# Chapter 3
# Jesus and Moses

The writer to the Hebrews, as we are continually discovering, is a man of one theme. That theme is the absolute and unquestioned superiority and pre-eminence of the Lord Jesus Christ above all comers. So far, he has stated and demonstrated his case as regards first, the prophets, and then, the angels. He has done this conclusively. Jesus, without question, is superior to any of the prophets and occupies a rank far above any of the angels. This is still comparatively early days in the epistle, however, and there is still a long way to go.

As we move now into the third chapter, the theme remains unchanged but the point of comparison is new. This time it is the superiority of Jesus over and above Moses. Let it be urged from the outset, however, that in no way is this intended to demean Moses. Moses is spoken of in the highest terms in Scripture. In his gracious providence God preserved his life from the very beginning (Exodus

2). God spoke to him 'in a flame of fire out of the midst of a bush' (Exodus 3:2) and commissioned him to royal service, saying to him, 'I am the God of your father, the God of Abraham, the God of Isaac, and the God of Jacob'. The effect of this upon Moses was that he 'hid his face, for he was afraid to look at God' (Exodus 3:6). To him was given the law on Mount Sinai (Exodus 20). He is described as 'very meek, more than all people who were on the face of the earth' (Numbers 12:3). Of him, God says, 'With him I speak mouth to mouth, clearly, and not in riddles, and he beholds the form of the LORD' (Numbers 12:8). It was under the leadership of Moses that the tabernacle was built (Exodus 26ff). He was there with Jesus on the mount of transfiguration (Matthew 17 and parallels). And in the course of his appearance in the gallery of faith in Hebrews itself, we learn of him that, 'He considered the reproach of Christ greater wealth than the treasures of Egypt, for he was looking to the reward' (11:26).

Interestingly, although the prophets were treated at the very opening of the letter, Moses himself was a prophet. Highly significantly, the messianic prophecy of Deuteronomy 18:15 speaks of the Lord Jesus in relation to Moses. 'The LORD your God will raise up for you a prophet like me [Moses] from among you, from your brothers—it is to him you shall listen'.

Before the Jesus-Moses account opens formally, however, our writer has something to say by way of earnest exhortation. This serves as a suitable prologue for what is coming.

## A call to consider Jesus (3:1)

The first word of the chapter is one which is always important whenever it occurs in the Bible: *'Therefore'*. As it has been said, whenever you come across a 'therefore', always ask yourself what it is 'there for'. It is a connecting word, drawing a deduction or conclusion or application from what has gone previously, and opening the way for what is to follow. It is a word which looks both backwards and forwards. We learned some precious truths from the end of chapter 2 concerning Jesus as 'a merciful and faithful high priest' (2:17), and the writer still has this in his mind. He will not permit any possibility of Jesus slipping from the forefront of the attention or affection of those to whom he is writing.

(1) *Notice how he speaks of his addressees.* They are '*holy brothers*'. He is having to write to them very candidly, without any beating around the bush. Things are needing to be laid on the line. No quarter is being given. This in no way detracts, though, from his Christian love for them or his desire for their spiritual best—indeed it is precisely on account of that love and desire that he writes as he does, for he is dealing with those who belong to the family of God. If he had not cared, then he would not have bothered, and could have left them to drift to their hearts' content. His manner towards them is very much that of the apostle Paul, when he urges the 'speaking the truth in love', with the aim of our mutual growing 'up in every way into him who is the head, into Christ' (Ephesians 4:15). This is how Christians are always to regard one another, and how pastors are to handle their flocks.

The noun '*brothers*' indicates one Christian's mutual belonging to and identity with other Christians in the bonds of divine grace and heavenly adoption. The adjective '*holy*' is a reminder of our having been chosen and set apart for God (the language of sanctification and consecration). The two words together lead to the next phrase: '*you who share in a heavenly calling*', that calling combining both our adoption as God's children and our holiness as we grow increasingly in likeness to Jesus. This '*calling*' is '*heavenly*' because it proceeds from heaven (in the eternal decree) and leads to heaven (in our eventual glorification). In each case, God is the fountain of it. It comes from above. It is a calling to the eternal blessedness of heavenly realities, not to the passing pleasures of this present world. It is something which Christians '*share*', in that while each and every sinner is loved personally and saved individually, we are not the only ones. Christians belong together—they are the church—and, as our writer will not hesitate to insist later on, we are to be careful not to neglect 'to meet together, as is the habit of some' (10:25). Be careful not to be among that 'some'. The word here for 'share' was translated 'companions' in 1:9, and is rendered 'partners' (of the fishermen) in Luke 5:7.

(2) *Notice how he speaks of Jesus.* He gives him this title: '*the apostle and high priest of our confession*'. We are already used in Hebrews to the thought of Jesus as 'high priest' (his office of priest, a truth which will be developed closely in the epistle in due course)—something which has both backwards reference to his once-for-all sacrifice for our sins at Calvary and present and future reference to his ongoing work of heavenly intercession. The addition here of the word '*apostle*', however, is something fresh. This is the only use of the word in regard to the Lord Jesus in the New Testament.

The fundamental meaning of the word 'apostle' is 'one who is sent'. It carries the sense of being an ambassador, and conveys a note of authority. Where Jesus is concerned, this links in with his office of prophet, making known the will of the Father to his people. In this respect, Jesus stands alone in being worthy of the name '*apostle*' (notice the use of the definite article here, '*the apostle*'), for, as he himself said to his disciples following his resurrection, 'As the Father has sent me, even so I am sending you' (John 20:21). Every subsequent 'sent one' owes their sending to Jesus, the 'sending one'— whether the New Testament apostles themselves (who were unique, for there is no continuing office of apostleship), or Christians as a whole, all of whom are 'sent' in the sense that we are charged with the proclamation of the gospel and are to serve Christ in the world.

The bringing together of both '*apostle and high priest*' in our present verse likely indicates that in Jesus the functions of both Moses and Aaron were brought together (even though Aaron will not appear by name until 7:11). Jesus is both. This would certainly fit in with the overall 'superiority of Jesus' theme of Hebrews. He it is (Jesus) who is the focus of '*our confession*', both our credal confession and our verbal confession, the word conveying the sense of mutual agreement in what is being confessed. The summons to '*consider*' him involves keeping him ever in our minds, thinking continually upon him, pondering and meditating upon him, beholding him by faith, having our hearts occupied with him—with the effects of relishing him, appreciating him, loving him, serving him, and glorifying him all the more. How altogether worthy the Lord Jesus Christ is of everyone's consideration, and no one's more so than from Christians—not an occasional or glancing thought, but a profound and prayerful meditation.

## Jesus and Moses compared and contrasted (3:2-6)

Our writer employs a basic twofold illustration concerning Jesus and Moses in order to demonstrate that Jesus occupies the higher ground: a building and a family, or, architecture and home. The argument focuses very much upon the word 'faithful'—not that Moses was unfaithful, but that the faithfulness of Jesus is of another order altogether. The closely woven threads of these verses may be unravelled in the following way.

- *Jesus and Moses: both faithful* (3:2). Of all the many suitable words that can be used of the Lord Jesus, faithful is one of the leading ones. It is this which is immediately to the fore here as the sentence of the opening verse of the chapter continues into the second: '*who was faithful to him who appointed him*'. It is God himself who appointed the Son to the work of salvation, in every respect of which the Son proved faithful. At no time did he relinquish the work, swerve from the work, or regret undertaking the work—and neither did he to any degree whatsoever leave the work unfinished or to be completed at another time. Jesus himself was able to say to the Father, 'I glorified you on earth, having accomplished the work that you gave me to do' (John 17:4). When actually upon the cross itself, he proclaimed, 'It is finished' (John 19:30). It is of the essence of being an ambassador that he be faithful to the task and trust committed to him. So Jesus was constantly engaged in his Father's business (Luke 2:49), working the works of him who sent him (John 9:4). Faithfulness is a supreme characteristic of the Lord Jesus Christ, a truth which means that we can rely on every word he ever spoke and every work he ever performed. He was faithful then and he is faithful now—'he remains faithful', even when 'we are faithless' (2 Timothy 2:13).

Moses also was marked by faithfulness: *'just as Moses also was faithful in all God's house'*. Way back in Numbers 12:7, God himself declared of 'my servant Moses' that 'He is faithful in all my house'. It would not be surprising if the writer to the Hebrews had this verse in mind at this point. By *'God's house'* is meant all that God gave and required Moses to do among and for his people Israel. He was not choosy, half-hearted or haphazard in his fulfilling of the divine commission first given to him at the remarkable scene of 'the bush (that) was burning, yet it was not consumed' (Exodus 3:2)—the commission to lead God's people out of their slavery and bondage in Egypt into the liberty and freedom of Canaan (even though Moses himself did not enter the promised land). He discharged faithfully before God all his responsibilities concerning the people. In Old Testament times no one was regarded more highly than Moses, and so it is very appropriate here that, in writing to the Hebrews, the faithfulness of this dear servant of God is emphasised clearly, *before* Jesus' superiority over him in this (and, by implication, in every other particular) is urged.

- *Jesus and Moses: Jesus is worthier* (3:3–4). Both are marked by faithfulness, indeed conspicuously so. Yet they are not thereby upon a level with one another. How so? *'For Jesus has been counted worthy of more glory than Moses'*. The mention of Jesus here by name is literally 'this one', though the reference is unquestionably to him. Moses, despite his pivotal role and outstanding qualities (something which will be brought out in 11:23ff), was a mere man, one who worked, as we have just seen, 'in all God's house', The Lord Jesus Christ, on the other hand, being both human and divine, is highly exalted above Moses, and for this simple reason: he has *'as much more glory as the builder of a house has more honour than the house itself'*. This is further elucidated as our writer continues, *'For every house is built by someone, but the builder of all things is God'*—another unmissable reference to the deity of the Lord Jesus.

It is invariably the case that an architect is worthy of greater respect than whatever he builds. The house that is built may be magnificent, but it is the architect who designed it who receives the chief honour.

The contrast is clear. Moses was a worker in the house, while Jesus is the builder of the house. Jesus as the builder was spoken of back in the Old Testament, when, speaking of him, the prophet announced that 'he shall build the temple of the LORD', adding, 'It is he who shall build the temple of the LORD and shall bear royal honour, and shall sit and rule on his throne' (Zechariah 6:12–13). Or, stating the contrast slightly differently, Moses served among the people of God, the church in the wilderness, while Jesus builds the living stones of the people of God into 'a spiritual house' (as Peter puts it, 1 Peter 2:5) and 'a holy temple in the Lord' and 'a dwelling place for God by the Spirit' (as Paul puts it, Ephesians 2:21–22). We could express it this way: Moses worked in the house (belonging to the family), whereas the house (the family) actually belongs to Jesus. Indeed, not only is Jesus the builder of the house, *but the builder of all things* (think back to 1:2).

In terms of the two—that is, the church in the wilderness and the church built by Jesus—there is a close and fundamental connection, for Scripture does not describe two separate churches (one in the Old Testament, one in the New), but rather, as the apostle states it, there is 'one body and one Spirit—just as you were called to the one hope that belongs to your call—one Lord, one faith, one baptism, one God and Father of all, who is over all and through all and in all' (Ephesians 4:4–6).

Remembering the danger, the writer of Hebrews judged those to whom he wrote to be in (that of selling out on Jesus and going back to the things that were past—back, so to speak, from fulfilment in Christ to ceremonies and rituals before him), this setting forth of Jesus' superiority over Moses would have been no academic matter. It may be that their affections were inclining more towards Moses than towards Jesus, more to 'the ministry of death, carved in letters on stone' than to 'the ministry of the Spirit' (2 Corinthians 3: 7–8), more to the 'glory in the ministry of condemnation' than to 'the ministry of righteousness (which) must far exceed it in glory' (2 Corinthians 3:9–10). That being so, it was too great a risk for our writer to let pass. Urgent counsel was needed, and that, not least, is what the letter to the Hebrews supplies. So concerned is our writer over the possible drifting of the Hebrews, what more powerful or persuasive argument could he employ than to direct their minds and hearts to the unwavering faithfulness and constancy of the Lord Jesus? In the face of all his trials and temptations from the evil one, as well as all his problems and disappointments from men, he was faithful through and through.

And so, on the writer continues.

- *Jesus and Moses: Jesus' superiority further defined* (3:5–6). Thus far in the argument of the present section, two truths have been clearly and firmly established. The first is, that both Jesus and Moses are characterised by faithfulness. The second is, that (notwithstanding this, neither backtracking from it) Jesus is worthier of greater honour than Moses. Now a third facet of truth is brought out, and needs to be observed closely. *'Now Moses was faithful in all God's house as a servant, to testify to the things that were to be spoken later, but Christ is faithful over God's house as a son'*. It is still Moses and Jesus who are being compared and contrasted. Particular note needs to be taken here of our writer's words. They are carefully chosen. In connection with Moses, these are *'in'* and *'a servant'*. In connection with Jesus, these are *'over'* and *'a son'*.

We noted earlier that a twofold illustration is used in these verses— building and family, architecture and home. It is the second of these which is now being developed. Moses' faithful service was *'in all God's house as a servant'*. This was a high honour, one in which he served with great distinction. It did not compare, however, with the distinction accorded to the Lord Jesus, whose faithful service was *'over God's house as a son'*. The contrast is so clear. There is all the difference in the world between being a servant and a son, as well as being in a house or over a house. In the case of Jesus, while he also was a servant and, on his own admission, 'came not to be served but to serve, and to give his life as a ransom for many' (Matthew 20:28—a truth brought out in detail by the prophet Isaiah in his passages concerning Jesus as 'the servant of the LORD'), yet, more than a servant who served the household of God, he is a son who is both over and belongs to that very family, even the eternal Son of God. This gives him an authority which was not Moses' portion—hence the *'over'* for Jesus compared with the *'in'* for Moses. This Lord Jesus Christ, as we learned at the very beginning of Hebrews (1:3), not only made 'purification for sins' (his humiliation at Calvary) but is now seated 'at the right hand of the Majesty on high' (his exaltation in glory). As with Jesus and the prophets and Jesus and the angels, so it is with Jesus and Moses—while there *is* a comparison, yet really there *is no* comparison!

What of the phrase, *'to testify to the things that were to be spoken later'*? This is stated of Moses, and it is God, of course, who would do this speaking *'later'*. Moses spoke the words which God gave him to speak, declaring the divine laws and commands, setting forth how the people were to live and worship, and so on. He did not come up himself with the truths he uttered. God communicated through him to his people. He was God's faithful witness, as all of God's servants (ourselves included, if we are Christians) are to be. But Moses did not say all that there was to be said—by which is not meant that he held things back that he should have delivered, or that he sold God's message short, but that God had much more yet to say long after Moses' ministry was over and gone, and to this Moses' ministry continually pointed.

Jesus was to say to a company of Jews on one occasion, 'If you believed Moses, you would believe me; for he wrote of me' (John 5:46). In other words, there was much more revelation still to come, until eventually the word of God was complete (the full Scriptures which we now possess). Supremely, the one who would deliver this revelation was to be the Lord Jesus Christ. He it is who declares, 'I am … the truth' (John 14:6). He it is who is 'the faithful witness' (Revelation 1:5). Much was in shadow in Moses' day, whereas with the ministry of Jesus the light of truth shone brightly. The shadows are now gone and the darkness is now past, where God's truth is concerned—for 'in these last days he [God] has spoken to us by his Son' (1:2).

## Making it personal (3:6)

There remains part of 3:6 still to consider, at the end of this section. It arises from the statement about Jesus being 'faithful over God's house as a son', and urges a serious note of self-examination combined with a choice note of consolation. *'And we are his house if indeed we hold fast our confidence and our boasting in our hope'.*

It is the gospel privilege of all those who have been saved by grace through faith (Ephesians 2:8), redeemed 'with the precious blood of Christ' (1 Peter 1:19), and 'born again' (John 3:7), that they belong to God's house—indeed, that *'we are his house'*, belonging to his family, 'members of the household of God' (Ephesians 2:19), part and parcel of 'the household of faith' (Galatians 6:10). Of such and to such, God says, 'I will be a father to you, and you shall be sons and daughters to me' (2 Corinthians 6:18). Indeed, back in the prophecy of Isaiah God declared something most exquisite when he said, 'I will give in my house and within my walls a monument and a name better than sons and daughters' (Isaiah 56:5).

There is, however an *'if'* included in this statement in 3:6, and it is attached to the verb *'hold fast'*. The phrase runs like this: *'if indeed we hold fast our confidence and our boasting in our hope'*. One of the abiding themes of Hebrews (one of the key reasons for it being written in the first place) is perseverance—the constant business, through thick and thin, of keeping on keeping on, for the word of Jesus stands true that 'the one who endures to the end will be saved' (Matthew 24:13). Not least this is the great purpose behind the famous roll-call of the heroes of faith, in chapter 11. So the verse presently before us for comment is not in any way intended to take a stab at the security of God's people (the doctrine we know as the final perseverance of the saints, so beautifully affirmed by Jesus himself in John 6:39–40 in the words, 'And this is the will of him who sent me, that I should lose nothing of all that he has given me, but raise it up at the last day. For this is the will of my Father, that everyone who looks on the Son and believes in him should have eternal life, and I will raise him up on the last day'). It is intended, however, to keep us on our mettle and to discourage us from growing slack or weary in the Christian life (often no easy task, knowing our own hearts). The momentous privilege of being God's *'house'*, carries with it the momentous duty of holding *'fast'*.

The true believer will show whether he or she is a true believer by continuing, enduring, holding fast. It is not that they will never experience any blips, never have any falls, never commit any sins, never know any doubts (sadly), but they will ultimately *'hold fast'*. Why? Because they will be held fast, kept by the power of God. It is not a passive business for the Christian, however. We are to press on with watchfulness, in obedience, with prayerfulness, in devotion, always concerned to 'grow in the grace and knowledge of our Lord and Saviour Jesus Christ' (2 Peter 3:18). The verb has a nautical use, as is found in Acts 27:40 of maintaining a firm course in making for the shore. This is what the Hebrews all needed to be doing, and so do we, all the way to heaven.

In particular *'our confidence and our boasting in our hope'* are singled out for our holding fast. Christians have a confident and boasting hope! What is in view here? By *'confidence'* we take the writer to mean confidence in God, confidence in the work of Christ, confidence in the gospel, confidence in the doctrines of the faith, and such like. The word *'confidence'* that is used here has a special reference to boldness in witness—a boldness which will arise, in great measure, from those confidences just listed as examples. By *'boasting'*, the thought would be of a boasting or glorying in the hope of the gospel—'Christ in (us), the hope of glory' (Colossians 1:27), 'waiting for our blessed hope, the appearing of the glory of our great God and Saviour Jesus Christ' (Titus 2:13), 'waiting for new heavens and a new earth in which righteousness dwells' (2 Peter 3:13), rejoicing 'in hope of the glory of God' (Romans 5:2), considering 'that the sufferings of this present time are not worth comparing with the glory that is to be revealed in us' (Romans 8:18), setting our 'hope fully on the grace that will be brought to (us) at the revelation of Jesus Christ' (1 Peter 1:13), looking 'not to the things that are seen but to the things that are unseen. For the things that are seen are transient, but the things that are unseen are eternal' (2 Corinthians 4:18). Hope can very easily wilt or grow dim. It is the Christian's business (in complete dependence upon the Lord, while continually girding up our loins) to see that it does not. Ultimately, Moses cannot help us. Only Jesus can do us any good.

It remains to mention that some manuscripts (and so some Bible versions) add at the end of 3:6 the words 'firm to the end'. It is a disputed matter, with pros and cons. It does not affect the essence of the matter, however, for although our version does not include these words (but mentions them in a footnote) we have laid stress upon the enduring to the end nature of our Christian profession if its reality is to be demonstrated. Profession and life must agree together. Hebrews is intensely personal. Says Jesus, 'If you abide in my word, you are truly my disciples' (John 8:31). Where do we stand?

## Warnings of grace (3:7–19)

Although Moses is only mentioned once more in the course of this chapter, and then not again until chapter 8, he remains very much among those present, since the historical events recorded by way of illustration in this section have to do directly with Moses' time.

It always remains true that one of the easiest things to do in the Christian life is to go backwards. Indeed, in order to be successful in this regard you don't actually have to do anything. It will happen easily enough, quickly enough and certainly enough on its own. By contrast, one of the hardest things to do in the Christian life is to go forwards, and to do so steadily, firmly and consistently. You have to go for it, work at it and endure to the end. This is one of the clearest and most repeated emphases and applications of the letter to the Hebrews. The verse we have just left, 3:6, has urged, with all seriousness and passion, the importance of holding 'fast our confidence and our boasting in our hope'. And the first word now of the present portion of the chapter, *'Therefore'*, establishes an immediate connection—one the recipients of the epistle needed, and so do we.

We may discern four warnings of grace in the course of 3:7–19, though once again the divisions are not in any way legalistic. Everything still continues to flow.

## (1) Remember the solemn example of the people in the wilderness (verses 7–11).

Our writer gets underway here with a quotation from Psalm 95 (yet a further drawing upon the Old Testament in his concern to keep those to whom he wrote from forgetting the New Testament). The psalm verses quoted are Psalm 95:7–11. Before we consider them, however, he makes a key statement with regard to Scripture itself. *'Therefore, as the Holy Spirit says'* (3:7).

Why is this so key? For at least the following three reasons. It affirms the *origin* of Scripture. The phrase, *'as the Holy Spirit says'*, is equivalent to 'God says', for the Holy Spirit is the third person of the Trinity—and, as the apostle Peter writes, 'For no prophecy was ever produced by the will of man, but men spoke from God as they were carried along by the Holy Spirit' (2 Peter 1:21). It affirms the *authority* of Scripture, for since it is the very word of God ('the LORD has spoken', Isaiah 16:13; 'This is the word of the LORD', Zechariah 4:6; 'every word that comes from the mouth of God', Deuteronomy 8:3, quoted by the Lord Jesus in Matthew 4:4; 'All Scripture is breathed out by God', 2 Timothy 3:16), it arrests us in our tracks, lays immediate and strong claims upon us, and demands both our attention and obedience. And it affirms the *relevance* of Scripture, for while the word of man has its day and then is gone, 'the word of our God shall stand forever' (Isaiah 40:8)—it is truth unchanged and unchanging from the God who is unchanged and unchanging, so never out of date, never for former generations only while not for ours. We had cause to remark early on in the commentary that our author takes a very high view of the Old Testament; but this is only part, of course, of the very high view he takes of Scripture as a whole (the whole Bible, so to speak). We should, without question, be imitators of him in this, with the highly practical result that we must 'be doers of the word, and not hearers only, deceiving (our)selves' (James 1:22).

So the example before us now (one which affirms all of these things—Scripture's origin, authority and relevance) is Psalm 95. Beginning with a fervent call to worship ('Oh come, let us sing to the LORD; let us make a joyful noise to the rock of our salvation!'), going on to affirm the excellence of Jehovah ('For the LORD is a great God, and a great King above all gods'), and giving a reminder of the grace of God ('For he is our God, and we are the people of his pasture, and the sheep of his hand'), the psalm then proceeds to take us back a long way to the experience and behaviour of the children of Israel during their years in the wilderness.

God had performed a most mighty work, having delivered his people from their bondage and slavery in Egypt ('with a mighty hand and an outstretched arm, with great deeds of terror, with signs and wonders', Deuteronomy 26:8). For a while things seemed to go well enough, but the rot soon set in. The people hardened their hearts against God, complained at what they considered to be his lack of proper provision for them on their journey, pined for the old life (and the old menu) of Egypt, and gave Moses continual grief. It must always be remembered that the journey from Egypt to Canaan need only have taken a few months. Instead it took forty years, on account of God's judgment upon the people for their unfaithfulness, rebellion and testing of him.

Now, at a time when the writer of Hebrews feared that something of an identical spirit was taking hold of (or showing signs of taking hold of) the people to whom he wrote, he urges them to 'remember, remember' what happened previously to their forebears, and not to commit the same sin and folly themselves this time around. He begins, with the psalmist, *'Today, if you hear his voice'* (3:7). He brings it right up to date, right to their own door, in a manner that could not ring more contemporarily with them. And the same 'today' brings it right to the door of God's people now. God's word always has the immediacy of 'today, this moment, right now, present duty, something that cannot wait and should not be left'. That is its nature, whether it is being read or preached. Though old, it is ever new. Though ancient, it is ever modern. Though long ago established, it is ever fresh. Scripture is, in a word, God's *'voice'*, and, as we are about to see, it is addressed not least to our *'hearts'*.

He continues: *'do not harden your hearts as in the rebellion, on the day of testing in the wilderness'* (3:8). A hard heart is one where the truth of God and the gospel makes no impression, is listened to without proper attention, dismissed without interest, with nothing of its appeal to mind, heart, conscience and will getting though.

The particular reference must clearly be to the occasion recorded in Exodus 17 when the people were in an especially quarrelling and grumbling mood (fundamentally against God, although they took it out on Moses), over their thirstiness and the lack of water—which led to God directing Moses to strike the rock and water would come out of it, which it did. Things had even come to the point where the people were asking, 'Is the LORD among us or not?' (Exodus 17:7).

This was outright rebellion, nothing less. Significantly, Moses named the place where it took place both Massah (meaning 'testing') and Meribah (meaning 'quarrelling'), as a lasting testimony to what had taken place there. What strong charges those are: putting God to the test and quarrelling with him, the Almighty, the covenant God. The one charge presumed upon him, the other refused to trust him. Their hearts took a turn against God, forgetting his mercies, slighting his commandments, discarding his judgments. They walked by sight rather than by faith, conveniently being unmindful of the provisions the Lord had made for them previously. Sadly, such summed up the history of their demeanour in the wilderness. Such an attitude on the part of men (and, worse still, on the part of God's people) is the height of sin, and will go neither unnoticed nor unpunished by God. Of it, God declared, *'where your fathers put me to the test and saw my works for forty years'* (3:9). Despite one token of grace, one abundant supply, one exhibition of divine patience after another, the people's attitude did not improve. The length of time indicated here only serves to make the people's unbelief an even greater sin than it would have been anyway.

English Bible versions vary over whether *for forty years* belongs (as we have it in our version) at the end of the sentence which began in verse 7, or with the beginning of the sentence which begins in verse 10. The difference is not immense, and good sense is given either way. The presence of the conjunction *'Therefore'*, however, which comes next, makes the rendering we have before us in the version taken for this commentary the more suitable one.

*'Therefore I was provoked with that generation, and said, 'They always go astray in their heart; they have not known my ways'* (3:10). They had certainly seen God's ways, day in and day out, year after year, but they chose not to observe them, not to take notice of them—in a word, to disregard them, as if they were nothing at all from no one at all. What an abiding lesson is here: the danger of seeing God's ways but not observing them, receiving from God yet never being thankful to him, presuming upon God but reckoning to owe him nothing. Such a stance will not go unpunished—it did not do so then, and it will not do so now. It is a provocation to God, a stirring of his anger, a grieving of his nature, hence his terribly solemn and far-reaching pronouncement, *'As I swore in my wrath, "They shall not enter my rest"'* (3:11). Those words from heaven record the wages of their sin. The verb *'swore'* is very solemn, indicating God's settled resolve and purpose. His decision concerning them was irreversible.

In the immediate context rehearsed in Psalm 95, what God calls *'my rest'* is the rest he had for them in the land of Canaan, the promised land, 'a land flowing with milk and honey' (Deuteronomy 26:9). The generation that came out of Egypt died over the course of the years traversing round and round in the wilderness, whereas the new generation that was born during those years was the one which entered in. At the end of the day, the rebellious ones excluded themselves. In no way could God be blamed, for he was the offended one, and they had not been in the least bit concerned about offending him. Reader, take note, whether you are a Christian or not. 'Do not be deceived: God is not mocked, for whatever one sows, that will he also reap' (Galatians 6:7).

## (2) Beware 'an evil, unbelieving heart' (verse 12).

This is the second of the four warnings of grace, and both words are important, and important together—both warning and grace. Hebrews is very much an epistle of warning, and this present verse is a classic case in point. It is also very much an epistle of grace, for it is so full of the Lord Jesus Christ, the one 'full of grace' (John 1:14). And even though this particular warning is both sharp and direct, it is delivered with pastoral grace. This is evident in the writer using the word *'brothers'* (compare 'holy brothers' back in verse 1). He does not shout his warnings to them or throw his warnings at them, but comes in the spirit of brotherly love and pastoral affection, as always befits every minister of the gospel and pastor of the flock. He is concerned for them. He yearns over them. He desires the very best for them. He cannot bear to see them in danger of wandering away from the truth, away from the gospel, away from the Lord. In a word, he loves them. May all who lay any genuine claim to being called of God in preaching and pastoring be of like spirit.

'Take care, brothers, lest there be in any of you an evil, unbelieving heart, leading you to fall away from the living God'. The call, 'Take care', leads into a close application of the departure from God just evidenced in the historical retrospect of the previous verse, which quoted from Psalm 95. As if to say, this is what happened to them— make sure it doesn't happen to you. When writing his first letter to the Christians at Corinth, the apostle Paul dealt in similar vein. 'Now these things [the events in the lives of God's people of old] took place as examples for us, so that we might not desire evil as they did' (1 Corinthians 10:6). This highlights the importance of learning from history, especially spiritual history; and we can only learn from it effectively if we study it carefully. We shall never learn if we are casual about 'taking care'. The number of times in political and national life when people speak about 'learning the lessons' or 'lessons must be learned'—but it doesn't always follow that that is what happens. Let it be better among the people of God.

But of what are the people addressed in Hebrews (and us, with them) to be taking care? Our writer continues, *'lest there be in any of you* [in any one of you, for, as the saying goes, there's always one, and it only takes one individual to affect for ill an entire congregation or company—remember Paul's teaching 'that a little leaven leavens the whole lump' (1 Corinthians 5:6)] *an evil, unbelieving heart* [literally, 'an evil heart of unbelief'] *leading you to fall away from the living God'*. Tragically, just such a heart led to the exclusion of countless precious souls from the land of promise. Behind it lay a total lack of confidence and trust in God, *'the living God'*.

The crucial duty lying behind this warning is that expressed in Proverbs 4:23, 'Keep (or, 'guard') your heart with all vigilance, for from it flow the springs of life'. As to why this heart-guarding duty (each guarding his or her own) *is* so crucial, Jeremiah furnishes the answer in the famous 17:9 of his prophecy: 'The heart is deceitful above all things, and desperately sick; who can understand it?'. Which of us can truly understand our own heart? It follows and wanders. It waxes hot and cold, obedient and disobedient. It responds and rebels. It requires us to be constantly on the watch, as a guard worth the name must always be.

What, precisely, is *'an evil, unbelieving heart'*? What is not intended here is the unbelieving heart of the unconverted sinner. Rather our writer intends the unbelieving heart of the one who has professed faith in the Lord Jesus Christ. At one time all looked well, but in due course things changed, and changed very much for the worse. There was an apparent departure from the faith, a denying of the truth, a ceasing to walk in the ways of godliness, a failure to uphold and esteem the name of the Lord, a doubting of God's wisdom in his dealings or his ability and willingness to perform his promises—and such like. The word for this is 'apostasy'—and the word used here in verse 12 translated *'fall away'* (or, 'depart') is the Greek word from which our English word 'apostasy' derives. It begins in the heart and then develops and shows forth in the life.

We must not pre-empt here the highly important teaching which will comprise further uncompromising warnings on this theme in chapters 6 and 10. Those passages must wait their turn, when we come to them. But this is a strong salvo fired across the bows of those to whom Hebrews was first addressed, and it loses none of its force now that it comes our way also. This is not something which happens accidentally. There is everything of the deliberate about it. When someone no longer holds firmly to the faith as they once did; when they no longer love the Saviour, desire his glory, gather with his people as in days previously; when they turn aside from the gospel, are careless where holiness and separation from the world is concerned; when they turn back to their old ways, old haunts, old associates—all of this does not just 'happen', still less happen overnight. Thought goes into it. The will is centrally involved. It amounts to nothing less than desertion. By and large, they know exactly what they are doing (even if it may have been building up for a long while). No wonder our writer begins this verse with the heartfelt cry concerning taking care of our hearts. Indeed we must. It is a matter of life and death. Moreover, never must the glorious Bible doctrine of the final perseverance and preservation (both) of the saints be made an excuse for living as we please, easing up, or taking our own course when we have professed to belong to *the living God*.

All of this is what happened to the Israelites in the wilderness, the illustration of which has already been provided in this third chapter. God had most certainly manifested himself to his people of old as *the living God*—choosing them, redeeming them, leading them, providing for them, exercising remarkable longsuffering towards them, and so on, unlike the 'gods' of the nations all around, including Egypt itself where God's people had been held in bondage. It made their sin of departing from him all the more gross—after all that he had been to them and after all that he had done for them. They had committed idolatry, spiritual adultery and multiple unfaithfulness to God's covenant. No wonder they died in the wilderness and never saw the promised land. Yet this is no ancient danger or experience only. It is ever with us—and, potentially, ever within us. Back to the guarding of the heart! The only alternative to apostasy is to 'cling (or, 'cleave') to the LORD (our) God' (Joshua 23:8)—the very duty to which Joshua, Moses' successor, exhorted the leaders of Israel towards the end of his life.

## (3) Encourage one another to 'keep on keeping on' (verses 13–15).

In the previous verse our writer addressed himself to 'any of you'. Now he employs the phrase *'one another'*. We might note the distinction as follows. The first expression looks the individual in the eye and speaks of his duty concerning himself. The second expression, while still eyeball to eyeball, places the individual in the context of his relationship with other believers. It is the contrast between 'you' (the individual) and 'us' (the congregation)—or, the Christian and the church. Each Christian is responsible for himself. Equally, every Christian is responsible for his brothers and sisters. There is the personal duty and there is the corporate duty. This third warning (still of grace) has an eye to the corporate.

*'But exhort one another every day, as long as it is called 'today', that none of you be hardened by the deceitfulness of sin'* (3:13). This is reminiscent of Galatians 6:1: 'Brothers, if anyone is caught in any transgression, you who are spiritual should restore him in a spirit of gentleness', as well as the major picture Paul uses of Christians being many members of the one body (the church) of which the sole head is the Lord Jesus Christ (this is worked out in detail in 1 Corinthians 12). The verb *'exhort'* is made up of two words, the effect of which is to strengthen the meaning, priority and urgency of what is being bidden here.

This sense of mutual care and responsibility will go a long way towards preventing folk from falling into the danger that has been outlined since verse 7—this whole danger of apostasy. It is so much easier to talk to others about someone who you fear is going astray than it is to speak with them face to face. Yet here a daily (in other words, continual) duty is laid upon each individual Christian to 'look out for' his brothers and sisters in Christ. This is done chiefly in the context of the local church, and highlights the regular New Testament expectation that every Christian will actually belong to a particular congregation of God's people, and will not neglect 'to meet together, as is the habit of some' (10:25).

Mutual encouragement (by both word and example) is of inestimable value in assisting to keep one another on the 'straight and narrow', so that there is no falling away. Each one counts, and must know that they count. They will never know this if no one takes interest in them or expresses care and affection for them. We are to hold each other up, draw alongside one another, warn, assist, exhort one another in a manner of meekness, and not live to ourselves only. And this is not to be 'put on' for special occasions, but is something God requires of us *every day, as long as it is called "today"*. The time will come in the purposes of God when *'today'* will end and the season of mutual encouragement to perseverance will be over. But that is not yet.

It is challenging to note the recurrence of the words 'one another' in the New Testament, highlighting the varied nature of our responsibilities towards one another. It covers, for example, mutual prayer ('pray for one another', James 5:16), mutual love ('love one another', John 13:34), mutual care ('care for one another', 1 Corinthians 12:25), mutual encouragement ('encourage one another', 1 Thessalonians 4:18), mutual edification ('build one another up', 1 Thessalonians 5:11), mutual instruction ('instruct one another', Romans 15:14) and mutual peacekeeping ('be at peace with one another', Mark 9:50). Well may we cry out, 'Who is sufficient for these things?' (2 Corinthians 2:16)—to which the only answer is, 'our sufficiency is from God' (2 Corinthians 3:5).

The verse continues, *'that none of you may be hardened by the deceitfulness of sin'*. Whether or not any of those to whom Hebrews is addressed had already fallen into this state of deception, we have no way of knowing. Certainly, however, the writer could see it coming if things continued as they were—it was on the horizon, and the horizon was drawing ever closer. So, with a true pastoral heart, he speaks up now, rather than waiting until things have gone too far for remedy. Even the apparently softest of hearts can be hardened terrifyingly quickly.

The phrase *'the deceitfulness of sin'* is striking, and recalls both Romans 7:13 ('that sin might be shown to be sin') and 11:25 of Hebrews itself ('the fleeting pleasures of sin'). It is in the nature of sin to be deceitful, not least because the one who himself is the deceiver is none other than the devil. He is the deceiving one and he weaves webs of deceit, seeking (as he did with Eve and then Adam in the Garden of Eden) to lead us into sin, painting sin in attractive colours yet hiding its miseries and consequences. Sin promises good and delivers evil.

Where the unbeliever is concerned, sin's deceitfulness is seen in making the sinner feel that sin doesn't matter, that God does not see it, and that there is nothing to be feared as a result of it. That, of course, is where 'sin' and 'God' are acknowledged in the first place, otherwise the very idea of something called 'sin' or of answerability to God does not occur to a person. In such a case, sin has become even more successfully deceitful! Where the believer is concerned, sin's deceitfulness is evident in such areas as these: it is a light thing, it can quickly and easily be forgiven, it can be kept private and so need not compromise a public Christian testimony, or this or that particular thing isn't really sin at all (when, in truth, it is). Beware the temptation to take such a view, and be on the lookout to warn and help fellow believers who show danger signs of going that way. If we always saw sin in its true colours, then we would, when tempted, run a mile from it, and encourage others to do the same.

Sin would take us away from Christ in a moment, if given free rein. This matter of apostasy is not some sort of 'straw man' that doesn't really exist but is just set up to frighten us. Strange though it may sound to put it this way: maybe there are times when we need to be frightened, pulled up short, in order to realise that if we 'loosen up' in the things of Christ, we play with serious fire. It is no use resting (or lounging) upon some past profession of him if now we have nothing to show for it day by day. Self-distrust (which does not have to be the robber of assurance) is a needful characteristic, much despised. The words of 2 Peter 1:10 are ever relevant: 'Therefore, brothers, be all the more diligent to make your calling and election sure', as are the words of Paul when he writes, 'Therefore let anyone who thinks that he stands take heed lest he fall' (1 Corinthians 10:12).

*'For we share in Christ, if indeed we hold our original confidence firm to the end'* (3:14). What is meant by this mutual sharing (or, partaking) *'in Christ'*? At one level it may refer to the mutual interest that all believers have in the Lord Jesus Christ, by grace through faith—the union which is the spring of all our true joys and pleasures. This would fit both the immediate and wider context of Hebrews, with this emphasis we are finding of mutual responsibility and mutual encouragement among Christians. It has this fundamental (we might even say, organic) basis: we belong to Christ, are united to him, and so we belong and are united to one another in the family of God, the church. It is the union of the branch to the vine, where the whole nourishment and support, indeed the very life, of the branch depends upon the vine—not the union of the ivy on the old garden wall, where the ivy has its own roots and merely clings to and around the wall as it climbs up it.

Paul expresses this truth when he writes, 'because we are members of his body' (Ephesians 5:30), gathering up the thought of our double union—first with the Lord Jesus and, consequently, with other Christians. At another level it may go a little further and touch upon our (that is, Christians') participation in all the blessings of 'such a great salvation' (2:3), covering both that which we already enjoy even while still upon the earth and that which awaits us in the glory when 'we will always be with the Lord' (1 Thessalonians 4:17). Interestingly, the verse immediately following that just quoted reads: 'Therefore encourage one another with these words'.

This sharing in Christ will be proved at the last *'if indeed we hold our original confidence* [the beginning of our confidence] *firm to the end'* [not just beginning, but continuing and ending the life, walk and triumph of faith]. A similar thought will be expressed by our writer when we come to 6:11, 'And we desire each one of you to show the same earnestness to have the full assurance of hope until the end'. The great passion of the true Christian is to *'hold ... firm'*, to 'continue in the faith, stable and steadfast, not shifting from the hope of the gospel' (Colossians 1:23), all to the glory of God. The evidence of true conversion and true piety is to persevere, to maintain ardour and devotion to the Redeemer and his cause.

This third warning of grace concludes with the following words, again quoting Psalm 95:7–8: *As it is said, "Today, if you hear his voice, do not harden your hearts as in the rebellion"* (3:15). This, however, is no vain repetition. The warning of the danger of failing to endure, giving up part way through the Christian life, slackening our pace for heaven is so real and so serious that it can never be stated too often. So having made his point very clearly about mutual encouragement (what we called, 'keeping on keeping on'), our writer enforces things once again. Consider what happened to your forefathers, is his message. Don't let it happen to you. Let there be no heart rebellion against the Lord, no putting him to the test, no provoking him to displeasure. Hear his voice in his word, follow in the way of his commandments, delight yourself in all his ways, doing so both today and every day. Without question, this exhortation to the Hebrews then is equally as much the Lord's exhortation to us now, for, recalling 1 Corinthians 10:6 again, 'these things took place as examples for us, that we might not desire evil as they did'.

## (4) Keep your eye clearly and firmly on the goal (verses 16–19).

The fourth and final warning of grace looks to the future—the rest that God provides—and prepares the way for the fuller treatment of this theme shortly in chapter 4.

The hearing of God's voice, so much to the fore in the Psalm 95 quotation, is the very thing that was neglected by Israel during the years in the wilderness. They exhibited less and less interest in hearing God speak to them through Moses, and were more and more concerned to follow their own whims and devices. So the Hebrews now receive a rapid series of hot shots fired straight across their bows. Here they are:

- 'For who were those who heard and yet rebelled?' (3:16)

- 'Was it not all those who left Egypt led by Moses?'

- 'And with whom was he provoked for forty years?' (3:17)

- 'Was it not with those who sinned, whose bodies fell in the wilderness?'

- 'And to whom did he swear that they would not enter his rest, but to those who were disobedient?' (3:18).

It is immediately observable how questions are raised and then answered, one by one, coming out here as three sets, each one arising out of the previous one. This question and answer approach is a very appropriate way of rendering this whole short passage. The facts are shattering. The ones who heard and rebelled are the very ones whom God had led out of Egypt under Moses' leadership. It was they who provoked God, year after year after year, and as a result of their sin they perished in the wilderness.

And it was again this very same company, these disobedient ones, to whom God swore *that they would not enter his rest*. In the event, not even Moses himself entered the promised land (not that he was among the rebellious ones). Joshua was appointed by God to take his place. How could those who had been so wonderfully favoured by God turn against him in this way? Well might we ask, were it not that we know our own hearts, how weak we are, how fickle we can be. Times do not change, and neither do hearts. We trust the Lord, we distrust him. We listen to him, we refuse to hear him. We follow him, we draw back from him. We obey him, we disobey him. Is that not true? It was amazing that God put up with the people for as long as he did, and it is even more amazing that he shows such patience and longsuffering to us also.

The great key to endurance and perseverance revealed here is not to forget the goal (the ultimate goal, that is) of the Christian life, the celestial city that awaits us at the end of our present earthly pilgrimage. The Israelites redeemed from Egypt increasingly lost sight of where they were heading. Their minds wandered back to the days in Egypt, recalling the food with relish, but forgetting the hardship. It seems that their hearts still felt the pull of 'the old', and experienced less and less of the joy of 'the new'.

It was said famously of one of old that heaven was in him before he was in heaven. Sadly, such a thing could not be said of these folk— but can it be said of us? Are we consciously pressing on to glory—that is, pressing on to God? However far off the goal might sometimes appear (on the far horizon or even beyond the far horizon of our desires, longings and expectations), is it real to us? Remember again, from earlier in the commentary: 'Christ in (us), the hope of glory' (Colossians 1:17). Add on, 'When Christ who is your life appears, then you also will appear with him in glory' (Colossians 3:4). The key thing the Israelites failed to do highlights for us an area where we who now profess Christ as Saviour and Lord must not fail.

*'So we see that they were unable to enter because of unbelief'* (3:19). The word *'unable'* is very strong and final. In the light of their rebellion their entering into God's rest in Canaan was quite literally an impossibility. God would not allow it. Trust in God was abandoned. They declared of themselves whether they belonged to him or not. Unbelief is a killer, and deprives of all possession of covenant blessings. Whenever this happens, as was observed in connection with 3:11, God is not to blame.

It ought to be added that the teaching of this passage in Hebrews is not that true believers either can or will fall finally away from grace or fail to reach our heavenly inheritance. 'The Lord knows those who are his' (2 Timothy 2:19). Rather what is written here is in line with such very solemn teaching as is expressed by Paul, when he wrote, 'Examine yourselves, to see whether you are in the faith. Test yourselves. Or do you not realize this about yourselves, that Jesus Christ is in you?—unless indeed you fail to meet the test!' (2 Corinthians 13:5). It is the solemn unvarnished truth that while we are saved through faith, we are lost through unbelief.

Here, then, are these four warnings of grace (or gracious warnings):

(1) Remember the solemn example of the people in the wilderness.

(2) Beware an 'evil, unbelieving heart'.

(3) Encourage one another to 'keep on keeping on'.

(4) Keep your eye clearly and firmly on the goal.

The only sure indication that someone who says they are a Christian really is a Christian is that they press on, even when along the way (sadly) they may experience seasons of spiritual coolness. Even when they backslide, in due course they return to the Lord, they are brought back. Ultimately, through fair weather and foul, on and on they go. They 'grow in the grace and knowledge of our Lord and Saviour Jesus Christ' (2 Peter 3:18). They keep right on to the end of the road. It is only someone who professes to be or who appears to be a true believer who can commit apostasy. An unconverted person cannot do it, since, as we have seen, it involves a person falling 'away from the living God' (3:14), failing to hold their 'original confidence firm to the end' (3:16), and ending up departing from God in 'unbelief' (3:18).

Thankfully it did not happen literally to every single one of the Israelites in Moses' day, neither is apostasy the end result of every professing Christian who goes astray in our own day. But these warnings are needful. This is a vital matter, and they are intended to keep us from being either hypocrites now or castaways at the last. It is not for no reason that our writer began this chapter by calling us all to 'consider Jesus' (3:1). The only safe way to heaven is to keep our eyes, minds and hearts fixed upon him.

# Chapter 4
# Rest, the Word and
# the Saviour

Chapter headings in our Bibles should never cause us just to assume that one subject is finished with and another is taken up, for very often that is not the case. We have now in Hebrews an instance of that very thing. Although we move from chapter 3 to chapter 4, two things in particular do not change. First and foremost, the overall theme is unaltered, namely, the superiority and pre-eminence of the Lord Jesus Christ. Indeed, this theme will never change throughout the entire epistle, for with it our author begins, continues and ends. In the second place, the specific aspect of the unfolding of that theme that is being handled also remains unchanged, and that is Jesus' superiority to Moses. The very opening of this new chapter, *'Therefore'*, demonstrates this.

The chapter falls naturally into three parts: verses 1–11, 12–13 and 14–16. The first revolves around the word 'rest'; the second has important things to say about the word of God; the third reveals most exquisitely the heart of Jesus.

## Four rests (4:1–11)

It is worth recalling two things from Hebrews so far, as regards why it needed to be written in the first place: the danger of falling short in the Christian life and the importance of keeping on. The writer does not let go of these twin truths. The exhortation now continues, with the key word being 'rest'. The word occurs eight times in the course of this section, with 'rested' once and 'it' (referring to this 'rest') once also. We cannot miss it! We shall discover, furthermore, a choice instance here of the ever-abiding relevance of God's word—for the promise concerning rest that is expounded in this chapter is just as applicable to us now as it was to those to whom it was first made. Unravelling the passage carefully, we discover four related 'rests'.

### (1) God's rest

The chapter commences in this way. *'Therefore, while the promise of entering his rest still stands'* (or, 'being left', 'still remaining') (4:1). This is being kept to the fore, and necessarily so, because in the days of God's people of old they failed to keep it to the fore. They let it slip to the back of their minds, until it had disappeared out of their minds altogether. The result of that forgetfulness is what prompts the words that follow: *'let us fear lest any of you should seem to have failed to reach it'* (the words *'Let us fear therefore'* are actually the opening words in the original, and the verb *'fear'* lends weight and solemnity to what is written here). They forgot, and as a direct result of their forgetting, they came short of *'entering his* [God's] *rest'.*

With respect to this rest being spoken of as God's rest, *4:4* needs to be noted at this point. *'For he* [God] *has somewhere spoken of the seventh day in this way: "And God rested on the seventh day from all his works"'* (compare the end of 4:3, *'although his* ['the', which, of course, are God's and no one else's] *works were finished from the foundation of the world'*). The quotation is from Genesis 2:2, when, having created all things out of nothing in six days, with each of those days having their evening, God came to the seventh day, a day with no evening. 'So God blessed the seventh day and made it holy, because on it God rested from all his work that he had done in creation' (Genesis 2:3). As in 2:6 of Hebrews, the word *somewhere* does not imply that our author was uncertain where in Scripture to locate the quotation; rather, he regarded it as such a well-known text among those to whom he wrote that, if they wished to, they could easily look it up for themselves. The Genesis verse quoted here does not imply that God ceased to do anything, once creation was finished. Far from it! He is the sovereign God who rules all things, fulfils his purposes and glorifies his name. He is the ever-active God!

God's own rest is his both in the sense that he himself enjoys it (it is, we might say, part of his delight in being God, as he beholds the excellence, beauty and order of all that he has made, rejoicing in the work of his own hands), and that he invites us to share it and enjoy it with him. How we are to do that immediately becomes apparent.

## (2) Gospel rest

The good news of the gospel was not something that was suddenly 'new' with the days of the New Testament. It had been preached from earliest days. Its first expression was in the very context of the fall of mankind into sin, as found in God's delightful and gracious words recorded in Genesis 3:15: 'I will put enmity between you and the woman, and between your offspring and their offspring; he shall bruise your head, and you shall bruise his heel'. This is a clear reference to the Lord Jesus Christ's great victory over Satan (the devil, the serpent) at Calvary and with the empty tomb. Thereafter, the gospel continued to be preached throughout the Old Testament. Although much of this was through types, shadows and symbols, many of these were crystal clear. Moreover, this 'gospelling' is evident in every genre of Old Testament literature (the historical books, psalms, wisdom literature, prophets and so on). Page after page of Scripture, right from its start, declares God's grace and mercy for the sinner and calls upon sinners to repent, believe and be saved. This approach—drawing arguments from the Old Testament—is quite deliberate, for the letter is addressed to Hebrew Christians, who, being themselves in danger of slipping back, need to see clearly that the Old Testament itself furnishes them with ample reasoning why they should adhere firmly to the things of Christ.

That is why our writer now says: *'For good news came to us* [the people to whom he is writing] *just as to them* [the people of old, their forefathers], *but the message they heard* [literally, and strikingly, 'the word of hearing'] *did not benefit them'* (4:2). And why was this? What is the explanation? We are told that it was *'because they were not united by faith with those who listened'*. This echoes precisely what we have already read in 3:19: 'they were unable to enter because of unbelief'. It is their unbelief which gives the game away. They heard with their ears, but the message was not profitable to them because it was *'not united by* (or, 'mixed with', 'did not meet with') *faith'*. It did them no good. They did what many people, sadly, are doing all the time: hearing, but not believing. For God's word, his gospel, to profit us when we listen to it, it must be received with meekness (James 1:21), we must tremble at it (Isaiah 66:2), it must pierce 'to the division of soul and spirit, of joints and marrow' and discern 'the thoughts and intentions of the heart' (4:12 of our present chapter). This had not happened with countless souls of those who had been delivered from Egypt yet died in the wilderness. They had heard, heard, and heard again, but they did not have ears to hear for there to be any lasting spiritual profit (Matthew 13:9). They had trifled with it instead of taking it seriously. Let us not be among such! How is it, dear reader, with your hearing and believing the word of God, the gospel of salvation?

The message of the gospel is good news in itself, but it only becomes good news to those who listen to it as they believe what they hear. Whether the message, at one moment, focuses upon the call 'prepare to meet your God' (Amos 4:12) or 'flee from the wrath to come' (Luke 3:7); or at another moment, the ringing call to respond to the summons to 'repentance toward God and ... faith in our Lord Jesus Christ' (Acts 20:21); or again, 'Seek the LORD while he may be found; call upon him while he is near' (Isaiah 55:6)—it demands a response, and the only response that is right and safe is always to trust and obey whatever God says.

There are such great blessings in hearing the gospel. But there are great dangers as well. Does that appear a strange thing to say? Yet the dangers are apparent—such as, preferring your own way of works rather than God's way of grace; being awakened to feel your sin, but never actually casting yourself upon the Lord Jesus; deciding you will wait until another time, a more convenient season, a later invitation; accepting the gospel in your mind, but never knowing its power in your heart or in your life. Beware the dangers—and be careful to avoid them!

*'For we who have believed* ('the believing ones') *enter that rest'* (4:3), testifies our writer. The contrast with those who had not believed the word of salvation is made clear. Unbelief bars us from the rest of the gospel, while faith gives us the entrance in. The *'we'* indicates those whom Paul designates 'those who are of the household of faith' (Galatians 6:10), that is, the true church of Christ. It is through believing in the Lord Jesus that we are saved (remember the famous reply to the Philippian jailer, 'Believe in the Lord Jesus, and you will be saved, you and your household', in response to his question, 'Sirs, what must I do to be saved?', Acts 16:30–31).

The rest the gospel provides (the centre of which is being right with God, with all our sins pardoned, and all things being made new) is only for believers. It cannot be otherwise. That is why the point is being pressed here, for the writer to the Hebrews continues to have this lingering fear that some (at least) of those to whom he wrote had never truly had the saving root of the matter in them. Consequently, as a true pastor of souls, he has no option before the Lord but to challenge them. It is, not least, through such exhortations and warnings as Hebrews supplies that the grace of God establishes us in the faith, keeps us from falling, and secures us against being lost after all. We have every reason to be thankful for them.

It may be worth adding, that in taking the truth of God's rest at the end of creation and referring it now to the rest the gospel provides for those who believe upon the Lord Jesus, our writer is not taking liberties with Scripture. Rather, he is following it wherever it leads, making the proper connections it suggests, drawing the appropriate conclusions it requires—and this constitutes a very desirable and correct manner of handling the word of God.

With this in mind, up comes a quote from Psalm 95 once more (and not for the only time in this third chapter): *'as he* [God] *has said, "As I swore in my wrath, They shall not enter my rest"'*. The fact that it is God's rest ensures that he receives all the glory. It is not man's rest, but the gift of God to sinners. You can only enjoy God's rest by entering into it—which is to say, you can only possess the blessings of salvation by laying hold of them through faith. Faith is the way 'in'— and, bearing in mind that Hebrews is written to encourage not only self-examination but also perseverance, faith is equally the way 'on'. Our writer wishes to be sure that those whom he addresses have both 'come in' and are 'going on'. Have *you*? Are *you*?

## (3) Canaan's rest

This is the third aspect of the theme of 'rest' which is being explored here. The thread of verses 5–8 reminds us of the historical background to all of this. The repetition, almost straightaway, of Psalm 95:11 in *4:5* (*'And again in this passage he said, "They shall not enter my rest"'*) recalls the wilderness wanderings on the way to the land of Canaan. Certainly it remains tragically true that *'those who formerly received the good news failed to enter because of disobedience'* (4:6), and it may be that this raises a question which ought to be addressed at this point. It might be suggested that since nearly all the adults who came out of Egypt died in the wilderness and so never arrived in Canaan, did the promises of God thereby fail in their accomplishment? It might look that way, but that is not actually the case. Rather, it is appropriate to say that God's original promise with respect to him bringing his people out of Egypt and into Canaan (Exodus 6:6–8 is a choice expression of this) was his promise to Israel as a people, and not of necessity to all of that particular generation. If it had been so, then a legitimate question could be raised concerning the divine promise. But it was not like that. Indeed, the word of the LORD to the people through Moses in Exodus 19:5–6 makes very plain the divine requirement: 'Now therefore, if you will indeed obey my voice and keep my covenant ...'. Yet, sadly, most of them neither obeyed God's voice nor kept his covenant. Consistently it is their unbelief and disobedience which is given as the reason for their not entering in. So it was the next generation which experienced the fulfilment of the divine promise, a promise which in no way did God fail to perform.

Notwithstanding all of this, yet in gospel terms the opportunity to enter into God's gospel rest still remains: *'Since therefore it remains for some to enter it'*. How so? For this reason: the day of grace still continues, the invitations of grace still are issued, the blessings of grace are still freely available—for, in one word, it is still *'Today'*.

Psalm 95 is still fully in use here: *'again he* (God) *appoints a certain day, "Today", saying through David so long afterward, in the words already quoted, "Today, if you hear his voice, do not harden your hearts"'* (4:7). God's words in this psalm, *'through David'* (note that carefully—*'saying through David'*—even though David is not mentioned at the head of this psalm in the book of Psalms), obviously came long after the events in the wilderness back in the book of Exodus. *'Today'*, however, though spoken of here as *'a certain day'*, is an ever present day, so long as it lasts. And currently, it still lasts.

Our writer has been dealing with things which took place in the days of Moses and under his leadership. He now glides smoothly to Joshua, who was Moses' successor, taking up the mantle and leading into Canaan those who made the entry. (That it is Joshua who is referred to here—not Jesus, as in at least one translation—is clear. Jesus is the Greek form of the Hebrew name Joshua).

The point is this. Even when the people of Israel entered Canaan under Joshua (and in so doing they did indeed enter into a real and tangible rest), they did not thereby experience the fullness of God's gospel rest. That is the meaning of *4:8*: *'For if Joshua had given them rest, God would not have spoken of another day later on'*. You could enter Canaan and not be saved (shades of Paul in Romans 9:6–7, where he writes, 'For not all who are descended from Israel belong to Israel, and not all are children of Abraham because they are his offspring'), just as you can attend church and be associated with God's people and not be saved. Many, Jesus tells us, will say to him, 'Lord, Lord', but those who 'will enter the kingdom of heaven' are those who do 'the will of my Father who is heaven'. To those who prove merely to be of the 'Lord, Lord' brigade (profession without possession), he will declare, 'I never knew you; depart from me' (Matthew 7:21–23). Otherwise, if Canaan in Joshua's day was all there was, why would God, *'so long afterward'*, be giving David Psalm 95 to write, with its call, *'Today, if you hear his voice, do not harden your hearts'*? It would be redundant. Yet here the quotation is—before the Hebrews' (and before our) very eyes and ears!

Still, however, one more layer of 'rest' remains in this section.

## (4) Heavenly rest

This is the focus of verses 9–11. They begin, *'So then, there remains a Sabbath rest for the people of God'* (4:9). The word *'a Sabbath rest'* forges again the link, already established in this chapter, with the days of creation—a link still further in evidence with what follows: *for whoever has entered God's rest has also rested from his works as God did from his'* (4:10). Just as we noted above, that it is possible to appear to belong to the company of the church, yet not to do so in reality because of not being saved, so even when you are truly saved and rightly rejoicing in sure possession of the Lord Jesus Christ's gospel rest, still that is not all there is to God's rest. There is more. And it is that 'more' which is found in the statement here concerning *'a Sabbath rest'*.

This is the only New Testament occurrence of this word. It is a different word from that translated 'the Sabbath', and does not refer here to our keeping of the weekly Sabbath. To this weekly keeping we are bound, of course, according to the abiding validity and force of the fourth commandment of the moral law (Exodus 20:8–11)—though now on the first day of the week since the resurrection, the Lord's Day, in light of the principle of the day changed but the Sabbath preserved. Rather, the word here is taking a longer view, looking forwards to the eternal, never-ending Sabbath rest of heaven, when we shall enjoy God himself and his rest of salvation for ever and ever in purity and delight. The weekly Sabbath here on earth is the foretaste of this (and sometimes a glorious foretaste, making us wish that we were already there); but it is only a foretaste. That is the fullness, this is the taste.

Heaven will be the perfect Sabbath, with nothing whatsoever to spoil or hinder it. Indeed, heaven will be one long and unbroken Sabbath (though by no means implying an endless time of doing nothing, for while we shall have ceased from the labours we engage in on earth, as Revelation 14:13 makes clear, heaven will certainly not be a place of idleness, inactivity or boredom, but rather of worship, fellowship and service). We shall be entirely taken up with enjoying God, with never any weariness or staleness. Our cup will continually be full of joy and bliss. That is what is before us. That is, for every Christian, the end of the journey which has no end. That is the *ultimate* gospel rest, God's rest, for all the people of God. That is the 'better country, that is, a heavenly one' which the Lord's dear ones desire (Hebrews 11:16). That is the new creation: 'But according to his promise we are waiting for new heavens and a new earth in which righteousness dwells' (2 Peter 3:13). As Job expresses it, very beautifully: 'There the wicked cease from troubling, and there the weary are at rest' (Job 3:17). A sweet repose! What an encouragement this is to seek the Lord's blessings upon our present earthly 'sabbath rests', that they may partake more and more of the character, serenity and delights of the heavenly one. And the fact that it is described here as *'God's rest'*, rather than 'our rest', is a beautiful reminder not only that it is his gift, but that it is his gift of himself to us, for ever.

So, not at all surprisingly, the next words we read are these: *'Let us therefore strive to enter that rest, so that no one may fall by the same sort of disobedience'* (4.11). The verb *'strive'* has the sense of 'make haste, be in earnest, labour, show diligence, exert all energy, engage every endeavour'—maybe even, colloquially, something like 'go for it with all speed and at all costs', and certainly the very opposite of settling in to things as they are at present, with no thought of things that are yet to come. Many an obstacle and difficulty does and will arise against us in this striving, and it is no use us drifting in a slack way through the Christian life as if there was no war on. The Lord Jesus spoke precisely to the point in saying, 'Do not labour for the food that perishes, but for the food that endures to eternal life, which the Son of Man will give to you' (John 6:27). The direction of our labouring distinguishes clearly the true believer from the dubious one.

It is true that Joshua, in leading the children of Israel into Canaan, led them into a rest; yet it was strictly a temporal and earthly rest. It was never a perfect or a final rest. There was always a further rest for God's people to look forward to. Jesus leads his redeemed into an eternal and spiritual rest. There is a very great difference. How earnestly we need to keep pursuing 'the holiness without which no one will see the Lord' (12:14). We have the offer of heaven. Let us be sure we do not fail to lay hold of it. For, as should be evident, the gospel rest and the heavenly rest belong inextricably together. You cannot have the second without the first—which is to say, first you must be saved from your sins if ever you would entertain any hope of entering God's spotless heaven, where no sin is found. So do not despise the message of salvation, for if you do not enter into that rest (the rest of the gospel), you will not enter into the other rest (the rest of heaven), and the very word of grace which invited you will become the terrible word of judgment which condemns you. If the earthly Sabbath holds no pleasure for you, how could you ever be at home in the heavenly one?

## The mighty word of God (4:12–13)

The key to establishing the connection between these two verses and the passage we have just considered is found in the small but telling word *'For'* (actually the second word in the original). Our author's point is this: the people of old had been marked by disobedience (3:11). But disobedience to what? Specifically, disobedience to the word of God. They had been given a whole range of divine commands which required not only their careful attention but also their resolute obedience. God had spoken his word of command (his word of covenant command, we might call it) through those whom he had raised up to declare it in his name. They had rejected it, however, and taken their own course in preference to it. That, therefore, will bring consequences. It always does.

We are taught here four essential truths concerning the word of God: what it is, how it works, what it does, and where it leads. Let us follow these through, one by one.

## (1) What this word is

It is called *'the word of God'* (4:12), and comprises the whole of Scripture (although we recognise, of course, that the people of the Old Testament did not have our complete Bible, because of when they lived—and, moreover, the Bible was still being written even as this letter to the Hebrews was written and first read). The phrase itself, though, *'the word of God'*, is used to refer to Scripture as an entirety (beginning with Genesis 1:1 and concluding with Revelation 22:21, and encompassing everything in between). This is the ultimate meaning of the phrase in 4:12 of Hebrews. It is a well-chosen description, for the Bible proceeds from God's mouth, it expresses his will, and it is his special manner of manifesting himself to us, communicating with us, and dealing with our souls. The very word 'word' implies speaking, and the expression 'for the mouth of the LORD has spoken' is familiar Bible talk (in, for example, Isaiah 1:20, 40:5 and 58:14).

In this connection, there is an important distinction to observe. The first is, that God has spoken, as a result of which the Bible is a closed book. There is nothing missing from it, nor anything to be added to it. It stands complete. The second is, that God still speaks, as a result of which the Bible is an opened book—not to receive further material, but rather that as it is read and preached God 'speaks' through it by his Holy Spirit to our minds, hearts, consciences, emotions (or, affections), wills and our lives. This truth is immediately confirmed by what comes next.

## (2) How this word works

The language here is vigorous. *'For the word of God is living and active, sharper than any two-edged sword'.* Think of the sword first of all. It is not a regular sword which is in mind, for such would ordinarily have a sharp side and a blunt side. Both sides of the sword of God's word, however, are sharp. It cuts with them both. It cannot be avoided. It can be relied upon at all times to do its work. It cannot fail. It is the sharpest sword imaginable, and is all cut and thrust. Not surprisingly, Paul calls it 'the sword of the Spirit' (Ephesians 6:17), in his exposition of the armour of God which the Christian is to take up and put on, for victory.

It has been suggested that there is a symbolism in the fact of it being a *'two-edged sword'*, namely that it has a judging edge and a saving edge. This may be a reasonable inference in itself—think, maybe, of the word of the gospel which we proclaim and commend with lip and life being 'to one a fragrance from death to death, to the other a fragrance from life to life' (2 Corinthians 2:16)—but this is unlikely to have been in our writer's mind at the time.

Two other words are used to describe this sword: *'living and active'.* This is no rusty, cast-off sword, superseded by more recent or better weapons. It is both *'living'* (lively, strong—the old word is 'quick') and *'active'* (continually at work, never missing its mark, inescapable, effective, powerful—indeed the word which *'active'* translates here provides us with our English words 'energy' and 'energetic', and the word of God is certainly energetic—you only have to feel what it is like to be on the receiving end of it!).

It is very appropriate to note that both of these things, *'living and active'*, are wonderfully and constantly true of God whose word this is. That should not surprise us. Furthermore, it should guarantee our full confidence in the Bible, our complete assurance of the truth of the gospel, enabling us to testify with Paul, 'For I am not ashamed of the gospel, for it is the power of God for salvation to everyone who believes' (Romans 1:16). Not to be confident in this way, not to have this assurance, would be to cast grievous aspersions upon God, who is 'the God of truth' (Isaiah 65:16); whose 'word is truth' (John 17:17), 'shall accomplish' all that God purposes and 'shall succeed' in all that God sends it out for (Isaiah 55:11), and 'remains forever' (1 Peter 1:25); and 'who never lies' (Titus 1:2).

## (3) What this word does

The two verbs, *'piercing'* and *'discerning'* speak volumes. This 'living and active' word of God, 'sharper than any two-edged sword', pierces and discerns.

The first thing it does is that it pierces: *'piercing to the division of soul and of spirit, of joints and of marrow'*. With its sharpness it pierces right to the very vitals of a person: *'soul and spirit'* speaks of every innermost and secret recess of a man, while *'joints and marrow'* carries the sense of 'all the way through'. (It is not necessary in this verse to seek to establish any particular distinction between the two pairings, in terms of the relationship between the concepts of 'soul' and 'spirit', on the one hand, and 'joints' and 'marrow' on the other, as some might be inclined to do. Our author is not going down that road here). God's mighty word pierces through hypocrisy, lies, deceit, pretence, unbelief and false assurance. It acts with laser force upon our consciences, penetrating every layer of ourselves which nothing else reaches. Nothing can stand successfully in its way. Nothing can hold out against it. It destroys all 'arguments and every lofty opinion raised against the knowledge of God, and take(s) every thought captive to obey Christ, being ready to punish every disobedience' (2 Corinthians 10:5–6). There is no safe hiding place from God and his word.

The second thing it does is that it discerns: *'and discerning the thoughts and intentions of the heart'*. To 'discern' is to discover, to reveal, to find out, even to expose. It can also mean to pass judgment, or be a sure and severe critic. We might (in our sad pride and folly) congratulate ourselves at times that no one can see our real motives, no one can open the curtain on our real thoughts, no one can understand our real emotions. Yet we forget the most important thing of all: God can—and does! And the chief way in which he does so is through his word. How it searches us out! Whenever we come into contact with it in any way, it sets about its *'discerning'* work, bringing all *'the thoughts and intentions of the heart'* (our hearts) into view before us, showing us to ourselves as we really are, stripping away from us all our false assessments of our attitudes and performances, and leaving us without defence or excuse before the all-seeing and all-knowing God. Continually it drives us to God for pardoning and sanctifying grace.

This leads directly to the fourth essential truth we have in 4:12–13 concerning the word of God.

## (4) Where this word leads

Where it leads is this: to our complete exposure before God, to our standing utterly revealed before his eye. *'And no creature is hidden from his sight, but all are naked and exposed* (or, 'laid bare, uncovered'—the image is of the throat bared to the sacrificial knife) *to the eyes of him to whom we must give account'* (4:13). We are face to face here with the divine omniscience and omnipresence in all its glory, for 'the word of God' in verse 12 has now given place to God himself in verse 13. This is to be expected, for God's word cannot be separated from God! God's word brings us and keeps us under God's eye, into God's sight, before his searching and scrutinising gaze. It leaves us in no doubt that it is with God (and not with men) that we have to do. So many people think only (and think desperately) of what other people think of them, how they are regarded, how highly they are rated, when all the time the only one whose judgment is of any significance is God himself. We are reminded of 1 Samuel 16:7: 'For the LORD sees not as man sees: man looks on the outward appearance, but the LORD looks on the heart'. Whatever we may try to hide from ourselves and from others, we cannot hide anything from God. His is the all-seeing eye.

The *'no creature'* leaves no one out. It is all-inclusive for mankind in every generation, and from the youngest to the oldest, from the newest born to the veteran. Words like *'naked and exposed'* show that no stone is left unturned. When the word of God gets going, it gets going, and none can stop it, prevent it, or even slow it down.

And because (as we noted in verse 12) this word is both 'living and active, sharper than any two-edged sword', it is always getting going. It never sleeps. It never rests. Our every encounter with it will bring results—and so many of those encounters, of course, will be full of and running over with abundant blessings. Let God's word truly be 'a lamp to (our) feet and a light to (our) path' (Psalm 119:105).

The final note struck in this section—the description of God as *'him to whom we must give account'*—transports us beyond today and lands us on the judgment day. 'For we will all stand before the judgment seat of God ... So then each of us will give an account of himself to God' (Romans 14:10, 12). There will be a reckoning. The fact that that judgment seat is also termed in the New Testament 'the judgment seat of Christ' (2 Corinthians 5:10) points us to the only one who can be our help and defence on that day, and urges us (if we have not done so already) to make haste to him right away, trusting him only (the crucified and risen one) for the pardon of all our sins and to reconcile us to God. Very strikingly, Revelation 1:16 declares concerning Jesus, 'from his mouth came a sharp two-edged sword'.

## A further sight of the heart of Jesus (4:14–16)

When commenting upon 2:14–18, a passage we described as one of the most precious paragraphs in the entire epistle, we dwelt upon the heart of Jesus—that it is condescending, conquering and compassionate. Coming now to comment on 4:14–16, we can only say that this also is one of the most precious paragraphs in the entire epistle—and that is no vain repetition to say so. It reveals what has been described as the heart of Christ in heaven towards sinners on earth. To begin with, however, a note is needed on why the writer to the Hebrews pens these words at this point.

He begins with *'Since then'* (or, 'Having therefore'), so the *'then'* or the 'therefore' immediately establish a connection. He is not branching out here on something that is so new that it has nothing at all to do with what he has just been saying. The connection is surely as follows. Since setting off on the theme of Jesus' complete superiority over Moses, our author has had some hard (at times, even threatening) things to say—along the lines of 'lest there be in any of you an evil, unbelieving heart', 'that none of you be hardened by the deceitfulness of sin', 'strive to enter that rest, so that no one may fall by the same sort of disobedience', and 'all are naked and exposed to the eyes of him to whom we must give account'. This is strong speaking. Our author is not one for beating around bushes, but is rather one for calling spades spades. Neither, however, is he a man for a 'one note samba'. So, after this straight talking, there now comes rich comfort and pure encouragement—indeed, the richest comfort and the purest encouragement imaginable. And it all focuses directly upon the Lord Jesus Christ. Moses has now dropped out of the picture entirely. What we have here is Jesus, all Jesus, and no one besides Jesus. Now we see 'no one but Jesus only' (Matthew 17:8). He, and he alone, is the one in whom our possession of eternal, heavenly rest is both secured and secure. How is it possible for any of us poor sinners to enter God's rest? Only because, as we are now to see, Jesus is already there for us.

The Christ-centred focus here is upon Jesus as our great high priest, and we may single out three aspects of his priesthood.

## (1) Jesus is our exalted high priest

The section begins, *'Since then we have a great high priest who has passed through the heavens'* (4:14). This is not the first reference to Jesus' high priesthood. In 2:17 he is described as 'a merciful and faithful high priest in the service of God', while 3:1 speaks of him as 'the apostle and high priest of our confession'. Take a moment to refer back to the comments on those two verses. Now, however, the subject is taken up again with gusto, and will recur in increasing detail, and from different angles, as the letter proceeds.

Several details stand out. Jesus is *'a great high priest'*. The contrast between Jesus' high priesthood and that of the Old Testament high priests will follow in earnest from chapter 5, but immediately the word *'great'* strikes us. It applies (and is applied) only to him. He does not rank in line with other high priests, but rather, in this as in everything else, Jesus stands alone. His high priesthood is beyond compare. It is unique. He is the greatest of all high priests. He is the incomparable high priest.

This greatness is enforced further in the recording of the fact that he *'has passed through the heavens'*. There is much here. In particular, the language declares Jesus' exaltation. In the matchless messianic expressions of Psalm 24, the gates and ancient doors of heaven have been lifted up and opened wide, 'that the King of glory may come in' (Psalm 24:7). And in he has gone, in his ascension, enthronement and coronation, having been glorified in the Father's 'own presence' with the glory that Jesus had with the Father 'before the world existed' (John 17:5). There, in the highest glory, in the place of supreme honour and choicest affection (compare 'he sat down at the right hand of the Majesty on high' in 1:3), our *great high priest* dwells, with the greatness of his person and work far surpassing all others.

What precisely is indicated by this actual passing *'through the heavens'*—in particular, what is the significance of *'through'*? The Hebrew word for 'heaven' is plural, while in the New Testament heaven appears at various times in both singular and plural forms. So *'the heavens'* here refers to heaven, while the addition of *'through'* informs us that Jesus is in the very 'heaven of heavens', the eternal dwelling place of God. Very likely there is an intended contrast with the high priests of old, who (and that only once each year) entered into the holy of holies (the most holy place) in the temple. Jesus, however, is 'a minister in the holy places, in the true tent that the Lord set up, not man' (8:2). He 'has entered … into heaven itself, now to appear in the presence of God on our behalf' (9:24). Nothing could keep him out!

Our exalted high priest is named here as *'Jesus, the Son of God'*. This is hugely significant, for it gathers up in a few words both his humanity and his deity. He is *'Jesus'*, the name given in the announcement by 'an angel of the Lord' concerning his incarnation— 'and you shall call his name Jesus [meaning 'Saviour', 'God saves'], for he will save his people from their sins' (Matthew 1:20–21). He is *'the Son of God'*, the Word who became flesh (John 1:14), very God of very God. His own heart towards us is a true expression of the Father's heart towards us. This assurance of his two natures (truly and really man, truly and really God) is a further statement of proof where his exalted position is concerned—one with God, one with man, having come to earth for a season to accomplish and provide our salvation, he has now returned to the glory, where he presents his merits before the throne on our behalf and will one day receive us to himself. While he remains *'the Son of God'* (for he is that eternally), he still bears in heaven his name *'Jesus'*. The very contemplation of that truth should be a blessing and comfort to us. He is there in heaven for us!

So it fits perfectly for the writer now to say, *'let us hold fast our confession'*. The writer to the Hebrews is very fond of 'let us'! It is one of his trademarks. Holding fast (compare, holding firm) is a note we found in 3:6 and 3:14. Here it is again. It is a reminder of the call to steadfastness and perseverance which is a hallmark of this letter, and, indeed, a fundamental reason why it was ever written in the first place. We have every cause and ground to *'hold fast our confession'*, in the light of all that Jesus is, all that he has done, and where he now resides. To cast aside our profession, to draw back, to 'drift away' (2:1), to ease up, would be the craziest and most foolish thing we could ever do. We have a mighty saviour, advocate and high priest, now exalted in heaven, and actually there for us. What sense could it ever make to turn away from him, when our whole business and priority should be to cleave to him, to keep looking to him (12:2), and to make him known to others so that they would cleave to him as well. Our *'confession'* is both within our hearts and upon our lips.

## (2) He is our sympathising high priest

4:15 is unspeakably exquisite. *'For we do not have a high priest who is unable to sympathize with our weaknesses* (or, 'infirmities')', is how it begins. Straightaway we need to note (and enjoy!) a feature of Greek grammar. We have here what is called a 'double negative'—*'we do not have ... who is unable'*—and the purpose of a 'double negative' is to assert a 'strong positive'. That is to say, *'we do not have a high priest who is unable to sympathize with our weaknesses'*—no indeed! What we certainly *do* have is a high priest who is most wonderfully and gloriously able *'to sympathize with our weaknesses'* (all of them), even though (as will be asserted in a moment by our author) he is absolutely sinless.

This is of great practical importance for us from day to day, for we might doubt, left to ourselves, whether one who is so exalted, so glorious, so without compare, could ever really be interested in us, bothered about us or concerned for us. But he is! Far from forgetting about us, he continually 'takes thought for (us)' (Psalm 40:17). He is not remote from us but present with us. This very section of the chapter which speaks so clearly of Jesus' exaltedness now speaks equally clearly (and very movingly) of his compassion. There is nothing cold, unfeeling or aloof about the Lord Jesus. Tenderness and kindness belong to him. Recall how Paul entreats the Corinthians with an argument drawn from 'the meekness and gentleness of Christ' (2 Corinthians 10:1). Every dear child of God may testify with the bride in the Song concerning Jesus, 'His left hand is under my head, and his right hand embraces me' (Song of Songs 2:6).

The very reality of Jesus' humanity is all the persuasion we need of his encompassing ability to sympathize with us, feel with us, know with us the experience of weakness. That is in no way to assert, of course, that the Lord Jesus Christ ever was or is weak in himself. There is nothing weak about him. He is our strong Saviour, 'mighty to save' (Isaiah 63:1), never allowing us to be snatched out of his hand (John 10:28), 'able to keep (us) from stumbling and to present (us) faultless before the presence of his glory with great joy' (Jude 24). Yet time and again in the course of his life on earth he experienced real and felt weakness—laid in the manger as a baby, hungry after his forty days in the wilderness being tempted by the devil, weary and thirsty at the well, fast asleep in the boat on the lake during the storm, weeping and in great turmoil and anguish at the grave of Lazarus, spending nights in prayer before the Father 'with loud cries and tears' (5:7), and 'crucified in weakness' (2 Corinthians 13:4). He has not forgotten all of this now that he is in heaven. As a result, all of our weaknesses stir his compassion all the more. We may dare to go further: even our sins (though they grieve him deeply) awaken his compassion towards us as well. Such is the amazing perfection of his love towards us. All of this greatly endears him to us as the very Saviour and Comforter we require.

The verse continues, *'but who in every respect has been tempted as we are, yet without sin'*. There is a much over-used phrase these days along the lines of having 'been there, done that, seen everything'. Taking that, and putting it to higher and better use, we may apply it (to our great blessing) to our Lord Jesus Christ. The verb *'tempted'* can have different connotations. It carries the dual sense of 'tried and tested' and 'tempted to commit sin'. We say very carefully that the Lord Jesus has known, and remembers, both (though his temptations, unlike ours, came altogether from without and never from within him). He was tried, tested and tempted many a time, in matters like shortcutting the cross, bearing with his disciples' slowness, facing continual opposition from the religious authorities, and having to face false accusations and charges. He spoke very movingly of his disciples when he said of them, 'You are those who have stayed with me in my trials (or, 'temptations')' (Luke 22:28).

Yet at no time did he succumb. He would not budge. It was always a case with him of *'yet without sin'*. We commented at 2:17–18 on the importance of Jesus being both tempted *and* remaining sinless. Take a moment to re-visit that portion of the commentary. It is necessary to insist that the fact that Jesus never sinned does not in any way hamper, reduce, or, worse still, cancel out his sympathy. It is the yielding to temptation which constitutes the sin, not the being tempted itself. The Lord Jesus Christ, though sorely tested and often bombarded with temptation, never yielded. He was, is, and remains altogether holy. Satan had 'no claim' on him (John 14:30). This is the key thing, for, as we remarked in connection with the end of chapter 2, if Jesus *had* actually submitted even to one single temptation he would have become a sinner as we are and would himself have been in need of mercy and pardon. He would have been in exactly the same boat as all the priests and high priests of Old and New Testament times. Such a thought is appalling, indeed unthinkable, and it would have meant that there is no salvation for us, since we need a thoroughly *sinless* Saviour, one who is totally 'without blemish or spot' (1 Peter 1:19). Jesus is that one!

The *'in every respect'* gives us further encouragement. There are depths here which it would be unwise for us to try to fathom. It does, at the very least, assure us that there was nothing merely of a surface nature about Jesus' temptations, neither were they selective. The devil, not least, will have come at Jesus from every quarter he (the devil) could think of. Our Saviour will have experienced testings and temptings far more brutally than we do—for he is pure and holy while we are all too familiar with defeats and failures. Yet even our many weaknesses and infirmities wonderfully and graciously stir Jesus' abiding and heartfelt compassion towards us all the more. Let that very truth act as a very weighty encouragement to us against sin, since it so grieves his holy heart. May our hearts be warmed with the knowledge that Jesus not only knows everything about us but cares for us to a degree beyond our imagining. And let us be sure always to keep at the front of our minds that we have the very best of all friends in the Lord Jesus Christ.

## (3) Jesus is our inviting high priest

With another 'let us' our writer draws a most magnificent application from all of this. *'Let us then with confidence draw near to the throne of grace'* (4:16). How inviting this is! Is it too good to be true? By no means!

Think of the divine throne. Here are some verses from the Psalms which speak of it. It is 'in heaven' (11:4), 'his throne for justice' (9:7), 'forever and ever' (45:6), 'his holy throne' (47:8), 'established from of old' (93:2), 'established ... in the heavens' (103:19). In Jeremiah 17:12 it is described as a 'glorious high throne', while Revelation 4:5 records, 'From the throne came flashes of lightning, and rumblings and peals of thunder'.

In the light of all of this, we might well feel that it is altogether unapproachable for poor sinful ones like ourselves, since thrones speak so readily of sovereignty and majesty. Yet, amazingly, for all of its glory, holiness, eternity and everything else, the divine throne has become for us 'the throne of grace'. We come to a throne, but may approach it without terror, bow in adoration before 'him who sits on the throne and ... the Lamb' (Revelation 5:13), and be assured of a welcome every time we come—so long, that is, that we come in and though the Lord Jesus Christ, and pleading *his* merits and sacrifice, and nothing of our own. It is not a throne upon which is written the awful word, 'go!', but the blessed word, 'come!'. It is the throne from which grace is dispensed to God's people, from which it flows, in a never-ending supply. What foolish ones we are whenever we stay away, question the invitation, or doubt the welcome.

Our drawing 'near to the throne of grace' is to be 'with confidence'. Because (as verse 14 taught us) Jesus (*our* Jesus) has entered into heaven, the way is open for us, through him, to approach that very heaven because of our union with him. The access for us is free. All the necessary payment has been made already on our behalf by our Saviour. Nothing remains outstanding. *We* may come *to* the throne because *he* is there *on* the throne. And while our coming 'with confidence' does not imply or involve coming lightly, cheaply, coarsely, brashly, vulgarly, or in any other such manner which would be entirely out of place, it does mean exactly what it says: 'with confidence'. And that means boldly, thankfully, unhesitatingly, humbly, devotedly, needily, hopefully and believingly, saying all that we need to say and asking all that we need to ask, pouring out our hearts before him. Our confidence is not in ourselves (how could it be?), but is wholly in the Lord Jesus Christ—he who 'himself bore our sins in his body on the tree, that we might die to sin and live to righteousness' (1 Peter 2:24), he who 'suffered once for sins, the righteous for the unrighteous, that he might bring us to God' (1 Peter 3:18), and he who (returning to Hebrews) 'suffered outside the gate in order to sanctify the people through his own blood' (13:12). We are blessed and accepted 'in the Beloved' (Ephesians 1:6).

Then, when we come, what do we come for and what awaits us? The answer is the same in both cases: 'that we may receive mercy and find grace to help in time of need'. Frankly, we never experience a moment in our lives when we are not in need of divine mercy and grace; and here at the throne, mercy awaits and grace abounds, ever needful by us and ever timely for us. Indeed, *'help in time of need'* is very much 'timely help'.

The mercy to be received and the grace to be found is manifold. It includes pardon for daily sin (1 John 1:7), lifting up for those who are downcast (Psalm 42:11), help in the vital work of the mortification of sin (Romans 8:13), assistance in the right regarding and joyful keeping of the Lord's Day (Isaiah 58:13–14), spiritual assurance (Romans 8:15–17), increase of faith (Luke 17:5), the undertaking of various family responsibilities and relationships (Ephesians 5:22–6:4), revival (Habakkuk 3:2), developing every spiritual virtue and grace (Galatians 5:22–23), guidance in matters small and great (Psalm 25:4–5), and longing for heaven (Revelation 7:15–17).

These examples are merely illustrative, and nothing like exhaustive! Come on any and every matter to *'the throne of grace'*. Do not hold back or stay away. Never imagine that you have come too often or have outgrown the need to keep on coming. Everything is available for us, for ever, in the Lord Jesus Christ. This is the sure way to persevere. Do not fall into the trap of some of those to whom Hebrews was first written—wandering away from Christ, returning to old ways, being satisfied all over again with former things.

The harder you find the Christian life, then the more (not the less) do you require divine mercy and grace, and the more (not the less) do you need to be found before God's throne. Keep on coming to it, day by day. Let us not be strangers but frequenters. It is the very best place to be! Moreover, should you be reading this commentary and yet are still not a Christian—you too must come to this throne of grace— come now, come straightaway, come without delay to the inviting and welcoming Saviour of sinners. And if you're not altogether sure whether you have ever come or not, then make sure work of it—come again!

# Chapter 5
# Jesus and the priesthood

A familiar sight when approaching a town or city is a sign announcing that the place is 'twinned' with a town or city in some other country. Leviticus in the Old Testament is a book very much about priests, high priests, altars, sacrifices, blood and the like. Hebrews in the New Testament is a book very much about the same things. We could say that they are 'twinned'. In a wonderful way they link together, they form a pair of Scripture books. Each one helps greatly in the explanation of the other. We would not wish to be without either of them.

There is a very significant difference between the two books, however, and it is this. Leviticus, when dealing with these matters, is all the time pressing and straining forward to the Lord Jesus Christ, in whom they all find their fulfilment. Hebrews, on the other hand, presents this fulfilment, setting forth as it does in such splendid fashion the Lord Jesus Christ as, for example, *the* high priest, *the* altar and *the* sacrifice. All the intricate details of the Old Testament ceremonial law come to completion and fruition in the Lord Jesus. He stands alone. We would remind ourselves, with thanksgiving and joy, that he is 'a merciful and gracious high priest' (2:17), the 'high priest of our confession' (3:1) and 'a great high priest' (4:14), which leads precisely to where we now are in the letter.

Coming to chapter 5 of Hebrews, our writer, still in pursuit of his grand theme of the absolute superiority and unquestioned pre-eminence of Jesus over everyone and everything, delves into a fresh area. The angels have been considered, and so has Moses. Now it is the turn of the Old Testament priesthood—in particular, at this point, the high priesthood, represented in Aaron, who is named for the first time in the letter in 5:4. There was no office in the religion of Judaism which possessed greater standing or commanded greater reverence than that of the high priest (the chief priest, for he was of higher rank and office, and even wore more costly and magnificent dress, than the other priests), so we are not surprised that this letter focuses here upon it.

If we should wonder what the point of this comparison between Jesus and Aaron is, it should be sufficient in jogging our memories to recall that—as the author of Hebrews perceived it—those to whom he wrote were in grave danger of preferring to go back to the past (to the types and shadows) rather than stay in the present (with its lights and beauties). They showed alarming signs of setting the Old Testament priests, sacrifices and so on over and above the Lord Jesus who, through his own person and work, has made it abundantly clear that they are all finished with. They are no more. Since Christ has come they have no continuing place. Their function is at an end. We might say that the people were wanting to abandon 'Hebrews' and return to 'Leviticus', which would have been a very bad step. That is why he writes here as he does. They need to grasp that the Lord Jesus Christ, the Messiah, is *the* high priest—even though his priesthood was of another order from that of the former ones, and though while he was on earth he did not function as a priest in the Jerusalem temple.

The chapter divides into two parts. In verses 1–10 the subject of the high priesthood is handled—first from the human side (5:1–4) and then with respect to the Lord Jesus (5:5–10). Then in verses 11–14 a series of warnings and applications is supplied, which continue into chapter 6.

## Human high priests (5:1-4)

Five characteristics are given of the Old Testament high priests. We shall note and comment on them in order.

(1) They are chosen from men and act for men. *'For every high priest chosen from among men is appointed to act on behalf of men in relation to God'* (5:1). There are a number of important things to note here.

They were all from *'among men'*. They came from the 'priestly tribe' of Levi, from the body of the people. Very importantly, they partook of the same nature as those for and to whom they ministered. This was essential. This was not a work put into the hands of angels (who do not share our humanity, neither are they familiar with our temptations), neither did it belong to young boys (who would lack the necessary experience and ability). It was from the men of Israel that the priesthood (and therefore, of necessity, the high priesthood) came. In the case of Aaron, the first high priest in Israel, we read these words from God to Moses: 'Then bring near to you Aaron your brother, and his sons with him, from among the people of Israel, to serve me as priests' (Exodus 28:1). He was set apart with his whole family for the priesthood. Sacred garments were prepared for him, and he was anointed and consecrated to his office by Moses. When a high priest died, one of his sons would succeed him. Again, this is what happened with Aaron. He died at the age of 123, at which point, on the divine command, the office passed to his son Eleazar (Numbers 20:22–29).

Being *'chosen from among men'* they were *'appointed to act on behalf of men'*. They represented the people and did not merely act for themselves. Yet this acting for Israel as a whole was very concretely a ministry for them *'in relation to God'*. As will shortly be explained, the nub of things was that they were to all intents and purposes mediators—not between men and men, however, but between men and God. Already these truths are bursting towards the Lord Jesus Christ, but we must remain for the time being with the human high priests of old. The words *'chosen'* and *'appointed'* are each significant. Neither allows for any sense of self-importance, arrogance or pride. High priests did not hold this office on their own account, as if they were naturally 'someone'. They were not in it for their own glory or prestige or name. Rather, it was something which was solemnly laid upon them, required of them, and for the performance of which they were accountable not to men but to God.

(2) They were occupied with a specific work, which was *'to offer gifts and sacrifices for sins'*. They did not come empty handed. They came to God for men. The phrase *'gifts and sacrifices'* is amplified at various points in Leviticus. That book opens with details of the laws and procedures for the burnt, grain, peace, sin and guilt offerings (all of which in their different ways point to and speak of Christ and his work on the cross at Calvary). Another Old Testament book, Numbers, speaks of the daily, Sabbath and monthly offerings, and then goes on to enumerate the offering and sacrificial arrangements for the various annual feasts (such as Passover, Weeks, Trumpets and Tabernacles).

There is an unmissable connection between the two phrases in 5:1, *'in relation to God'* and *'for'* ('on behalf of') *sins'*. God is altogether holy. This was impressed unforgettably upon the prophet Isaiah on that day in the temple, when he heard the heavenly seraphim calling to one another, 'Holy, holy, holy is the LORD of hosts; the whole earth is full of his glory' (Isaiah 6:3). Man, in contrast, is altogether sinful, 'for all have sinned and fall short of the glory of God' (Romans 3:23)—notice, 'have sinned' (it is our very nature to be sinners) and 'fall short' (do continually, as a result). Neither the people of the Old Testament, nor us, nor anyone else can just approach God on our own. We are all by nature 'alienated from the life of God' (Ephesians 4:18). So how can God in his holiness ever have anything to do with us in our sinfulness, apart from visiting upon us the judgment we deserve? The answer is found in sacrifice, without which the problem of our sins having separated us from God (Isaiah 59:2) would remain completely unresolved. Our writer will have so much to say about this (not least in chapters 9 and 10), but he is laying his stall out even here.

All those Levitical sacrifices, followed by the one gospel sacrifice. All the Old Testament high priests, followed by our one 'great high priest' (4:16). Sin can only be dealt with by a sacrifice for it. God's holiness (which cannot have any fellowship with sin) and his justice (which must punish sin) can only be satisfied on the basis of a sacrifice for sin. The Old Testament sacrifices foreshadowed this, but only the Lord Jesus Christ's sacrifice of himself actually accomplishes that satisfaction. So once again, what utter folly on the part of the Hebrews even to entertain the least thought of going backwards to the old days, when all the provision for them was made by God in the gospel!

A passing application is worth making. We have been noting here that it was proper to the office of a priest to present sacrifices for sin. It follows therefore (contrary to the ideas of many) that it is always absolutely improper to give the title 'priest' to a minister of the gospel. He proclaims Christ's sacrifice once offered, but offers no sacrifices himself. He declares the blood that has been shed, but sheds no blood himself. He preaches the word, but does not contribute to its writing.

(3) They were in a position to be pastorally sensitive in their dealings. *'He can deal gently with the ignorant and wayward, since he himself is beset with weakness'* (5:2). They were men, remember, from among men. They were not supermen. They were not unusual men. They were men of like passions and like weaknesses, men of fellow feeling, with those to whom and on behalf of whom they ministered, prone to identical ups and downs, sharing infirmities with them, sinners like them, facing trials and temptations like them, capable of falling like them and subject to dying like them. A crucial detail of this awaits us in the very next verse. They were to be men of sympathy and compassion, a sympathy and compassion born out of their own hearts and their keen awareness of their own weak humanity. They were to *'deal gently'*, have compassion, be capable of pity, suffer

with, not lording it over people, but bearing patiently with them, seeking to lead them into the right way, seeking to demonstrate the appropriate balance between over severity or over tolerance (the word has in it the sense of 'due measure'). Sadly, this is something which Aaron very conspicuously failed to do in the incident of the golden calf, when Moses was receiving the law on Mount Sinai from God (Exodus 32). The same may be said of Eli, who dealt so roughly with Hannah when she was in such anguish of soul (1 Samuel 2). What a challenging word this is to those who have the sacred responsibility of the ministry of the word and the pastoring of God's flock in our own day. And what a startling reminder it is to us not to put our trust and reliance upon mere men, even when they are spiritual leaders. 'Our help is in the name of the LORD, who made heaven and earth' (Psalm 124:8).

Those among whom the high priests ministered are described as *'the ignorant and wayward'*. The first of those two words is literally 'the ones not knowing', and speaks of those who sin unintentionally rather than deliberately. This may be, perhaps, because they are still very young in the faith or have not been taught adequately. Interestingly, Leviticus 4 records particular sacrifices which were to be offered for those who sinned unintentionally. The second of them carries the sense of 'being led astray', which belongs rather in the realm of deliberate sin: knowing what you're doing, yet still doing it ('Keep your heart with all vigilance', Proverbs 4:23), wandering out of God's prescribed path of holiness ('For this is the will of God, your sanctification', 1 Thessalonians 4:3), or falling in with bad company and as a result taking a wrong course (walking 'in the counsel of the wicked' and standing 'in the way of sinners', Psalm 1:1).

(4) They needed to have their own sins dealt with, as well as the sins of everyone else. *'Because of this he is obligated to offer sacrifice for his own sins just as he does for those of the people'* (5:3). The connection between this and the previous statement is immediately obvious. The very fact that the high priest himself was 'beset with weakness' (not just 'touched' with it but 'beset' by it, not just scratched with it on the surface but affected with it deep down—interestingly, the same

verb which is translated 'surrounded by, compassed about with' in 12:1 regarding the 'cloud of witnesses', and carrying the literal sense of 'lying around') placed him in the position of a sinner; and, being a sinner, his own sins had to be dealt with, along with everyone else's. The verb here, *'obligated'*, a present tense carrying the force of strong necessity—he 'had to' do this, he was 'bound' to do it, he 'had no option' but to do this, he 'was under a moral obligation' to do this— serves further to underscore this truth. No one else was in a position to deal with the high priests' sins, so they had to see to it themselves.

Nowhere is this better illustrated than on the Day of Atonement itself. This is recorded in Leviticus 16. It happened only once a year, and was the occasion when the high priest entered not merely into the outer court of 'the tent of meeting' (the tabernacle, and later the temple), nor even into the holy place, but right into the Most Holy Place, the very 'holy of holies' (compare 9:7). It was required by God that 'Aaron shall present the bull as a sin offering for himself, and shall make atonement for himself and for his house' (Leviticus 16:11). He was a sinner among sinners and offering the sacrifice not only for their sins, but also for his own. Moreover, as this Leviticus chapter makes clear, sacrifice needed to be brought for his own sins first of all, before that of the people, in order that no guilt was remaining upon him. He had to have the favour of God upon him, if the people (through the sacrifice he brought on their behalf) were to be brought into that same position.

(5) They did not appoint themselves, but served only by divine calling and appointment. *'And no one takes this honour for himself, but only when called by God, just as Aaron was'* (5:4). This links directly with the statement laid down back in verse 1, with those two verbs 'chosen' and 'appointed'. Given that it is entirely with God to choose who he will receive into fellowship with himself, it is not surprising that it is equally entirely with him to choose who he will appoint as high priest for the work of acting 'on behalf of men in relation to God' (verse 1). The phrase *'this honour'* gives a rich sense of what an honourable office the high priesthood was. It involved approaching God, having familiar dealings with him, seeking his favour towards

and his blessing upon his people, and more besides. The high priests were never self-appointed, but always God-appointed. What man would ever dare to offer any sacrifices for sin (whether his own or others') if he was without the assurance that God had called him to do this? It was not a case of a young boy being asked what he wanted to do when he grew up, and him replying that he wanted to be a high priest. The tribe of Levi was the priestly tribe, and it was from the house of Aaron, Moses' older brother, that the high priests came. We noted Exodus 28:1 above.

When this divine appointment was challenged, trouble followed. It certainly did for Korah and company, who, after they had 'assembled themselves together against Moses and against Aaron', were told straight by Moses. 'You have gone too far! For all in the congregation are holy, every one of them, and the LORD is among them. Why then do you exalt yourselves above the assembly of the LORD?' … Therefore it is against the LORD that you and all your company have gathered together. What is Aaron that you grumble against him?' (Numbers 16:3, 11). For them to take issue with Moses and with Aaron (who was the divinely chosen and appointed high priest) was to take issue with God, and Moses (the divinely chosen and appointed leader of the people of Israel) was having none of it. The striking incident recorded in the following chapter (Numbers 17) of the budding of Aaron's staff served as a further divine authentication of the ministry to which God, and God alone, had called Aaron as high priest—hence the phrase in our present verse, *just as Aaron was*. He was very much a case in point, although the same applied to all his successors in office.

## Jesus our high priest (5:5-10)

As a bridge passage (to use a musical term) between verses 1–4 and 5–10, the following stark contrasts stand out between the many human high priests and the one great high priest, the Lord Jesus Christ, whereby the abiding Hebrews theme of the supremacy of Jesus is kept in central focus. In the light of the five characteristics just considered, the following is true:

(1) While they were chosen from men and act for men, *this is*

*supremely and uniquely true of Jesus*. 'But when the fullness of time had come, God sent forth his Son, born of woman, born under the law, to redeem those who were under the law, so that we might receive adoption as sons' (Galatians 4:4). Compare Hebrews 1:2–3.

(2) While they were occupied with a specific work, involving the offering of sacrifices for sins, *this is supremely and uniquely true of Jesus*. '... as Christ loved us and gave himself up for us, a fragrant offering and sacrifice to God' (Ephesians 5:2). Compare Hebrews 10:11–12.

(3) While they were in a position to be pastorally sensitive in their dealings, *this is supremely and uniquely true of Jesus*. 'This was to fulfil what was spoken by the prophet Isaiah: "Behold, my servant whom I have chosen, my beloved with whom my soul is well pleased. I will put my Spirit upon him ..., a bruised reed he will not break, and a smouldering wick he will not quench"' (Matthew 12:17, 18, 20). Compare Hebrews 2:17–18.

(4) While they needed to have their own sins dealt with, as well as the sins of everyone else, *what is supremely and uniquely true of Jesus is this*: 'He committed no sin, neither was deceit found in his mouth' (1 Peter 2:22). Compare Hebrews 4:15.

(5) While they did not appoint themselves, but served only by divine calling and appointment, *this is supremely and uniquely true of Jesus*. God declares of him, 'Behold my servant whom I uphold, my chosen, in whom my soul delights' (Isaiah 42:1). Compare Hebrews 10:5, the very point which the letter now takes up.

Our author begins, then, with the last of the five matters just enumerated. The *'So also'* supplies the connecting link. *'So also Christ did not exalt himself to be made a high priest'* (5:5). Jesus being spoken of here as *'Christ'* is significant, giving the writer another opportunity to demonstrate to those to whom he wrote that Jesus is the true Messiah, the Anointed One, the long-expected One. The verb *'did not exalt'* signifies 'did not take upon himself the honour', 'did not glorify himself', 'did not put himself forward', even though he is greatly exalted and glorified in it and by it. When uttering his matchless prayer which we have preserved for us in John 17, Jesus said something which touches directly upon this. His words were these: 'I glorified you on earth, having accomplished the work that you gave me to do' (John 17:4). Notice that carefully. It was not a case of 'the work I decided to do' or 'the work that I took it upon myself to do', but, choosing his words quite deliberately, it is 'the work that you gave me to do'. It could not be otherwise, for while there is no wedge that can ever be put between the will of the Father and the will of the Son—remember Jesus' words in John 10:30, 'I and the Father are one'—yet as the Son Jesus delighted to obey the Father in all things. This will come out very clearly and strongly in chapter 10 of Hebrews, when Psalm 40 is quoted—but that is for then, not here. For now, it is to be emphasized that he took nothing upon himself, but accepted the office and honour given to him by the Father.

The verse continues: *'but was appointed by him who said to him, "You are my Son, today I have begotten you"'*. We are back with this quotation from Psalm 2:7, which we first met as early as 1:5. Take a moment to review the comments made there. The divine appointment relating to Jesus' high priesthood is unquestionable, and it is this psalm verse which declares and describes his call. Of no one else could it be said in the same way that he was called and appointed by God. It was in every sense a heavenly calling. That Jesus is here referred to by the Father as *'my Son'*, testifies forcibly to the Father's acknowledgment of him as our high priest, his pleasure in him, and his acceptance of all that he accomplished.

And neither was it an appointment made nor a calling given in 'time', but rather in 'eternity'. So the sentence begun, though not concluded, in 5:5 proceeds: *'as he says also in another place, "You are a priest for ever, after the order of Melchizedek"'* (5:6). This is another psalm quotation—in this case Psalm 110:4. It makes here its first appearance, but it is the first of several. Indeed, this is really the key Old Testament text undergirding the entire purpose and argument of the letter to the Hebrews. We shall meet it again, twice, in chapter 7, though its essence pervades so much of what is yet to follow. Moreover, Psalm 110:1 is a verse which appears in the Gospels (as, indeed, it did here in Hebrews at 1:13). The psalm is full of reference and application to Christ.

Melchizedek must wait until later. The point, however, of the psalm quotation at this stage (and in conjunction with that from Psalm 2) is in order to link together both the Sonship and the Priesthood of the Lord Jesus Christ. He who is God's Son is our great high priest. He who is our great high priest is God's Son. The force of that truth, in the light of our writer's chief theme, cannot be missed. This, not least, demonstrates the glory of Jesus' priesthood—it was not expressed in outward show and ceremony, but consisted in God's own words of declaration.

Two other aspects may also be highlighted. The first is that, as both Son and Priest (in both of which he is unique), Jesus is seated 'at the right hand of the Majesty on high' (1:3). He is there both as God and man, and 'the one mediator between God and men' (1 Timothy 2:5). The second is that, unlike the many priests of old, this one priest belongs not to the Levitical priesthood (which was not around when Jesus was appointed in eternity), but to the priesthood which is *'after the order of Melchizedek'*. That is to say, there is nothing temporary about Jesus' priesthood. Rather, it is an eternal priesthood—a priesthood which belongs to him still, and ever shall do. It has been his for as long as he has been God, and will be his for as long as he will be God. And in both 'directions' that is for ever!

The section continues. *'In the days of his flesh, Jesus offered up prayers and supplications, with loud cries and tears, to him who was able to save him from death'* (5:7). He is a real man with real experience. Just as the divine appointment of the Lord Jesus Christ to the high priesthood has been demonstrated in 5:5–6, so now the suitability of Jesus for this office and work and his successful execution of it is now the focus. *'In the days of his flesh'* refers to his incarnation and the days that followed for him here on the earth, when 'the Word became flesh and dwelt among us' (John 1:14), when he was 'born in the likeness of men' (Philippians 2:7). The true nature of Jesus' humanity has already been to the fore in 2:9, 14, 17 and 4:15, and is essential for him to be 'a merciful and faithful high priest' and to be able 'to sympathize with our weaknesses'. If he were somehow less than true man, these things could not apply. He was (and remains) of the most tender and sensitive disposition, thoroughly approachable, ready to help—a real man for real men.

In the Gospel accounts we find regular instances of Jesus being a man of prayer. In this he demonstrated his continual dependence upon the Father. So, for example, Mark 1:35 records that, 'rising very early in the morning, while it was still dark, he departed and went out to a desolate place, and there he prayed'. There was nothing 'one off' about this occasion. Another classic instance is Luke 6:12: 'In these days he went out to the mountain to pray, and all night he continued in prayer to God'. The most extended record of Jesus praying is, of course, John 17, where his prayer occupies the entire chapter and is one of the high points of the whole of Scripture. Significantly, it is often referred to as his high priestly prayer, and illustrates very movingly the truth stated of Jesus in 7:25 of our letter, about his continual intercession for 'those who draw near to God through him'—in other words, his own church. His entire earthly life was very much a season of prayer and supplication.

The detail supplied in 5:7, however, that he *offered up prayers and supplications, with loud cries and tears*, is not a merely general statement regarding the years of his humiliation, during which he was exposed to the sorrows and trials of human existence, but has a particular reference. That must surely be to his experience in the Garden of Gethsemane. Never throughout 'the days of his flesh' to that point had there been an occasion to match it. With his disciples Jesus had come 'as was his custom, to the Mount of Olives' (Luke 22:39). The shadow of Calvary was enveloping him increasingly, with the awful sense of what was before him as he approached ever nearer to the cross. The weight of the sins that he was to bear; the consciousness of the wrath and judgment of God upon sin; the realisation that he, the sinless one, was about to be 'made ... to be sin' (2 Corinthians 5:21); the prospect of redeeming 'us from the curse of the law by becoming a curse for us—for it written, "Cursed is everyone who is hanged on a tree"' (Galatians 3:13); the pressing knowledge of all that awaited him in the hours of darkness at Calvary, when he would be separated for a season from the felt comforts and supports of both the Father and the Holy Spirit (Matthew 27:46)—all of this, and more, was an unimaginably heavy burden. So, not surprisingly, he gave himself to prayer. And what praying it was—*'prayers and supplications* [no great distinction need be forced between these two words], *with loud cries and tears'*, the latter words signifying the intensity of the former words and recalling 'the words of my groaning' (Psalm 22:1) and 'the anguish of his soul' (Isaiah 53:11). The conflict grew fiercer as the cross came closer.

By *'loud cries* ('strong crying') ' is intended the lifting up of the voice in an intense manner of calling for help, while *'tears'* signifies what is obvious to the word. It is not out of place to remark that while it is not recorded in the gospel accounts that Jesus actually wept in Gethsemane, there is no reason to doubt that he did. There are several other precious accounts of Jesus weeping (most notably at the grave of Lazarus in John 11 and over Jerusalem in Luke 19). Our blessed Saviour is not dry-eyed. Moreover, this teaches us along the way that it is not an unmanly thing to weep. How can it be, when 'Jesus wept' (John 11:35), and there was never a manlier man than he. Our tears here will, in their own way, make heaven even more sweet, for there 'God will wipe away every tear from (our) eyes' (Revelation 7:17).

Jesus' prayer in Gethsemane began, 'Father, if you are willing, remove this cup from me' (Luke 22:42). It is noteworthy that he uses the intimate Trinitarian word, 'Father', while the 'cup' which he asks to have removed is the cup of suffering and anguish which he is already facing and is shortly to face even more furiously. He addressed himself in this manner to the Father as *'him who was able to save him from death'*. The words are, literally, 'out of death' (with which, compare Matthew 26:38, 'My soul is very sorrowful, even to death'). While this could carry the sense of wishing to bypass the very experience of death, at least 'death on (of) a cross' (Philippians 2:8), yet the Lord Jesus Christ, who 'came into the world to save sinners' (1 Timothy 1:15) and who in so doing was accomplishing the Father's will, is unlikely to have been thinking primarily of this. Indeed, no sooner has he asked for the removal of the cup than he utters the matchless words of submission and repose, 'Nevertheless, not my will, but yours, be done'. And immediately following that 'there appeared to him an angel from heaven strengthening him' (Luke 22:43). This angel is, without doubt, one of the great unsung heroes of the Bible. He was there for Jesus, but because he was there for Jesus he was there for us also, for whom Jesus was shortly to die.

So on Jesus strode to the cross. It puts us in mind straightaway of words we shall encounter in 12:2 of Hebrews: 'who for the joy that was set before him endured the cross, despising the shame, and is seated at the right hand of the throne of God'. There is an important lesson for us here in regard to Christian experience, and it is this. Our assurance of the omnipotence of God, indicated in Jesus' request to the Father for the removal of the cup of suffering, is always to be linked with our resting in the sovereignty of God, indicated in his readiness for God's will with him and for him to be done. The opening verses of Psalm 116 are appropriate for meditation at this point.

How are we to understand the final phrase of verse 7: *'and he was heard because of his reverence'*? It reminds us of Jesus' words in John 11:42, 'I knew that you always hear me'. Yet in what way was Jesus *'heard'*? Clearly God did not keep his Son from being crucified, for it was central to the provision of salvation that Jesus died for sinners. God 'did not spare his own Son but gave him up for us all' (Romans 8:32). What God did do, however, is that he delivered his Son from the power and dominion of death. He did not 'let (his) holy one see corruption' (Psalm 16:10). He did not allow it to be possible for death to gain any victory over the Lord Jesus Christ. The grave was not permitted to keep him. And all of this was accomplished in the resurrection. 'God raised him up, loosing the pangs of death, because it was not possible for him to be held by it' (Acts 2:24). In magnificent fulfilment of the prophecy in Psalm 68:18 (drawn upon by Paul in Ephesians 4:8) Jesus led captivity captive. He defeated death in its own domain, rose again from the dead, ascended up on high, and reigns now exalted in glory. So in this far higher and richer sense, Jesus' request that the Father would *'save him from death'* was indeed answered. His is 'the power of an indestructible life' (7:16). Indeed, we may make bold to say that Jesus' very prayer to be saved *'from* ('out of') *death'* may itself have been a prayer for his resurrection *after* his crucifixion and burial.

That still leaves *'because of his reverence'*, which is given as the reason for which Jesus' prayer was heard. The word translated here *'reverence'* is full of meaning. It gathers up the sense of 'godly fear, devoutness, reverent awe, total submission'. Behind all these is the root sense of concern for the honour of God in association with carefulness to submit to his will and pleasure. Without question, the Lord Jesus was characterised in this way, hence his 'not my will, but yours, be done'. Arising from this concern and carefulness, his prayer in Gethsemane was both heard and answered. Jesus was sustained in the terrible work of dying and was raised triumphantly from the abode of the dead. In the words of 13:20, 'the God of peace ... brought again from the dead our Lord Jesus, the great shepherd of the sheep'. What a terrible thing sin is, that it required such suffering and sorrow on the part of the Saviour; what an appalling thing the wrath of God upon it is, that he visits it with such a punishment as the death of his spotless Son; what a terrifying thing the lot of the wicked is, who refuse to call upon the name of the Lord for salvation; and what a glorious thing that eternal salvation is which the Lord Jesus has purchased for sinners through his death and resurrection.

It must not be supposed, when our prayers are answered in a way which was not in our mind when we prayed, that they have not been answered or have been disregarded. We may ask for a particular deliverance which does not come (not, at least, straightaway). But other rich favours may come instead, enabling us to bear up under pressing burdens we desired to be lifted—favours such as assurances of God's love towards us, supporting strength for us to keep on going, opportunities to testify of the Lord's upholding grace and overruling wisdom. No prayer from the heart, prayed in faith, is ever lost or wasted. Has not our God promised us, 'I did not say to the offspring of David, "Seek me in vain"' (Isaiah 45:19)? Moreover, we may learn from the example of our Saviour cited here by our writer that it is peculiarly appropriate to give ourselves to prayer when we are approaching death—and praying, not least, that we shall be given grace to honour God in our dying, for we know not exactly what we shall face in going through that experience, or how it will come to us. Dying grace is a needful prayer request for us all.

*'Although he was a son* (better, 'Son', with a capital, for the name belongs to him in a unique sense; the translation 'Son though he was' has been proposed to catch the full force here, Son in his very nature), *he learned obedience through what he suffered'* (5:8). Amazing! Reference has already been made (2:10) to Jesus being made 'perfect through suffering', and attention is drawn to the comment there. Though so exalted a person, and being aware of it ('knowing that the Father had given all things into his hands, and that he had come from God and was going back to God', John 13:3), Jesus was completely willing to learn by personal experience what was involved in being obedient through suffering. Indeed, it is so often God's purpose *with us* to teach us obedience through suffering—a lesson we do not necessarily learn so readily through other means. Sometimes people can be mystified by the concept of Jesus having to 'learn' anything, since he is the eternal Son of God. It must be kept continually in mind, however, that he who is altogether God became also altogether man, and it is a mark (and necessity) of the reality of his manhood that he 'learned', and that among the different things that he learned is that *'he learned obedience'.* Herein is an aspect of him taking our nature upon him and 'being born in the likeness of men' (Philippians 2:7). In this, he entered the full circle of human experience, with the single exception of him being sinless.

This is brought to our attention in the Gospels from the earliest days of Jesus' incarnate life. So in Luke 2:40 we are taught that 'the child grew and became strong, filled with wisdom', and in verse 52 of that same chapter that 'Jesus increased in wisdom', and in both instances mention is made of God's favour being upon him. None of this is in any way in conflict with the glorious truth that 'in (him) are hidden all the treasures of wisdom and knowledge' (Colossians 2:3), or the pervading truth in the book of Proverbs that Jesus is what we might call 'wisdom personified'. Oh blessed Saviour, who *'learned obedience through what he suffered'*!

It is not that the Lord Jesus was not naturally obedient, or that there was ever in him any tendency to resist the law of God or the pleasure of the Father. Far from it! He himself declared, 'My food is to do the will of him who sent me and to accomplish his work' (John 4:34). But it was *'through what he suffered'* that, humanly speaking, *'he learned obedience'*. It is the very nature of obedience to submit to the will of another rather than to please yourself. Paul affirms that 'Christ did not please himself' (Romans 15:3).

The whole process for Jesus, throughout his whole life, of persevering all the way to Calvary in fulfilling his Father's will (which was equally his own will, settled before the world's foundation in the eternal covenant, and with the Holy Spirit also being fully party to it all), refusing any temptations put in his way by the devil or men to deviate one jot from that course, keeping his focus on the one great matter of securing for us eternal 'redemption through his blood, the forgiveness of our trespasses, according to the riches of (God's) grace' (Ephesians 1:7), and triumphing over every foe of his and ours, was part and parcel of this cycle of 'suffering, learning, obeying'. It belongs at the very heart of his work as our Saviour and Mediator, is unique to him, was carried to the utmost limits, and all links in with the great argument unfolded by Paul in Romans 5:19. 'For as by the one man's [Adam's] disobedience the many [us] were made sinners, so by the one man's [Jesus'] obedience the many [us] will be made righteous'. Where Adam failed, and brought us all down with him, Jesus prevailed and raises us all up with him. Jesus' obedience was for our disobedience.

In all of this, our Lord Jesus provides us with a powerful example, 'so that (we) might follow in his steps' (1 Peter 2:21). For 'whoever says he abides in him ought to walk in the same way in which he walked' (1 John 2:6). The way that our heavenly Father frequently appoints for us to learn greater and more fruitful obedience is the way of trial and suffering. The way in which the master went is the way in which his servants must often go. True gospel obedience involves both sacrifice and self-denial. It is not attained easily or without demands being made upon us. And while Jesus' obedience was unique and for our salvation, our obedience is a mark of our union with him, a means of bringing glory to him, and a part of our sanctification as we grow more and more into his likeness.

This leads directly into the next verse, which begins, *'And being made perfect'* (5:9). This is not a reference to moral perfection, for that belonged to Jesus anyway. Rather, the meaning is that he became thereby perfectly fitted, matured, qualified, suited and equipped—in a word, complete—for his designed and appointed work as our high priest. He is perfection itself. The word can also carry the sense of 'consecrated', and considered in this light sets forth clearly the pre-eminence of Jesus' priesthood over those who preceded him. We may put it this way. They (the Old Testament men) were consecrated through the process of the sufferings of those beasts which were offered up in sacrifice. Jesus, in contrast, was consecrated through his own sufferings. We are reminded of his own words, 'And for their sake I consecrate myself' (John 17:19).

As a result, *'he became the source of eternal salvation to all who obey him'*. 2:10 spoke of him as 'the founder of their salvation' (see comment in that place), but the thought here is a little different. The word *'source'* makes its only New Testament appearance here, and while 'founder' is in the context of 'bringing many sons to glory', this different word indicates how it is that any sinner can have salvation at all. It is from him, through him and in him alone. He is the one who has 'obtained (purchased, acquired) with his own blood' (Acts 20:28) all those whom the Father 'gave (him) out of the world' (John 17:6). The 'great salvation' (2:3) is described here as *'eternal salvation'*—a lovely, sweeping phrase which goes all the way 'back' to when God 'chose us in him [Jesus] before the foundation of the world' (Ephesians 1:4), having 'loved (us) with an everlasting love' (Jeremiah 31:3), and reaches all the way 'forwards' with the gift to us of 'eternal comfort and good hope through grace' (2 Thessalonians

2:16). Herein is displayed the grandeur of God's gift of salvation. It is no small thing, neither was it provided in a small way.

And we cannot miss (yet again) a contrast between the old and Jesus' priesthoods. The former priesthoods (in the days of Aaron and others) provided pardon and forgiveness until the next sacrifice (as we might say). Jesus' priesthood, focused as it is upon his Calvary sacrifice of himself, has provided us with a pardon and forgiveness which never wears out, but lasts for ever—literally eternally. So why would these Hebrews (or anyone else, for that matter) ever hanker after the former high priests when they have such a glorious high priest in Jesus? It would make no sense at all!

There is this significant caveat, however—namely, that this eternal salvation of which Jesus is the source is exclusively for *'all who obey him'.* Only such (though all such) are on the receiving or beneficial end of Jesus' high priestly work. This is not to introduce some form of justification by works, as if we can render some form of obedience which merits or qualifies us for salvation. It is never that way, neither can it be. Rather, it is what Paul denotes 'the obedience of faith' (Romans 16:26). Furthermore, it recalls Jesus' words to his disciples when they were together in the upper room, 'If you love me, you will keep my commandments' (John 14:15); and it dovetails with his further remark in that same upper room context, 'Whoever abides in me and I in him, he it is that bears much fruit, for apart from me you can do nothing' (John 15:5).

This would have been very pertinent for those to whom Hebrews was written, for obedience to the Lord Jesus (stemming, as it must, from heartfelt love to Jesus) appeared to be fading. It is no less pertinent for all of us. Love to Jesus must be kept lively (compare Revelation 2:4–5), in order for obedience to Jesus to be kept vigorous. Perseverance *in* the faith is always a prime evidence of belonging *to* the faith. In consequence, the psalmist's urgent plea, 'Search me, O God, and know my heart!' (Psalm 139:23), needs regularly to be upon our lips, for the promise of 5:9 is not for those who continue to live in sin.

This immediate section upon Jesus our high priest concludes with another reference to him *'being designated a high priest after the order of Melchizedek'* (5:10). This truth was quoted in 5:6 from Psalm 110:4, so why is it repeated so speedily? Part of the answer is that it is so central and fundamental to everything that is being written in Hebrews, but something else can be said. Jesus being *'designated'* (the word can even mean 'saluted') in this way was spoken of him before ever he came into the world. It is mentioned again following verses 7–9 (which have been dealing with the *incarnate* Jesus) to underscore that what was declared of old has now been fulfilled. He was to be a priest. He has become a priest. He remains forever a priest. Hence (and we shall learn more of this later, when things should become much clearer) his high priesthood is no mere earthly office but is *'after the order of Melchizedek'*, the one who in a remarkable and mysterious way prefigured the Lord Jesus as a priest-king. Again it is being emphasised that Jesus' priesthood stands alone. But these things must wait for the end of chapter 6 and through chapter 7. For now, our author has some practical shots to fire across his readers' bows.

## Warnings and applications (5:11–14)

There is no doubt about it. All this doctrine about Jesus, the high priest, and Melchizedek is taking us into deep things. The writer of Hebrews is aware of this. What troubles him, however, is that far from being in a state to be taught and to appreciate the deeper currents of Christian faith and doctrine, his addressees seem to be losing all appetite and enthusiasm for such things. So he puts the present matters 'into a siding' for the time being, prior to returning to them in due course, and seeks meanwhile to impress upon the folk the extreme seriousness of their cooling off, wandering away and dampening down in their life and walk. Divine warnings are constantly needful for us in the Christian life for, sadly, we can all too easily lose our fire, take our eyes off the Saviour and, before we know it and without having planned for it, come a cropper. It is a Christlike hallmark of a true pastor that he senses when those in his charge are in danger of doing this. Our writer shows himself, as previously, to be a true pastor.

*'About this* (or 'whom', though it is preferable to take it here as neuter rather than masculine) *we have much to say, and it is hard to explain, since you have become dull of hearing'* (5:11). The sequence of words is striking: *'much to say... hard to explain ... dull of hearing'.* We are not surprised to be told that upon these matters just being treated there is *'much to say'.* Deep and demanding things are not to be dealt with in a swift or summary way. They need time. They require detail. They have to be approached from various angles. So far these truths have only been introduced. As for the fact that they are *'hard to explain'*, there is something almost encouraging here, which assures us that we should not (and need not) be surprised if we do not immediately grasp the whole business first time around, or, as it were, in the first lesson. This does not imply that the writer of Hebrews himself had difficulty in understanding what he was writing about, that he was unable to communicate truth plainly and clearly to them, or that the entire business was ultimately unexplainable. But it will certainly not help if those who need to be taught prove to be *'dull of hearing'* (literally, 'in the hearings'—a phrase which is not intended as an insult to their intelligence or to imply that they were all of a low IQ, but is a sorrowful comment on the waning of the people's desire for the things of Christ and, indeed, something of an increasingly manifest tendency to cast those very things off, to leave them behind and not pay attention to them any more).

That it was not always so with those originally receiving this letter is clear from *'have become'.* They were not always in this state, but have come into it—like those believers addressed in Galatians who to begin with 'were running well' but had slowed their pace significantly (Galatians 5:7). Maybe we can recall, or even now know, folk who fit this bill. Once they looked so hopeful, but then everything which had waxed started to wane. How diligently, therefore, do we need to pay careful attention to ourselves, lest we go the same way. The proud boast, 'such a thing would never happen to me', can very easily be the prelude to just such a thing happening to you, for 'God opposes the proud, but gives grace to the humble' (James 4:6). The word *'dull'* is translated 'sluggish' in 6:12, and that helps us to catch the sense here. It recalls the state and attitude of the sluggard in the book of

Proverbs, not the least of whose problems was that he could just no longer be bothered; everything was too much trouble.

If we would take this seriously as addressed to us also (as indeed it is), this is a moment to pause and ask ourselves some personal questions. Questions like: 'Am I as keen on learning about the Lord Jesus as once I was? Is he as precious to me as before? How is my appetite (and digestion) for spiritual food? Do I delight to be taken further out into the depths of the word of God?' There are many snares in this area for us to avoid if we truly are going to remain among those who persevere. In the old phrase, in the Christian life there are no gains without pains, particularly if we are going to grow rather than remain as we are or (inevitably) otherwise lose ground. Wholeheartedness in the things of God is what is required. For this there is no substitute, and we deceive ourselves if we imagine there is. It is those 'who hunger and thirst for righteousness' whom Jesus pronounces to be the blessed ones, 'for they shall be satisfied' (Matthew 5:6). Or, as it is strikingly expressed elsewhere, 'The soul of the sluggard craves and gets nothing, while the soul of the diligent is richly supplied' (Proverbs 13:4).

## (1) Where they ought to be

The illustration the writer uses in order to press home the point he has just made comes from the classroom: *'For though by this time you ought to be teachers'* (5:12). We take it from this remark that these Hebrews had been 'on the road' for long enough as Christians to have been relishing all that they could possibly glean for themselves or be taught by others of the richest seams of Scripture, delving into its ocean for beautiful and costly pearls, mining its depths for fine and priceless gold. They possessed the Old Testament, and (as 2:1–3 has already made plain) the things of the gospel had been taught and confirmed among them. They had been blessed with countless privileges, favours and opportunities. This should have been true to such an extent that, if need be, they could teach others all that they had learned. This reminds us of the husband and wife team of Aquila and Priscilla, of whom we read that they took Apollos aside 'and explained to him the way of God more accurately' (Acts 18:26). While some in Christ's church will be called and furnished to be 'the pastors and teachers, to equip the saints for the work of ministry, for building up the body of Christ' (Ephesians 4:11–12), yet every Christian has a responsibility for others, and this will sometimes include and involve explaining to them patiently and clearly the meaning of Scripture. Much of this will be done in the home from day to day, as parents bring up their children 'in the discipline and instruction of the Lord' (Ephesians 6:4). Every Christian home should be 'a little Bethel' ('Bethel' meaning 'the house of God', Genesis 28:17, 19). Another example is neighbour to neighbour or friend to friend. Yet, wherever we seek to *'be teachers'*, we cannot teach others what we do not know ourselves.

## (2) Where they actually were

This is what was giving such cause for concern to the pastoral heart of our author. They should have been ready to be teachers, but they were not. Yet it was worse than that, as is now made plain: *you need someone to teach you again the basic principles of the oracles of God* [compare 'living oracles', Acts 7:38] '. This is the alarming thing, and is the direct result of their having become 'dull of hearing'. Not only had they not 'gone on'—they had, in reality, 'gone back'. They had not 'progressed'—instead they had 'regressed'. Things were not looking good at all. In fact, they had gone back, they had regressed, so far, that they were virtually back in the nursery class! They needed to be taught all over again from first principles. The word *'principles'* is 'rudiments' or 'elements', which are here described in relation to *'the oracles of God'*, indicating the very vitals and essentials of the faith, of the divine utterances, set forth in holy Scripture. They were back to the 'ABC'. They were no longer grasping the basic truth that the things of the Old Testament ceremonial law were temporary, all of them pointing and leading to the Lord Jesus Christ—and he has now come and fulfilled them all! The writer's actual phrase rather piles it on, 'the rudiments of the beginning of the oracles of God', which rather implies not only back to the beginning but back even beyond that, even to spiritual babyhood!

Not satisfied with that, things are immediately pressed home even further. '*You need milk, not solid food*'. Children begin with '*milk*', but they do not stay with it. They advance to '*solid food*', and, if they show no inclination to do so and all they wish to do is to remain on a milk diet, then alarm bells start ringing with their parents and medical help will likely be sought. The situation can suggest there is something potentially serious the matter. The same applies in the spiritual realm. When a sinner is converted they begin, both doctrinally and in experience, with the milk of God's word. Yet it will be a healthy sign of their conversion being genuine that they will, before long, desire to advance to meaty matters. If this does not show signs of happening, then (as in the physical realm) concern is raised. Equally, when a believer has been going on well with the Lord over (maybe a lengthy) period of time, and then their spiritual appetite starts to wane and they show a preference for their earlier 'milky' days, then this is not a good sign at all. It appears that the Hebrews (or some of them) were in this position. They had begun well. They had been running well. They had been giving encouraging signs of growing in both 'the grace and knowledge of our Lord Jesus Christ' (2 Peter 3:18), keen on the word of God, taken up more and more with the Lord Jesus Christ, pursuing the way of holiness (and so on), but now they were 'hitting the buffers' and setting off backwards. And this was very much to the alarm and dismay of the one now writing this letter to them. Things must be rescued before it is too late, is very much the spirit of urgency in which he writes.

As a mark of his sincere affection for them, he proceeds to tell them why this is so serious: *for everyone who lives on milk is unskilled in the word of righteousness, since he is a child* ('infant', 'baby')' (5:13). It is one thing for a child to be a child, whether physically or spiritually. This is what is expected. To remain a child, however, is not what is expected, and certainly not to remain continually upon a liquid diet of milk. One fundamental reason why this is so is that there will be no development of abilities, maturity or strength. Paul needed to write to the Corinthians along these very lines: 'But I, brothers, could not address you as spiritual people, but as people of the flesh, as infants in Christ. I fed you with milk, not solid food, for you were not ready for it. And even now you are not ready, for you are still of the flesh' (1 Corinthians 3:1–3).

What does it mean to be *'unskilled* [that is, inexperienced] *in the word of righteousness*? The phrase *'the word of righteousness'* has been variously interpreted, but most likely it relates to 'the oracles of God' mentioned in the previous verse. Losing, as it seems they were, their grip upon the fundamentals of the faith, the Hebrews were losing their skills in understanding, discerning, handling, commending and upholding the true gospel and were travelling backwards from adulthood to childhood. The truth we need to keep hearing is, 'do not be children in your thinking … but in your thinking be mature' (1 Corinthians 14:20).

### (3) Where they need to get back to

With the intention of jolting them and bringing them back to their senses, our writer continues his counsel. *'But solid food is for the mature'* (5:14), and it is high time they were getting back to it (compare 6:1 which will be coming up shortly). Children tend to look forward to growing up. Adults may sometimes, sentimentally, wish they could become children again, or dwell and talk longingly about their childhood (people, places and possessions), but in their wiser moments know that such an eventuality is neither possible nor profitable. In spiritual matters it is never a good thing to return to childhood. It is true, of course, that the Lord Jesus speaks about 'childlikeness' being a mark of true Christian discipleship, but (as many a preacher has pointed out) that is not to be confused with 'childishness'. The problem with the Hebrews is that they were returning to the latter. It is the *'solid food'* of Scripture (its doctrines, commands, promises and blessings) which promotes spiritual maturity. Depart from this, and trouble follows.

Maturity in the things of God, nourished by the word of God, is *'for those who have their powers of discernment trained by constant practice to distinguish good from evil'*. This should be for all believers, and not only for some select few who are regarded as 'keen'. The verb *'trained'* suggests regular practice and vigorous exercise such as an athlete might engage in—in other words, some effort has been put into it, it has not just happened by sitting still. The phrase *'powers of discernment'* is, literally, 'faculties'. This involves the mind and conscience and affects the heart and life, and will assist in enabling a greater and surer ability *'to distinguish good from evil'*, whether in matters of truth (right and wrong teaching), morals (right and wrong behaviour), or anything else. Those things which are *'good'* are nourishing to our minds and hearts and upbuilding to our lives for the Lord, full of beauty and consolation, while those things which are *'bad'* are damaging and unhelpful in every way. The former will be embraced while the latter will be rejected. Remembering the two recent mentions of 'the oracles of God' and 'the word of righteousness', this *'discernment ... to distinguish good from evil'* can only be achieved by patient and persistent love for, study of and obedience to Scripture itself. In contrast to these Hebrews, how are we doing? Standing still or moving on? Remaining children or growing up? Staying with milk or digesting meat? I ask you, dear reader, how are *you* doing?

# Chapter 6
# Built on firm foundations

We left chapter 5 on the note of the importance of Christian maturity. The spiritual life is not a place where we can afford to stand still. As with our pilgrimage as a whole, we need to be constantly moving on—or, as the apostle Paul so vividly urges it, 'But one thing I do: forgetting what lies behind and straining forward to what lies ahead, I press on toward the goal for the prize of the upward call of God in Christ Jesus'. Very significantly, and absolutely in tune with where we are in Hebrews, he adds immediately, 'Let those of us who are mature think this way' (Philippians 3:13–15). We also noted that this growth towards maturity cannot be achieved without serious commitment to Scripture, otherwise we remain on milk long after we should have progressed to solid food.

The *'Therefore'* with which chapter 6 begins leaves us in no doubt that our writer has not yet said all that he has to say upon this subject.

The Hebrews needed more help, instruction and challenge here, and so do we all. How gracious of God that he condescends to us in this way, patiently bearing with our slowness to learn, and continually taking pains with us, in order (bit by bit) to 'present everyone mature in Christ' (Colossians 1:28).

This is a very intricate chapter, even more so than some of the other chapters, so we must proceed carefully. The first three verses, to which we now come, follow on without a break from the end of the previous chapter.

## A goal to pursue (6:1–3)

*'Therefore let us leave the elementary doctrine of Christ and go on to maturity'* (6:1). It appears that those to whom Hebrews was first written needed a good shaking. They were going backwards rather than forwards, and it was high time they got a grip and did something about it. No more rot could be allowed to set in. We noted 'the basic principles of the oracles of God' (5:12), those rudiments, those essentials of the faith, which form the foundation of all that Christians believe. It is always important (in the Christian life as well as in housebuilding) to lay a good, firm foundation. Rock is needed, not sand (Matthew 7:24–27). Yet it is no use leaving things at the foundation stage. You cannot, in buying a home, move in to the foundations. You need the house. So, for the Christian, while a sound grasp of foundational teaching is required before you can go on (or grow on) to anything else, there must be the going (and the growing) on. Those 'basic principles' are mirrored again in this phrase *'the elementary doctrine'* (literally, 'the word of the beginning'), while the addition of the words *'of Christ'* indicate that nothing is more necessary than clear and scriptural views of the Lord Jesus Christ, in all the glories of his person and work. How we understand and regard him is all important—as Jesus insists in his famous question, 'What do you think about the Christ?' (Matthew 22:42). The divine revelation in the gospel of the full glory of Christ (no longer a matter of types and shadows) must be laid hold of with understanding and enthusiasm, and the readers must be content with nothing less.

What might *'the elementary doctrine of Christ'* contain? It will (and must) contain great truths like the two perfect natures (divine and human) in the one person of the Lord Jesus; the historical facts of his miraculous incarnation, sinless life of obedience to the law of God, sin-bearing death on the cross, burial in the tomb, physical resurrection from the dead, glorious ascension, present ministry and coming again; the vital summons to 'repent and believe in the gospel' (Mark 1:15), with its insistence upon the twins of repentance and faith; the assurance that he alone 'came into the world to save sinners' (1 Timothy 1:15) and that he only is 'the way, and the truth, and the life' and that 'No one comes to the Father except through (him)' (John 14:6); and that in the Lord Jesus the worst of sinners may 'have redemption through his blood, the forgiveness of sins, according to the riches of (God's) grace' (Ephesians 1:7).

Our writer's *'let us'* shows pastoral wisdom and grace as he identifies himself with the people, rather than setting himself in a lordly or patronising manner above them, while the verb *'go on'* means literally 'let us be carried (forward)', (a word, evidently, which is taken from a sailing ship's progress before the wind). The implication is that this is not something to be done in their own energy or under their own steam but as they are enabled by God. The thought behind this is surely that this 'energy' and 'steam' is dependent upon the Holy Spirit, for he is the one within the Godhead who in a special manner is our teacher, maturer and sanctifier. Without the Holy Spirit there will never be any progress worth the name in the Christian life. The call to *'leave'* these beginning or elementary doctrines is not, of course, a call to abandon or deny them or forget all about them, for every deeper doctrine of the faith is built upon them. But they are the beginning, they are the elementary things, they are where we start, and there is so much more to learn and so much further to travel, both in knowledge and experience.

Remembering, then, what we have just observed about the importance of the foundation, yet the need to build upon that foundation, this opening verse continues with the charge *'not laying again the* ['a', there is no definite article] *foundation'*. A foundation is laid once, not twice or several times. Concerning the foundation of Christian life and doctrine, the writer now lists six subjects, grouping them in three pairs: *'the foundation of repentance from dead works and of faith toward God* [first pair]*, and of instruction about washings, the laying on of hands* [second pair]*, the resurrection of the dead, and eternal judgment* [third pair]*'* (6:1–2). How are these six features in their three pairs to be understood? The clearest way is to view them as presenting, one after the other, the beginning, the continuing and the ending of the Christian life—or, as we may put it another way, the way in, the way on, and the way out of that life.

## (1) The way in to the Christian life

Repentance and faith are fundamental to everything in becoming a Christian. They belong together, as the two faces of a coin. They represent the two sides of conversion. During the course of his most moving farewell with the Ephesian elders, Paul reminded them how he had testified 'both to Jews and to Greeks of repentance toward God and of faith in our Lord Jesus Christ' (Acts 20:21). In the wonder of the conversion of a sinner to God, repentance leads to faith and faith follows repentance. They make a pair. True conversion requires both to be present.

Repentance has been described as a medicine with various ingredients, among which would be a true *sight* of our sinfulness in the sight of God ('Against you, you only, have I sinned and done what is evil in your sight', Psalm 51:4); a deep sense of *sorrow* on account of our sin ('For godly grief (or, 'sorrow') produces a repentance that leads to salvation', 2 Corinthians 7:10); a genuine conviction of *shame* at the contemplation of our sin ('Let us lie down in our shame, and let our dishonour cover us. For we have sinned against the LORD our God', (Jeremiah 3:25); a heartfelt *confessing* of our sin before the holy God ('If we confess our sins, he is faithful and just to forgive us our sins and to cleanse us from all unrighteousness', 1 John 1:9); and a determined *forsaking* of all known sin, the Lord himself being our helper ('Whoever conceals his transgressions will not prosper, but he who confesses and forsakes them will obtain mercy'), Proverbs 28:13).

Why is the reference here in 6:1 specifically to '*repentance from dead works*'? Hebrews provides the only occurrences in the New Testament of the phrase '*dead works*' (it reappears in 9:14). It sets forcefully before all readers of this epistle (then and now) that the natural state of all mankind is that of being 'dead in … trespasses and sins' (Ephesians 2:1), 'alienated from the life of God' (Ephesians 4:18). It is also the natural manner of all mankind, left to themselves, to seek to be right with God by their own means (works) rather than by God's means (grace). But these human works are '*dead works*' in every sense of those words, 'For by works of the law [our doings, our efforts, our contributions, our obedience, our anything] no human being will be justified in his (God's) sight' (Romans 3:20). This works two ways: sin can only produce works that are dead, while a dead soul can only produce works that are sinful. Either way, the sinner's condemnation is certain, insofar as ever saving ourselves is concerned. It is, therefore, in the nature of true repentance that the sinner recognises this, acknowledges that of himself he has and can do no good thing, and casts himself upon God alone for mercy, laying hold eagerly of the divine assurance that 'with you (God) there is forgiveness, that you may be feared' and that 'with him is plentiful redemption' (Psalm 130:4, 7). The 9:14 occurrence points us directly to the sinner's refuge from '*dead works*' to 'the blood of Christ', our only plea.

With repentance belongs faith, so the second part of this first pair is, not surprisingly, '*faith toward God*'. We turn *from* sin (repentance) *to* Christ (faith). Each is incomplete without the other. Faith leaves all of self behind and clings only to Christ, receiving and resting upon him alone for complete salvation—that 'great salvation' of 2:3. With mind, heart and will the Lord Jesus Christ alone becomes the sole object of the repenting sinner's trust and affection, with the result that the believer can say with confidence, in these matchless words, 'My beloved is mine, and I am his' (Song of Songs 2:16).

In which case, why does our writer speak here of '*faith toward God*' rather than of 'faith in Christ'? The truth is that there is nothing strange in this, for while it is 'through faith' (in Christ, that is) that we are saved, which faith 'is not (our) own doing; it is the gift of God, not a result of works, so that no one may boast' (Ephesians 2:8–9), yet it is faith in Christ which brings us, reconciles us, to God. There is no other way of reconciliation, for 'in Christ God was reconciling the world to himself' (2 Corinthians 2:19). Would you be right with God, with sins forgiven and adopted into his family? It can only be through his Son, for 'there is one [that is to say, only one] mediator between God and men, the man Christ Jesus, who gave himself as a ransom for all' (1 Timothy 2:5–6).

## (2) The way on in the Christian life

Proceeding to the second of the three pairs, we are confronted immediately with matters which have been differently interpreted. Help is at hand, however, so long as we remember this 'way in, way on, way out' framework which the three pairs cover. This is the middle one, belonging to the ongoing Christian life. In sum, before we examine the details, it is safest to say that this second pair has to do with the Christian's life in the church, in the Spirit.

First off is *'and of instruction about washings'*. The strong contender for the meaning of this phrase is to refer it to Christian baptism, that being presented here in contrast with all the Jewish ceremonial washings of the Old Testament with which the Hebrews would be very familiar. Christian baptism is 'in the name of the Father and of the Son and of the Holy Spirit' (Matthew 28:19). That is to say, it is Trinitarian. It speaks of our union with the Lord Jesus Christ. As for the Jewish ceremonial washings, these are mentioned in 9:10, in the context of 'gifts and sacrifices … that cannot perfect the conscience of the worshipper, but deal only with food and drink and various washings' (9:9–10). The Lord Jesus thoroughly 'perfect(s) the conscience of the worshipper', and the washing aspect of baptism highlights this. Paul enlarges somewhat upon this: 'But when the goodness and loving kindness of God our Saviour appeared, he saved us, not because of works done by us in unrighteousness, but according to his own mercy, by the washing of regeneration and renewal of the Holy Spirit, whom he poured out on us richly through Jesus Christ our Saviour' (Titus 2:4–6). To focus the point we are making: all the former instructions relating to washings (many of which occur in the course of Exodus, Leviticus and Numbers) are now finished with because of all that Jesus has accomplished and provided for the sinner who comes to him. Moreover, 'the blood of Jesus (God's) Son cleanses us from all sin' (1 John 1:7), and the tense of 'cleanses' there is 'goes on, carries on, keeps on cleansing'. The old ceremonies only dealt with bodies. Jesus deals with the whole person.

The word here in 6:2, *'washings'*, may be rendered 'baptisms'. However, it is not the word used elsewhere in the New Testament for baptism as a Christian ordinance. Consequently, this is something that is urged against our interpretation given above, along with the fact that the word here is plural, whereas whenever and wherever baptism is mentioned it is always in the singular. Neither of these objections need derail us, however. The plural 'baptisms' matches the plural 'washings', while it may also refer to many baptisms—that is to say, such as on the day of Pentecost, or the plain fact that in ordinary circumstances all Christians will be baptised.

Along with this, rather than apart from it, it may be appropriate to mention 1 Corinthians 12:13, with its grand reminder that 'in one Spirit we were all baptized into one body'—the point here in Hebrews 6 being that having been born again by the Holy Spirit (for that is what Spirit baptism is), ushered into the Christian life by means of repentance and faith (remember the first pair in 6:1), and united thereby to the Lord Jesus Christ, baptism with water is the appointed outward sign of all that has taken place and sets the individual believer firmly in the context of belonging to the church and so being part of the body of Christ, as Scripture terms it.

The companion to the *'instruction about washings'* is *'the laying on of hands'*, and to that we now come. The practice of laying hands on individuals is a familiar one from the New Testament, and has several associations. It is connected with baptism itself (for example, in Samaria in Acts 8 and Ephesus in Acts 19); as an act of blessing or benediction (Jesus with the children in Matthew 19:13—and goes all the way back to Genesis 48:14 with Israel (Jacob) and his grandchildren); in respect of the healing of the sick (note Mark 6:5, when Jesus 'laid his hands on a few sick people and healed them', and

Acts 28:8, when Paul, ministering to Publius' father on the island of Malta, 'visited him and prayed, and putting his hands on him healed him'); and accompanying the setting apart of people for particular service in the church of Christ (examples include the apostles with the 'seven' in Acts 6, Saul and Barnabas being commissioned for missionary service in Acts 13, and Paul's reminder to Timothy in 2 Timothy 1:6 of what had happened earlier in his (Timothy's) life).

We learn from such examples as these that *'the laying on of hands'* was a symbolic action, related, not least, to divine blessing and divine gifts. In this connection it is inextricably linked with the gift of the Holy Spirit and his ministry and enabling. This gives us the clue to its appearance here in Hebrews. Thinking in terms of the principle of 1 Corinthians 12:27 ('Now you are the body of Christ and individually members of it'), those who have been converted (repentance and faith) and baptised (and so added to the church) have been brought into a life of mutual ministry and service one to another, none living for themselves but each to their brothers and sisters in the church family. 'Let each of you look not only to his own interests, but also to the interests of others'—urged upon the solid basis of Christians having 'this mind among yourselves, which is yours in Christ Jesus' (Philippians 2:4–5).

This has a very contemporary application to our own day, when there can be a tendency in some quarters to 'sit light to' or even 'get on without' the church. This is quite wrong. Christians belong to the church, by definition, and while there are times when church life and experience can present all sorts of difficulties and heartbreaks, those whom the Saviour has purchased by his blood and to whom he has given his Holy Spirit not only belong together but positively need each other. It is in the context of the ministry and fellowship of the local church that we prosper and flourish—not when we decide to 'keep to ourselves' or 'go it alone'. Always keep the right balance between (on the one hand), 'And the life I now live in the flesh I live by faith in the Son of God, who loved me and gave himself for me' (Galatians 2:20), and (on the other), 'Christ loved the church and gave himself up for her' (Ephesians 5:25). Very significantly, Paul continues: 'that he might sanctify her, having cleansed her by the washing of water with the word, so that he might present the church to himself in splendour, without spot or wrinkle or any such thing, that she might be holy and without blemish' (Ephesians 5:26–27), reminding us that just as the Lord Jesus knows and loves each one of his own individually, he regards us as well very much in terms of our togetherness. We are his 'one flock', and he is our 'one shepherd' (John 10:16).

So repentance and faith, the first pair, speak of 'the way in' to the Christian life, and washings and laying on of hands, the second pair, speak of 'the way on' in that life. We come now to the third, and final, pair.

## (3) The way out of the Christian life

The Christian life is unique. It begins, as all of life does, and it continues. Only in one sense, however, does it end. That is to say, it ends its earthly span (when we die), but essentially it never ends. What does the Lord Jesus say to his own? 'I give them eternal life' (John 10:28). 'Because I live, you also will live' (John 14:19). So this final pair, while speaking of 'the way out' of the Christian life, speak ultimately of this life that has no end. We shall change our place (moving from earth to heaven), but we shall not change our company (that of Christ and his people).

6:2 continues, then, with *'the resurrection of the dead, and eternal judgment'*. These belong to that part of doctrine which is often labelled 'the last things'. What they must never be allowed to become are the last things we ever consider. They should be in the forefront of our minds continually.

By this third pair is meant that momentous event at the end of the present age when the bodies of all who have died, believers and unbelievers, will rise from their graves (or wherever else they have been placed after death), be united with their souls, and all will 'stand before the judgment seat of God' (Romans 14:10). This same judgment seat is also called 'the judgment seat of Christ' (2 Corinthians 5:10)—a striking testimony to the deity of the Lord

Jesus. In between a person's death and resurrection is what we term 'the intermediate state'. During this period, bodies and souls are separated from one another. Bodies are laid in their graves, but souls will be in one of two places (and only in one of two places). The souls of the righteous (Christians) pass immediately upon death into the presence and enjoyment of the Lord Jesus in heaven, whereas the souls of the unrighteous (those who are not Christians) pass immediately upon death into the miseries of hell, where God is known and experienced only in his wrath. Then, at the resurrection spoken of here in Hebrews, the souls and bodies of the righteous are reunited, as are the souls and bodies of the unrighteous, and divine judgment takes place—'those who have done good to the resurrection of life, and those who have done evil to the resurrection of judgment', declares Jesus in John 5:29. The Father has given authority to the Son 'to execute judgment', the previous verse declares.

So many glorious prospects await every true Christian after death. Being with Christ (Philippians 1:23), being like Christ (1 John 3:2), seeing his face (Revelation 22:4), worshipping and serving him with purity of heart and motive, being sheltered with his presence, altogether satisfied in him, constantly refreshed from 'springs of living water' (Revelation 7:15–17), and wanting for nothing (Psalm 23:6)— these are just some of them.

The word *'eternal'* must be given its full value and not diminished in any way. Heaven is eternal, for all those who go there. Hell is eternal, for all those who go there. Both are final states and cannot be reversed. What (or, rather, who) makes the difference in terms of who goes where is the Lord Jesus Christ himself. Our writer to the Hebrews, all the way through his detailed letter, never tires of setting Jesus forth in all his fullness and sufficiency as the only one who can deal with our sins, reconcile us to God, keep us through life and present us safe on heaven's golden shore. Many things in the Old Testament spoke to this end in types, images, pictures and so forth, but only in Jesus are all these things fulfilled. They were shadows, he is reality. So once you have the reality, what can possibly be the point or the advantage in returning to the shadows—for that is all part of what the Hebrews appear to have been in danger of doing. As for us, our business is to lay full hold upon the Lord Jesus Christ, never looking elsewhere, ever confident in him and on increasing tiptoe of expectation for when we shall behold the one whom our souls love (as Song of Songs 3:3 expresses it).

These opening two verses of Hebrews 6 are very full, and (as we have discovered) not always easy to understand. In order to keep on the right lines, however, we must keep in mind all the time this 'three pair' framework for the Christian life. Beginning with 'the way in', we repent of our sins and believe upon the Lord Jesus Christ. Continuing with 'the way on', we are baptised, added to the church, and enjoy the rich and manifold ministry of the Holy Spirit. At the end, so far as this present life is concerned, 'the way out' through death leads on to resurrection and judgment. Judgment always has a heavy ring to it, and, indeed, it needs to, for many would ridicule it. Remember this, however, dear reader, if your heart and hope is set 'fully on the grace that will be brought to you at the revelation of Jesus Christ' (1 Peter 1:13). Remember what? 'There is therefore now no condemnation for those who are in Christ Jesus' (Romans 8:1).

It is very striking that the writer to the Hebrews denotes all these six things as elementary doctrine. The truth is that they dig deep. But that is not the point he is making. By 'elementary' he does not mean simple, easy or superficial. Nothing in Christian doctrine is really any of those things. He means 'fundamental', things that we learn first, that form the basis, the foundation, and upon which we then build as we go on to maturity. He is so concerned that the Hebrews grow up, and we should be equally concerned that we keep on growing up as well. So how thankful we are for Hebrews (and we trust they were thankful for it as well).

*'And this we will do if God permits'* (6:3). This has the spirit about it of 'go for it!' and 'let all take heed of it!'. Enough of this infancy. It is time to be grown men and women in the faith. The *'if God permits'* is not a 'let out', as if to say 'we'll do this if God allows us to, but not if he doesn't'. Such a reading of the verse would make no sense at all. It is rather an expression, needed at all times, of complete dependence

upon God in performing everything that is commanded and required of us. We are to leave certain things behind and press on to maturity, and the responsibility is wholly ours for doing so. Yet in that very acknowledgement, we admit that on our own and of ourselves we can do nothing. Never fear—divine help is always at hand for those who ask. Our problem? So often it is this: 'You do not have, because you do not ask' (James 4:2).

## A warning to heed (6:4–8)

We approach now a passage of the letter to the Hebrews which has presented great difficulties of interpretation over not only the years but the centuries. Our writer takes up the solemn theme of apostasy—a subject already broached in 3:12–14 and which will be revisited in 10:26–39 and 12:25–29. We have just been studying his words arising from his concern over the lack of progress in the Christian lives of those to whom he writes, and, more than this, the danger signs they are showing of actually going backwards. In the verses of the present section, however, something even worse seems to be in view—their potential abandoning of the Christian faith altogether, their going back beyond a point of no return, their complete ditching of Christ and the gospel. Could there be anything more serious or alarming than this? Red lights are flashing, and firm steps need to be taken, so that is what now happens.

The major question, and the one which has sparked the difficulties of interpretation, is this: who precisely are being spoken of here, these ones who cannot possibly be restored to repentance again? Are they true believers, or are they others (whoever 'others' are)? If they are true believers, then can true believers (after all) be lost? If they are others, then what has happened to them, since they appear to have had everything going for them at one time? In order to answer such questions correctly, we must first examine closely what is said of them. We shall proceed by way of their *description*, a *declaration* concerning them, the *explanation* of their case and an *illustration* to help us make sense of them.

## (1) Description

*'For it is impossible to restore again to repentance'* (6:4). While the original sentence does indeed begin *'For it is impossible'* in verse 4, the words *'to restore again* (or, 'renew') *to repentance'* do not appear until verse 6. In between the two we are given a sequence of five features or characteristics of the people who are here on the receiving end of the warning. All five relate to God-given blessings and privileges.

They *'have once been enlightened'*. The very word *'enlightened'* carries the sense of having been brought out of darkness into light (compare 1 Peter 2:9); or, as Paul puts it, receiving in the heart 'the light of the knowledge of the glory of God in the face of Jesus Christ' (2 Corinthians 4:6); or, with Paul again, 'having the eyes of your hearts enlightened' (Ephesians 1:18), and 'for at one time you were darkness, but now you are light in the Lord' (Ephesians 5:8). It is classic Scripture vocabulary for what is part and parcel of the mystery and miracle of the new birth. Moreover, the fact that the verb is in what is called the passive voice underscores that the enlightenment is God's work, and not something that anyone has done (or ever can do) for themselves. The folk here spoken of have been instructed in gospel truth and have come to a considerable understanding of it.

It has been held by some that there is a reference here to baptism, but it is not at all obvious that baptism was in any way in the author's mind when he wrote this. Such would be a strange intrusion, made no less strange by the mention in verse 2 of washings/baptisms.

They *'have tasted the heavenly gift'*. Since 'Salvation belongs to the Lord' (Jonah 2:9) and since it is 'by grace (we) have been saved through faith. And this is not (our) own doing; it is the gift of God' (Ephesians 2:8), it seems most natural to take this second feature as referring to the many blessings of God in salvation, all the grace and mercy of God towards sinners which comes down from heaven itself. For salvation, in all its rich abundance, is without question well spoken of as *'the heavenly gift'*. To *'taste'* implies personal experience, of whatever depth, along the lines of 'Oh, taste and see that the LORD is good!' (Psalm 34:8) and 'if indeed you have tasted that the Lord is good' (1 Peter 2:3). It does not, however, necessarily imply eating, for you can taste yet not eat, taste but not digest, and certainly taste while not being nourished.

As with baptism in the first feature, so it has been held by some that there is a reference this time to the Lord's Supper (because of the tasting), but it is no more likely in this case than it was in the above.

They *'have shared in the Holy Spirit'*. Following on immediately from the tasting of the heavenly gift, this third feature would appear to signify a personal experience of the work of the Holy Spirit (the concept of sharing has links with partaking), and so is suggestive of conversion as well as, maybe, some reception of one or more of the spiritual gifts which were in evidence in the church in the apostolic days (as, for example, in 1 Corinthians 12, or in Hebrews itself in 2:4). The purpose of these gifts was, not least, to act as confirmations and testimonies to the gospel's truth and power. It is to be noted that the word used here for *'shared'* [sharers, partakers] is a different one from that occurring in Colossians 1:12 ('who has qualified you to share in the inheritance of the saints in light') and 2 Peter 1:4 ('partakers of the divine nature'). In those two cases, without question, true Christians are in view.

They *'have tasted the goodness of the word of God'* (6:5). This may equally be rendered, 'who tasting the good word of God'. Whichever way we translate it, personal experience seems once again to be in view, while *'the word of God'* most likely refers to the good news of the gospel itself. God's word and gospel is most certainly good, for it proceeds from the good and gracious God, carries with it good and gracious benefits, and for all who receive it humbly through faith it issues in all manner of good and gracious fruits. As in the second characteristic above, *'tasted'* is the word used, not anything more. Does it remind us of Herod, of whom we learn, 'When he heard him [John], he was greatly perplexed, and yet he heard him gladly' (Mark 6:20)—gladly, but not savingly?

They have also tasted *'the powers of the age to come'*. This is the last of these five features the writer is employing in order to describe those to whom he refers. It takes us into the realm of the future, already begun to be experienced in the present. These *'powers of the age to come'* broke into the scene of time and history with the first coming of the Lord Jesus Christ. He himself said so in words such as, 'The time is fulfilled, and the kingdom of God is at hand; repent and believe the gospel' (Mark 1:15), and 'the kingdom of God is in the midst of (or, 'within') you' (Luke 17:21). There remains much more yet to come, however, and this will be associated with the second coming of the Lord Jesus Christ, for 'according to his promise we are waiting for new heavens and a new earth in which righteousness dwells' (2 Peter 3:13), the time when, according to his promise, God will make 'all things new' (Revelation 21:5).

The church lives in between these two comings, already experiencing much of *'the powers of the age to come'*, yet still very much as those who 'by God's power are being guarded through faith for a salvation ready to be revealed in the last time' (1 Peter 1:5). Paul speaks of this very eloquently when he says, 'And not only the creation, but we ourselves, who have the firstfruits of the Spirit, groan inwardly as we wait eagerly for adoption as sons, the redemption of our bodies. For in this hope we were saved' (Romans 8:23–24). The people under discussion before us had observed some of the marks of the breaking in of these kingdom powers—such as Jesus' miracles and signs, and the mighty works of the Spirit in the days from Pentecost onwards.

Summarising, the ones whom the writer to the Hebrews describes are 'those who have once been enlightened, who have tasted the heavenly gift, and have shared in the Holy Spirit, and have tasted the goodness of the word of God and the powers of the age to come'. These are the five features he chooses in order to describe them. Having done so, what does he now say of them?

## (2) Declaration

*'For it is impossible to restore again to repentance'* these very ones, *'if they then fall away'* (6:6). There is no 'if' here, notwithstanding English translations. Verse 6, continuing the sentence, reads 'and falling away'. It may be appropriate to render it 'when (or, 'after') they have fallen

away'. But what is the 'falling away' and why cannot such ever again be restored to repentance? Why is the outlook so bleak to the point of being completely hopeless?

We must take one thing at a time. It is necessary to observe, first of all, that at face value this fivefold description in 6:4–5 looks remarkably like a description of truly converted persons. Each of the five statements could be made of such. These things are true of them. But the thing is, that the very same things can *appear to be true* of others, when that is not actually the case. That is to say, many can show real indications of having been changed by the gospel (having a different mind, living a different life, pursuing a different goal, enjoying a different company—just like true believers), yet it is all appearance, and time shows that there was never any genuine change, any 'root and branch' change, at all. It seemed true, but time showed it to be false. And the time that showed it to be false was when they walked away, turned back in the opposite direction, denied the faith they had once espoused, openly and publicly rejected everything they had apparently stood for, 'made shipwreck of their faith' (1 Timothy 1:19), and even began to blaspheme the name of the Lord. To do such is to commit apostasy, and it is apostasy that is in view here.

This is *not* the same as backsliding. A backslider, who may go very far from the Lord and stay there for a long time (such that we have almost, if not completely, lost hope of them), returns, is brought back, eventually. He may fall into gross and even repeated sin, but he discovers upon true repentance that 'with (God) there is forgiveness' (Psalm 130:4), and he knows once more what it is to have restored to him 'the joy of (God's) salvation' (Psalm 51:12). In contrast, an apostate has gone for good. Apostates go away permanently, show their true colours, and never return. Such are those of whom the apostle John writes: 'They went out from us, but they were not of us; for if they had been of us, they would have continued with us. But they went out, that it might become plain that they all are not of us' (1 John 2:19). How true it is that all that glitters is not necessarily gold!

They are those whom Jesus pictures in the parable of the sower in Matthew 13:3–9. In that parable, different human responses to the gospel are pictured—some seed landing on the path and being eaten up by the birds, some on rocky ground with no depth of soil and so being scorched in the hot sun, some among the thorns which choke their growth, and, finally, some on good soil which produced a good crop of grain. The point is that for much of time it would be very difficult to tell the difference between all of them clearly. Things might look very much the same for quite a while. Time would have to be given in order to see what grew and proved fruitful and what did not. Much might have given hope of good prospects which would eventually prove to be unfounded. Early assessments would turn out to have been premature. Only the seed which actually fell on the good ground would end up producing the good harvest. What a terrible thing it is to be an 'almost' Christian—maybe not far from the kingdom of God, but never truly to have entered it. It is not surprising that Jesus concludes his parable with the challenging words, 'He who has ears, let him hear'.

To take another illustration from Jesus' teaching, the people here in Hebrews 6 are like the 'Lord, Lord' brigade of Matthew 7:21–23. He speaks there of many who in their time addressed him with what appeared to be great and genuine respect, saying, 'Lord, Lord—did we not do this and did we not do that, and all in your name', yet to them Jesus will declare the solemn words, 'I never knew you; depart from me, you workers of lawlessness'. While every true Christian will most certainly confess that 'Jesus is Lord' (as Romans 10:9 teaches), yet merely to call him by that name is no guarantee of anything. What is necessary, Jesus says, is to do 'the will of my Father who is in heaven'.

In Hebrews 6 terms, then: (1) being 'enlightened' can include spiritual experience which falls short of the new birth; (2) tasting 'the heavenly gift' can include a sense of gospel blessings without a heart reception of them; (3) sharing 'in the Holy Spirit' can include real movings of the Spirit in the mind and heart which do not equate with being made possessors of him; (4) tasting 'the goodness of the word of God' can include genuine pleasure being taken in God's Word without life submission to it; and (5) tasting 'the powers of the age to come' can include an acknowledgment of the truth of eternal things without having ever been transformed by the reality of them. Whereas in the case of another person, the same Hebrews 6 categories are the real thing—he is actually and truly born again, has received gospel blessings into his heart, is possessed and indwelt by the Holy Spirit, lives a life in cheerful and consistent obedience to God's word, and lives and longs for eternity. The former person—the one who looks to all outward appearances to be a true believer—ends up abandoning his profession of the Lord Jesus Christ (he professes, but time reveals that he does not possess). The latter person—the one who also looks to all outward appearances to be a true believer—actually is one and holds firm throughout his life and never departs from the Lord Jesus Christ (he both professes and possesses). But keep focused on the key point of these verses: for so much of the time you cannot tell the difference between them.

## (3) Explanation

It 'is impossible to restore again to repentance' these professors who have never possessed. Why? It sounds a very hard sentence to pronounce. The word 'impossible' is a very strong and dogmatic word. This is not its only appearance in Hebrews. We are told that 'it is impossible for God to lie' (6:18), 'it is impossible for the blood of bulls and goats to take away sins' (10:4), and that 'without faith it is impossible to please (God)' (11:6). The word speaks of something which can never happen, which admits of no exceptions. In the present case in chapter 6 it refers to the impossibility of restoring again to repentance those whose apostasy has been outlined. Why is it impossible? Why does it have to be impossible? For this reason: *'since they are crucifying once again the Son of God to their own harm and holding him up to contempt'.*

The writer's language here strikes as very daring. How can the Son of God be crucified again? In the literal sense of being put back upon the cross, he cannot. Calvary can never be repeated. Rather the meaning here is that they, by their deliberate and public abandonment of him after however long a time it might have been of professing to believe in him and follow after him, hold him up to ridicule and shame before all who knew them as 'supposed' Christians. When Jesus hung nailed to the cross, that is exactly how he was regarded by all the crowds who came to gape at him—an object of ridicule and shame, of utter contempt and disgust. That is what crucifixion was intended to make a person, and those in view here in 6:6 are, as it were, siding with Jesus' actual crucifiers. The gospel itself is brought into disrepute, and unbelievers tell themselves (and others) that they have every reason they require to pay no attention either to Christ or his gospel. Untold harm is done. This is judged by the Judge of all men to be so serious that there is no way back of repentance provided from it. Not only are the apostates themselves unable to repent, but God actually will not permit them to. It is not that God lacks the power to restore them, but that he refuses to restore them. They (or so it appeared) repented to begin with. There can be no renewing of that repentance following apostasy. For all such, most solemnly, 'there no longer remains a sacrifice for sins, but a fearful expectation of judgment' (10:26–27).

## (4) Illustration

Our writer will express from verses 9–12 that he has every hope that apostasy will not prove to be the case of those to whom he is writing. But before that he supplies a helpful and clarifying illustration of an agricultural and horticultural nature, whereby he sums up what he has been saying in the preceding verses and makes powerful application of it. *'For land that has drunk the rain that often falls on it, and produces a crop useful to those for whose sake it is cultivated, receives a blessing from God'* (6:7). Land enjoys drinking rain and producing crops. These are both 'useful' to those who work the land and a 'blessing' to the ground itself. *'But if it bears thorns and thistles, it is worthless and near to being cursed, and its end is to be burned'* (6:8). If, however, despite the rain, the land produces *'thorns and thistles'* rather than the good grain crop, that is neither useful to the workers nor blessed to the ground. The curse, rather than the blessing, of God is upon the land.

The language here will be very familiar to the recipients of Hebrews in terms of the Old Testament, and the book of Deuteronomy in particular. That book speaks of 'the land ... which drinks water by the rain of heaven' (11:11), as well as in terms of blessing and cursing, burning and judgment (passages in chapters 28, 29 and 32). There would also appear to be a reference to the 'thorns and thistles' which the ground would bring forth (Genesis 3:17–18), as part of the curse which came upon creation at the fall.

The solemn application of this to the case in hand that the writer to the Hebrews is dealing with is alarmingly clear and forceful. In contrast to the wonderful, gracious and everlasting blessings which accompany a sound and genuine conversion, there is no blessing whatsoever to be found in an untrue profession of Christ or an insincere acceptance of the gospel. We made reference earlier to Jesus' parable of the sower, and a further reference is appropriate. It is said there that, 'As for that [that is, that seed] in the good soil, they are those who, hearing the word, hold it fast in an honest and good heart, and bear fruit with patience' (Luke 8:15). Much in keeping with the perseverance theme of Hebrews, an essential mark of a genuine believer is that he or she perseveres, keeps going, does not turn back, and in making progress brings forth and evidences spiritual fruitfulness. Such is indicative of *'blessing from God'* resting upon them. To bring forth, in contrast, *'thorns and thistles'* is the sign, rather, of the absence of grace in the heart and life, and the very opposite of an indication of divine blessing and a sign of rejection by God.

It is true, as we have seen, that it may in some ways be difficult always to distinguish between those who have had a saving work of divine grace wrought upon them and those who, while having received many gracious influences and privileges, were never actually saved. But time will reveal it. The true will be made plain, and so will the false. The separation is described at the end of Jesus' parable of the sheep and the goats in Matthew 25. To some (the true ones) he will say, 'Come, you who are blessed by my Father, inherit the kingdom prepared for you from the foundation of the world'. To others (the false ones) he will say, 'Depart from me, you cursed, into the eternal fire prepared for the devil and his angels'.

As the apostle Paul states it, for those who are revealed as 'enemies of the cross of Christ', there is only one outcome: 'their end is destruction' (Philippians 3:18–19). Or as Jesus himself expresses it devastatingly: 'If anyone does not abide in me he is thrown away like a branch and withers; and the branches are gathered, thrown into the fire, and burned' (John 15:6).

## A word to encourage (6:9–12)

Notwithstanding all of this solemn and detailed talk of apostasy and no restoration to repentance, our writer now adopts a tone of warm pastoral encouragement, to the effect that he is hopefully persuaded that those to whom he writes are not and will not be among the apostates, but among the true people of God, the true disciples of the Lord Jesus Christ.

*'Though we speak in this way, yet in your case, beloved, we feel sure of better things—things that belong to salvation'* (6:9). His affectionate tone is immediately to the fore (*'beloved'*), assuring them, if assurance were needed, that he is very much for them and has not turned against them. The verb *'feel sure'* carries the sense of 'persuaded, firmly convinced'. It is reminiscent of the language of the apostle when speaking to the Romans (Romans 15:14) and to Timothy (2 Timothy 1:5). This does not make the foregoing warnings surplus to requirements in any way, however. As we have remarked earlier, the writer obviously felt sufficient concern that things, if left to do so, *could* go the way of apostasy, and he was not willing to stand by and allow that possibility to happen. So he stepped in with fervent warning, for 'Faithful are the wounds of a friend' (Proverbs 27:6). But now he combines it with encouragement, for while he would have them warned and stirred he would not have them overwhelmed and despairing.

He feels *'sure of better things'* where these dear ones are concerned, and these are the *'things that belong to salvation'*. By that is meant things well with their souls, rather than the opposite—that theirs are true professions and not false ones, that they are true possessors and not deceived ones. In Pauline terms, he is 'sure of this, that he who began a good work in you will bring it to completion at the day of Jesus Christ' (Philippians 1:6). He regards them very much as like the ground of verse 7 which 'receives a blessing from God', rather than that of verse 8 which is 'near to being cursed, and its end is to be burned'. It is interesting to note his use of 'better', a theme which recurs throughout the epistle in various ways (for example, 'a better hope', 7:19; 'a better covenant', 7:22; 'better promises', 8:6; 'better sacrifices', 9:23; 'a better possession', 10:34; 'a better country', 11:16; and 'a better life' or 'resurrection', 11:35).

What inclines our writer to this view of them? He proceeds to give us some of his reasons. *'For God is not so unjust as to overlook your work and the love that you showed for his sake in serving the saints, as you still do'* (6:10). This verse is full of the grace of God, and the evidences of that grace in the real lives of his tried and pressed readers. He recalls their Christian work, the details of which he will have been aware, although he does not set those details before us here; and he makes glad mention of their loving service of the saints (their love of the brethren, that is to say), a loving service which was continuing and which was being done not for its own sake but *'for his sake'*, that is out of love for God and for his glory. In this he is 'remembering before our God and Father your work of faith and labour of love' (1 Thessalonians 1:3). It is surely remarkable that the things we have done in the service of God, and with a sincere desire to promote his glory (even such things as the widow's offering of Mark 12:41–44 or the 'cup of cold water' of Matthew 10:42 given to a disciple) will not escape his notice or go unrewarded.

The really interesting thing, however, is the context in which he sets this work and loving service, namely the character of God. He asserts that *'God is not so unjust as to overlook'* it. He is not teaching here some form of salvation by works—far from it. Rather he is asserting the truth of 'faith working through love' (Galatians 5:6), or that 'faith apart from works is dead' (James 2:26), and that this is something which is pleasing and acceptable to God. He himself prompts it, takes notice of it and rewards it, though his rewarding is always all of grace.

*'And we desire each one of you to show the same earnestness to have the full assurance of hope until the end'* (6:11). The pastoral tone continues with this heartfelt expression of desire towards the Hebrews. He recalls them to *'the same earnestness'* they had shown earlier on, all part of his summons to them throughout this letter to endurance and perseverance, and not to allow any flagging or giving way. And what he desires for them as a company he wishes equally for them one by one—the *'each of you'* is a way of him addressing every individual 'by name', for it is regularly the case in a church or congregation that the health of the whole depends upon the health of the individual. Indeed, there is a fatherliness about his manner with them, as if he is dealing with his own family. This is how it is between a pastor and his flock.

There is helpful light shed here upon the effect that the Christian hope (future) should have upon the Christian life (present). In all the 'ins and outs' and 'ups and downs' of Christian experience it is all too easy to become enclosed in all that is going on and having to be faced right now, this moment or this week. This can readily lead to bondage to circumstances, particularly if your circumstances appear uncongenial in any way. Our writer brings the future directly into the present here, with his mention of having *'the full assurance of hope until the end'*. He does so by saying this: *'so that you may not be sluggish, but imitators of those who through faith and patience inherit the promises'* (6:12). The connection he establishes is clear. Faith and hope proceed hand in hand and feed off one another, all the way *'until the end'*. Our present persevering, holding fast, and pressing on (his repeated theme, warning against being *'sluggish'*) will be greatly energised, motivated and assisted by keeping our eyes firmly fixed upon the goal, upon what is promised, upon the end of the journey.

And what is that? As the great chapter 11 will demonstrate, with all its magnificent illustrations from generations of God's people, recorded for our imitation, it is 'a better country, that is, a heavenly one' (11:16). And who awaits us there and will welcome us home? The one who 'is the same yesterday and today and forever' (13:8). And his name? The Lord Jesus Christ. So rather than this heavenly hope being placed on the back burner of our lives, thoughts and priorities, let it shine brightly before us all day by day, keeping faith in exercise, patience consistent, assurance healthy and hope lively. As one of the choicest examples of those who did indeed *'through faith and patience* [a way of expressing faithful perseverance] *inherit the promises* [given by God to sustain our lives in him]*'*, the patriarch Abraham now makes his first major appearance in the letter to the Hebrews (although passing reference was made to him in 2:16).

Just before we launch into that however, it is worth (by way of review and application) to ask: what is the purpose of 6:4–12? This section has comprised both the direst warnings and the richest encouragements. How can we best benefit from it? By realising that it is here for at least these four reasons:

- To erect a warning sign alerting of the danger of slowing down, going back, or giving up in the Christian life—a sign announcing, 'Danger! Cliff edge! Don't go over!'

- To keep the true believer from presumption, though not to rob us of assurance

- To encourage close self-examination of and careful watch over our hearts

- To urge us to press on—for the fundamental reason that, where Christian profession is concerned, the proof that you are on God's road is to keep on it, the proof that you have been brought out of the bondage of sin is not to let any sin have dominion over you, the proof that you have the root of the matter in you is to cultivate its spiritual fruit, the proof that you love the Saviour is to love him more and more, and the proof that you are going to heaven is to arrive safely there.

## An example to follow (6:13–20)

Still the writer is unmoved from his central concern: encouraging his readers to 'keep on keeping on', not to slip into reverse gear, turn aside or drop out. He has just sought to stir them up to consider 'those who through faith and patience inherit the promises' (6:12). To this they might have responded, 'Very well, give us some incentives, something to help, to keep us going, to inspire us and encourage us'. To which he responds also with a 'Very well', and brings Abraham to the fore. This choice should not surprise us, for Abraham stands out as a bright and shining instance of both faith and patience, even when full allowance is made for the fact that he 'was a man with a nature like ours' (James 5:17). It is of Abraham that Paul wrote, 'In hope he believed against hope' (Romans 4:18)—hoping against hope, meaning hoping despite nothing to see and everything seeming to be against what was being hoped for. A couple of verses later (Romans 4:20), the apostle adds, 'No distrust made him waver concerning the promise of God, but he grew strong in his faith as he gave glory to God'.

We may gather up verses 13–20 under these three divisions: (1) God's promise and oath, (2) Abraham's patience and blessing, and (3) Jesus' position and provision.

## (1) God's promise and oath (6:13–14)

The covenant God is the promise-making, promise-keeping and promise-performing God. He is in every sense the God of the promises. And pre-eminent among those to whom he made firm promises was Abraham. Yet in drawing attention to this here, the writer to the Hebrews mentions not only the making of the promise but the manner of its being made. *For when God made a promise to Abraham, since he had no one greater by whom to swear, he swore by himself, saying, "Surely I will bless you and multiply you"* (6:13–14). Very strong emphasis is placed here upon God's veracity and truthfulness, his trustworthiness and unchangeableness, for his promises are completely unlike anyone else's. The rendering here of the Hebrew in the Greek text comes out literally (and forcibly) as, 'blessing I will bless you and multiplying I will multiply you', thus conveying the sense of God's blessing being without fail, without measure and without end. The *'Surely'* captures the potency of the divine promise.

The promise God made to Abraham (or, at least, the particular one which we are invited to consider here) is quoted from Genesis

22:17. The context of the promise as originally given was the divine assurance to elderly Abraham that his son Isaac (who had almost been sacrificed moments before) would be the one through whom his seed (or offspring) would come. The language of the promise is lavish (isn't the language of God's promises always lavish?): 'I will surely bless you, and I will surely multiply your offspring as the stars of heaven and as the sand that is on the seashore'. Abraham's very name was vitally associated with this promise, for when we first meet him in Scripture he is called Abram (which means 'father of height' or 'exalted father'), whereas with God's covenant promise to him came a change of his name to Abraham (which means 'father of a multitude', for God said to him, 'for I have made you the father of a multitude of nations', Genesis 17:5).

The remarkable thing, however, is what God accompanied the promise with—namely, an oath. Normally if someone swears an oath (as in a court of law) they swear in the name of someone greater than themselves. God, however, has no one greater than himself by which to swear. So what does he do? He reinforces, underscores, 'heavyweights' his promise with an oath made in the greatest name possible—his own! He announces his promise to Abraham with the words, 'By myself I have sworn, declares the LORD' (Genesis 22:16). This is taken up in Hebrews 6 with the words, *he swore by himself*. Other instances of God swearing by himself include Isaiah 45:23 (where the oath pertains to God saying, 'To me every knee shall bow, every tongue shall swear allegiance') and Jeremiah 22:5 (where God utters these words of warning for the prophet to declare to the king of Judah, 'But if you will not obey these words, I swear by myself, declares the LORD, that this house shall become a desolation').

The question may reasonably be raised as to why God made an oath at all in connection with his promise, for his promise was bound to be true and sure since it was *his own* promise, the promise of God and not of a man. So the reason is not that the oath made the promise more certain, for none of God's promises need to be 'made more certain'—they are certain! The answer to the query is threefold: the sheer condescension and kindness of God in doing this; the provision of a very striking reminder that God is indeed God, sovereign and true, whose word is never to be doubted for it is truth itself (note John 17:17 and Titus 1:2); and as a powerful additional 'strengthener' for Abraham's faith, for the patriarch was being required to believe something altogether amazing. Reflect again upon the circumstances in which the Genesis 22 promise was given—the severe test of Abraham's faith in being called to sacrifice Isaac, the son in whom all the covenant promises were bound up. This issued not only in Abraham receiving Isaac back in a manner approaching a resurrection (for that is how it is put in 11:19 of Hebrews) but in him seeing Christ's day and being glad (John 8:56—a reference to the typological significance of what happened on the mountain, which spoke of Jesus' substitutionary death and rising from the grave).

## (2) Abraham's patience and blessing (6:15)

What followed from God's promise and oath to his servant? *'And thus Abraham* ['he'], *having patiently waited, obtained the promise'.* This dovetails in precisely with the mention of 'faith and patience' in connection with God's promises in 6:12. Patience is a rich spiritual grace. Indeed it is one of the nine segments of the fruit of the Spirit (Galatians 5:22), reminding us that it needs to be cultivated in us by the Holy Spirit, for it will not grow or flourish naturally. What grows and flourishes naturally is impatience, which is the very opposite of the spiritual virtue.

It is important to remember that when this promise was first given to Abraham concerning the numerous posterity he would have, he was 75 years old (Genesis 12:4). Since then 24 years passed before he was told specifically of Isaac (Genesis 17:1), so by that time he was aged 99. And by the time Isaac was actually born (Genesis 21:3) Abraham was 100 and his wife Sarah was turned 90. Furthermore, when Isaac was probably somewhere in his teenage years, his father was tested in the momentous manner of the sacrifice (Genesis 22:2). What a catalogue of events! But still Abraham 'believed the LORD' (Genesis 15:6). He continued believing and waiting, believing and waiting, believing and waiting, even though he himself did not live to see this huge posterity with his own eyes nor the Messiah who was to descend from him; and in due time (for God always performs his every promise in due time, his own due time) *'having patiently waited, obtained the promise'*. He who had received the promise obtained it— the two are not the same thing. Abraham was unfailingly gripped in his mind and heart and soul that everything would happen as God had said and that his word would not fail. And, as expected, all that God had promised, he performed. He always does, for with him 'there is no variation or shadow due to change' (James 1:17). The wait was worth it, wonderfully worth it, even though it must at times have appeared endless to Abraham. It is, and will be, no different for us who now believe. That is how the Christian life is.

## (3) Jesus' position and provision (6:16–20)

This entire section, which has spoken of the character of God and the experience of Abraham, is moving resolutely forward to extol the glory of the Lord Jesus Christ. To reach that point, our writer is still impressing upon his readers' minds the truths already laid out.

*'For people swear by something greater than themselves, and in all their disputes an oath is final for confirmation'* (6:16). There is something fundamentally unreliable about man's promises and undertakings. This is because of his sinful nature, and tendency to be light with matters of the truth. This is why oaths are used. They should not be necessary, but they become so in a fallen world in order to bolster man's word and give it weight and (hopefully) truth. This is not, of course, a cast-iron guarantee, for there will no doubt be some from time to time who do not speak the truth even under oath. It is, at least, however, intended to deter such a practice. In such oath swearing, men do not swear by one another but *'by something greater than themselves'*—hence the name of God is invoked. The statement that *'in all their disputes an oath is final for confirmation'* is to say that this should settle the matter. Strictly, if God's name is used as a witness to the truth of what someone is testifying, that should be sufficient, for no higher authority exists beyond the authority of God himself, and it is the most serious matter to take God's name in vain. The third commandment is very searching: 'You shall not take the

name of the LORD your God in vain, for the LORD will not hold him guiltless who takes his name in vain' (Exodus 20:7).

The thought expressed in 6:13 continues to be reiterated as the section continues. *'So when God desired to show more convincingly to the heirs of the promise the unchangeable character of his purpose, he guaranteed it with an oath'* (6:17). Recall the comments above on why God made an oath at all in this matter, to which may be added the aspect highlighted here that it was to convince as certainly as possible *'the heirs of the promise'* (Abraham, his seed after him through Isaac, and ultimately the entire people of God) of *'the unchangeable character of his purpose'* (that he is to be believed without question to do all that he intends, that his eternal decrees and purposes must all be fulfilled, however much things appear to be working out to the contrary). In particular, in the present context, the reference is to his purposes to give his Son, the Lord Jesus Christ, who is the *ultimate* one in prospect in the promise to Abraham concerning his seed (Galatians 3:16 is the key verse which develops this). So *'he guaranteed it with an oath'*. This verb makes here its solitary appearance in Scripture and in a very beautiful way gives us the assurance of God's own personal guarantee of all his promises and purposes. Everything possible is being done in these verses to encourage and assure the people of God to trust God, precisely because he (alone) is trustworthy. 'Our God is in the heavens; he does all that he pleases' (Psalm 115:3).

The sentence continues: *'so that by two unchangeable things, in which it is impossible for God to lie'* (6:18). The *'two unchangeable things'* are the promise and the oath, they being the double establishing of God's truthfulness, the irrevocable deed of settlement (as it has been called) whereby the entire inheritance of grace is infallibly secured to each and every believer. The writer almost labours the point, it being so very important, since the world cannot imagine that God is unlike itself, and believers often struggle to believe God in all circumstances. 'God is not man, that he should lie' (Numbers 23:19). God himself is unchangeable (we call this the immutability of God), and so his promise and his oath must be like himself. It cannot be otherwise.

And to what end is all this, *'so that'*? An end not only for Abraham, but for the Hebrews who first received this letter, and for the rest of us who read it still: *'so that ... we who have fled for refuge might have strong encouragement* [such as prevails against all that is set against it, all that would rob us of it] *to hold fast to the hope set before us'*. Endurance, perseverance, keeping going continues unswervingly to be the writer's intensely practical and pastoral concern. He includes himself (*'we who have fled for refuge'*), but what is intended by *'refuge'*? It surely goes back all the way to the 'such a great salvation' of 2:3, and speaks of fleeing to Christ, trusting in him, coming into possession of all the riches of divine grace that are stored in him for everyone who believes. This figure would be consistent with the typology of the cities of refuge in the Old Testament with which the Hebrews would be very familiar (in Numbers 35, for example); the exquisite image of God's wings of refuge, expressed in the lovely and gracious words of Boaz to Ruth, 'The LORD repay you for what you have done, and a full reward be given you by the LORD, the God of Israel, under whose wings you have come to take refuge!', Ruth 2:12; the strong testimony and assurance of the people of God in every age, that 'God is our refuge and strength', Psalm 46:1; and, in the New Testament, the companion picture that the Lord Jesus uses of himself, when he says in a manner revealing his heart of love, 'How often would I have gathered your children together as a hen gathers her brood under her wings, and you would not!', Matthew 23:37.

This mighty combination of God's promise and his oath is intended to assist and enervate and give *'strong encouragement* (or, 'consolation')' to the Hebrews and to us, therefore, *'to hold fast to* [lay hold of, seize] *the hope set before us'*. The identity of this *'hope'* arises from the present experience of 'Christ in (us)', which is 'the hope of glory' (Colossians 1:27)—being with him, being like him. He himself is our hope ('Christ Jesus our hope', 1 Timothy 1:1). Although much ridiculed by those who know nothing about it, this truly is the one hope worth having, the hope at the very heart of the gospel of God's free grace, and the knowledge that it is absolutely guaranteed by God's 'two unchangeable things' is all the believer needs to know. May we never loosen our hold upon it.

The intricacy of the present thought continues right on to the end of the chapter. *'We have this as a sure and steadfast anchor of the soul'* (6:19). In these final two verses of chapter 6, our writer comes to focus again directly upon the Lord Jesus Christ. How can we be sure that any of us will ever make it to glory? How could the Hebrews know? How can we? We can know because our souls have been given *'a sure and steadfast anchor'*. The image of an anchor speaks of settledness, stability, something firm, well rooted, which does not suddenly disappear, however furious the storms, high the waves or strong the gales. The Christian hope is just such an anchor, holding firm in all weathers, reliably *'sure and steadfast'*. This is because of the one to whom and in whom the anchor is fixed, indeed the one whom the anchor actually is.

It is *'a hope that enters into the inner place behind the curtain'*, an expression which makes us think immediately of the holy of holies in both the wilderness tabernacle and (subsequently) the Jerusalem temple, where the high priest went on the annual day of atonement—which itself leads us on to think of the Lord Jesus Christ, and how it is recorded that immediately upon his death 'the curtain of the temple was torn in two, from top to bottom' (Matthew 27:51), signifying that the way into heaven is wide open for all who turn from their sins and believe and trust in him. The Saviour's work is completed, and accepted by the Father with delight. It links also with the reference we had back in 4:14 to our 'great high priest who has passed through the heavens, Jesus, the Son of God'. On the basis of his finished work, Jesus is now in heaven, our hope is secure, and the anchor will not move. How this should keep us calm in mind and heart amid all the tempests and storms of life. Our hope of heaven could not be more firm. Happy indeed are all who have fled to Christ for refuge, and laid hold upon the eternal hope of the gospel!

Relishing this from every possible angle, our writer continues: *'where Jesus has gone as a forerunner on our behalf'* (6:20). Having just spoken of 'the inner place behind the curtain', he now informs us that there (into heaven) not only has Jesus entered, but he has done so *'as a forerunner on our behalf'*. That is to say, having arrived there safely himself, he now awaits our safe landing into the harbour to be with him. Moreover, his presence there is the guarantee and security of our presence there—that, as Jesus prayed to his Father, 'that they also, whom you have given me, may be with me where I am' (John 17:24). This links in precisely with the great theme of Hebrews, namely the absolute superiority and pre-eminence of the Lord Jesus Christ in every realm, not least over the Old Testament priesthood—for of which of those high priests could it ever be said that they were forerunners? When the high priest of old entered the holy of holies once a year, no one followed him inside. Then having gone in himself, he came out again. Not so our Lord Jesus where the holy of holies in heaven is concerned!

The image of the *forerunner* draws this out significantly. This is the only appearance of this word in the New Testament, although in other Greek literature it is used in such contexts as advance groups of soldiers, scouts sent forward to investigate how things are, a quartermaster who goes ahead to prepare everything for the soldiers, or a herald who declares that someone is on their way. Fundamentally it refers, of course, to one who goes on ahead, but there is more to it than that. Not only has Jesus gone ahead of us, cleared the way for us, entered before us, into heaven, but now that he is there he is engaged continually on our behalf—making intercession for us (7:25), as he presents his merits for us before the throne; preparing for us the 'many rooms' in his 'Father's house' (John 14:2); governing and overruling all things for the ultimate good and growth of his church (Ephesians 1:22); and awaiting the arrival of each and every one of his purchased ones, that he may welcome us not as strangers but as friends, not as unknown but as known, as the sheep of his fold (John 10:16). It has about it the suggestion of the 'firstfruits', another image used in the Bible to convey the sense of 'Jesus first, his people to follow' (as, for example in 1 Corinthians 15:20, 'But in fact Christ has been raised from the dead, the firstfruits of those who have fallen asleep'). The *'on our behalf'* is a beautiful reminder of our complete dependence upon the Lord Jesus for everything, and the fullness and sufficiency of grace and blessing that resides for us in him. He is in glory that we may be there also. Our Saviour, friend and advocate awaits our arrival, which he himself has secured. Well may we each respond to him, 'Draw me after you; let us run' (Song of Songs 1:4).

There is one more thing to add before this chapter gives way to the next: *'having become a high priest forever after the order of Melchizedek'.* Not 'he will become', but *'having become'*—the significance of which is that it is on the grounds of his life and work that he has received this high priesthood. It is his present and permanent state and office, and one which he holds and exercises not for himself but for his people.

The mystery of Melchizedek is about to be revealed in chapter 7, to which we now proceed. As we do so, it is precious to note the use of the name *'Jesus'* in speaking here of the one who has entered heaven for us—'Jesus, crowned with glory and honour', 2:9; 'Jesus, the apostle and high priest of our confession', 3:1; Jesus, 'a great high priest who has passed through the heavens', 4:14; 'Jesus the guarantor of a better covenant', 7:22; 'Jesus, the founder and perfecter of our faith, who for the joy that was set before him endured the cross, despising the shame, and is seated at the right hand of the throne of God', 12:2. This is his dearest name to sinners, this is his warmest name to believers, this is his choicest name in glory—the name of 'my beloved' and 'my friend' (Song of Songs 5:16).

# Chapter 7
# Jesus and Melchizedek

Melchizedek at last! Without doubt, he is one of the 'mystery men' of Scripture. His name has already been mentioned three times in Hebrews, the first of these being at 5:6 in a quotation from Psalm 110:4 (a highly quoted psalm in the New Testament). Referring them to the Lord Jesus Christ our writer quotes these words: 'You are a priest forever, after the order of Melchizedek'. Straightaway we learn from this that the Hebrews references to Melchizedek bear upon the priesthood of Jesus. The two other mentions of Melchizedek thus far are in 5:10 and 6:20. In 5:11, following on immediately in thought from 5:10, our writer says that, 'About this we have much to say, and it is hard to explain', but he did not proceed with that explanation at that point. Why not?

From 5:11, as we have discovered, the writer has engaged in something of a 'digression', although a very important one—dealing with the Hebrews' little and slow progress in Christian growth, their need to advance into the deeper things of the faith, the great danger of apostasy they were facing, and a series of encouragements to them to hold fast their faith and hope until the end (in view of God's faithfulness to his divine promise and his divine oath). This interlude concludes with 6:20, with the statement concerning Jesus 'having become a high priest forever after the order of Melchizedek' (another clear reference to Psalm 110:4 without it being formally quoted).

So the scene is now set for the opening up of this subject, as chapter 7 begins with the words, 'For this Melchizedek'. This is a lengthy and detailed chapter, and is best handled in two parts: verses 1–10 and verses 11–28.

## Abraham and Melchizedek (7:1–10)

The curtain is about to be lifted on who Melchizedek is and why he is being made so much of in Hebrews.

### (1) The historical background

It needs to be stated that Melchizedek was a real person. He is not some character of fiction dreamed up to fit in with the teaching of Hebrews. He actually lived, and, moreover, had actual dealings with no less a Bible personage than Abraham, of whom the latter part of chapter 6 has been speaking.

*'For this Melchizedek, king of Salem, priest of the Most High God, met Abraham returning from the slaughter of the kings'* (7:1). Melchizedek makes only one personal appearance in the Old Testament, and that is recorded in Genesis 14. His name means 'king of righteousness'. He is also *'king of Salem'* (most probably short for Jerusalem)'; *'Salem'* means 'peace'. So as well as being 'king of righteousness' he is also 'king of peace', as 7:2 makes clear (*'He is first, by translation of his name, king of righteousness, and then he is king of Salem, that is, king of peace'*). The order is very significant, and is ever Scripture's order: first righteousness, then peace. In gospel terms, our first concern is to be made righteous by and before God, from which then our peace with God and the peace of God will flow. Isaiah 32:17 is precious

in this connection: 'And the effect of righteousness will be peace, and the result of righteousness, quietness and trust forever'. That is not all, however. Melchizedek is also described as *'priest of the Most High God'*, and so combines in himself the offices of both king and priest. Interestingly, this reveals that David was not the first king in Jerusalem, neither was Aaron the first priest whom God appointed.

Already this is highly suggestive of the Lord Jesus Christ, who is 'King of kings' (Revelation 19:16) and 'a great high priest' (Hebrews 4:14), and whose kingdom is marked by both righteousness and peace (Psalm 72:7). He 'shall execute justice and righteousness … And this is the name by which he will be called: "The LORD is our righteousness"' (Jeremiah 23:5–6); 'and his name shall be called … Prince of Peace' (Isaiah 9:6). We note that Melchizedek is the first person in the Old Testament to be called a priest. The designation of God as 'the Most High God' appears not only in Genesis 14:22 (in connection with him being the God of Abraham) but also in the Psalms and in the New Testament (in connection with him being the God of his people).

He *'met Abraham returning from the slaughter of the kings'*. What happened was this. A confederation of four kings went to war against the king of Sodom and four other kings (so it was four against five—their names are given in Genesis 14:1–2). The attacking kings won a victory over Sodom and Gomorrah, and among the 'prisoners of war' they carried off was Lot, Abraham's nephew. When news reached Abraham of this, he lost no time in gathering and leading 'forth his trained men, born in his house, 318 of them, and went in pursuit as far as Dan' (Genesis 14:14). They went after Lot's attackers and captors and routed them. 'Then he [Abraham] brought back all the possessions, and also brought back his kinsman Lot with his possessions, and the women and the people' (Genesis 14:16). This very event is highly suggestive of the victory of all believers in their warfare and conflict with their spiritual enemies.

It was then on the way home that this remarkable encounter took place between Abraham and Melchizedek. As the Genesis 14 narrative unfolds, Melchizedek 'brought out bread and wine' and blessed Abraham, while Abraham, for his part, 'gave him a tenth of everything'. These details the writer to the Hebrews takes up, saying of Melchizedek, *'and blessed him, and to him Abraham apportioned a tenth part of everything'*. The blessing itself was a sumptuous one: 'Blessed be Abram by God Most High, Possessor of heaven and earth; and blessed be God Most High, who has delivered your enemies into your hand!' (Genesis 14:19–20). This marks Melchizedek out as a worshipper of the true God and not of some heathen deity.

## (2) The spiritual application

It is important to understand that Melchizedek is not actually Jesus. That is to say, this is not a theophany (an appearance of the Lord Jesus Christ in the flesh before the incarnation). There are several of these in the Old Testament (examples include Jesus with Joshua by Jericho in Joshua 5, and Jesus in the fiery furnace with Daniel's three friends in Daniel 3), but this is not one of them. Melchizedek, we affirm, was a literal, physical, historical person in his own right; and anyway, the references in Hebrews to Jesus being 'a high priest forever after the order of Melchizedek' rather than Jesus being Melchizedek or Melchizedek being Jesus make this plain. This being said, however, Melchizedek is clearly a very striking 'type' of Jesus, a 'portrait' of Jesus, with the Lord Jesus as the full and perfect reality of all that Melchizedek portrays, as our writer now reveals.

*'He is without father or mother or genealogy, having neither beginning of days nor end of life, but resembling the Son of God he continues a priest forever'* (7:3). These statements concerning Melchizedek mean that we know nothing about his parents or family tree, not that he literally did not have such. They are covered in obscurity, and their details are not available to us. This is interesting in that the early chapters of Genesis in particular are full of genealogies, yet not for Melchizedek. He is only ever presented to us as a ministering priest. Yet our attention is drawn thereby to the resemblance this gives him to our high priest, the Lord Jesus: *'resembling the Son of God'* [note that: it is not that Jesus resembles Melchizedek, but the other way round— Melchizedek resembles, is made like, Jesus, though is inferior and subordinate to him]. As real man, Jesus had a mother, but no father.

As true God, he had a Father (capital 'F' for God the Father), but no mother. And while 'being found in human form' (Philippians 2:8), he is the eternal Son of God, whose 'years will have no end' (Hebrews 1:12, quoting Psalm 102:27), 'the same yesterday and today and forever' (13:8). There being no hint in Genesis of anyone following Melchizedek in his priesthood also directs our gaze to Jesus, for '*he* [Jesus] *continues a priest forever*', as Psalm 110:4 has insisted upon. In Old Testament days, the priests began their duties at the age of thirty, and ceased from them at the age of fifty. No such restriction here is placed upon Melchizedek's priesthood, giving yet another indication of the enduring and eternal nature of Jesus' priesthood.

Our writer continues: '*See* [consider, behold—a word sometimes used of a general reviewing an army, and implying a close inspection] *how great this man was to whom Abraham the patriarch gave a tenth of the spoils!*' (7:4). Abraham is not spoken of as 'a patriarch' (although he was one of a number), but as '*the patriarch*', signifying his significance in the purposes of God. Yet despite his own greatness and dignity (one of God's own chosen names is 'the God of Abraham', Exodus 3:6; while Abraham is described in Romans 4:11 as 'the father of all who believe', and in verse 16 of that same chapter as 'the father of us all'), the fact that he gave '*a tenth of the spoils*' to Melchizedek speaks rather of '*how great this man* [Melchizedek] *was*'. Indeed so! '*It is beyond dispute that the inferior is blessed by the superior*' (7:7). All the time, behind everything that is said, our writer's central focus on the superiority and pre-eminence of Jesus is evident. He never moves far away from it, if at all. If Melchizedek was a giver of blessings and a receiver of service, then how much more so is the Lord Jesus Christ! If the great Melchizedek was accorded such honour by such a one as the great Abraham, then how exalted and worthy of all praise is the Lord Jesus Christ.

Another aspect of things is now brought in to the picture, involving Levi. '*And those descendants of Levi who receive the priestly office have a commandment in the law to take tithes from the people, that is, from their brothers, though these also are descended from Abraham*' (7:5). But what does Levi have to do with things here? The Levites were ordained by God in Old Testament times to be the priestly tribe. As such, they received tithes from the other tribes, for they had no tribal land inheritance, unlike the others. Within the tribe of Levi, the office of priesthood belonged to Aaron and the males of his family line, with the other Levites assisting the priests and the high priest in tabernacle and (later on) temple duties. The system was that of the tithes received by the Levites from the people, a tithe of that was passed on by them to the priests. That way, everyone was provided for. That explains 7:5, which leads on to the pertinent application now about to be made regarding Melchizedek.

*'But this man who does not have his descent from them received tithes from Abraham and blessed him who had the promises* [God's promises having been given to Abraham more fully and clearly than to any of his predecessors]*'* (7:6). In blessing Abraham, Melchizedek was exercising his priesthood, while in paying tithes to him Abraham was acknowledging Melchizedek's priesthood, thereby signifying the patriarch's recognition that it was God who had given him the victory over the kings. Melchizedek had nothing to do with the tribe of Levi (and neither did Jesus, who, in terms of his human descent, was of the tribe of Judah, as verse 14 will say), so since this did not hinder Melchizedek from receiving a tithe from Abraham it will surely not in any way hinder Jesus from his superior priesthood. And if it be asked why Melchizedek was receiving the tithes from Abraham and bestowing the blessings upon him, then surely the answer is, plainly and simply, this: to draw us again to Jesus and away from everyone else—even the great patriarch Abraham, and this remarkable priest-king Melchizedek. In this, as in everything, Jesus stands absolutely alone.

But the point with Levi is not quite completed. *'In the one case tithes are received by mortal men* [those who are bound to die and will have successors]*, but in the other case, by one of whom it is testified that he lives* [is without end of life, compare 7:3]*'* (7:8). The *'mortal men'* are the Levites, while the *'one of whom it is testified that he lives'* is Melchizedek. No mention is made in Scripture of him dying—not because he never did, but in order to keep highlighting the ongoing nature of his priesthood. Jesus' priesthood, in contrast, is actually everlasting, for he says of himself, 'Fear not, I am the first and the last, and the living one. I died, and behold I am alive for evermore' (Revelation 1:17–18). To him, and to him alone, is our worship, devotion and service due.

Still there is more. *'One might even say that Levi himself, who receives tithes, paid tithes through Abraham, for he was still in the loins of his ancestor when Melchizedek met him'* (7:9–10). The teaching is this: there is a sense in which it could be said that when Melchizedek met Abraham, Levi was in Abraham's loins, albeit still some generations away, and so himself paid tithes through his distinguished ancestor (in biblical thinking, ancestors were considered to contain within themselves all their descendants who were to come after them, so the way of speaking here of Levi in connection with Abraham should not be regarded as strange). It is (so the argument here goes) as if both Abraham and Levi met Melchizedek. So? The same again: all are inferior to Jesus, and Jesus is superior to all. Jesus' high priesthood, which is forever, is not after the order of Levi but after that of Melchizedek, who is the greater of the two by far through being a priest-king, which was never the case with the Levitical high priests. Jesus is the exalted high priest over both of them.

Just as Levi was *'in the loins of his ancestor when Melchizedek met him'*, even so, but far more deeply and really, every true Christian is 'in Christ', for we died with him, are risen with him, 'reign in life' (Romans 5:17) through him, and shall be with him for ever. He is the one through whom God has blessed us in the gospel of his grace with 'every spiritual blessing in the heavenly places, even as he chose us in him before the foundation of the world' (Ephesians 1:3–4). He is the one at whose name 'every knee should bow, in heaven and on earth and under the earth, and every tongue confess that Jesus Christ is Lord, to the glory of God the Father' (Philippians 2:10–11). There is a lone majesty belonging to Jesus. He is the incomparable one.

## Jesus' unique priesthood (7:11–28)

Abraham now recedes from view and will not reappear until the mighty eleventh chapter of Hebrews, but Melchizedek remains very much in focus as the chapter continues both to explore and to demonstrate the total superiority of Jesus' priesthood over his. Melchizedek, in terms of his historical appearance in Genesis, is here one moment and gone the next, whereas Jesus abides for ever (and even now in heaven, 'at the right hand of the Majesty on high' (1:3) wears and exercises his priesthood, to the unimaginable and untold blessing of his people). In this major section of chapter 7 we may discern six outstanding excellences of Jesus' priesthood over every priesthood which came before him. This can best be brought out by the use of one of Hebrews' favourite words (as we have already seen): 'better'.

## (1) Jesus occupies a better office (7:11-14)

It must be the case that if the Levitical priesthood had been sufficient for everything that sinners ever need doing for us in our relation to God, there would never have been any need for a different or better office of priesthood. The one that there already was could have continued. But it was very far from sufficient, and so was superseded by that to which it pointed forward from its commencement: the priesthood of Jesus.

*'Now if perfection had been attainable through the Levitical priesthood (for under it the people received the law), what further need would there have been for another priest to arise after the order of Melchizedek, rather than one named after the order of Aaron?'* (7:11). It was this conspicuous lack of perfection in the Aaronic line (with special reference to its inability to do all that was needful) which was its fundamental undoing. True, it was ordained of God, and no aspersion is to be cast in any way upon the wisdom of his design. But God himself never intended the Levitical arrangement to go on and on and on. It was of limited duration, and served (albeit for a long time) a preparatory role for the coming of God's Son, the priest above all priests. It could not deal finally, once and for all, with sin. It could not put away sin. It could not achieve the end of reconciling sinners to God. It could not procure a righteousness for the sinner. It could not convey the gift of new spiritual life.

True, also, it was in the Levitical days that *'the people received the law'*, given to the people by God through Aaron's brother, Moses. Indeed, it was within the larger context of the giving of the law through Moses that God established the priestly and high priestly system involving Aaron. Yet both, in the wisdom and grace of God, both the law and the priesthood, had the Lord Jesus Christ (*'another priest'*, one of a different kind and order) continually in view. Regarding the law, Paul describes it as 'our guardian until Christ came, in order that we might be justified by faith' (Galatians 3:24), although it remains very much the rule of life for every Christian and plays a very significant role in our sanctification. As for the priesthood, the writer of Hebrews has been insisting with consistent force that Jesus' priesthood excels all others, and always will do; we have no need any longer of mere men to be priests, for our great high priest has done all things needful 'that he might bring us to God' (1 Peter 3:18).

*'For when there is a change in the priesthood, there is necessarily a change in the law as well'* (7:12). This underscores further what we have just been noting. There is an intimate connection between the priesthood and the law. Since the priesthood has undergone a profound change (from that of the Old Testament to that of the Lord Jesus Christ, for it was impossible for the Levitical priesthood to continue once Jesus' priesthood 'after the order of Melchizedek' (7:17) was brought in), so has the law—in terms, that is, of all of its commandments and arrangements for (say) the appointment, ministry and retirement of those earlier priests (for our writer is not here touching upon the moral law, the ten commandments, which abides in force, unchanged). This would not have gone down well among the Hebrews before they were converted (remember how Stephen was accused of preaching that Jesus would 'change the customs that Moses delivered to us', Acts 6:14; and how Paul was in danger of losing his life when accused of 'teaching everywhere against the people and the law', Acts 21:28). Now they needed to be reminded that Jesus excels all that came before, lest they return to their former beliefs and practices and abandon the gospel.

Because all of the former priests were sinful men, offering sacrifices for their own sins as well as for those of the people, and never able to offer sacrifices which would actually put away and deal with sin, another priesthood was required which *did not* involve sacrifices for the offerer himself and which *did* deal fundamentally and radically with sin. *That* priesthood is, and can only be, the priesthood of Christ, our Melchizedek. He has kept the law fully, has no sin of his own, and has offered on the cross a perfect sacrifice to accomplish salvation and redemption for his people. It truly is a case (to use a phrase which the apostle Paul used of a different matter) that, 'The old has passed away; behold, the new has come' (2 Corinthians 5:17).

*'For the one of whom these things are spoken belonged to another tribe, from which no one has ever served at the altar* [that is, exercised priestly functions]. *For it is evident* [that is, obvious, a known fact] *that our Lord was descended* [arose, has risen] *from Judah, and in connection with that tribe Moses said nothing about priests'* (7:13–14). How explicitly this highlights the difference and newness of Jesus' priesthood. We have noted earlier that Levi was always the priestly tribe under the old regime. The Lord Jesus, however, our 'great high priest who has passed through the heavens' (4:14), did not belong to that tribe, but was (in terms of his human genealogy) of the tribe of Judah (the tribe in connection with which *'Moses* [that is, the law] *said nothing about priests'*). Jesus' belonging to the tribe of Judah is stated prophetically as far back as Genesis 49:8–10, in the context of elderly Jacob's blessing upon his son Judah; it is re-iterated in the messianic promise inherent in God's covenant with David in 2 Samuel 7:12; it is confirmed in Micah 5:2; and it is made absolutely clear from the genealogies of Jesus supplied in Matthew 1 and Luke 3. That fact immediately sets him apart and puts him on his own—not 'a' priest, not even 'a' high priest, but 'the' high priest, who is in every way that you can think of more worthy of our confidence and love (not to mention our worship, for, significantly, the name Judah means 'praise').

## (2) Jesus possesses a better life (7:15–17)

Having just spoken in the previous verse of what is 'evident', our writer now states: *'This becomes even more evident* [obvious, clear]*'* (7:15). By *'this'* he is still dealing with the difference which Jesus' priesthood has over that which came before him. How does it become *'even more evident'*? In this manner: *'when* (or, 'since') *another priest arises in the likeness of Melchizedek, who has become a priest, not on the basis of a legal requirement concerning bodily descent, but by the power of an indestructible life'* (7:15–16). As is obvious, all the Old Testament priests and high priests died, one by one. As a result of this, and *'on the basis of a legal requirement* [literally, 'a law of fleshly command']*'*, the office was passed on to the next generation, and so things went on. This old requirement of the law no longer applies, not since Jesus has come and entered upon his matchless priesthood, one *'in the likeness of Melchizedek'*—that is to say, one which never ends. For Jesus never dies and so never passes on his priesthood to the next person in line. There *is no* next person in line, for his is *'the power of an indestructible* [endless, indissoluble—another word making its sole New Testament appearance] *life'*, for he is the eternal Son of God. As Romans 4:25 affirms, while Jesus 'was delivered up for our trespasses' (his death on the cross), he was then 'raised for our justification' (his resurrection from the tomb). 'God raised him up, loosing the pangs of death, because it was not possible for him to be held by it' (Acts 2:24).

To which is added a further reprise of the key test at this point in the extended argument, *'For it is witnessed of him, "You are a priest forever, after the order of Melchizedek"'* (7:17). Our writer appeals once again to this testimony of the Holy Spirit to Jesus through God's servant David. As our high priest, 'he always lives' (7:25). What a grand, strong, robust, reliable presentation of Jesus this all gives to us. His cross has been followed by his crown, and all our confidence can be placed securely in him—and so it must be.

## (3) Jesus introduces a better hope (7:18–19)

It might appear as if the writer to the Hebrews has a tendency to repeat himself. To think that, however, would be to do him a grave injustice. Remember how concerned he is to ensure that those to whom he was writing would not abandon Christ and the gospel by going back to their former ways in Judaism. And so, far from saying things several times when once or twice would do, he is at pains and goes out of his way to press vital things from every possible and available angle. No stone must be left unturned in this.

*'On the one hand, a former commandment is set aside, because of its weakness and uselessness (for the law made nothing perfect)'* (7:18–19). Our writer will just not let go of the crucial fact that the whole system of the Old Testament priesthood was fundamentally flawed. He does this here with the literary device of *'On the one hand'* followed shortly with *'but on the other hand'*.

What of *'On the one hand'*? Of those very legal requirements which regulated how the priesthood operated, it is stated with great frankness, *'a former commandment is set aside* [annulled, cancelled, as with a debt, a command, or someone's will]'. Why, for none but God himself has authority or right to do such a thing, as 10:28 makes clear? The answer is equally frank: *'because of its weakness and uselessness'*. And why was it so? With no less candour, the answer comes: *'(for the law made nothing perfect)'*. It was absolutely impossible for salvation to be effected for sinners in this way. It could not do the job. The priests were themselves sinners, and the law demanded perfection (although it could not *make* perfection). This is not a slur upon the law, of course, for the law is God's divine law and as such it is 'holy and righteous and good' (Romans 7:12), just as he is. The problem regarding the law resides in man (who breaks it), not in God (who decrees it).

Our writer is one for laying it on the line and speaking his mind. He is not shy or retiring where the honour of the Lord Jesus Christ is in any way at stake. So he continues with his *'on the other hand'*, which supplies the following glorious truth: *'a better hope is introduced, through which we draw near to God'* (7:19). The verb *'introduced'* contrasts strikingly with the 'set aside' of the previous verse. Now, in Christ Jesus, that which is perpetual and perfect has come. What, then, is this *'better hope'* which is ours as a result? Think of it this way: instead of us drawing near to God via types, shadows and men, we now come directly, personally and intimately through our Lord Jesus Christ. He, as 10:20 will tell us, is 'the new and living way'. He has not merely provided this way—he actually himself *is* the way. Jesus made this plain in the upper room when he said, 'I am the way … No one comes to the Father except through me' (John 14:6). We not only come to the Father through him in order to be saved, but continue all our lives to come through him. Continually we are to *'draw near to God'*, the very thing which we can only do through Jesus. 'But now in Christ Jesus (we) who once were far off have been brought near by the blood of Christ' (Ephesians 2:13). We are *never* beyond the need of our mighty and precious Saviour and Lord. Through him, having been brought into union with God, we now day by day enjoy communion with God. This is the sheer wonder of the gospel, for all those things which would keep us at a distance from God (our sin and guilt, God's own wrath upon us on account of that, and all other obstacles that could be named) have been gloriously removed. Outside of Jesus we are at an appalling distance from God, while in and through him that distance has been completely taken away.

It is absolutely true, of course, that some Old Testament believers enjoyed and experienced a deep and rich level of such communion, and were no strangers to vigorous spiritual hope. Theirs, as ours, was 'the assurance of things hoped for, the conviction of things not seen' (11:1). We only have to think of Enoch, who 'walked with God' (Genesis 5:24); of Abraham, whom Scripture calls 'a friend of God' (James 2:23); of Moses, 'whom the LORD knew face to face' (Deuteronomy 34:10); of David, who was 'a man after (God's) own heart' (1 Samuel 13:14); of Asaph, who testified, 'But for me it is good to be near God' (Psalm 73:28); or of Daniel, a 'man greatly loved' (Daniel 10:11). And these are only examples. Yet for all of this, they lived in the spirit of looking forward to the coming of the Messiah, whereas we live in the light of the Messiah having come. Now, under the new covenant of which Hebrews makes so much, we have access 'with confidence (to) draw near to the throne of grace, that we may receive mercy and find grace to help in time of need' (4:16). We may come into God's presence and dwell before his throne, and we do so on the basis of the Lord Jesus' altogether superior priesthood. So why would the Hebrews forget this or ignore it? And why would we?

## (4) Jesus guarantees a better covenant (7:20–22)

The nature and details of this *'better covenant'* (7:22) await us in the next chapter, but we are provided here with a strong marker concerning it. *'And it was not without an oath. For those who formerly became priests were made such without an oath, but this one was made a priest with an oath'* (7:20–21). To ground this, Psalm 110:4 is called upon once again as the sentence continues: *'by the one who said to him: "The Lord has sworn and will not change his mind* [that is the form of the oath], *'You are a priest forever'"* [that is the substance of the oath]'. It is the Father who swears of and to the Son.

Back in chapter 6 we were told about both God's promise and his oath regarding his covenant with Abraham. Here in chapter 7 the divine oath is mentioned again, this time with reference to the priesthood of Jesus (the Levitical priests of former times were ordained without any oath), and affirming that, since he is *'a priest forever'*, being of the order of Melchizedek and not of Levi, everything is firm and unchanging. The divine oath secures this; the thing cannot be altered. No more is there any waiting for another priest still to come. No more is it a matter of replacement or successors. The priest has come—the permanent priest. It is very striking, and must be noted carefully, how both the covenant and the priesthood were confirmed by the divine oath, thus indicating their supreme importance. The oath highlights them both, and is a comforting assurance to the oft-pressed people of God of 'the unchangeable character of (God's) purpose' (6:17). 'God is not man, that he should lie, or a son of man, that he should change his mind. Has he said, and will he not do it? Or has he spoken, and will he not fulfil it?' (Numbers 23:19). Hope in God could not possibly be more well founded.

There now follows a verse which requires particularly close attention, especially because of a crucial word in it. *'This makes Jesus the guarantor of a better covenant'* (7:22). The crucial word is *'guarantor'*. This is the only New Testament appearance of a word which may also be translated 'surety'. Such a person is one who stands in the place of another and acts for them when they cannot act for themselves. It is a legal word for someone who 'stands surety' or 'provides guarantees' or 'takes responsibility for the debt' for someone. It was said of the 'former commandment' concerning the priesthood that it was 'set aside because of its weakness and uselessness' (7:18). The Lord Jesus Christ, however, is 'the mediator of a new covenant' (9:15), involving a new priesthood (his own) with new promises and new blessings. Moreover, not only is Jesus the mediator of this new covenant (as the one, willingly, through whom we are reconciled to God and our broken fellowship with him on account of our sin is restored), but he is also the *'guarantor* ('surety')*'* of it (as the one, willingly, through whom, for our benefit, the covenant is established, permanent and sure, and through whom all supplies of daily grace are treasured up and provided). No weakness or uselessness can ever attach to this. It will never be subject to annulment. This truly is *'a better covenant'*, upon which much more will be said in the course of chapter 8.

Exploring this figure of the 'guarantor/surety', what may be said? It may be considered from two perspectives: on God's part and our behalf. On God's part we might feel guarantees are hardly necessary, since God is God and can and must always be trusted to keep his word and his promise. He will never be untrue to himself. Yet he condescends to us in this in order that we may believe in him with stronger confidence and firmer faith, never questioning or doubting him in anything. On our behalf, we might say to ourselves something like this: 'what if I sin, what if I backslide, what if I am unfaithful— what happens then? Am I out of the covenant? Is it all over for me with God?' To which the answer is a resounding 'No!'. 7:22 assures us that God's covenant and all its promises neither rest nor are they suspended on our faith, our obedience, or our anything, but wholly upon Jesus' obedience for us and the gift of faith in him. He personally stands as the *'guarantor'*, the surety, that the covenant (and our place in it through grace) will stand. In the light of which, how beautiful it is to see this covenant described in 13:20 as 'the eternal covenant'. Could anything be more sure than that? In what better hands could the eternal interests of our souls be placed?

## (5) Jesus exercises a better ministry (7:23–25)

Fundamental to this is the fact that Jesus is 'the living one' who is 'alive forevermore' (Revelation 1:18), whereas one of the most marked features of all of the Old Testament priests and high priests is that, one by one, they died. *'The former priests were many in number* [they had to be, 83 high priests altogether according to Jewish records, from Aaron to the destruction of the Jerusalem temple in AD70, for the reason now to be stated], *because they were prevented by death from continuing in office* [their death settled the matter, so one was regularly following another], *but he* [Jesus] *holds his priesthood permanently, because he continues forever'* (7:23–24). As 7:16 put it, his is 'an indestructible life'. Because Jesus never dies his priesthood never dies. He truly is 'a priest forever' (7:21). If any were to object and say, 'but Jesus did die', that is, of course, true. The answer to the objection is immediate, however. Yes, he died, but his death (unlike theirs) in no way prevented him from continuing as a priest. His death was his offering of himself as both priest (who offered the sacrifice) and victim (who himself was the sacrifice). Yet after his death and burial, he rose again and *'he continues forever'.* His death was not the end of his priesthood, for that abides continually (*'he holds his priesthood permanently'*). This has been the basic Melchizedek argument all along. See now, however, what treasures flow from this truth.

*'Consequently, he is able to save to the uttermost those who draw near to God through him, since he always lives to make intercession for them'* (7:25). What a consequence indeed. Because he was made priest with an oath (7:20), because of the Father's purpose not being open to alteration (7:21), because Jesus is 'the guarantor of a better covenant' (7:22), and 'because he continues forever' (7:24), great and magnificent consequences follow. This is surely one of the most exquisite verses in the entire letter, or, for that matter, in the entire Bible! It is in the very warp and woof of Jesus' person and work that *'he is able to save'.* That is why he became incarnate. The angel announced to Joseph that the son to be born of Mary was to be called 'Jesus, for he will save his people from their sins' (Matthew 1:21). Jesus stated of his own mission that, 'the Son of Man came to seek and to

save the lost' (Luke 19:10). The Samaritans, subsequent to the meeting of Jesus with the woman at the well, testified, 'we have heard for ourselves, and we know that this is indeed the Saviour of the world' (John 4:42).

That *'he is able to save to the uttermost'* could be rendered something like 'to the entirety'—that is to say, entirely, completely, absolutely, totally, perfectly, for all time. We are saved from sin, saved from Satan, saved from death's power and sting, saved from curse, saved from hell, saved from despair, saved from the wrath and condemnation that is coming upon the world—and all of that not temporarily but permanently. That 'great salvation' (2:3) is comprehensive. Nothing is lacking from it that is needful to it. And it belongs to all *'those who draw near to God through him'*, for only such are saved. There is a reminder here of Jesus' lovely word of grace, 'All that the Father gives me will come to me, and whoever comes to me I will never cast out' (John 6:37); there are shades here of, 'everyone who calls on the name of the Lord will be saved' (Romans 10:13); and there is a recollection here of, 'But now in Christ Jesus you who once were far off have been brought near by the blood of Christ' (Ephesians 2:13). The emphasis is upon the new and intimate relationship which exists, through Jesus, for us with God.

Yet the climax of verse 25 still awaits, and it is this: *'since he always lives to make intercession for them'*. Jesus' interceding (praying) in heaven for his people is the continuing, the ongoing, aspect of his high priestly work, and is one of every true believer's richest consolations. The Calvary part is finished (John 19:30), while this priestly part continues. The earthly and heavenly aspects of Jesus' priestly work, while distinct, are together part of the one whole. This work of 7:25 is not engaged in by means of words, however, unlike our own intercessions, but by Jesus' very presence on his Father's throne, and the constant presenting there of all the merits of his obedience and sacrifice while he was here on earth, on our behalf. And the fact that *'he always lives'* is quite obviously essential to this work. It could not be done by the former priests who had died, but requires the living one who abides forever. The apostle Paul rejoices triumphantly in this when he writes in Romans 8:34, 'Who is to condemn? Christ Jesus is the one who died—more than that, who was raised—who is at the right hand of God, who is interceding for us'. This intercessory work of our priest and mediator is a wonderful assurance to us of his continuing (indeed, unceasing) love and care for us. 'As for me, I am poor and needy, but the Lord takes thought for me' (Psalm 40:17)—one of the most precious verses in the psalms.

Two questions may quite properly be asked concerning Jesus' intercession for us: *what does it consist of*, and *what are the benefits of it?* As to *what it consists of*, his great prayer recorded for us in John 17 gives us the vital clues—matters such as our being kept safe, that we may know the blessing of unity together in the faith, have his joy fulfilled in us, be protected from the evil one, be sanctified; and this too, as he prays to the Father that we 'may be with me where I am, to see my glory that you have given me because you loved me before the foundation of the world' (John 17:24). And this is only for starters where his praying for us is concerned. Ultimately, we may be confident that these intercessions cover absolutely everything that is needful for us, as he grants to us day by day to 'receive mercy and find grace to help in time of need' (4:16). And when is it not a time of need for us?

As to *what the benefits of it are*—knowing that the Father always hears the Son ('Father, I thank you that you have heard me. I knew that you always hear me', John 11:41–42), we may be sure that it is on this account that our sins are forgiven, our prayers are answered, blessings are showered upon us, our services are accepted, we are not overwhelmed with sorrows or overcome by trials, and (in the light of John 17:24 quoted above) that we ever arrive safely in glory. And while our 'great high priest who has passed through the heavens, Jesus, the Son of God' (4:14) prays individually for each one of his people, for he knows us each by name, he is equally concerned to intercede for his church as a whole, for she is his bride whose beauty (his own beauty put upon us) he greatly desires (Psalm 45:11). To all of which, how do we respond? We respond in the language of Romans

8:31: 'What shall we say to these things? If God is for us, who can be against us?'.

## (6) Jesus exhibits a better character (7:26–28)

The final section of this extremely full chapter takes us even higher still into the wonders of Jesus' priesthood and priestly character. Again, in order to draw this out as strikingly as possible, contrast is drawn between Jesus and the priests and high priests who preceded him.

*'For it was indeed fitting* [suitable] *that we should have such a high priest* [none other could ever possibly meet our need or reach us in our extremity], *holy* [set apart by the Father, while one with the Father, being God's 'holy one', Psalm 16:10, in every way pleasing to him], *innocent* [blameless, having nothing in him of a harmful or sinful nature], *unstained* [undefiled, 'made like his brothers in every respect', 2:17, 'yet without sin', 4:15; 'a lamb without blemish or spot', 1 Peter 1:19, who 'committed no sin, neither was deceit found in his mouth', 1 Peter 2:22], *separated from sinners* [not remote or aloof from us in the sense of not wishing to have to do with us, but rather separate, distinct, set apart from us in our sin, yet very present with his comforts, his compassion, and his preserving grace], *and exalted above the heavens* [where now he dwells in unspeakable glory, being risen, ascended and glorified, and to which destination he will bring us in due time, not only to see but also to share in his glory, that where he is we may also be]*'* (7:26).

It is worth, in the light of this, stressing again how *'fitting ... a high priest'* Jesus is for us. No other high priest could ever possibly avail. His *holiness* provides for our lack of it. His *innocence* is the ground of our acquittal before God's judgment seat. His *stainlessness* is a great encouragement to us to have every confidence and trust in him in our approaches to God. His *separateness* (which, as we have just noted, does not mean distance from us in the sense of making him inaccessible to us) is a glorious reminder of his majesty and beauty, his worthiness and excellence. His *exaltedness*—the exaltedness of the one who was made 'for a little while lower than the angels', 2:7—is a spur to us, through all the ups and downs of daily life (and of Christian experience), to 'seek the things that are above, where Christ is, seated at the right hand of God', and to keep our minds, hearts, affections and longings fixed there, 'not on things that are on the earth' (Colossians 3:1–2).

The concept of Jesus being so fitting and suitable for us is pursued in the closing two verses of chapter 7. *'He has no need, like those high priests, to offer sacrifices daily, first for his own sins and then for those of the people, since this he did once for all when he offered up himself'* (7:27). We are familiar already from Hebrews with the truths being expressed here, but once more this is no vain or needless repetition. It has direct relevance to the writer's present emphasis, and is wonderfully encouraging. There was the constant succession of former high priests, offering sacrifice after sacrifice, bringing animal after animal, shedding blood after blood, day after day after day. There was no end to it. And before they could offer a sacrifice for anyone else's sin they had to offer one for their own sin. In a terrifyingly relentless way, they were all in it together. But such was never the case with the Lord Jesus Christ. He, bearing all the character marks just now set forth in verse 26, offered up only one sacrifice, for that was all-sufficient and needed no (indeed, could not have any) repetition. By this single, *'once for all'*, sacrifice, Jesus made 'propitiation for the sins of the people' (2:17).

Of this sacrifice which Christ offered, two things stand out here: *'he did this once for all'* and (the very next words) *'when he offered up himself'*. The *'once for all'* motif will appear again in 10:12, which states that Jesus 'offered for all time a single sacrifice for sins'. It affirms both the completeness, the effectiveness and the unrepeatableness of his own sacrificial work upon the cross, while at the same time indicating beyond dispute that the entire sacrificial system that pertained until that time is now abolished and redundant. This truth is underscored all the more magnificently by the fact that in this sacrificial work *'he offered up himself'*. No longer ordinary men offering animals in sacrifice, but the Son of God offering himself, he who 'loved us and gave himself up for us, a fragrant offering and sacrifice to God'

(Ephesians 5:2). What the many sacrifices over centuries could never accomplish, this one sacrifice has done for ever and ever. The one sinless priest has done on his own what the many sinful priests could never do. How this sets forth the glory of the Lord Jesus Christ.

*'For the law appoints men in their weakness* [physical, spiritual, moral] *as high priests, but the word of the oath, which came later than the law, appoints a Son who has been made perfect forever'* (7:28). The interrelated matters of priesthood, law and oath have already been dwelt upon by our writer. Here he presses home this great truth: the weakness of the high priests of old, appointed to their office in accordance with the divine law and pleasure, have been totally superseded by the divine oath appointing Jesus and the perfection of his own sacrifice. The law came before the oath (for the law was given at Sinai, when God's people were in the wilderness, while the oath was given in Psalm 110, much later on). Had that which was put in place by the law (concerning priests and sacrifices) been all that could ever be needed for us in our sins, then the oath would not have been necessary. We have been learning clearly enough from Hebrews so far, however, that the law was not all that was needed. Consequently, we are very thankful for the oath that followed, and for all that our Lord Jesus Christ has done for us in his one unrepeatable sacrifice 'when he offered up himself'. That oath secures for us Jesus' permanent continuance for us in the office of high priest.

Although there is no mention here by name of Melchizedek, he would still appear to be in the mind of the author of Hebrews, not least because of the Psalm 110:4 flavour both to the concept of the divine oath ('The Lord has sworn and will not change his mind', 7:21) and to *'a Son who has been made perfect forever'* ('You are a priest forever, after the order of Melchizedek', 7:17). The Son's being *'made perfect forever'* incorporates the active obedience of his life (keeping the law perfectly on behalf of us law-breakers), the passive obedience of his death ('He himself bore our sins in his body on the tree', 1 Peter 2:24), his glorious resurrection from the dead (opening up for us the door of eternal life) and his entering 'into heaven itself, now to appear in the presence of God on our behalf', 9:24. It should not be considered strange that Jesus is referred to here as *'a Son'* rather than as 'the Son'. The relationship of God the Son to God the Father is unique, and does not always require the definite article for us to be reminded of that.

What a chapter this has been, with all these 'betters'. All the promises and provisions of the gospel are fixed upon the firmest foundation imaginable. Let us examine ourselves to enquire whether or not we are resting and trusting wholly and only in the Lord Jesus Christ, in the light of all that he is, all that he has done, and all that he continues to do, so ample, rich and free.

# Chapter 8
# The two covenants


Hebrews, as we have already discovered, is very much a letter of warning. It is also, equally, very much a letter of encouragement. These two features, warning and encouragement, are both essentials for believers if we are to make progress in a balanced and consistent way in our Christian lives. In Hebrews, the balance is exactly right. A vital ingredient in biblical encouragement is comfort. To this end, our writer is continually at pains to prove to us and to assure us that all our true and lasting comforts are found (and found only) in the Lord Jesus Christ—our matchless high priest. He will not let go of this— and not surprisingly, since the excellence and glory of our high priest is central not only to Hebrews but to all of Scripture's unfolding of his person and work. And so he continues this golden thread as we move into chapter 8, a major part of which concerns Jesus being high priest of a better covenant than was the case with the high priests of old. This comes particularly to the fore in the second part of the chapter (verses 7–13), but to begin with we shall explore the comforts in Christ which are displayed in the earlier part of the chapter (verses 1–6).

## Jesus our high priest (8:1-6)

The opening phrase, *'Now the point* [the main point, main idea, crown or summary] *in what we are saying is this'* (8:1), establishes the clear connection with what has been set out before. The writer is both summing up and moving on, both gathering up things which he has already written and building upon that to develop further things that remain to be said. The theme (a grand one!) continues to be the high priesthood of Jesus, concerning which we may note where he is, what he is, and what he offers.

### Where our high priest is

Verse 1 continues: *'we have such a high priest, one who is seated at the right hand of the throne of the Majesty in heaven'*. This is not a new thought in Hebrews. As early as 1:3 we were told of Jesus that, 'After making purification for sins, he sat down at the right hand of the Majesty on high'; 4:14 began, 'Since then we have a great high priest who has passed through the heavens'; while 10:12 will affirm that 'he sat down at the right hand of God'. It speaks in particular of the perfection of his atoning work, and recalls again his 'It is finished' of John 19:30. When, in the Old Testament, the high priest had slain the sacrificial lamb and taken the blood into the holy of holies, he always stood. Jesus, himself *the* sacrificial lamb 'without blemish or spot' (1 Peter 1:19), when he had offered the sacrifice, went into heaven and sat down. How this should have commended the Lord Jesus afresh to the Hebrews, and how it should draw out our own hearts anew in adoration and devotion.

The 'we have' of 4:14 is repeated here in 8:1, and is the comforting and assuring language of personal possession—this Jesus, this high priest, this heavenly seated one, is ours, he is mine, we belong to one another. This same wonderful truth and blessed assurance is set forth in terms of great delight in these words elsewhere in Scripture: 'My beloved is mine, and I am his', and 'I am my beloved's, and his desire is for me' (Song of Songs 2:16 and 7:10).

Assurance (while possessed in different measures by different believers at different times) is highly desirable and contributes significantly to the stability, joy and effectiveness of our daily worship, walk and warfare, to the glory of God. Our writer has already drawn attention to its desirableness in 6:11 ('And we desire each one of you to show the same earnestness to have the full assurance of hope until the end'), and he will do so again in a most practical manner in 10:22 ('let us draw near with a true heart in full assurance of faith'). To know, and to know that we know, the reality of this *we have* can sometimes make all the difference in the Christian life between pressing on and feeling like giving up, especially when trials and temptations are pressing relentlessly upon us and forever knocking at our door.

Little words mean a lot in the Bible, and that is true of *'such'* here— for as we have observed earlier in the commentary, Jesus' position specifically *'at the right hand'* of God's heavenly throne expresses his majesty, glory, honour and exaltation, as well as indicating that to him belongs the Father's chief pleasure, affection and delight. What a contrast this presents with all the high priests who had preceded him. In consequence, let us never doubt the adequacy of salvation, the sufficiency of Christ, or the Father's complete approval and acceptance of his Son's work.

There is this aspect also—that while the former high priests exercised their priesthood for a limited time and only upon earth, the high priest who is ours (Jesus) exercises his priesthood eternally as it continues now and forever in heaven. And he does so (as the Melchizedek teaching has made so crystal clear) not only as a priest but as a king as well. So, once again, the comparison between Jesus and the other high priests proves to be no comparison at all—Jesus is totally and eternally unique.

## What our high priest is

He is *'a minister in the holy places, in the true tent that the Lord set up, not man'* (8:2). There is much to relish in this statement. Jesus is '*a minister*', which is to say that he ministers, he has and exercises a ministry. He was a minister when he was on earth, and now that he is in heaven he remains a minister. Thankful for all his ministry here below, how thankful we should be also for all his ministry continuing above. He remains active, and his activity is on our behalf, ministering for us and ministering to us. We know from other Scriptures the richness of this ministry. It includes his appearing in the presence of God for us (9:24); his ceaseless intercession for us (recently mentioned in 7:25), as well as his preparing a place for us in the 'many rooms' of his 'Father's house' (John 14:2); his defending of his church in the face of all her enemies and opponents ('I will build my church, and the gates of hell shall not prevail against it', Matthew 16:18); and his provision of ministers for his church on earth ('the pastors and teachers, to equip the saints for the work of ministry, for building up the body of Christ', Ephesians 4:11–12).

This ministry is '*in the holy places*'. This may be rendered 'of the holy things' or 'of the sanctuary'. Most likely is the latter, which fits with our ESV's translation, and speaks of heaven itself, the place of God's glorious presence (compare 4:14 again). This place of ministry is further called '*the true tent*', true not as opposed to false but in contrast with what is only a copy or representation of it. The adjective '*true*' is also in order to contrast Jesus' settled ministry in heaven with the moveable ministry of the priests in the tent, the tabernacle, during the many years of the wanderings in the wilderness. This heavenly tabernacle is '*the true tent that the Lord set up, not man*'. Men set up the tent in the wilderness. God has established the heavenly tabernacle. This interpretation is confirmed by the reference in 9:11 to 'the greater and more perfect tent (not made with hands, that is, not of this creation)', as well as by 9:24, where our writer declares, 'For Christ has entered, not into holy places made with hands, which are copies of the true things, but into heaven itself, now to appear in the presence of God on our behalf', and serves further to highlight the superiority of Jesus' ministry over that of anyone and everyone else. His very presence there is the proof not only that his Calvary sacrifice has been made but also that it has been accepted by the Father and is effective for us. Moreover, his heart of love and compassion towards us which Jesus evidenced while on earth is undiminished now that he is in heaven.

All of this (for the Hebrews and, just as much, for us) is intended to lift our eyes, affections and joys up from the earth (where they all too easily are prone and content to dwell), that we may fix them upon our great and glorious high priest, glory in him, be confident in him, delight in him 'with joy that is inexpressible and filled with glory' (1 Peter 1:8). Without being simplistic, it is surely true that the more we are taken up with the Lord Jesus Christ, the better will be the spiritual shape that we are in, the firmer will be our assurance of his and our mutual belonging, and the greater will be the honour that we are to him. This is why it was so important for these Hebrews who first received this letter that they should hold fast to Christ and not slip back towards those who came before him, for such a move would be returning into the murky shadows when, in the gospel, they have been brought into the brightness of the light. The point for them should not be lost on us either.

## What our high priest offers

As verse 3 opens we are transported back in thought and theme to 5:1 with the key phrase 'gifts and sacrifices'. *'For every high priest is appointed to offer gifts and sacrifices; thus it is necessary* [a matter of necessity] *for this priest also to have something to offer'* (8:3). Before sin entered into the world there was no need for offerings of this nature to be made. After the tragic entrance of sin, however, that is what the priests of old offered. So, the argument here runs, if Jesus is truly our high priest then he must have *'gifts and sacrifices'* to offer as well. And so he has! The singular *'something'* is significant, however, rather than 'somethings', for it is in the nature of Christ's priestly work that he 'offered for all time a single sacrifice for sins' (10:12), distinguishing himself in that from the many sacrifices offered by the many priests before him. There was no need for him to offer more than this one sacrifice, for he 'put away sin by the sacrifice of himself' (9:26). There is no further offering required beyond this one offering when he was here on earth, no need for him 'to offer himself repeatedly' (9:25), for this single offering of himself was 'a fragrant offering and sacrifice to God' (Ephesians 5:2), whereby 'we have redemption through his blood, the forgiveness of our trespasses, according to the riches of his grace' (Ephesians 1:7).

*'Now if he were on earth, he would not be a priest at all, since there are priests who offer gifts according to the law'* (8:4). Jesus' sacrifice of himself was made on earth, for, as 1 Peter 2:24 puts it, 'He himself bore our sins in his body on the tree' ('the tree' referring to the cross at Calvary). But—as Hebrews has insisted again and again—he is 'a priest for ever' (7:20) because of being 'after the order of Melchizedek' (7:17), and his priestly work and ministry is now carried on in and from heaven itself (refer back to 8:1). Had he remained on earth, Jesus could not have officiated as a priest, for he was not of the priestly tribe. Furthermore, his remaining on earth would have implied that his work was incomplete. Even at the time of writing Hebrews the earthly priests continued their work (*priests who offer gifts according to the law*), not realising that their work is now redundant, for the great high priest, the Lord Jesus Christ, now glorified in heaven, has completed and brought to an end all that they and their forebears had been doing for so long. The many priests of the tribe of Levi have given way to the one priest of the tribe of Judah (7:14), the priest-king who lives forever. They were all, we might say, 'from the earth', while he is 'from heaven' (1 Corinthians 15:47).

This is focused in the next two verses. *'They serve* [present tense, their ministry still continuing when our author wrote] *a copy and shadow* [a shadowy copy?] *of the heavenly things* [rather than the heavenly realities themselves]. *For when Moses was about to erect the tent* [the tent or tabernacle in the wilderness], *he was instructed by God, saying, 'See that you make everything according to the pattern that was shown you on the mountain'* [a quotation from Exodus 25:40, referring to the divine directions he received when he was on Mount Sinai, with nothing being left to Moses' own ideas or designs—note Exodus 25:8–9, as well as, 'Thus all the work of the tabernacle of the tent of meeting was finished, and the people of Israel did according to all that the LORD had commanded Moses; so they did', Exodus 39:32] *(8:5).*

These instructions which God gave to Moses have a significance which goes far beyond the building of the tabernacle itself. We may say that when Moses was with God at the top of Sinai, God did two things: first he revealed to him the law and then he revealed to him the gospel. The first he did in the giving of the commandments. The second he did in the providing of these detailed instructions for the design and building of the tabernacle—for the tabernacle, in the many types and pictures it includes, shows very remarkably the gospel themes of sin and salvation, sacrifice and offering, priesthood and high priesthood, all of which bear upon Jesus the high priest who is being set forth in the present verses. If it be asked how the pattern of the tabernacle was actually shown to Moses (that is, how he actually knew what the pattern was so that the tabernacle could be erected accordingly), answers have been various: Moses received the pattern in a vision, some form of model of it was given to him, or that he received some form of 'verbal' instructions. The fact is that we do not know because we are not told. What we do know (because 8:5 says so) is that however Moses received the instructions, he received them from God. That must suffice.

The words *'copy and shadow'* merit comment. A copy of something (maybe a building plan, vehicle design or landscape drawing) is exactly that—a copy, not the thing itself. A shadow of something requires the 'something' to be there, or there would be no shadow—but, similarly, the shadow is not the thing itself. The danger our writer perceived among the Hebrews (we observe again) was that they were showing far too much interest in returning to copies and shadows and seemed, dangerously, to be losing interest in and grip upon the realities in the Lord Jesus Christ of which the earlier things were the copies and the shadows. The famous call to be 'looking to Jesus' (12:2) is what is really throbbing all the way through the entire book, long before it is actually stated in that verse. It is so easy (for all of us) to be side-tracked and distracted from heavenly realities, to have our vision blurred and clouded from a lively and soul-thrilling sight of Christ by faith, to be bogged down and impeded by the things of this world—in other words, in our own ways to be taken up with copies and shadows of one sort or another, and to lose the need and desire to have the Lord Jesus Christ at the centre of all things in our lives, for him to be 'all, and in all' (Colossians 3:11). Let us be on our guard!

'*But as it is* ('now')', our writer continues, as he presses home his theme and prepares to deliver some vital teaching upon the subject of covenant(s), '*Christ* ('he') *has obtained a ministry that is as much more excellent than the old as the covenant he mediates is better, since it is enacted on better promises*' (8:6). Mention was made of Jesus being a minister in 8:2; and just as his ministry is superior ('*much more excellent*') to the ministries of those who came before him as priests, for reasons already supplied, so also '*the covenant he mediates*' (compare 7:22, 'guarantor, surety', and 9:15, 'mediator') is superior ('*better*'). Why? The clue is in that word 'better' (recall all those 'betters' we discovered in chapter 7)—'*since it is enacted on better promises*'. Jesus is not only priest but mediator also, and mediator because he is a priest, for it is by his priestly office and work that he exercises his role as mediator. That mediatorial work will be examined more closely when we come to comment on 9:15.

The over-arching reason for Jesus' ministry being '*much more excellent*' is that he himself is more excellent. Indeed, he is the most excellent of all. No other priest, high priest or ministry comes near to challenging comparison with him or his, whether in character, fitness, effectiveness or anything else. The statement that he has '*obtained*' this ministry is a strong assertion carrying the sense of achievement and accomplishment. The verb '*enacted*' has a legal sense, implying the secure establishment of the covenant through Christ: it has been legislated by divine authority and so it must stand and is not subject to alteration. The '*better promises*' are displayed here and there in Hebrews itself—including the purifying of 'our conscience from dead works to serve the living God' (9:14), and our drawing 'near [that is, to God] with a true heart in full assurance of faith, with our hearts sprinkled clean from an evil conscience and our bodies washed with pure water' (10:22). Moreover, they will be opened up in the second section of this present chapter in the context of the major Old Testament quotation there. Covenants and promises belong together. Many of the promises of the first (old) covenant pertained (though by no means exclusively) to material things, such as times and seasons, length of life, peace and prosperity. Those of the second (new) covenant pertain primarily and essentially to spiritual things, as will be seen.

So again the call rings out loud and clear to the backward looking Hebrews: don't go back, hold on to the Lord Jesus Christ, be careful not to lose what you have been given, be sure to let all your joy and all your confidence continue to abound only in him. The same applies to us. Remember that little word we drew attention to when commenting on verse 1, 'we have *such* a high priest'. Indeed we do! You may have loved ones in heaven, but think often upon this which is best of all: Jesus, our high priest, is in heaven—and him, through grace, 'we have'.

8:6 is a link verse between the chapter so far and that which is immediately to follow. Thus far the excellency of Jesus' priesthood has been demonstrated above that of former priestly and sacrificial arrangements, while there now follows a demonstration of the excellency of the new covenant above the old.

## Covenants old and new (8:7-13)

This second section of chapter 8 has seven verses, no less than five of which comprise a substantial quotation from the prophecy of Jeremiah. This is a significant move by our writer, for it directs the Hebrews to the Old Testament as a means to get them to accept from their own prophet the New Testament themes that very prophet was writing about. The crucial word is 'covenant'. This is a pivotal section in the letter to the Hebrews and needs to be approached carefully so that we understand it correctly. We shall comment upon it by way of asking five questions, all of them to do with covenant(s).

### (1) What is a covenant?

In ordinary terms a covenant is a solemn and binding agreement between one party to it and another. In biblical terms it is much more than that. It has to do with a sovereign dispensing of grace on God's part. It is not a mutual agreement as a result of negotiations hammered out between God and another party or parties until they can agree terms, but rather is something entirely on God's side, of God's pleasure, and on God's terms. The language of Scripture is that God says, 'I will make, I will establish' (the Hebrew is 'I will cut') a covenant. Of course, he makes it with people, as we shall see in a moment, but their responsibility is to accept and obey his instructions, as given and received, not to question them or seek to adjust them or negotiate upon them. It is a promise with conditions attached, and this in no way compromises God's sovereignty, which remains intact at all times.

## (2) What is the first (old) covenant?

*'For if that first covenant had been faultless, there would have been no occasion to look for* ['no place would have been sought', there would have been no need, God would not have provided] *a second'* (8:7). We might answer immediately that it is the Old Testament itself, but that would be an inadequate reply. Certainly within the pages and history of the Old Testament several covenants are mentioned. The chief ones are these.

First, God made with Adam in the Garden of Eden before the Fall what we refer to as the Covenant of Works. This is recorded in Genesis 2, although the word covenant does not appear. In this covenant God promised that he would give Adam life on the condition of Adam's perfect obedience. 'And the LORD God commanded the man, saying, 'You may surely eat of every tree of the garden, but of the tree of the knowledge of good and evil you shall not eat, for in the day that you eat of it you shall surely die' (Genesis 2:16–17). This covenant had no mediator since there was no need for one. All was well between God and man. Their fellowship was unsullied.

At another time God made a covenant with Noah after the flood, which is recorded in Genesis 9. Once the flood waters had receded and Abraham and company had come out of the ark, 'Noah built an altar to the LORD' (Genesis 8:20), upon which he sacrificed various burnt offerings. We then read: 'And when the LORD smelled the pleasing aroma, the LORD said in his heart, 'I will never again curse the ground because of man' (Genesis 8:21). This was rapidly followed by: 'Then God said to Noah and to his sons with him, "Behold, I establish my covenant with you and your offspring after you"'. The sign of this covenant was the rainbow: 'And God said, "This is the sign of the covenant that I make between me and you and every living creature that is with you, for all future generations: I have set my bow in the cloud, and it shall be a sign of the covenant between me and the earth"' (Genesis 9:8–9, 12–13). This covenant is sometimes seen as a 'type' of what we refer to as the Covenant of Grace.

A third significant covenant mentioned in the Old Testament is that which God made with Abraham, which is recorded in Genesis 17. At this time, when Abraham (then still called Abram) was 99 years old, 'the LORD appeared to Abram and said to him, "I am God Almighty; walk before me and be blameless, that I may make my covenant between me and you, and may multiply you greatly"'. On hearing this, 'Abram fell on his face. And God said to him, "Behold, my covenant is with you, and you shall be the father of a multitude of nations"'. Abram was then renamed Abraham, meaning 'father of a multitude', by God. This covenant also involved God's gift to Abraham and his descendants of 'all the land of Canaan, for an everlasting possession' (Genesis 17:1–5, 8).

One other covenant might be mentioned, and that is the one which God made with David, recorded in 2 Samuel 7. Its nub is found in these words of God to King David: 'And I will make for you a great name … Moreover, the LORD declares to you that the LORD will make you a house. When your days are fulfilled and you lie down with your fathers, I will raise up your offspring after you, who shall come from your body, and I will establish his kingdom … And your house and your kingdom shall be made sure forever before me. Your throne shall be established forever' (2 Samuel 7:9, 11–12, 16).

These various covenants have been mentioned in order to demonstrate that God deals with men by covenants. The triune Jehovah is the covenant making, covenant keeping and covenant remembering God. None of these covenants, however, with Adam,

Noah, Abraham, or David, is the one referred to here in 8:7 as *'that first covenant'*. So what is this reference to? We need look no further than two verses on, where, in part of the Jeremiah 31 quotation, we read: *'not like the covenant that I made with their fathers on the day when I took them by the hand to bring them out of the land of Egypt'* (8:9). This is clearly a reference to the Mount Sinai covenant, the one made by God in connection with the Exodus and the giving of the law, in the days of Moses. This solemn occasion is referred to again in 12:18–21. The confirmation of this covenant is found in Exodus 24, verses 4–8 of which teach that is was validated by blood.

### (3) What is the second (new) covenant?

There is no doubt over the answer to this question, in the total context of chapter 8 and what has gone before it. *'Behold, the days are coming, declares the Lord, when I will establish a new covenant with the house of Israel and with the house of Judah'* (8:8). It is that covenant of which the Lord Jesus Christ is both 'guarantor' (7:22) and 'mediator' (9:15)—the covenant we often refer to as the covenant of grace. Reference might be made to the words of the Saviour at the last supper. When taking the cup, he said, 'This cup is the new covenant in my blood' (1 Corinthians 11:25).

### (4) How is the first (old) covenant at fault?

That it is somehow at fault is clear from the language used. We have already noted that 'the covenant (Jesus) mediates is better' (8:6), and that 'if that first covenant had been faultless, there would have been no occasion to look for a second' (8:7). We are told, *'For he* [God] *finds fault with them* [it?] *when he says* [to them, the people originally addressed]*'* (8:8), and we shall learn at the end of the chapter that, *'In speaking of a new covenant, he* [God] *makes the first one obsolete. And what is becoming obsolete and growing old is ready to vanish away'* (8:13).

So in what way is this first covenant at fault? In answering this question, we must beware of a danger. The old covenant is not to be disparaged or disregarded. Yes, it was not 'faultless'. Yes, it became 'obsolete'. Yes, it grew old and vanished away. But it was not nothing at all. Most importantly, it was God's covenant, setting forth his righteous requirements. It included blessings for obedience and curses for disobedience. God made it graciously with his people—'not like the covenant that I made with their fathers on the day when I took them by the hand to bring them out of the land of Egypt' (8:9) is a beautifully tender statement.

Its fault, its weakness, its temporariness lay in this: (1) By and large, the people did not obey or keep this first covenant (as we have already seen in Hebrews), so the key fault lay with them; (2) It focused chiefly (while certainly not entirely) upon physical blessings rather than spiritual ones, although it was by no means devoid of spiritual blessings; (3) It set a standard before the people of Israel, one of perfect righteousness, which it was impossible for them to reach, for it provided no enabling for them to do so—it was 'weakened by the flesh' (Romans 8:3); (4) It was unable to justify (provide justification) for sinners, for 'it is evident that no one is justified before God by the law, for "The righteous shall live by faith"' (Galatians 3:11, incorporating a quotation from Habakkuk 2:4), and, 'For by works of the law no human being [flesh] will be justified in his sight, since through the law comes knowledge of sin' (Romans 3:20); (5) Its essence was God saying to the people, 'I will, if you will'—but they wouldn't; (6) It was powerless to supply the new regenerate heart issuing in a rich relationship and fellowship with God, which will be made clear in the course of God's words through Jeremiah.

It was 'old' because it was being replaced by 'new'. It was 'first' because it was being followed by 'second'. You cannot have a 'new' if there has been no 'old', and you cannot have a 'second' if there was never a 'first'. It was because the first covenant was not without fault that there was need for the second covenant which was without fault.

## (5) How is the second (new) covenant better?

This brings us to the heart of the matter, and to the reason why the writer to the Hebrews employs a highly relevant and significant prophecy from Jeremiah. 8:8–12 of Hebrews quotes Jeremiah 31:31–34. Interestingly, this is the longest Old Testament quotation to be found anywhere in the New Testament. It is a most remarkable passage, which not without reason has been described as being among the most profound passages in the Old Testament. That is no overstatement. It is a glorious declaration from God concerning what he will do, who he will do it for, and what will be the benefits to those on the receiving end of it. It abounds in grace and hope, and serves as a stirring and further reminder to the Hebrews not to be so crazy as to 'give up' on the gospel. It should stir us similarly! We shall see that there is both a negative ('not like', 8:9) and a positive ('For this is', 8:10) concerning this new covenant. As regards the positive, one thing in particular shines out, and that is the gracious and decisive initiative of God, seen in the following sequence of divine 'I wills': 'I will make', 'I will put', '(I will) write', 'I will be' (all in 8:10), 'I will be merciful' and 'I will remember' (both in 8:12).

*'Behold, the days are coming, declares the Lord'* (8:8). *'Behold'* is always an arresting word in the Bible, calling us to be ready to take special note of what is about to be said. So it is in this instance. What coming days are intended here? Remembering that God spoke these words in the days of the prophet Jeremiah (who spoke them as God's appointed mouthpiece), we understand the reference to be to the fact that the days prophesied in Jeremiah 31 of God making this new covenant have now arrived. The Hebrews were living in those days— and so, much later on, are we. The days when Jeremiah ministered were not good days spiritually. As the Lord's prophet he was very much up against it. The word of the Lord was not being well received.

They were days when God said of his people such sorrowful things as these: 'Be appalled, O heavens, at this; be shocked, be utterly desolate, declares the LORD, for my people have committed two evils: they have forsaken me, the fountain of living waters, and hewed out cisterns for themselves, broken cisterns that can hold no water'; 'Yet I planted you a choice vine, wholly of pure seed. How then have you turned degenerate, and become a wild vine?'; and (perhaps most poignantly of all), 'Can a virgin forget her ornaments, or a bride her attire? Yet my people have forgotten me days without number' (Jeremiah 2:12–13, 21, 32).

For God—in those days—to utter the matchless words of him

making a new covenant, must have been like a shaft of light in a dark tunnel, a glimpse of sunshine after a cloudy day, a sight of spring blossom after a dreary winter. This was a glorious prophecy indeed. It spoke, surely, of mercy triumphing over judgment (James 2:13). God had a future for his people after all, despite everything. And in and through the Lord Jesus Christ, those promised days have finally arrived.

Why, specifically, does God say, *'when I will establish a new covenant with the house of Israel and with the house of Judah'*? Given that long before Jeremiah's day (let alone New Testament times) Israel and Judah had been divided kingdoms (going right back to after Solomon's death), the covenant being made with both Israel and Judah signifies the unity of all God's true people and their being 'all one in Christ Jesus' (Galatians 3:28, and the context there). It has in mind the 'great multitude that no one could number' (Revelation 7:9), and that 'in Christ God was reconciling the world to himself' (2 Corinthians 5:19). Thus the reference is to God's people as a whole, the entire church of elect believers taking in both Jews and Gentiles, memorably denoted in Galatians 6:16 as 'the Israel of God'.

We noted above the fact stated in 8:9 about the new covenant not being like the one which God made with his people at Sinai, and the reasons why this first covenant was not without fault. It is now added: *'For they did not continue in my covenant, and so I showed no concern for them, declares the Lord'*. God's showing of *'no concern for them'* [paying no heed to them, not regarding them] means that he left them to carry on in their disobedience—not himself forsaking his own covenant or casting them off for ever, but leaving them (as we might say) to taste their own medicine and have their own way, in order that they might discover where having their own way would get them. It would not get them favour and blessing from God. Neither will a similar tack on our part secure such favour and blessing for us either. No wonder Paul emphasised to the Ephesians the importance of looking 'carefully then how you walk, not as unwise but as wise, making the best use of the time, because the days are evil' (Ephesians 5:15–16). This call to God's people remains as needful as ever.

There now follows, in words of sublime divine grace, the nature of God's new covenant blessings which have come to pass through the Lord Jesus. The details of 8:10–12 expand upon the truth stated back in 8:6, that 'the covenant he [Jesus] mediates is better [than the old, that is], since it is enacted on better promises'. The especially noteworthy feature of these new covenant blessings (this 'great salvation', harking back to 2:3) is that they are inward and spiritual rather than outward and material. Such is the predominant nature of gospel privileges and delights.

*'For this is the covenant that I will make with the house of Israel after those days, declares the Lord'* (8:10). The expression here is very beautiful and can properly be translated, 'For this is the covenant that I will covenant', both noun and verb coming from the same root. This is the 'prologue' to the essential blessings listed. It is striking that nowhere in these verses is the Lord Jesus Christ mentioned by name. This need not concern us, however, for (as we remind ourselves yet again) since he is the new covenant's surety and mediator, he is the very heart, life and assurance of all these blessings. These blessings may be gathered up under four divisions: a new nature from God, a new relationship with God, a new intimacy with God and a new experience of grace.

### A new nature from God

*'I will put my laws into their minds, and write them on their hearts'.* God's law is God's law. It always has been and it always will be. The people of God in the Old Testament already had the law. It is not that God was cancelling that law (we are speaking of what we call the moral law, the ten commandments, of Exodus 20 and Deuteronomy 5), or writing a new law. Moreover, not only God's people but all mankind have God's law—it is for everyone, not only for some. This moral law of God is unchanging. It does not shift with the times, fluctuate with the markets, or change with the weather. It is not to be subject to the whims of society or the preferences of governments. It abides. So, since it is the same moral law, what is different about it in the new covenant?

The answer is that, in a manner and to a degree outstripping anything that came before, God says he will *'put my laws into (our) minds'* and he will *'write them on (our) hearts'*. It is an internalising process, whereas under the old covenant God had written his law upon 'two tablets of stone' (Deuteronomy 5:22). It makes us think of God's word through Ezekiel: 'And I will give you a new heart, and a new spirit I will put within you. And I will remove the heart of stone from your flesh and give you a heart of flesh. And I will put my Spirit within you, [note carefully the consequence now following], and cause you to walk in my statutes and be careful to obey my rules (or, 'judgments')' (Ezekiel 36:26–27). What is being spoken of is nothing less than the mighty and effectual operations of the Holy Spirit both upon and within the minds and hearts of believers, as a result of which they (we) walk in the ways of the Lord, regulated by the word of the Lord, and all to his own glory. Without this Spirit wrought work nothing truly real and lasting is accomplished in the soul.

It should not be overlooked that both *'minds'* and *'hearts'* are mentioned. This dual emphasis should always be observed. God's truth enters our minds as we are taught by the Spirit (reflect upon 2 Corinthians 2:9–16). The mind is never bypassed, for by means of it we are instructed and gain understanding ('the renewal of your mind', Romans 12:2; compare Ephesians 1:17–18, 4:23). That which the Spirit of God graciously deposits in our minds, however, must also affect our hearts (reflect upon Ephesians 3:14–19). It is mind and heart in connection, neither one being without the other—the mind clear, the heart warm—the precious things of God and the gospel being both 'known' and 'felt', as God works in us according to his good pleasure and grace.

What is in view here is far more than respect for God's law, more than committing it to memory, more than speaking it out loud, more than legislating for it. This is nothing short of the grand gospel doctrine of the new birth (regeneration, being born again)—which is not for one moment to say that no one in Old Testament days was ever born again, for of course they were, of which Hebrews 11 will leave us in no doubt. Many individuals most certainly were regenerate. Just to take a few examples, we cannot possibly imagine folk like Enoch, Abraham, Ruth, David, Esther or Isaiah (along with many others) being anything other than regenerate. The way of justification and salvation was exactly the same for believers in 'the old days' as it is for believers in 'the new days'—by grace alone, through faith alone, in Christ alone. Many, however, it seems, were only ever on the 'outside' of God's law, and never possessed it in their minds or on their hearts. The point is that a heart so engraved acknowledges, delights in and freely and willingly obeys God's law. Paul declares this, speaking of himself but on behalf of all Christians, when he testifies, 'For I delight in the law of God, in my inner being' (Romans 7:22), while at the same time being very aware of the struggle he still has (and we still have) with sin. There is no room here for the Christian, or in the church, for any antinomianism (rejecting God's law, picking and choosing among God's law, living without or above God's law, or denying it its proper place as God's rule for our holiness in the great business of our sanctification). Let such never be given 'house room' among us. One of the choicest characteristics of a true Christian and a true church is deep and heartfelt love for, obedience to and upholding of God's law.

### A new relationship with God

There's more, as God continues: *'and I will be their God, and they shall be my people'.* This is really the 'motto' of the covenant and of the covenant relationship, and brings to mind the words of Psalm 144:15, 'Blessed are the people to whom such blessings fall! Blessed are the people whose God is the LORD!'. It is at the very centre of all the covenant blessings enumerated here in Hebrews 8. It is familiar covenant language, going right back to the days of Moses (Exodus 6:7); finding magnificent expression in 2 Corinthians 6:16, where the apostle quotes from Leviticus 26:12; and climaxing in Revelation 21:3, where John 'heard a loud voice from the throne saying "Behold, the dwelling place of God is with man. He will dwell with them, and they will be his people, and God himself will be with them as their God"'.

Here, in words which should continually cause us wonderment that such a thing can ever be, God covenants to be our God and, equally, covenants to take us as his people. It is reminiscent of somewhat similar language in the Old Testament, expressing this mutual relationship of God and his people—even, we might dare to say, their possession of one another. Compare, 'But the LORD's portion is his people' (Deuteronomy 32:9), and, '"The LORD is my portion", says my soul' (Lamentations 3:24). Nothing more could be required for us.

Certainly the key thought here is 'relationship'. This relationship between God and his people is much richer and fuller under the new covenant—not least because it has been brought about by Jesus' sacrificial and priestly work at Calvary, concerning which our writer has been so emphatic. It is described in manifold ways in Scripture. Two of the most precious are Father and children, and Shepherd and sheep. Our consciousness of this new relationship should itself feed and assist that very love for and obedience to God's law which has just been mentioned. It was one thing for the Israelites to be in a special relationship with God (to them God said, 'You only have I known of all the families of the earth', Amos 3:2), and for them to boast about it. It is another thing to 'walk in the light, as he is in the light' (1 John 1:7), and to keep in step with the gospel summons, 'So, whether you eat or drink, or whatever you do, do all to the glory of God' (1 Corinthians 10:31).

### A new intimacy with God

*'And they shall not teach* [there is a very strong negative here: 'not' is 'by no means'], *each one his neighbour and each one his brother, saying, "Know the Lord", for they shall all know me, from the least of them to the greatest'* (8:11). Two different words are used in this verse for 'know'. The first (*'Know the Lord'*) carries the sense more of knowledge as opposed to ignorance; the second (*for they shall all know me*) indicates more of knowledge involving acquaintance with the person or thing known.

The essence of being a Christian is that we know God, for while it is true that 'The secret things belong to the LORD our God', it is equally true that 'the things that are revealed belong to us and to our children forever, that we may do all the words of this law' (Deuteronomy 29:29). It is not that we know various things about God (many who are not Christians may be in that position, even though many will have been taught falsely concerning him and end up with woefully wrong ideas, creating a god of their own making, very far removed in every way from the true God). Rather it is that we actually know him. This is personal. Just as 'The fear of the Lord is the beginning of knowledge' (Proverbs 1:7), even so the relationship of every believer with God is a lifetime's experience (we may even say an eternity's experience) whereby we continually 'press on to know the Lord' (Hosea 6:3). There is no end to this knowledge, for there is no end to God. Always there are deeper depths to plumb and higher heights to explore. This is part of the sheer romance and adventure of the Christian life—and to think that many who are not Christians pity us!

One of the joys of knowing God is that it is the privilege and possession of all who belong to him, *for they shall all know me, from the least of them to the greatest*. The babe in Christ and the veteran of the long and often arduous race are together in this blessedness, and each can be an example and a blessing to the other. True, some will know the Lord more closely than others, but this highly personal intimacy with God belongs to boys and girls, young men and women, and those of all ages.

There is a testing point for us here. Ask yourself how well you really know the Lord, how acquainted with him you are, how deeply you understand his ways. We were reminded in 3:8–9, in the quotation from Psalm 95, that even though God's people of old saw God's works, that did not stop them from putting him to the test, provoking him, or from receiving this rebuke from him: 'They always go astray in their heart; they have not known my ways'.

What is meant by people not teaching their neighbours and brothers? It is not intended to imply that any Christians can reach the position of being 'know-alls' regarding God, incapable of being taught anything more by anyone (although occasionally we might meet some who think like that of themselves!). Neither does it in any way run contrary to 'the work of ministry' (Ephesians 4:12), the office of 'pastors and teachers' (Ephesians 4:11), or respect for and submission to appointed leaders who 'are keeping watch over your souls' (Hebrews 13:17). It serves rather as an enforcing companion to the *'they shall all know me, from the least of them to the greatest'*, commented on above. Here is an intimacy, a fellowship, a communion with God such as has never been known before. It is a reminder also (looking back to God's 'I will put' and 'write' of verse 10) that at the end of the day what we know of God, what we understand of the Scriptures, what we really appreciate of salvation, what we most deeply relish of the covenant, is taught us by God himself, through his Spirit, however much we are indebted to him (as indeed we are) for our human teachers of these things.

### A new experience of grace

We come to the final verse of this major Jeremiah quote. It is (to use a very poor analogy) the icing on the cake. *'For I will be merciful toward their iniquities, and I will remember their sins no more'* (8:12). Again there is a forceful negative: 'and their sins I will by no means remember more'. Central to the new covenant with which our writer is presently dealing is the sacrificial work of the Lord Jesus Christ upon the cross at Calvary. There was an abundance of grace available for sinners in the Old Testament, and many were those precious, though otherwise perishing, souls who availed themselves of it, 'without money and without price' (Isaiah 55:1)—that is to say, the gift of God's free grace. There was even 'grace in the wilderness' (Jeremiah 31:2). Moreover, it was all available (and only available) in and through Jesus to whom those who were saved in those days looked forward in humble and expectant faith. It is the actual fulfilment of that looking forward which was in view in Jeremiah's ministry, when God spoke through him of the new covenant; and the fulfilment has taken place, for Christ has done his work.

At the time when Jeremiah prophesied the thought of divine mercy and forgiveness was not new. The psalmist rejoices in the comfort of the knowledge that 'with you [God] there is forgiveness, that you may be feared' (Psalm 130:4). The prophet relishes the truth that he is given by God to declare, that 'though you [God] were angry with me, your anger is turned away' (Isaiah 12:1). Jeremiah gazes delightedly forward to this scenario: 'In those days and in that time, declares the LORD, iniquity shall be sought in Israel, and there shall be none. And sin in Judah, and none shall be found' (50:20). Yet (as Hebrews insists) there was never through the old covenant priests and sacrifices the fundamental and final 'putting away' of sins. Instead the annual day of atonement led to 'a reminder of sin every year' (10:3). Things are altogether different as the glorious result of Jesus' priestly and sacrificial work.

The position now, for God's own people, is this. The reach of God's pardon is immeasurable. Every sin that we commit—whether from yesterday, today, tomorrow or at whatever point in the future—is completely pardoned by God, on the sole basis of Jesus' Calvary work, for this work is absolutely accepted and delighted in by the Father. As we shall find when we come to 9:14, 'the blood of Christ' actually purifies 'our conscience from dead works to serve the living God'. This is how Jesus could say to the Father, 'I glorified you on earth, having accomplished the work that you gave me to do. And now, Father, glorify me in your own presence with the glory that I had with you before the world existed' (John 17:4–5).

The truth that God himself utters (and promises), *'I will remember their sins no more'*, takes some getting hold of. It is momentous. We hardly dare to believe it. But it is the word of our 'God, who never lies' (Titus 1:2), so we must believe it. Not to believe it would be greatly to dishonour God. It must never be used, though, to allow us to take anything less than the most serious view of sin. The old covenant from Sinai was not without many gracious aspects, but contained nothing quite to match the glorious abundance of divine promises contained in the new. It must follow also from 8:12 that whereas the old covenant was broken, that can never be so with the new. It is unbreakable. Herein, not least, is its newness.

With all of this said—that the new covenant brings for us a new nature from God, a new relationship with God, a new intimacy with God, a new experience of grace—our writer is able to gather things up so far in his discussion of the two covenants with the closing verse of the chapter. *'In speaking of a new covenant, he makes the first one obsolete. And what is becoming obsolete and growing old is ready to vanish away'* (8:13). There is more than one word in the New Testament for 'new'. In the present instance the word is not 'new' is the sense of 'novel', but refers to something which cannot be affected by the passage of time, something which in consequence will never change. 'New' and 'old' stand here in clear distinction from each other. The old covenant is replaced (or overtaken) by the new covenant, but nothing will ever replace (or overtake) the new.

The new covenant represents the fullest and most luxurious flowering of grace. It relates vitally to the heart rather than to external obedience. It rests, as we have seen, upon better promises. It relies utterly upon the Lord Jesus Christ—his perfect obedience, not our imperfect obedience or wretched disobedience. In response to the old covenant given by God through Moses, the people said, 'Go near and hear all that the LORD our God will say and speak to us all that the LORD our God will speak to you, and we will hear and do it' (Deuteronomy 5:27). Notice that: they said, 'we will hear and do it'. But, of course, they didn't. The Lord Jesus Christ, in contrast, has heard and done all of the Father's will and work, and has done so on our behalf.

Since the old covenant was God's covenant (he made it, he established it, he set its terms, he determined who it would be with), then it is only with God to make it *'obsolete'*. No one else could do this. He announced what he announced through Jeremiah concerning his new covenant, and the writer to the Hebrews has just restated the very words of God. The intrinsic weakness of the old covenant is vividly present in the reference to it *'growing old'*, something which can never be true of its replacement. It has to follow that something which *'is becoming obsolete and growing old is ready to vanish away'*. Its time is up. It has served its purpose. It is the same with a worn-out garment, an ancient building, a decayed tree, or a passing generation. And what replaces the old? The new!

# Chapter 9
# The copies and the realities

Connections are very important in Scripture. In the instance now before us, the connection between this and the previous chapter is clear from the outset (not least remembering that as originally written the Bible had no chapter and verse divisions, so our writer was not in that sense moving from chapter 8 to chapter 9—he was just carrying straight on). The connection of thought surrounds the theme of covenant. As we have been seeing, the writer to the Hebrews has been contrasting the first (or old) covenant with the second (or new) covenant. 'In speaking of a new covenant, he makes the first one obsolete' (8:13). While in 9:1 the word 'covenant' is supplied in our English translation (for it does not appear in the original, which reads simply 'Now even the first'), it is obvious that it is the covenant which is meant, not 'the first' anything else. And behind this connection is the most fundamental connection of all, for there is no change of theme, neither will there be, since our writer is a one-theme man. We know very well by now what that theme is, and there is none

like it: the absolute superiority, pre-eminence and excellence of the
Lord Jesus Christ. No theme can compare with this, for none can
compare with him. So, notwithstanding the vanishing away of the old
covenant, it presents many points of instructive teaching for us in the
total biblical display of our Saviour. To some of these our writer now
turns.

The argument of the chapter divides into several natural sections,
which we shall consider one by one, in the following way: a tour of
the tabernacle (verses 1–5), the activity of the priests (verses 6–10),
the superiority of Jesus (verses 11–14), the will and the blood (verses
15–22), and the two appearings (verses 23–28).

## A tour of the tabernacle (9:1–5)

'*Now even the first covenant had regulations for worship* (or, 'ordinances
of service') *and an earthly place of holiness*' (9:1). From its very
beginning the first covenant (the one, remember, given by God
through his servant Moses on Mount Sinai) contained '*regulations for
worship*'. These were extremely detailed, as the book of Exodus reveals.
Nothing was left to be done as man pleased. All was to be done as
God ordered, according to his appointment. This is as it should be,
for he alone is the one who is to be worshipped, and so it lies with
him and not with us to determine how he should be worshipped. We
call this, historically, 'the regulative principle' of worship, whereby we
worship him according to his specific command and requirement,
needing this always as our warrant for everything that we render to
him. And while these worship regulations are different in many ways
under the new covenant (no more priests, altars, sacrifices, festivals,
for example), the principle still abides. Why? For while the old
covenant has given way to the new (it '*had* [note the tense] *regulations
for worship*'), God himself has not changed in any way. He remains as
eternal, as holy, as sovereign, as glorious, as ever he was. It is still with
him, and only with him, to declare how he is to be worshipped, and
to show us (consequently) what worship is pleasing and acceptable to
him, and what worship is not.

The putting into practice of these '*regulations for worship*' under '*the *first covenant*' was intimately related to what is here described as '*an earthly place of holiness*'. The next verse will reveal that this refers to the Old Testament 'tent' or 'tabernacle'. Note here in 9:1 its identity as being '*earthly*' and '*a place of holiness*'. By '*earthly*' is meant worldly— not in the sense of worldly being opposed to spiritual, but belonging to this world, material, here on this earth, all of which the tabernacle was, even though it was one of the chief glories of the Mosaic covenant, and even a type of the eternal Son of God becoming incarnate. Yet it was only here for a season and was destined to pass away. By '*a place of holiness* [a sanctuary]' is indicated, by way of reminder, the holiness of God and the holiness of the activity of worship (compare Psalm 29:2, 'Ascribe to the LORD the glory due his name; worship the LORD in the splendour [beauty] of holiness').

Having made this initial statement regarding worship under the first covenant, the writer now proceeds to develop the theme, in readiness for drawing the contrast between things as they were and things as they now are in and on account of Jesus' person and work.

'*For a tent* (or, 'tabernacle') *was prepared* (8:2). The divine instructions for the building of the tent, or tabernacle, in the wilderness are recorded for us in Exodus from chapter 25 onwards ('Moreover, you shall make the tabernacle', 26:1). When this work was completed, we read that, 'According to all that the LORD had commanded Moses, so the people of Israel had done all the work' (39:42); 'Then Moses blessed them' (39:43); and, most exquisitely of all, 'Then the cloud covered the tent of meeting and the glory of the LORD filled the tabernacle' (40:34). Very significantly, whenever the people of Israel in the course of their years of wilderness wanderings stopped in their journey and pitched camp, the tabernacle (which was portable) was always erected in the centre of the camp (Numbers 2:2), demonstrating the truth of the Lord God Jehovah dwelling in the midst of his people.

This tent /tabernacle had two parts or sections to it, divided from one another by a curtain. They are denoted in this passage of Hebrews as '*the first section*' (literally, 'the first') and '*a second section*'. The former part was *'called the Holy Place'*, while the latter was *'called the Most Holy Place* [the Holy of Holies, the Holiest of all]'.

In *'the first section … were the lampstand and the table and the bread of the Presence'*. These items of furniture each had their own use and significance. As for *'the lampstand'*, its design and the instructions for its making are given in Exodus 25:31–40. It was made of pure gold, had three branches out of each side of the central stem (so six branches in all), and included 'cups made like almond blossoms', all of it 'of one piece'. There were also 'seven lamps for it' (one on each of the side branches and a seventh at the top of the stem). These seven lamps were kept alight day and night. Exodus 26:35 informs us that this lampstand was 'on the south side of the tabernacle'. The gospel picture here reminds us of Jesus, who is our light, walking in the midst of the seven golden lampstands in Revelation 1, where the lampstands (or candlesticks) are his church. The fact that the branches were made of one piece with the lampstand itself suggests the oneness of Jesus and his people, while the supplying of the lamp with oil which was poured first into the stem and then went through the several branches is illustrative of Christ receiving the Holy Spirit and then communicating the Spirit to his people.

On the north side of the Holy Place of the tabernacle was *'the table'*, and on this table was *'the bread of the Presence'* (literally, 'the setting forth, or presentation, of the loaves' and sometimes called 'the showbread'). These two items belonged very much together. There were a dozen loaves, arranged in two rows of six, and replaced every Sabbath by freshly baked bread. We learn from Exodus 25:23–30 that the table was made of acacia wood and was overlaid with pure gold. The bread was baked with 'fine flour' (Leviticus 24:9). The gospel picture this time focuses upon the church's communion with God, the twelve loaves being suggestive of the twelve tribes as well as the twelve precious stones in the high priest's breastplate.

*'Behind the second curtain* (or, 'veil') *was a second section called the Most Holy Place'* (8:3). This was no ordinary curtain. It was made 'of blue and purple and scarlet yarns and fine twined linen … with cherubim skillfully worked into it' (Exodus 26:31). This is that very

curtain or veil of which we read immediately upon the death of Jesus on the cross: 'And, behold, the curtain of the temple was torn in two, from top to bottom' (Matthew 27:51). The question might arise in our minds: if this is the second curtain, where is the first? The answer is that the first curtain would be the one through which it would be necessary to pass on the way from the outer court of the tabernacle into the Holy Place. It is not, however, our writer's concern here to give an exhaustive description of the tabernacle, but only to draw attention to those features of it which serve his purpose.

The Most Holy Place contained further items of furniture, again each having its own use and significance. These our writer designates *'the golden altar of incense and the ark of the covenant'* (8:4). Above the latter *'were the cherubim of glory overshadowing the mercy seat'* (8:5). The altar here mentioned is described in Exodus 30:1–10. Like the table, it was made of acacia wood and overlaid with pure gold. It was square, portable, and upon it Aaron burned 'fragrant incense'. No 'unauthorized incense' was to be offered upon it (the preparation of the correct incense made with the appropriate spices is dealt with in Exodus 30:34–38). This altar was 'most holy to the LORD'.

It is the case that while Hebrews 9:3–4 places this golden altar unquestionably in the Most Holy Place, two verses in Exodus imply its presence on the Holy Place side of the curtain (those verses are 30:6, 'in front of the veil', and 40:26, 'before the veil'). How so, since it could not have been in both places, on either side? The point does not bother our author, but is best explained by saying that the association between the altar and the ark ('And you shall put the golden altar for incense before the ark of the testimony', Exodus 40:5) was so intimate that although, strictly, it was in the Holy Place, it was reckoned, virtually, to be part of the furniture of the Most Holy Place. On that annual Day of Atonement, when the high priest went into the Holy of Holies, he took in there with him incense from this golden altar (see Leviticus 16:12–13). Incense speaks, among other things, of prayer, and Hebrews lays due emphasis upon Jesus as our great intercessor who (as we shall see in 9:24) now appears 'in the presence of God on our behalf', and who (as we have already seen in 7:25) 'always lives to make intercession for' us. His intercession is most certainly fragrant.

Of immense significance, and full of meaning, is *'the ark of the covenant'*. Exodus 25:10–22 records its pattern and construction. Once again both acacia wood and pure gold are involved. It is fair to say that it was the most important of all the furniture in the tabernacle. It was a box or chest. When the Israelites were on the move, travelling in the wilderness, the ark led the way, going before them and carried by the priests by the poles which were prescribed for the purpose. In a very striking manner it represented the presence of the living God of the covenant in the midst of his people, something which is very much an abiding reality. In Exodus 25:22 God gave this promise to Moses, 'There I will meet with you, and from above the mercy seat, from between the two cherubim that are on the ark of the testimony, I will speak with you about all that I will give you in commandment for the people of Israel'. It was of the essence of the very glory of Israel. That being so, it was a devastating moment in Israel's history when the ark was captured by the Philistines in battle (1 Samuel 4 has the account of how this happened), and a corresponding joy when it was unexpectedly returned to them (1 Samuel 6). After David established his capital in Jerusalem the ark was housed in a tent (see 2 Samuel 6); subsequently, after Solomon had built the temple, it was placed in the temple's inner chamber (see 1 Kings 8).

Our writer now draws our attention to the contents of *'the ark of the covenant'*. They are three: *'in which was a golden urn holding the manna, and Aaron's staff that budded, and the tablets of the covenant'*. Comment is necessary on each one, for all are highly significant and recall very substantial moments in the earlier history of God's people.

Beginning with *'a golden urn holding the manna'*, this took the recipients of Hebrews back (and takes us back with them) to God's miraculous provision of manna for his people to eat in the wilderness. Read all about it in Exodus 16. Sadly, 'the whole congregation of the people of Israel grumbled against Moses and Aaron in the wilderness' (16:2), complaining especially about the lack of diet compared with what they had been used to back in Egypt, 'when we sat by the meat pots and ate bread to the full', and charging Moses and his brother with bringing them 'out into this wilderness to kill this whole assembly with hunger' (16:3). The Lord was quick to respond, saying 'to Moses, "Behold, I am about to rain bread from heaven for you, and the people shall go out and gather a day's portion every day, that I may test them, whether they will walk in my law or not"' (16:4). In the event, they did not come out of the test very well. The manna itself (the word means 'What is it?', which is what the people said when first they saw it, 16:15) was 'a fine, flake-like thing, fine as frost on the ground' (16:14), 'like coriander seed, white, and the taste of it was like wafers made with honey' (16:31). Moses instructed Aaron, '"Take a jar, and put an omer of manna in it, and place it before the LORD to be kept throughout the generations". As the LORD commanded Moses, so Aaron placed it before the testimony to be kept' (16:33–34). We are told, 'The people of Israel ate the manna forty years, till they came to a habitable land. They ate the manna till they came to the border of the land of Canaan' (16:35). The manna in the urn was a lasting testimony to God's gracious provision and his unchanging unfaithfulness, and recalls to us the words of the Lord Jesus Christ, 'Truly, truly, I say to you, it was not Moses who gave you the bread from heaven, but my Father gives you the true bread from heaven. For the bread of God is he who comes down from heaven and gives life to the world' (John 6:32–33); 'I am the bread of life' (John 6:35).

Next to be mentioned among the contents of the ark is *'Aaron's staff that budded'*. Read all about it in Numbers 17. In a very striking episode (after, sadly, the people had been grumbling again), 'The LORD spoke to Moses, saying, "Speak to the people of Israel, and get from them staffs (or, 'rods'), one for each fathers' house, from all their chiefs according to their fathers' houses, twelve staffs. Write each man's name on his staff, and write Aaron's name on the staff of Levi [the priestly tribe, remember]. For there shall be one staff for the head of each fathers' house. Then you shall deposit them in the tent of meeting before the testimony, where I will meet with you. And the staff of the man whom I choose shall sprout. Then I will make to cease from me the grumblings of the people of Israel, when they grumble against you'" (17:1–5). All of this was done, the result being that, 'On the next day Moses went into the tent of the testimony, and behold, the staff of Aaron for the house of Levi had sprouted and put forth buds and produced blossoms, and it bore ripe almonds' (17:8). The people were suitably humbled, saying to Moses, 'Behold, we perish, we are undone, we are all undone' (17:12). This budding staff of Aaron's was a lasting testimony to God's unflinching holiness, righteousness and justice, mixed with his enduring grace, mercy and lovingkindness.

The next words we read regarding the ark's contents are, *'and the tablets of the covenant'*. The reference is to the two tablets of stone which God gave to Moses on Mount Sinai containing the ten commandments (the Decalogue), 'written with the finger of God' (Exodus 31:18). This gives particular significance to the ark being named *'the ark of the covenant'*, for this law instructed the covenant people how to behave towards the covenant God; it impressed upon them the need for them to be covenant keepers and not covenant breakers. Moreover, in the Exodus verse just cited the 'tablets of stone' are also called 'the two tablets of the testimony'—a further reminder, then and now, that in his law the holy God testifies (and testifies permanently, since, as we have urged already, the ten commandments abide) to the holiness he looks for in the hearts and lives of his people, both individually and together. He it is who says, 'You shall therefore be holy, for I am holy' (Leviticus 11:44), which is then quoted in the New Testament in 1 Peter 1:16.

Do not be foxed by any apparent contradiction between what is stated here in Hebrews 9—namely that there were these three items kept in the ark—and the statement in 1 Kings 8:9 that, 'There was nothing in the ark except the two tablets of stone that Moses put there at Horeb [another name for Sinai]', where the context is the ark being brought to the newly built temple in the days of Solomon. Any contradiction is only apparent, for the Hebrews reference is to when the ark was in the wilderness tabernacle, not when it was in the temple.

One further feature is now mentioned by our writer. *'Above it* [the ark] *were the cherubim of glory overshadowing the mercy seat'* (9:5). God had instructed Moses, 'You shall make a mercy seat of pure gold … And you shall make two cherubim of gold; of hammered work shall you make them, on the two ends of the mercy seat … The cherubim shall spread out their wings above, overshadowing the mercy seat with their wings, their faces one to another … And you shall put the mercy seat on the top of the ark … There I will meet with you, and from above the mercy seat, from between the two cherubim that are on the ark of the testimony, I will speak with you' (Exodus 25:17–18, 20–22). The word 'cherubim' is the plural form of 'cherub', and these winged figures are described here in 9:6 as *'the cherubim of glory'* because of the glorious presence of God appearing above the mercy seat intimated there at the end of the Exodus quotation. The glory belonged to God, not to the cherubim. On a number of occasions in Scripture God is spoken of as 'enthroned upon the cherubim'; Psalm 80:1 is a lovely example of this.

The word for *'mercy seat'* is itself important. In what we call the Septuagint (the Greek translation of the Old Testament, sometimes called the LXX) the word is regularly used to render a Hebrew word meaning 'covering' (keep in mind that the mercy seat was above the ark, as a covering for the ark). It has been suggested, however, that there is a deeper meaning to be discovered than this. Picturing things as they were in the Most Holy Place, there was the holy law of God *in* the ark and the glory of God's presence *above* the ark, with the mercy seat *between* the two. So? This is surely a gospel picture, for the Greek word itself translated here 'mercy seat' is one of the great gospel words, and signifies 'a place of propitiation', speaking of the turning aside of God's wrath from us and upon his Son in our place. Indeed, in Romans 3:25 the Lord Jesus is actually referred to as the one whom 'God put forward as a propitiation [same word as for 'mercy seat' in Hebrews 9:5] by his blood, to be received by faith'. When thinking about 'the mercy seat', we cannot help thinking also about 'the throne of grace', of which so much was made back in 4:16, the place where God meets with us and we with him.

All of us as sinners are condemned by the law of God, we are under its curse for being law-breakers. As such, we are barred from God's holy presence, we have no access. How, then, may such access be found? Only in God's provision of the Lord Jesus Christ, 'in who we have redemption, the forgiveness of sins' (Colossians 1:14), in a word, 'mercy'. God's abundant grace and mercy 'covers' all our sins. This well serves our writer's focused purpose of urging those to whom he wrote not to backtrack from Jesus and the gospel, not to return from grace to works, not to hanker after the old covenant now that it has been superseded by the new (which it was intended it should do from the start). And it preserves the constant gospel emphasis of the Scriptures, with every book of the Bible (each in its own way) pointing to Jesus—he who, on the day of his resurrection, spoke of how 'everything written about (him) in the Law of Moses and the Prophets and the Psalms must be fulfilled' (Luke 24:44).

Having said all this, our writer now makes the following remark. *'Of these things we cannot now speak in detail'.* This rather abrupt looking statement might prompt the question, if he doesn't mean to speak in detail of these things, why does he mention them at all? Where do they actually come in his overall argument? How do they fit? In what way do they help? The immediate answer to him not going into any more detail than he has done is the obvious one: he has said as much as he feels it necessary to say in order to make his point, and that to have said more would risk concealing his point. But what of 'his point'? What precisely is it? It is as just stated in the previous paragraph: everything in the Old Testament pointed to Jesus, and not only pointed to him but vigorously strained forward towards him—the truth the Hebrews seemed in such danger of missing or abandoning.

9:1–5 follows very suitably the discussion in chapter 8 concerning the two covenants, and prepares the ground well for the treatment about to follow in the present chapter concerning priesthood, sacrifices and matters pertaining to the Day of Atonement, matters which took place within the tabernacle. We might say that in the features the writer has touched upon thus far in chapter 9 he has been dealing with the types and the figures, whereas in what he is about to move on to as the chapter unfolds further will be concerned with fulfilments and realities. He has spoken of the shadows, but now will come to the substance. The Hebrews needed urgently to see the distinction, and so always do we. If all they saw was the tabernacle and its furniture, they were missing the main sight. In a word, since it was intended to show them the Lord Jesus, then if they did not see him, they really saw nothing at all. We (like them) rejoice in the types, but we (as they needed to do) must rest in the Saviour.

## The activity of the priests (9:6–10)

Following this concise tour of the tabernacle, the scene is now set for our writer's detailed exposition which follows, not only in this chapter but through much of chapter 10 as well. We have been reminded of the tabernacle in its structure, whereas now we are brought to consider it in terms of the activity which went on in it in the days of the Old Testament ministries (the priests into the Holy Place and the high priests into the Most Holy Place), and how all of this was in preparation for the unique ministry of the Lord Jesus Christ, the 'high priest forever after the order of Melchizedek' (6:20). The people of old gloried very much in the priestly office and the tabernacle with all its furniture. How important it is now, writes the author of Hebrews, that the people of God should glory rather in the Lord Jesus Christ. And so must we.

'*These preparations* (or, 'things') *having thus been made*' (9:6), is how this next section begins. This links back to 9:2 and the mention there of 'a tent (being) prepared', and serves to invite us inside the tabernacle to observe what went on. First up is the activity of the priests in the Holy Place: '*the priests go regularly into the first section, performing their ritual duties*'. The meaning of '*regularly*' in this context is variable, for they had both daily duties and weekly duties. The word means 'at all times'—that is to say, at all appropriate times, at all the times when the occasion required.

A helpful passage which gives a very clear account of their varied duties is 1 Chronicles 23:24–32.

For their duty was to assist the sons of Aaron for the service of the house of the LORD, having the care of the courts and the chambers, the cleansing of all that is holy, and any work for the service of the house of God … to assist with the showbread, the flour for the grain offering, the wafers of unleavened bread, the baked offering, the offering mixed with oil, and all measures of quantity or size … to stand every morning, thanking and praising the LORD, and likewise at evening, and whenever burnt offerings were offered to the LORD on Sabbaths, new moons and feast days, according to the number required of them, regularly before the LORD. Thus they were to keep charge of the tent of meeting and the sanctuary, and to attend the sons of Aaron, their brothers, for the service of the house of the LORD.

A further part of this 'charge of the tent of meeting' was keeping the lamps burning on the golden lampstand (recall 9:2) and the burning of incense on the altar of incense (recall (9:4). These are detailed in Exodus 27 and 30 respectively. Notice how everything was to be done with such care, in order to ensure that all that was done for the Lord and in the name of the Lord was as he wished. So it should always continue to be in the church of God.

The sentence continues: *'but into the second* [that is, the second section, the Most Holy Place] *only the high priest goes* [there was no admittance here for the Levitical priests as a whole]*, and he but once a year* [on the Day of Atonement, the tenth day of the seventh month, described in detail in Leviticus 16]*, and not without taking blood* [the blood of sacrifice]*, which he offers for himself* [as a sinner needing pardon and forgiveness] *and for the unintentional sins of the people* [for, high priests or not, they were all in it together as sinners in the sight of the holy God] (9:7). Twice before we have had reference to this dual responsibility of the high priest, bringing sacrifices for both his own and the people's sins (first in 5:3, then again in 7:27). The word rendered here *'unintentional'* has the literal meaning 'ignorances', and speaks of those sins committed without prior intent or as a result of human weakness (recall the reference to 'the ignorant and wayward' in 5:2). This was in contrast to deliberate sins, sinning 'with a high hand'

(Numbers 15:30). Leviticus 16:17 records God's instruction that no one else was to be in the tent of meeting from the time the high priest went in until the time he came out. He had to be there alone. We cannot help thinking of the Lord Jesus, who, with regard to the cross, uttered these solemn words: 'I have trodden the winepress alone, and from the peoples no one was with me' (Isaiah 63:3).

The way to God is always by blood, always by sacrifice, and the whole nature (as we have seen) of all the sacrifices and all the blood which could not put away sin was to point forward continually to the one sacrifice and the one shedding of blood (on the cross at Calvary) which both could and has. The high priests of the Old Testament were incapable of dealing with the peoples' sins (for they could not even deal with their own); and the sacrifices they brought were equally incapable of doing so because they lacked the perfection which God required. How striking it is that the Day of Atonement, which we could term the high point of the whole Jewish year, revealed at its very heart the ultimate inadequacy of all that was done upon it, year in and year out.

'*By this the Holy Spirit indicates that the way into the holy places is not yet opened as long as the first section is still standing*' (9:8). There is a beautiful and clear (if incidental) reference here to the inspiration of Scripture by the Holy Spirit. 'For no prophecy [referring ultimately to the whole of Scripture] was ever produced by the will of man, but men spoke from God as they were carried along by the Holy Spirit' (2 Peter 1:21). He it is who gave the Bible writers the words to write, and he it is who interprets to us what they have then written. He is ever our teacher, and always has been the teacher of the people of God, the revealer of spiritual truth. 'A person cannot receive even one thing unless it is given him from heaven' (John 3:27). In the present case, he is revealing the imperfection of the Old Testament system (hence the becoming obsolete of the old covenant, 8:13). Look back to 8:5, and Moses being 'instructed by God' in all the matters pertaining to the tabernacle. For so long as the necessity remains for all the business of the priests in the Holy Place and the high priest in the Most Holy Place, '*the way into the holy places is not yet opened*', which is to say there was no freedom of access, no liberty of entrance, into the very presence of God for all. However, the *'not yet'* is full of hope and promise—what was not then open to all would be, once 'Christ appeared as a high priest of the good things that have come' (9:11).

You can see how all of this fits like a glove into the concern of the writer to the Hebrews that they should not slip back into the old ways now that the Messiah has come and all the types and shadows are fulfilled. This was no time to be going backwards—and it never is! So it will not be long before the writer is joyfully declaring, 'we have confidence to enter the holy places by the blood of Jesus, by the new and living way that he opened for us through the curtain, that is, his flesh' (10:19–20). Yes, *'the way into the holy places'* was not open *then*, but it is *now*, and Jesus himself says, 'I am the way' (John 14:6). And later in the New Testament, Peter writes that the people of God constitute 'a holy priesthood, to offer spiritual sacrifices acceptable to God through Jesus Christ' (1 Peter 2:5).

The present line of thought continues: *'(which is symbolic for the present age)'* (9:9). The word translated *'symbolic'* here is actually 'parable'. This underscores helpfully what we have just been seeing and saying. One thing and another about the tabernacle (with its two sections) and the priesthood (with their set ministries) all serve to show their temporary and typological nature. They are parables or pictures, full of symbol and instruction, pointing on to things beyond themselves which will come to pass in due time. They served this function for those who lived in those days, and continued to do the same for those who were around in the days of the letter to the Hebrews (not least if the temple was still standing in their day) and who were being addressed in this letter. As for ourselves, they enable us to see with richness and clarity the way in which God's purposes unfold, the purposes of the God who not only knows, but actually ordains, the end of things from the beginning, that we may thereby give him all the glory as the God of our salvation.

*'According to this arrangement, gifts and sacrifices are offered that cannot perfect the conscience of the worshipper'.* In contrast, as we shall see shortly, the result of Jesus' sacrifice is to 'purify our conscience'

(9:14). Why does our writer bring in the subject of *'the conscience of the worshipper'* here? The conscience takes us inside a person. It speaks of personal knowledge, conviction and answerability for thoughts and actions. That very thought reminds us that since every part of us is defiled by sin, every part of us needs to be cleansed from sin. Titus 1:15 relates this specifically to our minds and our consciences. The sacrifice of Jesus reaches our innermost beings with its cleansing power and fits us for communion with him—something which (as has been insisted all along in this discussion in Hebrews) the former sacrifices just could not possibly do. With all those former things, sin and guilt continually remained. There was no relief from them, no hiding or resting place, no intimacy with God, no 'fellowship with the Father and with his Son Jesus Christ' (1 John 1:3). For all those who put their hope and trust in *'this arrangement'* rather than in the one to whom *'this arrangement'* points, there was no salvation. The many throughout Old Testament days (and there were many) who were truly saved were enabled through faith (which 'is the gift of God', Ephesians 2:8) to look right through *'this arrangement'* to the Saviour himself. Like Abraham of old, they saw Christ's day and were glad (John 8:56).

The sentence begun in 9:9 runs on: *'but deal only with food and drink and various washings* [such as for the priests themselves, for which the 'basin' ('laver') in the tabernacle was provided, Exodus 30:17–19; the different parts of the burnt offerings, Leviticus 1:8–9; and the washing of the people themselves whenever they contracted defilement, Leviticus 15:8], *regulations for the body* [all of these speaking of external matters which were all part and parcel of the rites and ceremonies of the former days] *imposed until the time of reformation'* (9:10). By *'the time of reformation'* (an expression making here its only appearance in Scripture) is intended all that was spoken of in the Jeremiah 31 passage on the new covenant, dealt with in Hebrews 8—that is to say, the fulfilling in the Lord Jesus Christ of all that had gone before. In other words, our writer is telling the Hebrews, that time has now come. Calvary is the hinge and focus of it all. Those before Calvary looked by faith towards it. We who live after Calvary look by faith back to it. Either way it is Jesus only, for 'there is salvation in no one else, for there is no other name under heaven given among men by which we must be saved' (Acts 4:12).

## The superiority of Jesus (9:11–14)

With a resounding *'But'* (although *'Christ'* is the actual opening word of the verse) our writer launches forth with relish into a further setting forth of the superiority of the Lord Jesus Christ over all that has gone before him—especially, in the present context, the whole business of the tent/tabernacle and the activity that went on within it. The direct access for the sinner into the presence of God, which could not be provided under the former arrangements, is now gloriously available through Jesus, his person and his work. Everything that pointed to him and was promised in him has now become a reality— another persuasive to the Hebrews, should it be needed, not to return to what was and has now gone, but to cleave to that which is and abides for ever.

We may discern here five aspects of Jesus' superiority: his priesthood (verse 11a), his sanctuary (verse 11b), his sacrifice (verse 12a), his provision (verse 12b), and his results (verse 13–14). The sum of the whole is that we are so very much better off on account of him.

### Jesus' superior priesthood

*'But when Christ appeared as a high priest of the good things that have come'* (9:11). There is a great difference between good things promised and good things delivered. The Old Testament high priests, most notably on the annual Day of Atonement, dealt in good things still to come. The Lord Jesus, in his priestly work, brings *'good things that have come* (or, having come about)'. In the light, for example, of the application of the Jeremiah 31 passage that was presented in chapter 8, these *'good things'* are all the new covenant blessings. In Scripture's language of the doctrine of salvation, they include such things as regeneration, justification, reconciliation, adoption, sanctification and so on, going on ultimately to glorification. They are well expressed by the apostle when he writes of Jesus, 'whom God made our wisdom and our righteousness and sanctification and

redemption' (1 Corinthians 1:30), or, 'For all the promises of God find their Yes in him' (2 Corinthians 1:20).

In order to avoid any confusion, it ought to be mentioned (especially if any reader is using a different Bible version from the one upon which this commentary is based) that a variant reading translates *the good things that have come* as 'good things to come', looking still to something future. Should this rendering be taken, the reference will be either to these good things being future from the perspective of the Old Testament believers, or to them being future in terms of the final consummation of all things at the end of the age with the second coming of Jesus. There is no overarching reason, however, to depart from the rendering before us in the ESV, thinking of things that are already here. This makes good sense in linking in with the phrase 'until the time of reformation' in verse 11. That time, in Christ, has now arrived. Having said that, of course, whatever our present experience of new covenant blessings in and through the Lord Jesus, there is always more still to be experienced, for his fountain is ever full, and will remain so even throughout eternity. In that sense, *the good things* have both already come and are still to come. There is no end to them. We enjoy them and we shall yet enjoy them. We possess them and we shall yet possess them. We rejoice in them and we shall yet rejoice in them.

## Jesus' superior sanctuary

The same verse continues, *'then through the greater and more perfect tent (not made with hands, that is, not of this creation)'*. What is this *'greater and more perfect tent'* that our writer now refers to, through which Jesus went? A body of interpretation takes this to refer to the humanity of Christ, his human nature, but it would appear the wisest course to take it in the same sense as we took 'the true tent' in 8:2, namely, heaven itself. The tent spoken of there is described as the one 'that the Lord set up, not man', and that accords well with the description of the tent in 9:11 here as being *'not made with hands, that is, not of this creation'*. Moreover, in the 8:2 context the reference to 'the true tent' arises in direct connection with Jesus being 'seated at the right hand of the throne of the Majesty in heaven', which continues: 'a minister in the holy places, in the true tent'. This seems to be all of a piece and demonstrates the unity of 8:2 and 9:11. The Old Testament priests and high priests ministered in an earthly tent, an earthly sanctuary. The same is not true of Jesus, however, who ministers in a heavenly one, which in its nature must be *the greater and more perfect*. If it seems strange to speak of him passing *'through'* the tent (verse 11) 'into the holy places' (verse 12), for how can you pass through heaven in order to enter heaven?, the language is rather comparable to what we shall have in 10:20, 'through the curtain'. It draws upon the movement of the high priest on the Day of Atonement, who went through the Holy Place and into the Most Holy Place. Jesus has gone into heaven through the place of sacrifice (in his case, the cross), which is now to be brought to the fore in the words that follow.

## Jesus' superior sacrifice

Still in the same sentence, the thought continues into the next verse: *'he* [Jesus] *entered once for all into the holy places, not by means of the blood of goats and calves* [note the plural] *but by means of his own blood* [not meaning that he literally carried his sacrificial blood into heaven with him, but that it was 'by virtue of' it—the meaning of the *'by means of'*—that he entered in] *'* (9:12). There is much here. The nature of things prior to Jesus is that the priestly work went on and on, day after day, year in and year out. There was never any *'once for all'* about it. It knew no end. In contrast, Jesus *'entered once for all into the holy places'*, for his sacrificial work on earth was completed. Again, every time a sacrifice was offered in the Old Testament, the blood shed and offered was *'the blood of goats and calves'*—that is to say, they brought 'other' blood, for their own would have been no use at all. In contrast this time, the sacrifice that Jesus offered, the blood that he shed, was *'his own blood'*—the perfect offering, the perfect sacrifice, involving the perfect blood, 'the precious blood of Christ, like that of a lamb without blemish or spot' (1 Peter 1:19). This is the heart of the deep mystery of Jesus' priestly work. His entering *'once for all into the holy places'* was, as we learned back in 6:20, 'as a forerunner on our behalf'.

It is impossible to overestimate the importance and significance of 'blood' in Scripture. It runs all the way through the Bible, and the word is mentioned no less than nine times in this present chapter. As verse 22 will tell us, 'without the shedding of blood there is no forgiveness of sins'. All the blood offerings of all the countless animal sacrifices were illustrations rather than being themselves effective. In contrast, the blood of Jesus is mightily effective. As the apostle Paul declares, 'But now in Christ Jesus you who once were far off have been brought near by the blood of Christ' (Ephesians 2:13); and as the apostle John states, 'the blood of Jesus his [God's] Son cleanses us from all sin' (1 John 1:7).

## Jesus' superior provision

9:12 builds up to this great climax: *'thus securing an eternal redemption'*. The words *'thus securing'* are more strictly 'having secured', the point being that first Jesus secured *'an eternal redemption'*, and then, having done so on the cross, entered into the heavenly sanctuary. There he presents himself and his work upon our behalf, and the Father takes delight in it.

What is the import of *'eternal'* here (compare 'eternal salvation', 5:9, and 'eternal inheritance', 9:15)? The redemption (the root meaning of redeem, redemption and so on is release from bondage upon payment of a debt, so a purchase price for the people of God) which Jesus has secured for us is rightly called *'an eternal redemption'* for at least these three reasons: (1) It was planned from all eternity, 'even as he [God the Father] chose us in him [God the Son] before the foundation of the world' (Ephesians 1:4). (2) This provision is the cornerstone of the 'eternal gospel' (Revelation 14:6), the good news which deals with eternal matters as nothing else ever can or will be able to do. (3) It lasts to all eternity, in the sense that the benefits secured for us by Jesus at Calvary (and the empty tomb) continue for ever, they are permanent, they never wear out, for never will anything 'be able to separate us from the love of God in Christ Jesus our Lord' (Romans 8:39).

## Jesus' superior results

The lengthy sentence which now follows needs to be grasped in its wholeness. *'For if* [carrying the force here of 'since'] *the sprinkling of defiled persons with the blood of goats and bulls and with the ashes of a heifer sanctifies for the purification of the flesh, how much more will the blood of Christ, who through the eternal Spirit offered himself without blemish to God, purify our conscience from dead works to serve the living God'* (9:13–14). If we are expecting a question mark at the end there, we would be wrong. The writer to the Hebrews is not so much asking a question ('if such and such a thing is true, then how much more is something else true?'), but, rather, is making a grand statement: 'such a thing being so, then something else is even more so!'

His point is this, and it is as simple as it is profound. Since the entire Old Testament system of *'the sprinkling of defiled persons with the blood of goats and calves and the ashes of a heifer'* had the result of giving a ceremonial cleansing (*'sanctifies for the purification of the flesh'*), then all the more (*'how much more'*) will Jesus' sacrifice of himself on the cross, with the offering of his own blood, avail for something greater, internal and altogether more glorious (*'purify our conscience from dead works to serve the living God'*). Again, it is important to stress that our writer is not raising a question but is stating a conclusion, and a more magnificent conclusion could scarcely be stated.

What the old sacrifices could not do, Jesus has done. The result they could never secure, however many of them there were, Jesus, by his one sacrifice of himself, has done. There is no comparison. The one dealt only with *'the flesh'*, for it was external. The other deals with *'our conscience'*, and penetrates to the springs of things, deep down within us. Vast quantities of *'the blood of goats and calves'*, along with *'the ashes of a heifer'*, were impotent to obtain what Jesus secured on his own and without repetition. Regarding the former (the sprinkling of people with the blood), note the instance recorded in Exodus 20:21 in respect of the persons and garments of Aaron and his sons when being consecrated as priests. Regarding the latter (the sprinkling of people with the ashes), we have an instance set out as part of the laws of purification in Numbers 19 in respect of anyone who came into contact with a dead body.

It is insufficient for the flesh alone to be cleansed. The deeper need is for the work of God to be wrought upon the conscience, whereby sinners are convicted of guilt and shame before the holy God on account of their sin itself and their actual multiple sins, and are then brought to behold the wonder of salvation, the freeness of grace and the completeness of forgiveness from God, all found in and through the Saviour, the Lord Jesus Christ. Those who were truly converted in Old Testament days were those upon whom this greater work of God (the conscience work) was truly wrought and who looked by faith to this very Saviour. He, the undefiled one, offered himself for us, the defiled ones. He who was *without blemish* (both in the purity of his person and the holiness of his life) was delivered up for us, who are full of blemish. Further, it is stated that this offering was *to God*. Jesus' entire life had been one of unblemished obedience to God (the messianic words of Jesus from Psalm 40 will be quoted in 10:7, 'Behold, I have come to do your will, O God, as it is written of me in the scroll of the book'); and now his death on the cross, when he *offered himself without blemish to God*, was the climactic high point of that obedience, in every way pleasing to God.

With regard to this offering of himself (note how the expression *offered himself* indicates the voluntariness and willingness of the act—in contrast, the sacrificial animals had no say in the matter), we are told that Jesus did this *through the eternal Spirit*. While it has been argued in some quarters that this should be rendered along the lines of 'through his eternal spirit' (note the lower case 's' there), meaning something like 'by virtue of his very nature, power or personality', there surely seems every reason to retain the capital 'S' and see here an unmistakable reference to the Holy Spirit, and his mysterious involvement in the work of Christ upon the cross. Let it be remembered that upon Jesus rests 'the Spirit without measure' (John 3:34), and that time and again during his earthly ministry the Holy Spirit is mentioned in association with the Lord Jesus. So here in 9:14, the meaning would be that, in the offering up of himself and the shedding of his own blood, the second Person of the Trinity was greatly upheld, sustained and enabled by the third Person of the

Trinity, and that thereby all was wondrously accomplished that was accomplished.

The verse concludes: *'purify our conscience from dead works to serve the living God'*. Mention was made in 6:4 of 'repentance from dead works' (see the comment on that verse). Before us now is a reminder that our *'dead works'* cannot, do not and will not ever be of the slightest use in dealing with our sins and reconciling us to God. In the language of Hebrews here, our *'dead works'* can never bring us into the blessed position of being able *'to serve the living God'*—anymore than could the constant array of animal sacrifices offered on human altars by sinful priests. Indeed, what can *'dead works'* and *'the living God'* ever have to do with one another? The truth is that *'the living God'* needs to be served in a living way by those who themselves God has made 'alive together with Christ' (Ephesians 2:4). Those, consequently, who are still dead in sin and performing *'dead works'* can do nothing pleasing or acceptable to God. No small part of the wonder and glory of the gospel is that we are so transformed by the grace of God that we can now render what *is* pleasing and acceptable to him, as those who are God's 'workmanship, created in Christ Jesus for good works, which God prepared beforehand, that we should walk in them' (Ephesians 2:10). Here is a test of our 'deadness' or our 'liveliness'—our service of *'the living God'*.

## The will and the blood (9:15–22)

*'Therefore he is the mediator of a new covenant'* (9:15). Once again we are right at the centre of the message of Hebrews: the new covenant, and Jesus as its mediator. The specific newness of this *'new covenant'* is that it has completely superseded the old covenant, the one which has become 'obsolete' (8:12). Previously in Hebrews, as we have seen, Jesus has been styled the 'guarantor' or 'surety' of this new covenant (7:22). Now, for the second time, he is termed its 'mediator', the one who 'mediates' it (compare 8:6). The specific position of Jesus as *'the mediator'* of this covenant is a testimony to his honour and excellence. We are reminded of the statement elsewhere that

'there is one mediator between God and men, the man Christ Jesus' (1 Timothy 2:5).

A *'mediator'* is someone who intervenes between two sundered parties with a view to reconciling them. As the verse just quoted declares, it is a most appropriate term to use in connection with the Lord Jesus who reconciles sinners to God (1 Peter 3:18). Ordinarily a mediator needs to be completely impartial (think of the use of the word in employment relations, for example); he cannot take sides. Our Lord Jesus, however, is most gloriously partial—partial for the holiness of the offended God, and partial for the plight of the helpless sinner. The Father commits this work to him and takes divine pleasure in it; the sinner is bidden to trust in Jesus as the Saviour to put him right with God. Jesus became *'the mediator of a new covenant'* on the basis of his work that has just been described in verses 11–14: his sacrificial death, the shedding of his blood, the provision of full atonement for sin, and his entrance into the heavenly places. He alone is qualified for this title. No one else may claim it or share it with him. In this, as in all things, 'Christ is all, and in all' (Colossians 3:11).

Having made this fundamental statement, our writer proceeds to unfold something of the intents and outcomes of the new covenant. First to be mentioned is: *'so that those who are called may receive the promised eternal inheritance'*. The language of receiving a promised inheritance is very much covenant language. When, so very many years before Hebrews was written, God made a covenant with Abraham, similar language as this was used. Whether we recall God's promise to Abraham (then still called Abram), 'To your offspring I will give this land' (Genesis 12:7); or, later, 'that I may make my covenant between me and you, and may multiply you greatly' (Genesis 17:2); or, 'And I will give to you and to your offspring after you the land of your sojournings, all the land of Canaan, for an everlasting possession, and I will be their God' (Genesis 17:8); or, to mention just one more, 'I will surely bless you, and I will surely multiply your offspring as the stars of heaven and as the sand that is on the seashore. And your offspring shall possess the gate of his enemies, and in your offspring shall all the nations of the earth be blessed, because you have obeyed my voice' (Genesis 22:17–18)—it is the same every time. The language of covenant promise is the language of possession and inheritance. To that extent it was so with the old covenant—so how much more is it so with the new, since (as 8:6 so beautifully insisted), 'the covenant (Jesus) mediates is better, since it is enacted on better promises'. And what are these 'better promises'? See the comment on that verse, but remember, not least, that these 'better promises' take us all the way from the city of destruction (where we dwelt in our sin and misery) to the celestial city (where we shall reign with Christ in his eternal presence).

We must not overlook the doctrine of divine calling here also: *'the promised eternal inheritance'* (the 'great salvation' of 2:3, the 'inheritance that is imperishable, undefiled, and unfading, kept in heaven for you' of 1 Peter 1:4) will be received by *'those who are called'* (the 'holy brothers ... who share in a heavenly calling', 3:1). There is the outward call, and there is what we refer to as the effectual call. 'For many are called, but few are chosen', says Jesus at the end of the parable of the wedding feast (Matthew 22:14). This dovetails readily with the words of the Lord Jesus in John 6:37, where he declares that, 'All that the Father gives me will come to me, and whoever comes to me I will never cast out'. It does the same with the words of the apostle Paul in Romans 8:28, when he speaks of 'those who are called according to (God's) purpose'—and two verses later in what we refer to sometimes as 'the golden chain of salvation': 'And those whom he predestined he also called, and those whom he called he also justified, and those whom he justified he also glorified' (our glorification, our receiving of the inheritance of promise, being so certain and sure in the covenant that it can be stated in the past tense as a thing already accomplished). So great (and so gracious) is our glorious God, the God of our salvation! It can never be the case that the inheritance will be there with no one to possess it and enjoy it. The matter is expressed with particular exquisiteness in Isaiah 35:10, which states, 'And the ransomed of the Lord shall return and come to Zion with singing; everlasting joy shall be upon their heads; they shall obtain gladness and joy, and sorrow and sighing shall flee away'. Here is the great object and goal of God's everlasting covenant—that all, every one, of *'those who are called may receive the promised inheritance'*. That object and goal is most gloriously fulfilled through the one who *'is the mediator of a new covenant'*.

Still in connection with these intents and outcomes of the new covenant is what follows here in 9:15: *'since a death has occurred that redeems them from the transgressions committed under the first covenant'*. At his last supper with his disciples, as they gathered together so poignantly in the upper room in Jerusalem, Jesus said these words to them when he took the cup: 'This cup that is poured out for you is the new covenant in my blood' (Luke 22:20). It was by virtue of his death that Jesus acted as mediator of the new covenant, and that death was redemptive. Mention was made in 9:12 of Jesus' death 'securing an eternal redemption', and that truth is pressed home now. As has been insisted all along (in Hebrews itself, and so in this commentary), the redemptive, saving, work of Jesus upon the cross worked 'both ways' or 'in both directions'. That is to say, it covered *'the transgressions'* committed by all those living in old covenant days who looked on to Jesus as their Saviour, and it covers similarly all *'the transgressions'* of those who, living in new covenant days, look back by faith to all that Jesus accomplished on the cross. 'There is therefore now no condemnation for those who are in Christ Jesus' (Romans 8:1), and it does not matter at what point they lived. The cross (and resurrection) of the Lord Jesus Christ is the hinge of all history.

In order to make these deep and precious things as clear as possible, our writer now employs the illustration of a will. *'For where a will* [or 'testament', the same word thus far translated 'covenant', which can carry either sense depending upon the context] *is involved, the death of the one who made it must be established. For a will takes effect only at death, since it is not in force as long as the one who made it is alive'* (9:16–17). Readers will no doubt be familiar with the picture here. When someone makes a will (an important thing to do, rather than to leave things for others to sort out after you've gone), it can be changed as many times as they like during their lifetime. Someone can be 'brought in' to a will for an inheritance, and someone can be 'cut out' of a will and no longer receive what was originally intended for them. Either way, the will itself will only come into force when *'the one who made it'* is dead. You may know in advance that you are to inherit a vast amount of money, a business, a stately home, or whatever, in someone's will. But none of it will actually be yours until the will-maker has died and the will is at last *'in force'*. At that point, everything within the will is not only fixed and final but must be put into practice. No alterations can be allowed. So this is the illustration, but why is it given here?

We made the point much earlier in the commentary, that where God's covenant is concerned it is not an agreement which has been worked out mutually between parties. Rather, God alone has set the terms of *his* covenant and has, we might say, 'gifted' it to us. Like the will, however, this covenant requires a death to take place in order for all its benefits and blessings—all the inheritance—to be made over to those to whom it is promised (those named in the will). That is exactly what has happened in the gospel. There is the covenant (the new covenant). There has been a death (that of Jesus at Calvary). So the covenant (the will) is now fully in force and cannot be altered or annulled. All its legacies are freely available. All that the Lord Jesus Christ has secured for sinners by his death (the 'eternal redemption' of 9:12 and the 'eternal inheritance' of 9:15) is now fully and freely available for his people, to whom it belongs, comprising ultimately that 'great multitude that no one could number, from every nation, from all tribes and peoples and languages, standing before the throne and before the Lamb, clothed in white robes, with palm branches in their hands, and crying out with a loud voice, "Salvation belongs to our God who sits on the throne, and to the Lamb!"' (Revelation 7:9–10). And all have this in common—saved by grace!

All of this being so, our writer moves from the will to the blood, from the fact established that a will requires the one who made it to have died before it comes into force, to the fact that the covenant of God also hinges upon a death in order for the fullness of *its* blessings to come into force. *'Therefore not even the first covenant was inaugurated without blood'* (9:18). He begins with *'the first covenant'* before proceeding to the new covenant.

Back we go to Moses and the Sinai covenant. When it was *'inaugurated'*, the inauguration was *'not ... without blood'*, which is a way of saying that it involved a blood-shedding sacrifice. This event is recorded in Exodus 24, as our present passage goes on to affirm. *'For when every commandment of the law had been declared by Moses to all the people* [all that is contained in Exodus 20–23], *he took the blood of calves and goats, with water and scarlet wool and hyssop* [all this would have been in strict accordance with the divine command, not Moses making things up as he went along], *and sprinkled both the book itself* ['the Book of the Covenant', Exodus 24:7] *and all the people, saying 'This is the blood of the covenant that God commanded for you'* [quoting Exodus 24:8]' (9:19–20).

It is true that there are certain discrepancies between Exodus 24 and Hebrews 9. In Exodus, for example, oxen are mentioned, but not *'calves and goats'*; the blood is recorded as sprinkled upon the people but not upon *'the book'*; and *'water, scarlet wool and hyssop'* receive no mention. Does this present us with a problem? No. It is certainly the case that in the overall ceremonial system prescribed by God in the Old Testament these 'missing' items have their roles, and it may be that our writer was making a more broad-brush statement here in Hebrews 9, rather than fixing his thoughts exclusively upon the Exodus 24 narrative. If this is so, it accords with his major emphasis that blood sacrifice was of the essence where the old covenant was concerned, just as it is (he will shortly come on to say again) with the new. When we come in a moment to 9:22 he will tell us that 'under the law almost everything is purified with blood', and that may be taken to include *'both the book itself and all the people'*.

It is very striking that the blood with which Moses performed all this sprinkling is called *'the blood of the covenant'*. This highlights the fact that on the Exodus 24 occasion all that took place happened in connection with the people committing themselves to wholehearted obedience to all the words of the covenant. They declared 'with one voice' in Exodus 24:3, before the sprinkling, and after Moses had read aloud in their hearing all that God had spoken, 'All the words that the LORD has spoken we will do'. Indeed, the full quotation from Exodus 24:8 (upon the gist of which our writer draws in 9:20) reads, 'Behold the blood of the covenant that the LORD has made with you in accordance with all these words'.

*'And in the same way he* [Moses] *sprinkled with the blood both the tent and all the vessels used in worship'* (9:21). This was on a different occasion, of course, from that in Exodus 24 which has just been touched upon, and refers to the consecration and dedication of '*the tent and all the vessels*' once everything had been made according to the divine pattern. It is mentioned here to serve as a further underscoring of the importance of blood under the first covenant. And to press this even further, the writer of Hebrews continues: *'Indeed under the law almost everything is purified with blood'* (9:22). By *'under the law'* is meant the law of God given to Moses and delivered to and for the people. The phrase *'almost everything'* indicates that there were exceptions to this rule, although not many. Two such instances were the offering of fine flour rather than two turtledoves or two pigeons for the sin offering, which the poor person could bring (Leviticus 5), and the purification by fire and water of metal objects captured in war (Numbers 31).

The climax of the argument regarding the importance of the blood is now stated. All of these things were so (and necessarily so) for this crucial and fundamental reason: *'and without the shedding of blood there is no forgiveness of sins'*. Here is the stark nub: no blood, no forgiveness. And, remembering the 'how much more' line of reasoning which our writer used earlier in the chapter (see 9:14), what was the rule with all the Old Testament ceremonial (the type and shadow) is all the more the rule with the new covenant (the fulfilment and reality). It has always been the case, in God's dealings with sinful man and sinful man's relationship with God, that there must be '*the shedding of blood*' if there is to be *'forgiveness of sins'*. This is God's way, his only and his non-negotiable way. It may not be the way that proud man would choose, but therein lies the problem. Sin, and pride through sin, separate the sinner from God. Only blood shed in sacrifice can mend the breach, and the vast amount of blood shed under the old covenant continually strained forward to the once for all *'shedding of blood'* which is at the heart of the gospel of God's grace.

## The two appearings (9:23–28)

The whole thrust of this chapter so far (and of more of Hebrews than only the present chapter) has been building up to what now follows in these verses and then on into chapter 10. Here the Lord Jesus Christ is displayed in his all-sufficiency and glory.

*'Thus it was necessary for the copies of the heavenly things to be purified with these rites* [all the things we have just been considering], *but the heavenly things themselves with better sacrifices than these'* (9:23). There is a recollection here immediately of 8:5, where we were told that the priests of old 'serve a copy and shadow of the heavenly things', whereas Jesus is 'a minister in the holy places, in the true tent that the Lord set up, not man' (8:2). Now we understand about the purification of *'the copies of the heavenly things'*, but how are we to understand the need for *'the heavenly things themselves'* to be purified? On the face of it, this appears strange.

Something of a clue is provided in the fact that *'the heavenly things themselves'* were to be purified *'with better sacrifices than these'* (*'these'* being the former rites and ceremonies). The *'better sacrifices'* comprised the one sacrifice which the Lord Jesus, the mediator of the new covenant, made of himself, 'a single sacrifice for sins' which he offered 'for all time' (10:12). Without question it is *'better'*, for it did what all that went before it had not done.

But still a puzzle remains concerning the necessity for the purifying of *'the heavenly things'*. If they are heavenly, then surely they must be pure in their very nature and being (even as Jesus himself is), and so in no need of being purified. Since God dwells in heaven in all his purity and holiness, how can the place need purifying or cleansing? Yet 9:23 says exactly what it says. This is without question a difficult verse, and a variety of explanations have been offered from various quarters, but the truth being asserted here appears to be this. It is not that heaven itself is somehow in need of cleansing, for it has not been defiled. Rather we are to understand the *'better sacrifices'* as purifying heaven for our entrance in this sense: just as the earthly tabernacle was purified by the blood sacrifices that were offered there, in order that sinners might approach God acceptably, even so (by way of analogy) the heavenly places, on the basis of far *'better sacrifices'* than the previous abundance, are made open and accessible for all who rest upon the Lord Jesus, that we may dwell in the very presence of God and worship him 'with reverence and awe' (12:28).

The plural *'sacrifices'* in respect of Jesus' single sacrifice is a linguistic way of emphasising the very singleness of his sacrifice. His *one* sacrifice was in every way excellent, and replaced all the *many* sacrifices of old. By way of illustration, all the different burnt, grain, peace, sin and guilt offerings under the old covenant were both gathered up in and superseded by Jesus' sacrifice.

The writer continues with these deep things. *'For Christ has entered* [in his resurrection, ascension and glorification], *not into holy places made with hands* [the earthly tabernacle in the wilderness], *which are copies of the true things, but into heaven itself, now to appear in the presence of God on our behalf'* (9:24). Our writer eliminates the negative (*'not into'*) in order then to accentuate the positive (*'but into'*). Two things in particular, both of great beauty, merit comment. Jesus' entering into heaven was a magnificent occasion. It is especially precious to see it in the light of two texts concerning Jesus in John's gospel. John 13:3 records this: 'Jesus knowing that the Father had given all things into his hands, and that he had come from God and was going back to God'. Then there are his own words in John 17:4–5, 'I glorified you on earth, having accomplished the work that you gave me to do. And now, Father, glorify me in your presence with the glory that I had with you before the world existed'. This event of Jesus' return to heaven (from which he had come), is also magnificently set forth by prophecy in the second part of Psalm 24, with the glorious imagery of the gates lifting up their heads, and the ancient doors being lifted up, 'that the King of glory may come in' (Psalm 24:7).

The other thing which catches the eye with great joy is the

reference to Jesus appearing *'in the presence of God on our behalf'*. Interestingly, this is the second of four mentions of the verb 'appear' in fairly short compass in Hebrews 9. The first was in verse 11, 'when Christ appeared as a high priest of the good things that have come', referring to the wealth of new covenant blessings that are ours through him. The third will be along shortly in verse 26, referring to when he 'appeared once for all at the end of the ages', namely his life on earth leading to his death on the cross. The fourth will be in verse 28, speaking of when Jesus 'will appear a second time', looking on to his second coming. And in second place is our present instance here in verse 24, where the emphasis is upon the Lord Jesus appearing *'in the presence of God on our behalf'*.

That phrase, *'in the presence of God'*, carries the literal sense of 'before the face of God', and is an expression indicating great intimacy and (in the best and most spiritual sense of the word) familiarity. It is, of course, Jesus' presence there which is the guarantee of ours also, who are united to him, whereas the high priest of old entered the Most Holy Place always and only on his own, and that was it. Indeed, in title (we may say) we are there even now, in the gospel sense, for God 'has raised us up with him and seated us with him in the heavenly places in Christ Jesus' (Ephesians 2:6). All that remains (in one sense) is for us actually to arrive!

While no exposition is given by our writer of what Jesus is doing *'in the presence of God on our behalf'*, there is a clear link in thought and doctrine with 7:25, and the mention there of Jesus' constant intercession for us in heaven, that being (as we saw) part of his ongoing high priestly ministry. See further our comments on that verse. It is necessary to re-emphasise that he is not there with verbal pleading, neither is he having to persuade an otherwise unwilling Father to bless us. His very presence in heaven is the key thing necessary for us. He is our mediator, our advocate and our representative, who 'calls his own sheep by name' (John 10:3). The present active nature of this ministry is underlined with the use of the word *'now'*. It is from heaven that the Lord Jesus pours out his Holy Spirit upon us (Acts 2:33), supplies gifts for service (Ephesians 4:8), and looks forward with great joy and anticipation to welcoming us there to be with him for ever (John 17:24).

*'Nor was it to offer himself repeatedly, as the high priest enters the holy places every year with blood not his own, for then he would have had to suffer repeatedly since the foundation of the world. But as it is, he has appeared once for all at the end of the ages to put away sin by the sacrifice of himself'* (9:25–26)'. Holding all of this together, here is another reminder of (1) the many sacrifices (*'repeatedly'*) as opposed to the one sacrifice (*'at the end of the ages'*); (2) the annual Day of Atonement (*'every year'*) compared with the one Calvary event (*'once for all'*); (3) the blood brought by the high priests which was outside of themselves (*'not his own'*) and (in contrast) the blood of the one who was himself both priest and victim (*'the sacrifice of himself'*); and (4) the continual reminder of sins year by year (*'every year with blood'*) now replaced by the dealing with sin as a result of the perfect (and so complete and finished) work of the Lord Jesus Christ (*'to put away sin'*).

Two other comments need to be made. Firstly, the reference to *'since the foundation of the world'* is a solemn reminder of how sin entered the world so very early, and so how atonement was necessary from then on. This itself reminds us of the lovely description of Jesus as 'the Lamb (having been) slain from the foundation of the world' (Revelation 13:8, literal order of words in Greek). The writer is emphasising the central truth of the gospel that, if Jesus' sacrifice had been just like the sacrifices of old, *'then he would have had to suffer repeatedly since the foundation of the world'*. In other words, his sacrifices and sufferings would have gone on and on and on. Had that been the case, it would have argued for a fatal inadequacy and ineffectiveness in his work, as well as falling at the fence of the fact that a person *can* only die once anyway. His sacrifice, however, has been made, his sufferings are over, and he has entered into heaven. Herein is no small part of his glory.

Secondly, the reference to *'the end of the ages'* links in with what will be said in verse 28 concerning the reference there to Jesus' two appearings (his first coming and his second coming). There is an indissoluble link between these two events, for while, as has already been urged, the cross and resurrection provide together the hinge of history, it will be Jesus' return which will provide its climax. Everything prior to that first event was leading up to it, and everything after that leads up to the second event. The two need to be held together, as indeed they are in the sovereign purposes of God. Each is a revelation or a manifestation of him, and it is these two comings which themselves actually constitute '*the end of the ages*', giving it meaning and relevance. The actual phrase used here is reminiscent of other New Testament phrases, such as 'the close of the age' (Matthew 13:39, in Jesus' explanation of his parable of the wheat and the weeds), 'the end of the age' (Matthew 28:20, at the close of his great commission), 'the fullness of time' (Galatians 4:4, where Paul is treating of Jesus' incarnation happening at God's set time), and 'the last times' (1 Peter 1:20, dealing with Christ's work).

'*And just as it is appointed for man to die once, and after that comes judgment, so Christ, having been offered once to bear the sins of many*' (9:27–28), the magnificent argument continues. There is a fundamental statement here concerning the mortality of man, every man. Death is the great leveller. Here all mankind (male and female, young and old, rich and poor, great and small) are in the same position, and all the distinctions that are often made so much of between one person and another come to nothing. After death comes judgment, for 'we all stand before the judgment seat of God' and 'then each of us will give an account of himself to God' (Romans 14:10,12). God 'has fixed a day on which he will judge the world in righteousness by a man whom he has appointed; and of this he has given assurance to all by raising him from the dead' (Acts 17:31). It is impossible to escape death, and so equally impossible to escape judgment.

Very solemnly it is decreed that '*it is appointed for man to die once*'. This is the judgment '*appointed*' by God, for he it is who declares, 'the soul who sins shall die' (Ezekiel 18:4). Yet it was in order to deal with this very desperate predicament that we are all in, that Jesus came into the world in the first place. In the eternal plan of salvation it was determined that Jesus, as true man for our sakes (yet without sin), would *'die once'*, and in that death would face *'judgment'*, the divine judgment due upon us for our own sin. He has identified with our humanity in the most amazing way. The substitute has taken our place. The one who 'knew no sin' was 'made ... to be sin' for us. To what end? To this end: 'so that in him we might become the righteousness of God' (2 Corinthians 5:21). This is all God's doing. Christ has *'been offered once* [a single and unique sacrifice] *to bear the sin of many'*. This recalls the great testimony of John the Baptist concerning Jesus: 'Behold the Lamb of God, who takes away the sin of the world!' (John 1:29).

Jesus' second coming in its relation to his first coming is seen now in clear view: *'so Christ, having been offered once to bear the sins of many, will appear a second time, not to deal with sin but to save those who are eagerly waiting for him'*. Jesus' first coming was in order to deal with sin. Our writer has made plain how he has done this (*'having been offered once to bear the sins of many'*), and the fact that he is referred to here as *'Christ'* is a further thrust in the direction of the Hebrews to remind them that it is the Messiah he is writing about, the Messiah they are showing signs of abandoning. His second coming (when he *'will appear a second time'*) will be *'not to deal with sin'* (literally, 'without sin' or 'apart from sin'—identical wording with 4:15, though while there indicating Jesus' sinlessness, here indicating rather the sense in which it is translated in our version).

For what purpose, then, will it be? For another (though closely related) purpose, namely, *'but to save those who are eagerly waiting for him'*. The sequence is obvious: the first time, Jesus came to save sinners; the second time, he will come for those he has saved, in order to gather them to himself for ever. Such are attractively described as *'those who are eagerly waiting for him'*. These words form an essential part of the portrait (and test) of a true Christian—they wait *'eagerly'*, longingly, expectantly, for him. They long to see him. They long to be with him. Jesus, in his final promise recorded in Scripture, says to his church (his bride), 'Surely I am coming soon'; to which his church responds to him (her bridegroom), 'Come, Lord Jesus!' (Revelation 22:20). It is a precious truth that, having come the first time to humiliation, rejection, suffering and death, the Lord Jesus *'will appear a second time'* in victory and triumph, to honour and to glory.

What a grand day that of the return of the Lord Jesus Christ will be for all *'those who are eagerly waiting for him'*. On that day, Jesus will appear suddenly, personally, visibly, gloriously and inescapably (compare, for example, Acts 1:11 and Revelation 1:7). It will be the day of his and our vindication, the day of the coming together of bridegroom and bride, the day when 'we shall be like him, for we shall see him as he is' (1 John 3:2), the day when the transient things that are seen will give way to the eternal things which for so long have been unseen (see 2 Corinthians 4:18), the day (more than ever before) of 'joy that is inexpressible and filled with glory' (1 Peter 1:8), the day which will last for ever and ever, for 'full day' (Proverbs 4:18) will at last have dawned. The other side of the coin, of course, in biblical faithfulness, is that it will be a day of 'fearful expectation of judgment' (10:27 of Hebrews), for, without Christ as your Saviour, 'It is a fearful thing to fall into the hands of the living God' (10:31).

Before proceeding to the next chapter, the practical question does arise: how should we conduct ourselves in the meantime, since 'concerning that day or that hour [that is, as to when it will take place], no one knows' (Mark 13:32). One part of the answer to the question is that we should 'Stay awake' (Mark 13:37), 'be ready' (Matthew 24:44, 'for the Son of Man is coming at an hour you do not expect'), 'Watch' (Matthew 25:13). The other part of the answer is supplied by Peter, when dealing with this subject of Jesus' return: 'what sort of people ought you to be in lives of holiness and godliness, waiting for and hastening the coming of the day of God' (2 Peter 3:11–12). What a word to the straying Hebrews, and what a word to the rest of us. Are you, dear reader, *'eagerly waiting for him'*?

# Chapter 10
# No turning back

The wise teacher will know when to make appropriate use of repetition—not necessarily by merely repeating the same thing over again precisely as before, but going over the same ground, exploring a different angle, drawing out a fresh application, and so on, in order to press things home securely. In this, the writer to the Hebrews excels. As we move into a new chapter, there is, as we would expect by now, no change of fundamental theme. Still he is passionately and single-mindedly determined to set forth the absolute superiority of the Lord Jesus Christ, especially where his priesthood and sacrifice is concerned, over all that went before him and pointed to him in Old Testament times.

Chapter 9 ended on the note of Jesus' two appearings—his first (which has taken place) 'to bear the sins of many', and his second (which is yet to take place) 'not to deal with sin but to save those who are eagerly waiting for him'. In between these two appearings, (in other words, 'now' for the Hebrews and 'now' for us), the Christian lives of God's people, 'the ransomed of the Lord' (Isaiah 35:10 and 51:11), are being lived, from one generation to the next.

In broad terms, chapter 10 falls into three sections of differing lengths: verses 1–18, verses 19–25 and verses 26–39.

## A fourfold declaration (10:1–18)

### (1) A sheer impossibility (10:1–4)

The inadequacy of the shadows and the sufficiency of the realities continues to be opened up in this portion. Back in 9:11 we learned of 'when Christ appeared as a high priest of the good things that have come', and now we have this: *'For since the law has but a shadow of the good things to come instead of the true form* [image, actual manifestation] *of these realities'* (10:1). These two verses clearly belong together, indeed they mirror each other. To begin with there was *'a shadow of the good things to come'*, while now these good things have come—and the reason is that the Lord Jesus Christ, in all the matchless fullness of his person and his work, has fulfilled the types, dispersed the shadows, and shed forth his glorious light.

The *'shadow'* is related here to *'the law'*. This mention of God's law (the law of Moses, as it is sometimes called, although, of course, it was God's and not Moses') is because all the functions and ministries that the priests and Levites performed were laid down in the law. Every detail and requirement of that law had to be obeyed precisely. There was no room for adjustment or human preference. And so it was, until *'the true form of these realities'* arrived. Once Jesus had accomplished and completed his own sacrificial work, there was no place remaining (and there remains no place remaining) for any human priests, altars, sacrifices, or any such thing. Any who believe or practise otherwise are grievously mistaken.

As we have already learned in Hebrews, it was in the very nature of the former arrangement that *'it can never, by the same sacrifices that are continually offered every year* [and every day in many cases, although the annual Day of Atonement is still what is chiefly in view here], *make perfect* [in the sense of conformity to God] *those who draw near'*. How may we be sure of that? The answer is obvious: *'Otherwise, would they not have ceased to be offered, since the worshippers, having once been cleansed, would no longer have any consciousness* [or, 'conscience', referring to continuing guilt and fear of condemnation] *of sin?'* (10:2). In other words, if their sins had truly been dealt with as a result of all those sacrifices, the sacrifices could have ceased being offered there and then, and the people would have pressed forward in the full assurance that all was permanently well between themselves and God. There would have been neither need for nor point in continuing the sacrificial process. But cleansing was not available by these sacrifices themselves. No perfection was available. Indeed the result was the very opposite, for rather than deal with sin, the sacrifices reminded of sin. *'But* (or, 'But in fact') *in these sacrifices there is a reminder* [a calling to mind] *of sin every year'* (10:3). They reminded, but they did not remove.

It is not, for all their inadequacy, that there was no meaning or value at all in the many sacrifices (in the sense of God appointing something which was utterly meaningless and valueless), for by them the people were not allowed to forget the holiness and majesty of God, they were brought to a regular acknowledgment of their own sinfulness, and they had kept consistently in view before them the one to whom all the sacrifices pointed to. But their placing their hope in the sacrifices themselves was a false hope.

The question might be raised about sin in our lives compared with sin in the lives of God's people of old, since though sinners saved by grace we are sinners still. The position is this. In our own case, if we are Christians, it remains the case that (sadly) still we sin and still we need to be coming before God with 'godly grief' (2 Corinthians 7:10), asking for the fresh forgiveness of sins committed. No further sacrifice for sin is necessary on that account, however, and that is a fundamental difference between how things were before Calvary and how they are since Calvary. The matter is illustrated helpfully in the upper room instance of Jesus washing the disciples' feet. When he came to Peter, the disciple was keen to have not only his feet washed 'but also my hands and my head'. To him, Jesus replied, 'The one who has bathed does not need to wash except for his feet, but is completely clean' (John 13:9–10). The point is that, where sin in the Christian life is concerned, we do not go back to the beginning all over again and need a fresh sacrifice (after the Old Testament manner). What do we do? We go again, and as often as we need, to the fountain that remains open, 'to cleanse (us) from sin and uncleanness' (Zechariah 13:1). In other words, we avail ourselves afresh of the ongoing efficacy of Jesus' one sacrifice. We do not seek another, for 'the blood of Jesus (God's) Son cleanses [that is, goes on cleansing] us from all sin' (1 John 1:7).

We can picture the situation. Every year, on this special divinely appointed day (remember the Leviticus 16 account of it), the priest would go through all the prescribed rituals concerning both his own and the people's sins, only then the following year to do the same thing all over again, and the next year, and the year after that, and on and on, one year after another. Instead of their sins being put away, they were continually being brought to the fore. The burden of sin and guilt upon their consciences remained intact. There was no escape, except for those sinners who were enabled, through faith, to look 'through' the types and shadows to the reality. 'These are a shadow of the things to come, but the substance belongs to Christ' (Colossians 2:17). That is why our writer could speak in verse 1 of 'the good things to come'—they have come! A shadow has to have a substance or reality, otherwise there would be no shadow. Your shadow is a shadow of you, and if there was no you then you would cast no shadow. But the shadow is not the substance and should never be thought to be so.

'*For it is impossible for the blood of bulls and goats to take away sins*' (10:4). How could they possibly do so? They were never intended to do so! The sheer impossibility mentioned here is inevitable. Things could not be otherwise. The fact that the same thing (whatever it might be) has to keep on being done over and over again speaks volumes of its fundamental inadequacy. The plain fact is that '*bulls and goats'* were in no position to help sinners, however much of their blood was sacrificed, or how often. Although 'without the shedding of blood there is no forgiveness of sins' (9:22), other blood was needed. Another sacrifice would have to be offered. And to this the chapter now turns.

## (2) A rich provision (10:5–10)

We now revisit the coming of 'the good things', which is established by means of a very pertinent messianic scripture from Psalm 40. This gives us yet another instance of how the writer to the Hebrews illustrates and secures his case by bringing Scripture proof from the Old Testament. Let Christians never despise this extensive and highly significant portion of the whole Word of God. Our Bibles do not commence with Matthew's gospel!

*'Consequently, when Christ* [strictly, 'he', but unmistakably referring to Christ, he 'who is God over all, blessed forever' (Romans 9:5); the one who, 'though he was rich, yet for (our) sake he became poor, so that (we) by his poverty might become rich' (2 Corinthians 8:9)] *came into the world'* (10:5), provides a reminder of the event to which all that went before it in biblical revelation had been moving. 'And we have seen and testify that the Father has sent the Son to be the Saviour of the world' (1 John 4:14). Or as Paul states it, 'The saying is trustworthy and deserving of full acceptance, that Christ Jesus came into the world to save sinners' (1 Timothy 1:15). Notice in both of those examples the direct line between Jesus' coming into the world and the reason why he came into the world—to die.

What an utterly remarkable event the incarnation of the Lord Jesus Christ was. There is for us an eternity's worth of meditation to be found in it. Here something of the secret of what was being planned in the eternal counsels of the Godhead is revealed. We see the wisdom and grace of God the Father, the compassion and obedience of God the Son, and the complete involvement and concurrence of God the Holy Spirit in our salvation planned (in eternity), accomplished (on the cross) and applied (in the new birth). Here is mystery and miracle most gloriously combined. Here is divine and holy love.

The quotation which now follows (Psalm 40:6–8) is truly messianic. Although David wrote the psalm, its depths of meaning go far beyond anything that could apply to him. These are the very words of Jesus, hence *'he said'*. What did he say? *'Sacrifices and offerings you have not desired* [a further reminder that more of what had for so long been all too familiar is not God's design in sending his Son into the world], *but a body have you prepared for me* [a rich stating of the humanity of Christ, this is the wonder and mystery of the incarnation, that 'the Word became flesh and dwelt among us, and we have seen his glory, glory as of the only Son from the Father, full of grace and truth', John 1:14)]; *in burnt offerings and sin offerings you have taken no pleasure* [it was God himself, of course, who commanded these and other offerings, but by this statement from the psalm we understand that it was not his pleasure or intent that they would be the things which would accomplish the work of dealing with sin—rather, as we have seen, they foresaw the one upon whom the Father's pleasure rested, whose sacrifice of himself would do so, and would do so completely and forever] ' (10:5–6).

It ought to be noted (not least in order to avoid confusion) that if you look up Psalm 40:6 in your Bible you will not find the words *'a body you have prepared for me'*. What you will find is, 'but you have given me an open ear', or 'ears you have dug for me'. What explains this discrepancy? The reason is as follows. In the third century BC the Hebrew Old Testament was translated into Greek. We call this translation the Septuagint, or, for short, the LXX (the Roman number 70, since it is reckoned that the translation was the work of 70 Jewish scholars). It is often the case that the New Testament writers, when quoting from the Old Testament, use this Greek version rather than the actual Hebrew one. The writer to the Hebrews is one of these, and our present case with Psalm 40 is an instance of this. It has been suggested that the Greek version is merely a freer rendering of the Hebrew (combining the twin elements of hearing and doing), or that the ear is mentioned as being representative of the body (in that you would be unlikely to have an ear without a body). Whether this is so or not, the meaning intended is the same in either rendering, namely that of the Son's obedience to the Father's will—the very thing which is emphasized as the quotation now continues.

With all of this in mind, it is very striking to observe that four different words are used in respect of sacrifice here: 'sacrifices' and 'offerings' (verse 5), 'burnt offerings' and 'sin offerings' (verse 6). It would appear that these four terms cover all the main offerings which God required under the Levitical system (the peace, meal, burnt and sin offerings)—yet none of them, even taken together, gave God pleasure in the way that his Son's sacrifice did when it came to dealing with the problem of sin at its root.

*'Then I said, 'Behold, I have come to do your will, O God* [underscoring the Son's obedience to the Father in all things and at all times, and his pleasure and delight in rendering that obedience, not merely his consent to it], *as it is written of me in the scroll of the book* [there may be a hint here of the 'book' of God's eternal counsel, though it refers especially in the present context to the law of Moses, yet is also true ultimately of the entire body of the Old Testament Scriptures, the whole of which speaks of the Lord Jesus—'it is they that bear witness about me', John 5:39; 'These are my words that I spoke to you while I was still with you, that everything written about me in the Law of Moses and the Prophets and the Psalms must be fulfilled', Luke 24:44] (10:7). What a beautiful illustration and affirmation this gives us of the Lord Jesus' love of Scripture, and his giving himself with focus and precision to willing obedience to it, for the Father's glory and (wonder of wonders) for our salvation. May we all be like him in this—Christlikeness is exceedingly practical!

The *'will'* of God here, which Jesus came so willingly to do, is a reference to his gracious saving design of having a people who shall 'be holy and blameless before him' (Ephesians 1:4), 'a people for his own possession' (1 Peter 2:9), a favoured company to whom he gives 'a name better than sons and daughters' (Isaiah 56:5), a blessed gathering whose 'citizenship is in heaven' (Philippians 3:20), a bride for his Son at 'the marriage of the Lamb' (Revelation 19:7). Had God wished to accomplish this by animal sacrifices, then (we say reverently) he could have done so. But that was not his design. Rather, 'he did not spare his own Son but gave him up for us all' (Romans 8:32). It was the Son's delight to perform every single detail that was needful to fulfil the Father's exact requirements regarding the grand scheme of redemption.

What the writer does next is to make one or two remarks upon the Psalm 40 passage, to help us understand as clearly as possible its relevance to his over-riding theme. Moreover, what he writes here relates to what we learned in chapter 8 concerning the two covenants. *'When he* [Jesus, from whose lips the words of the psalm come] *said above, "You have neither desired nor taken pleasure in sacrifices and offerings and burnt offerings and sin offerings" (these are offered according to the law), then he added, "Behold, I have come to do your will"'(10:8–9).* This is no needless repetition of the verses that have just gone before, as is seen in what he is leading up to: *'He abolishes the first in order to establish the second'.* All the many and varied offerings that were *'offered according to the law'* are finished, done away with, the reason being that they belonged to the terms of the first (old) covenant, and that covenant Jesus has abolished *'in order to establish the second'.* The second (new) covenant is established through the sacrifice of Jesus upon the cross, and of this covenant he is the mediator (9:15). As Jesus said at the Last Supper (which was itself his institution for his church of the Lord's Supper), 'This cup that is poured out for you is the new covenant in my blood' (Luke 22:20). It might be objected that nowhere in this section is the term 'covenant' mentioned; yet while that is true, the whole concept of 'covenant' is surely in the background here, for every 'part' of Hebrews fits in precisely with the 'whole'.

*'And by that will we have been sanctified through the offering of the body of Jesus Christ once for all'* (10:10). The phrase *'once for all'* (a single word in the Greek) provides another fine statement of the complete and unrepeatable nature of our Saviour's sacrifice. In a heart-warming way our writer includes himself in what he writes here (*'we',* rather than 'you').

The important relationship between our justification and our sanctification is something we shall comment upon when we come shortly to verse 14, but an important marker on the subject is laid down here in the present verse. Jesus' offering himself for us at Calvary *'once for all'* purchases our redemption, for it is the offering of the one who (as he himself says) came 'to give his life as a ransom for many' (Matthew 20:28). That same blood, that same offering, however, provides us not only with cleansing and forgiveness but with sanctification also, in the sense that in being reconciled to God and brought into fellowship with him we are set apart (a basic meaning of sanctification) for him and to him. In this connection, 1 Corinthians 1:30 is important, where we learn that God (the Father) has made his Son both 'our righteousness and sanctification', the two together rather than either one without the other. It is also noteworthy that in verse 10 it is stated *'we have been sanctified'*, while verse 14 speaks of us *'being sanctified'*. Again, we shall reserve comment for 10:14. All of this, Hebrews here declares, is *'by that will'*, *'that'* incorporating the will of both the Father and the Son, who share one will. All that Jesus did was according to the will of God, from which he never departed.

## (3) A clear contrast (10:11–14)

We mentioned at the head of this chapter the benefit of well-chosen repetition, and the verses now under consideration are a classic example of that very thing. Here the writer to the Hebrews reviews and summarises some of the key features of the contrast between the priesthood of Old Testament days and that of the Lord Jesus Christ. It is almost as if he had two columns, one for each, in which these contrasts are highlighted.

*'And every priest stands daily at his service, offering repeatedly the same sacrifices, which can never take away sins. But when Christ had offered for all time a single sacrifice for sins, he sat down at the right hand of God'* (10:11–12). The contrast runs like this.

- There were many priests (*'every priest'*), each taking their turn, morning and evening, day by day, but only one Lord Jesus Christ (*'But when Christ'* [literally 'he', or with the sense of 'this one, this priest']).

- There were endless sacrifices (*'offering repeatedly the same sacrifices'*), but with Christ there was only one sacrifice (*'offered for all time a single sacrifice'*).

- The former priests stood up, with no mention anywhere of any seats in the tabernacle furniture, for their work was never finished (*'stands daily'*), whereas Christ, having offered his single and unique sacrifice, sat down (*'he sat down at the right hand of God'*) in the place of highest honour, all his work completed, divine justice satisfied, salvation absolutely secured (compare 1:3, 'After making purification for sins, he sat down at the right hand of the Majesty on high').

- The old covenant sacrifices, however many of them there were and however varied, could not deal with sin or in themselves provide forgiveness (*'which can never take away sins'*), while full and free forgiveness is available for the sinner on account of Jesus' sacrifice, as is indicated by the finished nature of his work (*'he sat down'*).

Although seated, we know very well already from Hebrews that our Lord Jesus Christ is in no sense inactive (remember 7:25). The emphasis being made is rather that of the end of his sacrificial work, with nothing to add to it in any way. It is done—as Jesus himself proclaimed, uttering 'It is finished' (John 19:30) from the cross. Yet our writer has something highly significant to add concerning Jesus in his regal seated state—namely that he is *'waiting from that time* [the time when he sat down in heaven] *until his enemies* [all who array themselves against him and seek to hinder or resist his purposes] *should be made a footstool for his feet'* (10:13).

A great deal has been made in this book so far of Psalm 110, particularly with respect to Jesus and Melchizedek. Strong shades of that psalm are present again now, for it begins with these words: 'The LORD [God the Father] says to my Lord [God the Son]: "Sit at my right hand, until I make your enemies my footstool"' (Psalm 110:1). In the latter verses of the psalm, moreover, David writes of Jesus that 'he will shatter kings on the day of his wrath', 'execute judgment on the nations', 'shatter chiefs over the wide earth', 'drink from the brook by the way' (that being a symbol of the conquering victor) and, finally, 'he will lift up his head'. This all hints at the final victory and glory that will come to the Lord Jesus at the final judgment, although that is not to say that it does not have 'partial' fulfilments along the way throughout history, for indeed it does.

As well as Psalm 110, there is an echo also of Psalm 8:6 ('you have put all things under his feet'), reference to which was made in 2:8 of Hebrews, where the comment was made that, 'At present, we do not yet see everything in subjection to him'. Yet there is no danger that Psalms 110 and 8 will not find their fulfilment—no danger at all, for Christ 'must reign until he has put all his enemies under his feet' (1 Corinthians 15:24). He who is prophet and priest is also king, 'King of kings and Lord of lords' (Revelation 19:16). That time must come to pass, announced in Revelation 11:15, 'Then the seventh angel blew his trumpet, and there were loud voices in heaven, saying, "The kingdom of the world has become the kingdom of our Lord and of his Christ, and he shall reign forever and ever"'. All those people, enemies of God all their lives, who dare foolishly and recklessly to make it known that on the last day they will have something to say to God when they see him, will have a surprise. In the language of Romans 3:19, 'every mouth (will) be stopped, and the whole world (will) be held accountable to God'.

It is worth pointing out that there are no less than four references in Hebrews to Jesus being seated, though each has its own nuance. In order of their appearance: in 1:3, it is stated in the context of his radiance and glory; in 8:1, in that of his superior priesthood; in 10:12 (our present instance), in that of the acceptance of his sacrifice; and in 12:2, in that of his perseverance and victory.

10:13 should be a verse bringing tremendous comfort and encouragement to every true believer—and Hebrews was written very much to be a word of encouragement, and remains so for all the Lord's people who read it and meditate upon it. Here is the promise of something we long for more and more as the days go on (and as they often become worse)—the complete vindication of the Lord Jesus Christ. And there is a further comfort and encouragement in that as well—for the day of Jesus' vindication will be the day of his church and people's vindication as well. In familiar Bible imagery, bridegroom and bride will be vindicated together. For this we must wait with patience, with the assurance that in this matter (as in every matter) our God will perform his pleasure in his own time.

*'For by a single offering he* [Jesus] *has perfected for all time those who are being sanctified'* (10:14). As promised when commenting upon verse 10, it is important to say something here about the relationship between our justification and our sanctification. The two are intimately related but fundamentally distinct. In 10:10 it was stated that 'we have been sanctified [note the tense] through the offering of the body of Jesus Christ once for all'. Now notice the tenses of the verbs in 10:14. With regard to Jesus' *'single offering'*, we are told that *'he has perfected for all time those who are being sanctified'*—*'he has perfected'* and *'are being sanctified'*. How do we square something which has been done and which is being done?

The answer is found in what might sound rather a riddle. We both are sanctified and are being sanctified. That is not to state a contradiction. Both parts of the sentence are true, and apply to every believer. It is the contrast between (as it is sometimes expressed) two things: 'definitive' sanctification and 'progressive' sanctification. The former ('definitive') is stated in the verse mentioned in connection with 10:10, namely 1 Corinthians 1:30, where we learn what Jesus has already been made to us. The trio of things there (righteousness, sanctification, redemption) cover the entirety of our Christian experience from conversion to glory, every single shred of which flows from and is dependent upon the Lord Jesus Christ. All of these wonderful things are found in him. None of them is found apart from him. And as the Father looks upon us in his Son (delighting in him, and so, on that account, delighting in us), it is as if we are not only righteous but (even now) holy and glorified as well. Such is the glory of gospel grace!

Yet we know all too well that, while being righteous (right with God) we are certainly neither sanctified (thoroughly holy) nor glorified (in heaven) yet. We *'are being sanctified'*, and will only be completely so (purified 'as he [Christ] is pure', 1 John 3:3) once we are in glory. The process is under way, though. It is 'progressive' in terms of our growing 'in the grace and knowledge of our Lord and Saviour Jesus Christ' (2 Peter 3:18), and will be brought to fruition by the work of the Holy Spirit in due time.

As for how our justification and our sanctification relate to one another while being distinct from one another, we could set things out in this way:

- It is God the Father who justifies us, but God the Holy Spirit who sanctifies us. Both of these works, of course, are in connection with God the Son and his work for us on the cross.

- Justification pardons and removes guilt, while sanctification subdues sin and removes pollution and defilement.

- Justification is unrepeatable and for ever (it has been described as the Christian's 'standing state'), but sanctification is gradual and progressive throughout our life.

- In the work of justification we play no part ('It is God who justifies', Romans 8:33), whereas in the work of sanctification we are very much involved (for example, soaking ourselves in Scripture, praying, resisting the devil, attending the means of grace, and much more), all in dependence upon the Holy Spirit ('the Spirit of holiness', Romans 1:4).

Only the justified will be sanctified, but all the justified will be sanctified—and both, from first to last, are entirely of divine grace.

## (4) A sure testimony (10:15–18)

We are back once again here with the new covenant passage from Jeremiah 31 (or, at least, selections from it) which our writer made so much of in chapter 8. Readers of this commentary may find it worthwhile to revisit the comments on 8:8–13. But this return to the prophecy is for a reason, and not merely for the sake of it. It is prefaced with another magnificent affirmation of the divine inspiration of holy Scripture, for rather than re-introducing the Old

Testament quotation with 'And as Jeremiah says' or 'As the prophet says', or some such thing, we have this: *'And the Holy Spirit also bears witness to us; for after saying'* (10:15), *'then he adds'* (10:17). This could not be clearer. Jeremiah wrote under the direct inspiration of God the Holy Spirit, and so did the writer to the Hebrews. In these days when even sections of the church (let alone the world as a whole) have loosened from the moorings and sailed away from this doctrine of Scripture, we need to trumpet it forth (whether people will receive it or refuse to hear it) and stand firm upon it. Let preaching recover that note of authority which, where the entire Bible is concerned, declares, 'thus says the Lord' and 'this is the word of the Lord'. And let that preaching be continually, closely and relevantly applied to the hearers, which is the very thing the writer of Hebrews is doing here with the material he uses from Jeremiah.

So what does the Holy Spirit say here, and to what does he *'bear witness'* [that is, proclaim the truth]? The answer is found in the fact that this section of Hebrews brings to a climax the entire argument which has been unfolding concerning the superiority of Jesus' priesthood and sacrifice over that of the Old Testament types and shadows of it, and the blessings of the new covenant as superseding all that preceded it under the old. It is as if our writer says, at the peak of his argument, 'this is really true—marvellous and true—even as God, by his Holy Spirit declared from the beginning': *for after saying, "This is the covenant that I will make with them after those days, declares the Lord: I will put my laws on their hearts, and write them on their minds", then he adds, "I will remember their sins and their lawless deeds no more"* (10:16–17). This is what has happened! This is exactly what God has done, just as he said he would do! In place of sins remembered (10:3) there is now sins no longer remembered; in place of external cleansing (10:2), there is now inward transformation. Never will another drop of sacrificial blood ever have to be shed. And so, true to his promise, in no longer remembering our sins, God keeps no record of them, he never brings them to mind. Moreover (as we have just seen in verse 14, and this also part of the Holy Spirit's witness now being mentioned), we are not only justified but sanctified also. So the Hebrews are urged with even greater urgency, as we might express it, to lay hold afresh of new covenant provisions and blessings, to hold firm to the good way of the gospel, to press on in the way of obedience and holiness, to keep (as we shall have it in 12:2), 'looking to Jesus'—and not to turn aside, go back or give up. Is that what you and I are doing?

Our writer does an interesting thing which can be seen upon a comparison of 10:16 with 8:10. In 10:16 God's laws being put on our hearts is mentioned before them being written on our minds, while in 8:10 it is the other way round. This does not present a problem, for New Testament writers sometimes exhibit a measure of 'flexibility' when quoting from the Old Testament, while always preserving carefully the sense. One suggestion for the difference in this case is that the divine order of operation (first addressing our minds before then renewing our hearts) is what is emphasized in 8:10, while the 10:16 order is a reminder to believers that a vital test of knowing whether God's law is truly written on our minds is to seek to discern how well it is engraved upon our hearts.

'*Where there is forgiveness of these* [that is to say, our 'sins' and our 'lawless deeds'], *there is no longer any offering for sin*' (10:18). So much has been insisted upon the single nature of Jesus' sacrifice and offering of himself, both priest and victim, upon the cross, its once-for-all-ness and the unrepeatable nature of it. He has done everything, accomplished everything—so much so that the Son could say to the Father, without any possibility of him being gainsaid, 'I glorified you on earth, having accomplished the work that you gave me to do' (John 17:4). Jesus had announced in Psalm 40, which we found quoted back in 9:7, that he had come to do the will of God, and that is what he has done. As a firm and immovable result of this doing of the divine will ('Christ, having been offered once to bear the sins of many', 9:28), '*there is no longer any offering for sin*' (how could there be, and what would be the point of it?). And the whole of it is 'according to the purpose of his [God's] will, to the praise of his glorious grace, with which he has blessed us [favoured us, accepted us] in the Beloved' (Ephesians 1:5–6). Is there anything more wonderful to rejoice confidently in than this, as we press on in our pilgrim path?

## A fivefold call (10:19–25)

We have now reached a very significant moment in Hebrews. Up until this point the writer has been unfolding with undiminished focus his great theme of the superiority of the Lord Jesus Christ. We have seen how Jesus is superior to the prophets and the angels, as well as to Moses and Aaron. It has been shown how Jesus' priesthood and sacrifice ('You are a priest for ever, after the order of Melchizedek', 5:6) is superior to all that went before him in the Old Testament days. We have been given a clear demonstration of the superiority of the new covenant over the old. In the process there has been much interweaving of one aspect of the over-arching theme with another. Now, from 10:19 onwards, the emphasis is more upon the application of this doctrine—though, as with much choice preaching, our writer's doctrine has been full of application and now his application is still full of doctrine. So it should be. Great privileges bring with them great responsibilities, and never more so than in the things of the Lord.

The key word which reveals this to us is *'Therefore'*, with which this new section begins. It is never enough for us, as Christians, merely to understand the truth. God's truth is powerful and relates to our lives at one point after another. So we must also make a suitable response to it—and that gratefully, willingly, wholeheartedly, self-denyingly and cheerfully. Our attitude must continually be that of Saul of Tarsus (Paul the apostle), 'What shall I do, Lord?' (Acts 22:10). Scripture always demands such a response.

The fivefold call, as we have termed it, is found in verses 22–25, and is preceded by what in musical terms might be called a 'bridge passage' in verses 19–21, which leads seamlessly from pre-10:19 to post-10:19. The entire passage (10:19–25) forms one huge sentence in the original Greek, although our English versions tend to divide it up into a sequence of shorter sentences. The 'oneness' of the whole, however, must be maintained intact as we comment upon it.

*'Therefore, brothers, since we have confidence to enter the holy places by the blood of Jesus'* (10:19). As already indicated, the *'Therefore'*

establishes the direct connection between what has already been in Hebrews and what is yet to come. It is the classic Bible word for doing this—a word which draws attention to the consequences of a thing or a truth, a word which prepares us for conclusions being drawn, a word which invariably leads straight into application. The writer preserves his affectionate address for those to whom he is writing, calling them *'brothers'* and uniting himself with them in what he is about to urge (*'we'*).

The concept of confidence was to the fore back in 4:16, in the exhortation, 'Let us then with confidence draw near to the throne of grace, that we may receive mercy and find grace to help in time of need'. It is returned to again here, much rich doctrine having flowed under the bridge since that earlier verse. In the light of the Lord Jesus having entered 'into the inner place behind the curtain', where he 'has gone as a forerunner on our behalf' (6:19–20)—or, as 9:24 put it, 'For Christ has entered, not into holy places made with hands, which are copies of the true things, but into heaven itself, now to appear in the presence of God on our behalf'—we too may now *'have confidence* [the word, it is maintained by some, can mean here 'freedom' or 'authorisation'] *to enter the holy places* [the innermost place of fellowship with God, which finds its ultimate fulfilment in heaven itself]*'*. And how may we come? Only by one way, and that is *'by the blood* ['by means of', speaking of his sacrifice on the cross, 'the blood of the [new] covenant', 9:20] *of Jesus'*. The use of what we might call Jesus' 'human' name here (*'Jesus'*) reminds us of the true and real humanity of the Saviour, dying as real man for real men (though he was at all points and at all times and in all ways 'without sin', 4:15). It was as a result of his own sacrifice upon the cross that Jesus himself entered *'the holy places'*, and on that same basis he has provided for us to enter also. Here is a further demonstration of the believer's union with Christ.

This one way is further described in what follows: *'by the new and living way that he opened for us* [the sense is of providing an access] *through the curtain, that is, through his flesh'* (10:20). Here is the magnificence of the new covenant, and, thereby, the glory of the gospel. Here is the hope of sinners and the joy of saints. It is reminiscent of Paul's sure word in Ephesians 3:12, 'in whom [Jesus] we have boldness and confidence through our faith in him'. Through his death (and his resurrection from the dead and his ascension into heaven), Jesus has opened, and opened wide, the way to God for us. The high priests of old could not do this, but our high priest has done it abundantly.

Of this way back to God, with our sins dealt with and reconciliation to God freely granted, we are told:

- It is *'new'*. This stands in contrast with the terms of the old covenant. It has been suggested that the word here rendered *'new'* means, literally, 'newly (or freshly) slain', and that this 'newly slain' way (or road) of access through Jesus is so expressed in contrast with the 'old slain' way (or road) of the former times which is now redundant.

- It is *'living'*. This is since Jesus is alive, and his is 'the power of an indestructible life' (7:16). He gives eternal life to all who come to the Father through him (John 6:40). He is *the* 'living stone', as a result of whom we are made 'living stones' (1 Peter 2:4–5). He is the one who is 'the living bread that came down from heaven', who declares, 'If anyone eats of this bread, he will live forever. And the bread that I will give for the life of the world is my flesh' (John 6:51).

- It is *'opened up for us'*. The verb can be translated 'consecrated, dedicated'. This has been done by the one who says of himself, 'I am the way, and the truth, and the life. No one comes to the Father except through me' (John 14:6), and who promises us, in tones of tenderness, assurance and grace, 'Because I live, you also will live' (John 14:19).

- It is *'through the curtain'*, which is immediately explained as, *'that is, through his flesh'*. The *'curtain'* reference must clearly be to the curtain in the tabernacle, and later in the temple, which separated the holy of holies, the most holy place, from the holy place, and which stood as a symbol of the sinner's inability to

have fellowship with God in his divine and holy presence—
and which curtain 'was torn in two, from top to bottom'
immediately upon 'Jesus (crying) out again with a loud voice
and (yielding) up his spirit' (Matthew 27:50–51). As a result we
may come before God and receive his gracious welcome. There
has been much discussion over the phrase *'through his flesh'*. The
most natural way of taking it, however, would be to understand
it in terms of Jesus having taken our nature upon him ('being
born in the likeness of men', Philippians 2:7), then, through his
sacrificial offering of himself (his death), having done all that
could ever be needful to give us access to God.

Our writer continues, *'and since we have a great priest over the
house of God'* (10:21). As has been insisted throughout Hebrews, Jesus'
priesthood stands entirely alone. There is none, ever, to compare
with it. Its greatness lies in the combination of Jesus' person (who
he is) and Jesus' work (what he has done). The words *'great priest'*
are really equivalent to *'high priest'*. Both appear together in 4:14,
where we were told that 'we have a great high priest who has passed
through the heavens'. That his priesthood is *'over the house of God'*
is a way of expressing his authority over, his rule of, and his care for
his church and people. 3:6 is a confirmation of this interpretation.
It carries a reminder that the Lord Jesus is 'head over all things to
the church, which is his body, the fullness of him who fills all in all'
(Ephesians 1:22–23). No one else shares this position with him, no
one is his fellow or companion—no angel, no man, no apostle, no
minister, no monarch, no parliament, no one at all. Christ's headship
and priesthood *'over the house of God'* is divine, supreme, exclusive,
complete and perpetual. It is his praise, his honour and his glory.
He calls into his house whom he wills, and whoever wishes to have
a place in the church must submit to him and acknowledge him as
both their Saviour and their Lord.

The 'bridge passage' is now complete, and the fivefold call in initial
application of all of this now follows, albeit with the same present
sentence still continuing. On the basis of the entire book of Hebrews
so far, and (in particular) in the light of the 'summary' of things just

given in 10:19–22, these next five exhortations and encouragements arise.

## (1) A call to fellowship with God (10:22)

This major sentence now proceeds: *'let us draw near with a true heart in full assurance of faith'* (10:22). Each of these five applications has the form of a *'let us'*—which is not intended to give the impression to the readers of Hebrews then or now that to do these things would be a good idea, though at the end of the day we are left to please ourselves. Far from it! The force of this way of putting things (as in 4:14, 'let us hold fast our confession', with which compare 10:23 coming up shortly), is very strong. It is as if the writer is giving the lead, setting the example, showing the way to one and all (not without some measure of command) to do these particular things.

The very essence of the Christian life is to know God and to have and to enjoy fellowship with him. We have been brought, through grace alone, into a relationship with God—not only as our Maker, which he was anyway, whether we acknowledged it or not, but now as our Redeemer (in salvation), our Father (in adoption) and our Portion (in everything, as Jeremiah signifies in Lamentations 3:24, '"The LORD is my portion", says my soul, "therefore I will hope in him"'). We have been given a new relationship with God, who has reconciled us to himself, when before we were estranged from him. Moreover, this fellowship (it is sometimes termed 'communion') is not only with God as God, but with each of the three persons of the Godhead (the Trinity) individually, Father, Son and Holy Spirit. The Trinitarian benediction of 2 Corinthians 13:14 expresses this beautifully as us experiencing and relishing in an ongoing way, 'The grace of the Lord Jesus Christ and the love of God and the fellowship of the Holy Spirit'.

This drawing near we are to do, not timidly or sheepishly or apprehensively, but *'with a true heart in full assurance of faith'*. By *'a true heart'* is meant genuinely, sincerely, desiringly, as opposed to falsely, proudly, or as those to whom these things do not belong. By *'in full assurance of faith'* is intended believingly, confidently, expectantly, as opposed to doubtingly, uncertainly or half-heartedly. These two features belong together, for only *'a true heart'* can possess *'full assurance of faith'*. This assurance, in the present context, is more than being certain we are Christians. It is, in a focused manner, an absolute and unswerving trust and confidence in the priesthood of the Lord Jesus Christ, the matchless worth of his sacrifice, and a wholehearted persuasion of him (and only him) as the one who has brought us to God. Any and all trust in rites, ceremonies, works and the like has been totally abandoned. All reliance upon men has been vigorously rejected. The newest or the weakest believer may come, for all believers may come—and not only 'may' come but 'must' come, for our very Christian life and health depends upon it.

This fellowship itself is nourished with praise and thanksgiving to God, reading and meditating upon his Word, seeking his presence and blessing in prayer, and attending dutifully and delightingly the means of grace. In sum, it involves nothing less than, 'by the mercies of God [in the light of them, in view of them], (presenting our) bodies as a living sacrifice, holy and acceptable to God, which is (our) spiritual worship' (Romans 12:1).

There is still more that pertains to this drawing near. We are to do so *'with our hearts sprinkled clean from an evil conscience and our bodies washed with pure water'*. There are two things here, though the verbs *'sprinkled'* and *'washed'* show an obvious connection. Taking them in order this is not the first mention in Hebrews of the conscience. It has already appeared in 9:9 and 14 (and compare 10:2, and our comments on each of these three verses). 13:18 will speak of the importance of having 'a clear conscience', very different from *'an evil conscience'*, which is one still burdened and polluted with the sense of unpardoned guilt, of having offended God, and which as yet has no solid ground or robust hope of forgiveness and reconciliation.

There is an important Old Testament background here in the book of Exodus. Both sprinkling and washing figured in the consecration of the priests in the Old Testament. They were (in order of events) washed with water (Exodus 29:4) and sprinkled with blood (Exodus 29:21). These things spoke of the need for the priests to be clean vessels, holy to the Lord. It is the same for us as Christians, and this cleansing and sanctifying is ours through Jesus' sacrifice of himself in our place. For us this is an internal cleansing and sanctifying, whereas for those of whom these things are recorded there in Exodus 29 it was purely external. As well as Exodus 29, there is likely here also the imagery from Exodus 24 which was given us back in Hebrews 9, with Moses sprinkling the people with the blood of the covenant when it was inaugurated at Mount Sinai. And Exodus 40 has relevance also, for we learn from that chapter that in the court of the tabernacle the altar of sacrifice (where the blood of the sacrificial victims was shed) and the laver (or basin, containing the water used for washing) were closely associated with each other.

The Christian's vital experience in this matter is touched upon by Paul, when he writes of 'the washing of regeneration and renewal by the Holy Spirit, whom he [God] poured out on us richly through Jesus Christ our Saviour' (Titus 3:5–6). We have been both washed clean from sin (by Jesus' sacrifice) and made new people (by the Holy Spirit). There may also be, in our writer's mind, the work of God pictured in Ezekiel 36:25, when God declares to his people, 'I will sprinkle clean water on you, and you shall be clean from all your uncleanness, and from all your idols I will cleanse you'. Notwithstanding the view of some, it is unlikely that there is any reference in Hebrews 10:22 to the gospel sacraments of baptism and the Lord's Supper.

## (2) A call to steadfastness in the gospel (10:23)

Paul proclaimed unreservedly, 'For I am not ashamed of the gospel, for it is the power of God for salvation to everyone who believes' (Romans 1:16), and exhorted Timothy to 'guard the good deposit entrusted to you' (2 Timothy 1:14). Jude challenged those to whom he wrote 'to contend for the faith that was once for all delivered to the saints' (Jude 3). The writer to the Hebrews is of the same mould as Paul and Jude, as is clear in this next verse. *'Let us hold fast the confession of our hope without wavering, for he who promised is faithful'* (10:23). We remind ourselves that this is not a new sentence in the original, but a continuation of the one begun in verse 19.

The call given here has already been given in 4:14, though here it is amplified. The verb to *'hold fast'* has an energetic ring to it, summoning us to determined, strenuous and persevering action and effort in the face of whatever hindrances, discouragements, oppositions or persecutions might appear in our way, whether from the world, the flesh or the devil. It is calling us to a most pressing duty. In what direction, and to what end? The maintaining and advancing *'the confession of our hope* [hope in Christ, hope in the gospel, hope of enduring to the end, hope of glory] *without wavering* [not an on and off business, not something to be engaged in when it suits us or when we have the time, not some matter only of little consequence, not a thing to be done either nervously or apologetically]*'*.

This hope was addressed back in 6:19, where it was described as 'a hope that enters into the inner place behind the curtain'. It is the gift of God, who is 'the God of hope' (Romans 15:13), and it is fixed upon the Lord Jesus Christ, for Christians are those who 'have hoped in Christ' (1 Corinthians 15:19). It may go without saying, but is being said anyway, that this holding fast can only be maintained successfully with divine aid. In the face of every duty and in the discharge of every responsibility of the Christian life, we are in continual dependence upon the triune God. The balance is well illustrated in Scripture's use of the verb 'keep'. For our part, we are given charges such as these: 'keep oneself unstained from the world' (James 1:27), 'keep yourselves from idols' (1 John 5:21), and 'keep yourselves in the love of God' (Jude 21). Behind all such biddings, however, rests this grand foundation: 'guarded (or 'kept') by God's power' (1 Peter 1:5).

The latter part of the verse, *'for he [God] who promised is faithful'*, is key to the whole work of the former part of the verse, *'hold fast the confession of our hope'*, and for this reason: neither faith nor hope, which are intimately related, would have any prospect of being maintained if it were not the case that the God in whom we trust and hope is the God of faithful promises. He is the promise making, the promise keeping and the promise performing God. He has proved his faithfulness to his promises time and again in the lives of his children, in his dealings with his church. If he were even once to prove himself unfaithful, then all would be lost. But such an eventuality can never possibly be. The unchangeable fact of the matter is that God is faithful. And this holding fast is not only something which is done personally and privately in our hearts, but rather something which gives vent in witness, preaching, evangelism, missions and a constant prayerful interest in and pleading for the spreading and prospering of the good news of the gospel to the ends of the earth. Let us always be 'prepared to make a defence to anyone who asks (us) for a reason for the hope that is in (us)' (1 Peter 3:15).

## (3) A call to mutual encouragement (10:24)

The long sentence continues. *'And let us consider* [give careful thought to, show some concern about, and so, ultimately, something along the lines of work out viable practical possibilities for] *how to stir up* [literally, 'provoke, arouse or incite', in the sense of providing motivation] *one another to love and good works'* (10:24). There is a reminder at the root of this third part of the fivefold call that although there is something intensely personal and individual in being a Christian (for 'the life I now live in the flesh I live by faith in the Son of God, who loved me and gave himself for me', Galatians 2:20), there is something equally intense which is corporate and communal (for 'Christ loved the church and gave himself up for her', Ephesians 5:25). Both of these aspects need continually to be borne in mind. Another biblical way of holding together these twin truths is to link Romans 14:7 ('For none of us lives to himself') with Philippians 2:4 ('Let each of you look not only to his own interests, but also to the interests of others'). 10:24 is an exhortation which aims to keep us from the selfish angle and encourage us to pursue the selfless one. It may be that in being fearful of the Hebrews wandering off from the firm moorings of the gospel, our writer also perceived a loosening of the bonds of mutual carefulness for one another among them. Certainly 10:32–34 implies that at one time this exhortation might not have been so necessary, for they were doing it anyway.

We are to be marked by 'a sincere brotherly love' and are to 'love one another earnestly from a pure heart' (1 Peter 1:22). Interestingly, in the calls so far we have had faith (verse 22), hope (verse 23) and now love (verse 24), recalling 1 Corinthians 13:13 ('So now faith, hope and love abide, these three; but the greatest of these is love'). There is implicit here a lovely portrait of Christian character. We are to be believing, hoping, loving people, as unworthy recipients of the grace of God in the gospel.

The putting of this into practice will involve and include many things, but that which is singled out in the present verse for special mention is the stirring up of *'one another to love and good works'*. The connection of *'love and good works'* is significant. They go together, for the one should always lead to the other. In a similar connection, the point is made in James 2:26 that 'faith apart from works is dead'. The Bible is always absolutely clear that a true Christian profession is to be fruitful. Without question, in every church there will be manifold opportunities both for the mutual stirring up of *'one another to love and good works'*, and the actual doing of the same ourselves.

In what might these *'good works'* consist? Here are just a few examples, for starters, after which no doubt every reader can extend the list. 'Contribute to the needs of the saints and seek to show hospitality' (Romans 12:13. 'Rejoice with those who rejoice, weep with those who weep' (Romans 12:15). 'Brothers, if anyone is caught in any transgression, you who are spiritual should restore him in a spirit of gentleness' (Galatians 6:1). 1 Timothy 4:12 gives this charge: 'set the believers an example in speech, in conduct, in love, in faith, in purity'. 'And we urge you, brothers, admonish the idle, encourage the fainthearted, help the weak, be patient with them all' (1 Thessalonians 5:14). And, of course, what begins within the church, among the brethren (for if the practice of 10:24 does not start there, where will it start?), does not end there, for we have a *'love and good works'* responsibility to all men. Galatians 6:10 makes this plain: 'So then, as we have opportunity, let us do good to everyone, and especially to those who are of the household of faith'. And where unbelievers are concerned, there is no higher good that we can do them than to speak to them of the Saviour and to show them acts of kindness.

## (4) A call to Christian assembling (10:25)

In a vital sense, what we have here is a further example of the
directive we have just been considering from the previous verse,
especially the stirring up of one another. We made the point then
that being a Christian and living the Christian life is not to be seen
as an isolated existence. Christ's people belong together, for we
belong to the church, his church. So this fourth call is, *'not neglecting
to meet together, as is the habit of some'* (10:25). In the first days of
the early New Testament church, following the day of Pentecost,
it is recorded of the believers that one of the things to which 'they
devoted themselves' was 'fellowship' (Acts 2:42). It is clear from the
verses that follow that statement that the fellowship they shared
and enjoyed together was both formal and informal—that is to say,
there was corporate worship, and there was the gathering in private
homes (both are mentioned in Acts 2:46). So it should be today, for
where these things are concerned, nothing has changed. God has
commanded it. Our spiritual health demands it. The love and unity
of believers requires it. An honourable and consistent Christian
testimony before the world necessitates it.

The verb *'neglecting'* has strong force and can carry the weight
of 'abandon' or 'forsake'. We note solemnly that it is the same verb
used by Jesus on the cross, when he said, 'My God, my God, why
have you forsaken me?' (Matthew 27:46). Happily, it is also the same
verb used in 13:5 of Hebrews, when God declares to us, 'I will never
leave you nor forsake you'. Moreover, to add to the seriousness of
the matter, the section of this chapter which will follow (10:26–31),
with its most solemn warnings about the dangers of apostasy (not for
the first time in Hebrews), serves as a warning light: the forsaking of
Christian assembling together on the Lord's Day can so easily end up
(dangerously more easily than any might think) in forsaking the Lord
himself altogether. The presence of *'as is the habit of some'* is enough to
suggest, again, that the Hebrews to whom this book of Scripture was
first addressed were giving serious cause for concern in this very area.

Absolutely central and vital to this is corporate worship together
on the Lord's Day in the Lord's house. There is no substitute for

this, both morning and evening. This is a timely reminder in these days when (not least, because of a weakening grip upon the moral law in general, and the fourth commandment in particular) many Christians are becoming wayward in this matter. We need a fresh burst of Psalm 122:1 ('I was glad when they said to me, 'Let us go to the house of the Lord'), as well as of Psalm 26:8 ('O Lord, I love the habitation of your house, and the place where your glory dwells'). On these occasions, we gather together as one, as the Lord's redeemed people, to worship and praise him, to seek his face in prayer, to hear his Word read and preached, and (when appropriate) for baptism and the Lord's supper. These are the choicest of occasions, and the Lord's Day is the first and the best day of the week, not least because of its blessed associations with the resurrection of our Lord Jesus Christ from the dead. Few things are more discouraging for a church family (and, not least, for the minister) than to discover different brothers and sisters in the fellowship absenting themselves from public worship without adequate reason. And, more importantly, such *'neglecting to meet together'* is disobedience to God and a slur upon his honour. So as a further aspect of our caring concern for one another, we are to be mutual encouragers against this danger of neglect, and to be on the lookout for each other should any show danger signs of it.

At other times there will be ample further opportunities for Christians *'to meet together'*. Obvious examples would be prayer meetings, open air gospel preaching occasions, hospitality in each other's homes, fellowship meals and mutual visitation.

This matter is not yet complete, however, as the fifth and final part of the fivefold call now reveals.

## (5) A call to expectant faith (10:25)

Still with the same sentence, begun in 10:19 and now drawing to its close: *'but encouraging one another, and all the more as you see the Day drawing near'* (10:25). Mutual encouragement is a great link throughout these exhortations (not least where the taking care not to neglect our meeting together is concerned), and now the writer adds a forceful argument to enforce the crucial nature of what he is saying. Our mutual encouragement of one another is something in which we are to engage *'all the more'*—which is to say, with greater urgency, with greater consistency, with greater affection, with greater exemplariness, with greater necessity. Why? For this reason: *'as you see the Day approaching'*.

What is this *'Day approaching'*? It must (and can) only be the day of the return of the Lord Jesus Christ at the end of the age, that day when he 'will appear a second time', as we had it in 9:28. This is 'the Day of the Lord', as it is so often termed in Scripture—the day the timing of which 'no one knows' (Mark 13:32); the day when (as the angels addressed the disciples at the time of Jesus' ascension into heaven), 'This Jesus, who was taken up from you into heaven, will come in the same way as you saw him go into heaven' (Acts 1:11); 'the day of the Lord' which 'will come like a thief in the night' (1 Thessalonians 5:2); 'the coming of the day of God' (2 Peter 3:12); the day when the cry will sound forth, 'Here is the bridegroom! Come out to meet him' (Matthew 25:6).

There is always the danger, in every age, that this truth (however firmly held) gets pushed onto the 'back burner' of our lives, thoughts and expectations. This should not be so! Even though the timing of this momentous event is entirely unknown to us, what we do know is that it will most certainly happen. So we are to live in constant longing and expectation for it, for in the most vital sense it is always the case that 'the coming of the Lord is at hand' (James 5:8). 'For salvation is nearer to us now than when we first believed' (Romans 13:11). The church's (the bride's) prayer should always and increasingly be, 'Come, Lord Jesus!' (Revelation 22:20).

## A threefold imperative (10:26–39)

This final section of the chapter subdivides into three, each containing an earnest imperative to the Hebrews and to us: verses 26–31, verses 32–34, and verses 35–39. Having expounded so richly the wonders of Jesus' sacrificial work (verses 1–18), and urged with clarity and passion some of the key duties that belong to those who have been saved (verses 19–25), the writer of Hebrews now, in the remainder of the chapter, leaves every reader in no doubt as to what are the consequences of rejecting the Saviour, having once accepted him (verses 26–39).

This is an exceedingly solemn portion of the word of God, yet at the same time it contains some precious encouragements and assurances. It reminds us that there is always the danger of us deceiving ourselves that we are truly converted and heading for heaven, when that might not be the case. In the light of this, therefore, we need to be scrupulous in examining ourselves in the light of Scripture, asking the Holy Spirit to search us out and make us clear to ourselves, that no self-deception would overtake us. Paul's summons to the Corinthians is ever relevant: 'Examine yourselves, to see whether you are in the faith. Test yourselves' (2 Corinthians 13:5). To possess full assurance from the Lord that we truly *do* belong to him ('The Spirit himself bear(ing) witness with our spirit that we are children of God', Romans 8:16) is a most blessed assurance indeed.

## (1) Watch out! (10:26–31)

This first portion presents challenging difficulties of interpretation, and is rather reminiscent of 6:4–6, bearing, as it does, upon the solemn subject of apostasy. We must approach it carefully. It follows on very naturally from 10:19–25, even if this is not immediately apparent. By way of reminder, those verses presented a fivefold call to Christians, in order to help keep us on the straight and narrow and to quell any thoughts or intentions of backing out on the Lord Jesus Christ and the gospel. Yet—and here is the vital connection between verses 19–25 and 26–31—if those calls go unheeded, if they are played fast and loose with, if anyone considers them to be of little relevance or importance, then the very apostasy now warned so vigorously against may all to easily come to pass. Hence the imperative: watch out!

'*For* [itself a word forming a connecting link with what has just been laid out] *if we* [the writer associates himself with those to whom he writes, though in no way implying thereby that they, still less he, have actually done what is about to be mentioned, although some of his readers may be dangerously close to it] *go on sinning deliberately after receiving the knowledge of the truth'* (10:26). What is in view here in the *'sinning deliberately'* is not the miserable day to day business of our daily sins and shortfalls, intensely serious though these are (and whenever and wherever sin *is* indulged, it can never be known in advance to what shipwreck it may lead, even if it did not seem an enormity at the time). Something else, rather, is intended here. We noted back in 5:2 a mention of those described as 'the ignorant and wayward'. They, too, sin, but not in a deliberate, knowing and relishing manner. Those who *'go on sinning deliberately'*, however, do. Their sinning is all the more serious (even though all sin in serious). They sin, we might say, with a high hand. Their sin is wilful. There is intent, there is forethought, there is insistence, where this sinning is concerned. It is rebelling against the light (Job 24:13), a deliberate rejecting of the gospel they professed to believe and the life of holiness they professed to live, a solemn and unashamed turning away from the Lord Jesus Christ and abandoning of allegiance to him.

This is confirmed by the continuation of the verse: it speaks of those who *'go on sinning deliberately after receiving the knowledge of the truth'*. This is not sin in the life of the unbeliever, nor is it sin on the part of the person who was only ever (at best) tenuously or half-heartedly attached to the things of Christ, the gospel and the church. This is not being taken unawares in a sin. Neither is it the backslider who is in view. The impression is given, rather, that here is one who appeared to be setting about Christian things with some seriousness, purpose and endeavour. But things were never as well with them on the inside as they appeared to be on the outside. Proverbs 2:13–14 has such in mind when speaking of those 'who forsake the paths of uprightness to walk in the ways of darkness, who rejoice in doing evil and delight in the perverseness of evil'. They even appear to boast about it, to flaunt it, to draw the attention of others to it (and, maybe as well, seek to lead others astray after them in the same way). Once they loved light, now they prefer darkness—the very language used in John 3:19: 'And this is the judgment: the light has come into the world, and people loved the darkness rather than the light because their deeds were evil'.

This, grievously, is apostasy with a capital 'A'. It is a complete about-turn, a casting aside, a resolute turning away. It is the precise opposite of persevering in the faith, 'hold(ing) fast the confession of our hope without wavering' (10:23), enduring to the end. The phrase *'the knowledge of the truth'* means more than a mere intellectual receiving and assenting to the truth of God and his Word. It implies something altogether more personal by way of that reception and assent—at the end of the day, some indication to all appearances of a person's conversion. After having been convinced of *'the truth'*, they have since rejected it. Mind, heart and will had all been involved in the reception. They are at least taken for being Christians. But that, it eventually appears, is all: they were *taken to be* Christians.

This is no small matter, anything but. What is to become of anyone who comes under the words just considered? The answer could not be more serious: for all such, *'there no longer remains a sacrifice for sins'*. This makes sense. For a person who at one time accepted Jesus' sacrifice for sin upon the cross, then to reject it, to cast it aside—what is he left with? He is left without a sacrifice, for there is no other. How can there be, since Jesus' sacrifice is the only one, and he cannot be sacrificed a second time? Our writer has been at such pains to leave no stone unturned in establishing this fact. None of the old sacrifices could deliver salvation, forgiveness, and (thereby) reconciliation with God. Rather, they all pointed to the Lord Jesus who could and did. Bells are ringing from 6:4 with regard to the impossibility of such souls being restored 'again to repentance'. All interest in Jesus' sacrifice is completely forfeited.

There is a further side to this also, for things get heavier and darker still. Not only does there remain no 'sacrifice for sins' for all those who abandon faith and return to unbelief, *'but a fearful* ('terrifying') *expectation of judgment* [indicating something which is inevitable], *and a fury of fire that will consume the adversaries'* (10:27). This is fundamental to the gospel message, so succinctly expressed in Jeremiah 21:8: 'Thus says the LORD: "Behold, I set before you the way of life and the way of death"'. It could not be clearer. By the grace of God in the gospel, the sinner is saved from 'the way of death' and placed securely on 'the way of life'. We are reminded of Jesus' words in Matthew 7:13–14, when he contrasts the way 'that leads to destruction' with 'the way ... that leads to life'. To depart wilfully and settledly from the way that leads to life is to choose by preference the only alternative—the way that leads to death. Twice in Proverbs (14:12 and 16:25) the warning is pressed: 'There is a way that seems right to a man, but its end is the way to death'. This shows the fatal nature of apostasy. To take the reckless course of turning away from the side of Christ and back to the side of his enemy is a road which only carries one-way traffic.

The end that faces the traveller on this road cannot be otherwise than is here stated. For *'a fearful expectation of judgment'* and *'a fury of fire'* is the only outcome that can ever await an unbeliever— whether he is an unbeliever who has never believed, or an unbeliever who once professed to be a believer. As 12:29 will declare, 'for our God is a consuming fire'. Romans 1:18 is terrifyingly stark in its words concerning divine wrath. 'For the wrath of God is revealed from heaven against all ungodliness and unrighteousness of men, who by their unrighteousness suppress the truth'. For some of the Hebrews it may be that the particular danger of apostasy facing them involved their leaving Christianity behind and going backwards to the Judaism they had left. The subject itself, though, is very much wider of application than that. Here is stated the final punishment and irreversible condemnation of the apostate. The plea of the psalmist David needs continually to be our own. 'Keep back your servant also from presumptuous sins; let them not have dominion over me! Then I shall be blameless, and innocent of great transgression' (Psalm 19:13). That is why it is in the interests of every believer to 'watch out!'.

For his next remark, our writer refers to an Old Testament principle. *'Anyone who has set aside the law of Moses dies without mercy on the evidence of two or three witnesses'* (10:28). That this is so is clear from a verse like Deuteronomy 17:6: 'On the evidence of two witnesses or of three witnesses the one who is to die shall be put to death; a person shall not be put to death on the evidence of one witness'. We might wonder, however, what that has to do with the present context. The answer is immediately provided. The context of that Deuteronomy verse is of 'a man or woman who does what is evil in the sight of the LORD your God, in transgressing his covenant, and has gone and served other gods and worshipped them' (Deuteronomy 17:2–3), and so is on very much the same lines as the sin of apostasy being dealt with at this point in Hebrews. If the punishment awaiting such a transgressor and idolater was a thing of such enormity under the old covenant, how much more will that be so, under the new covenant, for the one who does the same?

This is exactly the point the writer comes to. *'How much worse punishment, do you think, will be deserved by the one who has'* (10:29), is how he begins his answer. And the way he then develops it (in a sentence ending with a question mark) is in the straightest of straight talking language, language which links back with the phrase 'if we go on sinning deliberately' in verse 26. He presents a three-part word portrait of an apostate, in order to leave no one in any doubt concerning the appalling nature and folly of the crime. He is not content with leaving matters in general terms, but provides detail and colour. Let it not be thought that the holy God will deal more leniently with apostates in and after New Testament times than he did in the days of the Old.

Firstly, the apostate is described as *'the one who has spurned the Son of God'*. The verb *'spurned'* is very strong. It refers to 'trampling underfoot', and is the verb Jesus uses in Matthew 7:6 when using the illustration of pigs trampling pearls underfoot. Where this is engaged in with respect to Jesus, the meaning is to count him as worthless, as not even worthy of notice. It speaks of contempt for him, despising of him, completely disregarding him. Instead of him being 'all in all', he becomes 'nothing at all'. The very thought is appalling. It is to move to a position which is even worse than that referred to in Isaiah 53:2, where those are spoken of for whom Jesus 'had no form or majesty that (they) should look at him, and no beauty that (they) should desire him'. His exalted person as *'the Son of God'* is put entirely to one side, in such stark contrast to our writer's insistence upon his deity, supremacy and incomparable excellency. Remember

the magnificent panorama of this which was set out in the opening
chapter. It is as if everything that has been taught about Jesus here in
Hebrews is false. Watch out!

Secondly, the apostate is described as *'and has profaned the blood of
the covenant by which he was sanctified'*. The despising of Jesus' person
was the focus of the first part of this three part word portrait of an
apostate. The focus now is rather upon the despising of his work,
and, in particular, his sacrificial work on the cross which is at the very
centre of all that he has done for sinners.

Hebrews is rich in its references to Jesus' blood, as is Scripture as
a whole. We have read of it in chapter 9—'he entered once for all
into the holy places ... by means of his own blood, thus securing
an eternal redemption', verse 12; 'how much more will the blood
of Christ, who through the eternal Spirit offered himself without
blemish to God, purify our conscience from dead works to serve the
living God', verse 14. We have read of it in chapter 10—'Therefore,
brothers, since we have confidence to enter the holy places by the
blood of Jesus', verse 19. We shall read of it in chapter 12—'and to
Jesus, the mediator of a new covenant, and to the sprinkled blood
that speaks a better word than the blood of Abel', verse 24. We shall
read of it in chapter 13—'So Jesus also suffered outside the gate in
order to sanctify the people through his own blood', verse 12; 'Now
may the God of peace who brought again from the dead our Lord
Jesus, the great shepherd of the sheep, by the blood of the eternal
covenant ...', verse 20. And we are reading of it now in the verse
before us.

This reference to Jesus' blood (as with the others just quoted) is a
reference to his death, his sacrifice, on the cross at Calvary. Here it
was that the work of salvation was procured—where, 'For our sake
he [God the Father] made him [God the Son] to be sin who knew
no sin, so that in him [Jesus] we might become the righteousness of
God' (2 Corinthians 5:21). Yet just as the apostate 'spurned' Jesus'
person, so now it is said he *'profaned'* Jesus' work. To 'profane' is to
treat with irreverence, to deem something unholy and common. Yet
it is this very blood of the Saviour which has sanctifying power and

grace (*'the blood of the covenant by which he was sanctified'*). It cleanses the unclean, washes the unwashed, undefiles the defiled, and makes holy (sanctifies) the unholy. Yet the experience of these profaners demonstrates that theirs, tragically, was no more than an external sanctification, an outward dedication, a temporary allegiance. What a terrible course it is to take, which ends up with someone profaning 'the precious blood of Christ' (1 Peter 1:19), and what awful eternal consequences follow from it. Watch out!

Thirdly, the apostate is described as *'and has outraged the Spirit of grace'*. Without doubt, *'the Spirit of grace'* is the Holy Spirit, the third person of the Trinity, through whom, in the mystery of divine things, *'grace'* is given. And this gives a further dimension to the terrible nature and implications of apostasy. In the spurning of Jesus as 'the Son of God', and the profaning of his 'blood of the covenant', comes this dimension also—the outraging of the Holy Spirit! Maybe we would not readily think of the Holy Spirit ever being *'outraged'*. Remember, however, that he is the *Holy* Spirit, 'the Spirit of holiness' (Romans 1:4), and so we should not be surprised at the language the writer uses here. It is the special work (and the special delight) of the Holy Spirit to exalt the Son of God and to see him exalted in the life of every believer. So when the very opposite happens, it is to him a matter of outrage. It is an insult to each person of the Godhead, including the third.

This ties in very precisely with two other relevant Scriptures which bear upon the Holy Spirit. One is 'the blasphemy against the Spirit (which) will not be forgiven', as Jesus teaches in Matthew 13:31. The other is the 'sin that leads to death', of which John teaches in 1 John 5:16. Think it through carefully. People are being described here who at one time professed faith in the Lord Jesus Christ and claimed to be his disciples. Moreover, their testimony was received by others as genuine. No one can truly profess faith in Jesus or live consistently as his disciple without the Holy Spirit—first in the Spirit's work of regeneration, then in his work of sanctification. So whenever anyone who has made such a profession and made such a claim backtracks completely upon it, denies that it was ever so, and sets off in the opposite direction to that of faith and discipleship, is it any wonder that the Holy Spirit himself is *'outraged'*? Would we expect him to be otherwise? 'Therefore let anyone who thinks that he stands take heed lest he fall' (1 Corinthians 10:12). Watch out!

Whilst we have commented separately upon the three parts of this word picture of the apostate, it is important to keep in mind that they do constitute three parts of one whole, they belong together. And of them all together, the writer poses this searching question: 'How much worse punishment, do you think, will be deserved by the one who has spurned the Son of God, profaned the blood of the covenant by which he was sanctified, and has outraged the Spirit of grace?'. Yet he still has more to say, for the matter is so serious.

*'For we know him who said* [note the appeal to the unchanging truth of the unchanging God], *"Vengeance* [the sense of meting out full justice, rather than vindictiveness] *is mine; I will repay". And again, "The Lord will judge his people"'* (10:30). The two quotations are from Deuteronomy 32:35 and 36 respectively. Again, in an expression of his pastoral heart and concern for those to whom he is writing who are giving him concern, our writer uses the inclusive *'we'* rather than the more direct 'you'. It remains his hope and longing that those in danger of committing apostasy will not do it, that they will be brought back from the brink and prove to be 'the real thing' after all as Christians. Even so, however, the note of serious warning cannot be muted. Yes, there is grace from God, for he is 'the God of all grace' (1 Peter 5:11); but there is judgment also, for he is 'the Judge (who) is standing at the door' (James 5:9).

It was always the divine insistence in the Old Testament (with which the Hebrews were so familiar) that with obedience to God came blessing and with disobedience to God came curse. This was an inflexible truth, and a potent reminder of it is what lies behind the employment here of the Deuteronomy references, drawn from Moses' final exhortation 'in the ears of all the assembly of Israel' (Deuteronomy 31:30), urging them to faithfulness and away from any thoughts of apostasy. It was a needful reminder at the time, and remains so for every generation of God's people. It is as if, with the apostle Paul, our writer is saying, 'Do not be deceived: God is not mocked, for whatever one sows, that will he also reap' (Galatians 5:7). What intense care we all need to take, in order to ensure that we are neither hypocrites now nor castaways at the last.

The 'watch out!' section concludes with a further salvo of warning. *'It is a fearful* [scarcely could a stronger word be chosen] *thing to fall into the hands of* [the phrase signifies the complete helplessness of the one who so falls] *the living God'* (10:31). In terms of the reception of his grace, it is a most blessed thing to fall into God's hands, for it is the safest and most comforting place to be. But if we abandon him when once having cleaved to him, if we deny him when once having confessed him, if we speak blasphemously of him when once having honoured him, then it is indeed *'a fearful thing to fall into'* his hands. The wrath of God is an appallingly fierce thing to have to face. It is to be left to bear all the unimaginable infinity and intensity of his power and holiness and justice, with no hiding place from that storm, nowhere to run, no way of escape.

It remains true that 'with (God) there is forgiveness, that (he) may be feared' (Psalm 130:4), but that provides no liberty whatsoever for us to take him for granted, treat him as we like, or be 'on and off' with him. We are either for him or against him. 'But God's firm foundation stands, bearing this seal: "The Lord knows those who are his", and, "Let everyone who names the name of the Lord depart from iniquity"' (2 Timothy 2:19). He who is *'the living God'* (reread 3:12 carefully) will be met by us all—either as our Redeemer or else as our Judge.

## (2) Think back! (10:32–34)

Our writer now tries another (though complementary) tack in order to warn his readers against apostasy. This time he bids them think back to days of former joys, sufferings and assurances—days when they had a spring in their step and a song in their heart. There can be a great benefit in this exercise, particularly when the Christian is 'up against it', for it is a means of sharpening our often dull recollection of the kindness and faithfulness of God, who has daily followed us with his 'goodness and mercy' (Psalm 23:6). It is commended, for example, way back in Deuteronomy 8:2, where Moses exhorts the people to 'remember the whole way that the Lᴏʀᴅ your God has led you these forty years in the wilderness, that he might humble you, testing you to know what was in your heart, whether you would keep his commandments or not'. Indeed, the entire book of Deuteronomy is really what we might call a book of 'remembrance' or 'remembering'.

*'But recall the former days'* (10:32). On this basis he seeks to encourage them to better things. There is a savour here of the message of Jesus to the church at Ephesus in Revelation 2:4–5, with its mixture of warning and grace: 'But I have this against you, that you have abandoned the love you had at first. Remember therefore from where you have fallen; repent, and do the works you did at first. If not ...'. Faith, hope, assurance and obedience may hereby be revived and our Christian lives take choicer flight once again, for this remembering is intended, not least, to bring afresh to mind the divine support under trials, his love tasted through our afflictions, and his marvellous tendency to turn the worst of trials into the best of blessings.

What were they like, these *former days*? What characterised them? The verse continues with, *'when, after you were enlightened'*, this being a reference back to the time when God's work of grace was begun in their hearts, when they professed conversion and confessed Christ publicly and without shame, as those who had been 'turn(ed) from darkness to light' (Acts 26:18). In those days, and the ones that followed, their Christian lives were far from easy, but this did not deter them from pressing on. It is recorded of them here, *'you endured* [that is, they stood firm, they held fast, they did not faint or give way to discouragement] *a hard struggle* [the sense is of a conflict or contest] *with sufferings'*. They were immediately in the thick of the battle, as is regularly the case with new converts. There is not necessarily a honeymoon period!

If, as we are understanding to be the case, the recipients of Hebrews were (at least largely) those who had come to Christianity from Judaism, they will no doubt have received some harsh responses

from their once fellow Jews whom they had left behind, and this will
very likely have affected their acceptance in the local community,
their standing in society, and their entire family and business lives.
'Indeed, all who desire to live a godly life in Christ Jesus will be
persecuted' (2 Timothy 3:12). Their lives, quite literally, would
not have remained the same. They never do, once you become a
Christian.

This reference to their endurance of suffering, however, is
not left here as some mere vague statement, but is fleshed out
in what immediately follows. We learn of them *sometimes being
publicly exposed* [the image here is of being put to public shame and
disgrace, made a spectacle—'like the scum of the world, the refuse
of all things', 1 Corinthians 4:13] *to reproach* [insults and character
assassinations, very likely chiefly delivered verbally, on account of
their identification with the Lord Jesus—it is the same word which
is used by Paul of Jesus' own experiences, when quoting from Psalm
69:9 in Romans 15:3: 'The reproaches of those who reproached you fell
on me'] *and affliction* [persecutions, these suggesting physical violence
and cruelty, no doubt to intimidate them and draw them back into
their previous lives], *and sometimes being partners* [the word describes
fellowship and partnership, companions and sharers, standing loyally
side by side with one another] *with those so treated'* (10:33). They faced
trials individually, and were involved with one another's troubles
as well in their new relationship as brethren together. They knew
and demonstrated in practice the love of the brethren, one of the
privileges as well as one of the duties of the Christian life.

Their brighter (though tough) days are now further described.
*'For you had compassion on those in prison, and you joyfully accepted
the plundering of your property'* (10:34). The clear implication here
is that some of them, as part of their sufferings and afflictions, had
ended up *'in prison'*. When this happened, however, they were not
forgotten, abandoned or disowned by the others. Rather these others
rallied round and *'had compassion'* on the prisoners. When we come
to 13:3 we shall find the following exhortation to continue with this
compassionate ministry: 'Remember those who are in prison, as

though in prison with them, and those who are mistreated, since you also are in the body'.

This call to Christian compassion (including prison visiting) continues to be very relevant and applicable in our own day, whether involving visiting unbelievers in prison in order to take the gospel to them, or visiting Christians themselves who have been imprisoned through having had (in these godless days) to 'obey God rather than men' (Acts 5:29). From the way things are going, we may have to face this latter possibility more and not less. Should this happen to any of us, may our experience match that of the apostle Paul, who declared, 'But the Lord stood by me and strengthened me' (2 Timothy 4:17). It is appropriate also, in this context, to remember Jesus' own words in his parable of the sheep and the goats. 'Truly, I say to you, as you did it [including visiting prisoners] to one of the least of these my brothers, you did it to me' (Matthew 25:40).

Not only had the Hebrews been noted for this compassion, however. There was more: *and you joyfully accepted the plundering of your property'.* Presumably the meaning is that the authorities themselves (as well, perhaps, as other folk generally) had robbed them, helping themselves to, and in one way and another making off with, their goods and possessions, thereby leaving them in a bereft and plundered state, maybe even in poverty. Yet the emphasis here is upon the joyful manner in which the Hebrews bore with this; they *'joyfully accepted'* it, rather than complaining about it, bemoaning it or feeling hard done by. Whatever happened to them, they did not consider themselves to be the losers by it. And what explains their response? Our writer tells us, in reminding them: *'since you knew that you yourselves had a better possession and an abiding one'.* They focused clearly not on 'the things that are seen' (which 'are transient') but upon 'the things that are unseen' (which 'are eternal') (2 Corinthians 4:18). Their earthly possessions may have been taken from them, but they had a *'possession'* of a different order altogether.

This will come to the fore shortly in chapter 11, where we learn that the great motivation which again and again captured the hearts of God's people of old was to look to the future, to the inheritance, to the blessedness to come—'having acknowledged that they were strangers and exiles on the earth', 'seeking a homeland', desiring 'a better country, that is, a heavenly one' (11:13, 14, 16). Theirs was the inestimable benefit of heavenly mindedness. At that season in their lives they 'Set (their) minds on things that are above, not on things that are on earth' (Colossians 3:2). In every generation and in every circumstance, the Lord being our helper, his people are to do the same.

It must never be thought (or taught) that all your problems disappear the moment you become a Christian. Nothing could be further from the truth. The more likely scenario is that many of them will only just start at that point. Yet the heavenly hope is a great consolation and assurance at such times, hopefully becoming stronger and stronger as the years go by. Let the words of the Saviour be ever before us: 'lay up for yourselves treasures in heaven, where neither moth nor rust destroys and where thieves do not break in and steal. For where your treasure is, there your heart will be also' (Matthew 6:20–21). Read also his words a little earlier in the Sermon on the Mount, in Matthew 5:11–12. They tell the same story and urge our minds and hearts in the same direction of present joy in difficulties and future blessings in heaven.

Two words are used in 10:34 to describe this possession the Christian has—*'better'* and *'abiding'*. It must be *'better'*—not only for the obvious reason that it cannot be worse, but for the highly positive reason that when we enter into the fullness of it we shall 'be with Christ, for that is far better' (Philippians 1:23). To exchange earth for heaven can only be advantageous! It is also *'abiding'* (that is, remaining, enduring, lasting, permanent, without either change or loss), unlike so much of what we have and enjoy during this present life. The true believer's inheritance 'is imperishable, undefiled, and unfading, kept in heaven for (us), who by God's power are being guarded through faith for a salvation ready to be revealed in the last time' (1 Peter 1:4–5). We may appear sometimes to have nothing. The truth is, we possess everything (2 Corinthians 6:10). Be ready to let go of the movables, and to hold on tight to the eternals.

The only safe course for a Christian is to make consistent spiritual progress every day, with no slacking. So, having urged his original readers to 'watch out!', he proceeded to urge them with equal vigour to 'think back!', back to the days (still hopefully in their memories) when their profession of the Lord Jesus Christ was healthy, earnest and joyful, so very different from how it had become by the time they received this exhortation. Both of these calls, remember, are part of his plea to them not to backtrack from Jesus, but rather to be 'imitators of those who through faith and patience inherit the promises' (6:12).

Two of the three imperatives have now been given. One remains.

## (3) Press on! (10:35–39)

It has been maintained throughout this commentary that Hebrews, for all its solemn warnings, is very much a book of Scripture given to encouragement, and, especially, encouragement to endure, to keep going, to press on. It is this note of the need for endurance, perseverance, patience, 'stickability' and hope which is primarily to the fore in this final section of chapter 10.

*'Therefore do not throw away your confidence, which has a great reward'* (10:35). This is not, of course, self-confidence, or anything like it. It is, rather, confidence in Jesus, in the gospel, in the divine promises, in the reality of the heavenly hope—which breeds boldness and courage and a persevering spirit. In the face of all their 'reproach and affliction' (verse 33), and all that has accompanied it (verse 34), there would be a great and present danger of wondering if it was really worthwhile to carry on—the attitude of 'if this is what being a Christian involves, if this is where it gets me, why bother to continue?'. And with that mindset, it would be the easiest thing in the world for them to look back to their former days in Judaism and come to the conclusion that things were brighter there after all, and to return in that direction. This was the great mistake that the children of Israel made in the wilderness—an error which they so eloquently expressed in the words (spoken to Moses and Aaron but directed, ultimately, against God), 'Would that we had died by the hand of

the LORD in the land of Egypt, when we sat by the meat pots and ate bread to the full, for you have brought us out into this wilderness to kill this whole assembly with hunger' (Exodus 16:3).

Yet why would the Hebrews contemplate (still less, do) such a thing? They had been pointed to the fullness and sufficiency of the Lord Jesus Christ in his person and work, and that they had all things and abounded in him. To remind them of this, which seemed increasingly to be slipping from their mind and grasp, our writer has been setting forth in a methodical and passionate manner these things to them again. Salvation! Grace! Faith! Promises! Blessing! Reward! Yet have all his efforts been to no avail? He will not give up that easily, however. He desires that they 'be steadfast, immovable, always abounding in the work of the Lord' (1 Corinthians 15:58). In order to encourage the Hebrews to press on and endure, the writer himself presses on and endures in his pastoral and evangelistic concern for them.

He reminds them yet again of the *'great reward'* of the 'great salvation' (2:3)—the reward, that is, of God's grace, and never our merit, which accompanies the believing and embracing of the gospel—the reward which it is quite proper for the Christian to be thinking about and looking forward to. Faith and hope are twins that cannot be separated. You must never even try to separate them. No human merit is or ever can be involved. All is entirely of God's free grace from first to last, from beginning to end. But what a reward it is! The 1 Peter 1:4–5 text quoted above is proof of this, as are the words of the veteran (by that time) apostle Paul to his much younger 'true child in the faith', Timothy (1 Timothy 1:2): 'Henceforth there is laid up for me the crown of righteousness, which the Lord, the righteous judge, will award to me on that Day, and not only to me but also to all who have loved his appearing' (2 Timothy 4:8).

*'For you have need of endurance* [the word also conveys the sense of 'patience']*, so that when you have done the will of God you may receive what is promised'* (10:36). There is a glorious reward to come, but in the meantime there is an urgent need—and, consistent with the teaching of Hebrews all the way through, this great need is the

'*need of endurance*', more and more of it. In verse 32, the 'think back!' section, the writer recalled to them the days when they endured. Now, in this 'press on!' section, they need afresh to endure. This is for the vital reason that without the endurance there will be no reward. The reward is not bestowed half way through the race. To employ Paul's picture (2 Timothy 4:7), 'the good fight' must be 'fought' (to the end), 'the race' must be 'finished' (to the end), and 'the faith' must be 'kept' (to the end). There can be no dropping out along the way.

There can be no discharge in this present life from a wholehearted commitment to be doing '*the will of God*' in all things. Along similar lines, Paul called upon the Christians at Ephesus: 'do not be foolish, but understand what the will of the Lord is' (Ephesians 5:17); and he encouraged the Christians at Colossae: 'knowing that from the Lord you will receive the inheritance as your reward. You are serving the Lord Christ' (Colossians 3:24).

Endurance and apostasy cannot mix. This is made absolutely clear in the present verse, as the '*so that*' demonstrates. The sequence is clear—enduring, doing '*the will of God*', and then (and only then) receiving '*what is promised*'. If we are serious in our lives about doing God's will in all things, then this most certainly includes paying thorough practical attention to the call to endure. However difficult the course, heavy the trials, shattering the disappointments or brutal the persecutions, perseverance is the key in the Christian life. And in order to enable us so to do, 'the God of all grace' (1 Peter 5:10) undertakes to give us 'more grace' (James 4:6)—as often as we need it and as much of it as we need, from his unfailing supply. We are not left to our own devices—and neither were these Hebrews.

To '*receive what is promised*' is more precisely to 'receive (or, 'obtain') the promise'. It is striking (and challenging) to note that again and again in the lives of the Old Testament believers it was keeping their eyes firmly fixed upon the covenant promises of God that kept them going. This will become very apparent shortly when we move into chapter 11. Yet they died not having received the promise (11:39), that is, the ultimate fulfilment of it. This was not because somehow the promise had failed, for not one of God's promises will ever fail, but 'since God had provided something better for us, that apart from us they should not be made perfect' (11:40). In other words, all of God's people, whenever they or we live along the course of history, all belong together, all will receive the fullness of God's promises together, and all will be perfected together. Oh happy day! Recalling 10:23, 'Let us hold fast the confession of our hope without wavering, for he who promised is faithful'. This is what, at the end of the day, will separate the wheat from the chaff (Luke 3:17), the true believers from the apostates.

Our writer's skilful pastoral touch continues with further incentives for the people to endure. *'For* [a connecting word, about to draw a conclusion from what has just been written]*, "Yet a little while* [an emphatic 'very, very little while']*, and the coming one will come and will not delay"'* (10:37). The prophet Habakkuk is now quoted. Although he prophesied a long time before Hebrews was written (he ministered during the seventh century BC), this is a very suitable choice of Old Testament citation. His were difficult and discouraging days for the covenant people of God, and God raised him up for such a time as that, just as he did with the writer to the Hebrews in his own day. The quotation here is from Habakkuk 2:3 (with 2:4 about to follow in the next verse of Hebrews).

The fact that the Habakkuk reference reads, 'For still the vision awaits its appointed time', whereas the Hebrews use of it relates it to a person (*'the coming one will come'*), is explained by the fact that (once again) the quotation comes from the Septuagint translation rather than the Hebrew. This does not present any problem, however, for 'the vision' was always tightly bound up with a person, an individual, and that one was the very heartbeat of God's entire covenant promises—the Lord Jesus Christ. He is the Saviour and he is the Judge. 9:28 has already spoken of his two appearings—the one already passed (his incarnation, 'to bear the sins of many'), the other still to come (his return, 'to save those who are eagerly waiting for him'). Yet here is the firm assurance: *'the coming one will come'*, and, moreover, he *'will not delay'*. It is the certainty of the coming, and not merely the coming itself, which is being emphasised here, and it is a most needful emphasis.

Why is the second coming brought in at 10:37? As a spur to the Hebrews to keep going with Christ. Let it be the very same to us, knowing that the coming Saviour *'will not delay'* even one second beyond his appointed time, and that then all our sorrows and struggles will be over, and we 'shall dwell in the house of the LORD forever' (Psalm 23:6).

The Habakkuk quotation now continues: *'but my righteous one shall live by faith'* (10:38). Who is intended by *'my righteous one'*? The answer is in the quotation itself. God's *'righteous one'* is the *'one* (who) *shall live by faith'*. That is to say, the true Christian, the one who has been accounted righteous in God's sight, who has 'been justified by faith' (Romans 5:1), who has 'become the righteousness of God' (2 Corinthians 5:21), will live with faith in continual exercise, trusting and resting in the Lord. He does live and he *'shall live by faith'*. It is the one who can say, with Paul, 'the life that I live in the flesh I live by faith in the Son of God, who loved me and gave himself for me' (Galatians 2:20). All self-confidence and self-trust has been eliminated, and the Lord alone is our sure refuge. The truth about us now is that 'if we live, we live to the Lord, and if we die, we die to the Lord'. And what, for all such, is the conclusion and application of the matter? 'So then, whether we live or whether we die, we are the Lord's' (Romans 14:8).

The alternative to living by faith (too grievous to risk trying) is to go backwards. But of such a one the Lord says, *'and if he shrinks back, my soul has no pleasure in him'*. We know from Ezekiel that God has 'no pleasure in the death of the wicked, but that the wicked turn from his way and live' (Ezekiel 33:11). In our present Hebrews verse we learn that he *'has no pleasure'* [catch the force—*'no pleasure'* at all] in the person (whoever he or she is) who *'shrinks back'*. Such a one boasts in himself, rather than in the Lord, and congratulates himself on being saved, rather than giving all the glory to God. This is to rob the Lord of the praise and honour due only and entirely to him. We should not forget the Saviour's challenging words: 'For whoever would save his life will lose it, but whoever loses his life for my sake will save it' (Luke 9:24).

It is the mark of the truly converted one that he does not shrink back, turn aside, take up (after all) a position against Christ and the gospel, but keeps right on till the end of the road and arrives safely in glory. This is both the perseverance and the preservation of the saints. There is never any need to choose between those two words (perseverance and preservation). Both are true. Both apply. And both depend upon the Lord. Yet, having said that (and in order to leave us without any excuse), something needs to be added. While it is the Lord who preserves his people, we are to persevere (though we do so in the strength which the Lord supplies, for, as Jesus himself said, 'apart from me you can do nothing', John 15:5).

This tenth chapter closes with a statement of encouragement and hope. *'But we are not of those who shrink back* [this noun, here making its only New Testament appearance, captures the sense of withdrawal, hesitancy, turning tail, timidity, taking fright] *and are destroyed* ['to destruction'—recall verse 31], *but of those who have faith and preserve their souls* [who believe and are saved]*'* (10:39). For all his serious pastoral concerns about those to whom he was writing (and he has not held back from expressing them), our author clearly maintained a solid hope that it was and would yet remain well with these precious souls—just as any pastor does for the flock in his care as their under-shepherd. He did exactly the same in 6:9 after delivering the solemn warnings there concerning apostasy, when he wrote: 'Though we speak in this way, yet in your case, beloved, we feel sure of better things—things that belong to salvation'.

It is a terrible position to come to, if a pastor finally gives up hope for one who has professed Christ, however far from the Lord they might through some long season appear to be, and whatever grievous sin they may have committed. Again he uses the gracious and encompassing pronoun *'we'* in addressing them. In doing so, his words here may carry also the challenging nuance of, 'as for us, we are not among any shrinking back ones—and don't you be either!'.

Yet even in holding out hope that it is well with them through grace, still there is the reminder here of the end awaiting those who do give up on the Saviour and disown the faith: *'those who shrink back and are destroyed'.* Nothing but 'the punishment of eternal destruction, away from the presence of the Lord and from the glory of his might' (2 Thessalonians 2:9) awaits the shrinking back ones, if their shrinking back turns out in the end to be real apostasy, for from that there is no return. As will be said, terribly, of Esau in the next chapter: 'For you know that afterward, when he desired to inherit the blessing, he was rejected, for he found no chance to repent, though he sought it with tears' (11:17).

The only safe course is to *'have faith'* (and for that faith to be renewed in liveliness day by day) and to *'preserve (our) souls* (or, 'lives')' (that blessedness, the actual possession of eternal salvation, which is the opposite of destruction). The further on you are in the race (the last lap), the deeper you are into the match (the final set), the closer you are to the end of the fight (the final round), the less sense does it make to give up or drop out. Press on!

May we, through grace, be finished with the things of death and be totally consumed by the things of life. Which is a very appropriate note to strike before our writer launches into the next chapter, the chapter which in a wonderful way celebrates true and living faith, that faith which (having endured to the end) reaches the heavenly goal.

# Chapter 11
# Vistas of faith

The great eleventh chapter of Hebrews! This is probably the best known (at least on the surface) of all thirteen chapters of the book, and has provided an abundance both of challenge and encouragement to the people of God down the generations. Right at the outset, however, we must remember the overall theme of Hebrews, and, in the light of that, understand clearly the place that this chapter has in the unfolding of that theme.

Hebrews is concerned, above everything else, to set forth the matchless beauties and excellences, the superiority and pre-eminence, of the Lord Jesus Christ. In doing this, it is in line with the whole of Scripture, Old and New Testaments alike. Its particular angle upon this theme, though, is so to display Jesus as to encourage the original readers (and us, following them) to stay close to him, keep him always in clear sight, rely absolutely upon him, and never even dream of turning away from him or giving up on him. In a word, they (and we) must *endure*. In four words, they (and we) must *endure to the end*. We have remarked upon this many times in the commentary already. It has not gone away now, neither will it, right through to the conclusion of the letter.

Without question, the great subject of Hebrews 11 is faith. But not faith in some vague or philosophical sense (believing in someone, something, somewhere, somehow), but faith in the living God. It was from 'the living God' that the readers were warned not 'to fall away', as a result of there being 'in any of (them) an evil, unbelieving heart' (3:12). And as the chapter proceeds, our writer brings into view one after another some of the men and women of faith in the Old Testament, presenting them as real life examples of those who, through thick and thin, in good times and bad, in company or on their own, demonstrated faith of the calibre which endured to the end, faith which (although sometimes stretched to breaking point) did not fail, faith which time and time again proved the sufficiency of God and of his grace, faith which had an eye continually to the Lord Jesus Christ.

Three things further need to be said before we proceed verse by verse. The first is this. This eleventh chapter is more often than not spoken of as telling us about 'the heroes of faith'. This, however, is not strictly accurate. None of those who receive a mention in these verses ever had any personal thoughts of being a 'hero' or a 'heroine'. Nothing would have been further from their ambitions for themselves or their assessments of themselves. They had no wish to have their 'likenesses' hung on the walls of some portrait gallery of believers. They were not celebrities, and knew nothing of our present society's unwholesome preoccupation with such things. Each and every one of them, men and women alike, were people 'with a nature like ours' (James 5:17).

The second thing to say is this, and, although obvious, is still worth saying. The people of God who appear in the course of this chapter are only representative of believers. They were not the only ones! Neither is it in any way a slur on others who do not receive a mention. If every possible candidate had been named, imagine what length the book of Hebrews would have extended to! The fact is that those of whom we read here display between them a wide and valuable range of the different aspects and vistas of faith. We learn here of faith's varieties, faith's colours, faith's possibilities, faith's struggles, faith's victories, and much more besides. And all of this in the light of faith in action—not armchair faith, but battlefield faith; not presumptuous faith, but dependent faith; not always consistent faith, but often up and down faith; not imaginary faith, but real faith. And a close and prayerful study of this faith, in all its richness both of practice and of outcome, should be of immense help to those of us now who name the name of Jesus (as we trust it was, similarly, to the Hebrews of old) to persevere.

The third thing to say is by way of clarifying what 'faith' is being dealt with here. This is not a chapter primarily about what we term 'saving, or justifying, faith' (such as in Acts 16:31, 'Believe in the Lord Jesus, and you will be saved')—although all these men and women of faith listed here were saved souls. Rather chapter 11 is primarily concerned with what we refer to as 'continuing, or persevering, faith'. Expressing that another way, the chapter treats of the life of faith, faith as it is lived out by the believer, rather than the initial gift of faith, by which we are enabled to lay hold of salvation in the first place.

## Faith itself (11:1–2)

The chapter opens, not with a precise (still less, exhaustive) definition of faith as such, but rather with a rich statement of its nature—thereby setting out what it is that all the examples which follow exemplify. Indeed, these first two verses give us a sense of the 'tenses' of faith—its past, present and future (although not presented in that usual order).

### Faith's present

This is mentioned first. *'Now faith is the assurance of things hoped for'* (11:1). Our author mentioned at the end of the previous chapter that 'we [he included himself] are ... of those who have faith and preserve their souls' (10:39). What is this faith actually like? How does it work out? What does it look like?

The word here rendered *'assurance'* can bear a number of different translations. It occurs only five times in the New Testament, three of which are in Hebrews (the two others being 1:3, where the ESV translates it 'nature', with respect to the being and essence of God; and 3:14, where we had the translation 'confidence', with respect to holding it 'firm to the end'). The translations 'substance', 'reality', 'guarantee' and 'foundation' are also sometimes given for it. So which translation of the word should we favour here? They are not necessarily that very far apart from one another. We might dare to say that the thought here seems to be that faith gives present assurance of, present confidence in, present substance to and present guarantee concerning *'things hoped for'*. In that comprehensive sense we see something of faith's present. It is something in operation right now, for the present, day by day; and in being so, it brings us consoling and assuring certainty of what is yet to be. Even now, by faith, we lay hold of these future realities. Even now, through faith, we actually possess them. Even now, with faith in exercise, they are ours.

As for the *'things hoped for'* themselves, we have commented upon them at different points already. In sum, they are heavenly blessings now and heavenly blessings in store—all 'the immeasurable riches of (God's) grace in kindness toward us in Christ Jesus' (Ephesians 2:7).

## Faith's future

This first sentence continues: *'the conviction of things not seen'*. In the Christian life, faith and hope are intimately entwined. Romans 8:24–25 makes this plain: 'Now hope that is seen is not hope. For who hopes for what he sees? But if we hope for what we do not see, we wait for it with patience'. There is a direct link between these two phrases in 11:1. The terms *'assurance'* and *'conviction'* are like twins. We are both assured and convinced (or, persuaded) that all that is promised to us in the gospel (even though there is still so much of it that we cannot actually see) is absolutely real. Nothing divinely promised will ever turn out to be non-existent. By faith we sense them, taste them, and enjoy them, even though as yet they are still to come.

What are some of these things which are as yet still in faith's future, still *not seen*? Precious coming realities such as these: being completely delivered from every last vestige of sin (though at the present the weights of sin cling to us so closely, 12:1); possessing eternal life (though we know we have to die); being clothed in our resurrection bodies (though thus far we have never seen one and cannot conceive what they will be like); discovering that all of God's providences in our lives really have been full of wisdom and love (though for now we have to reckon with the devil and our own frail hearts that seek to tell us otherwise); and beholding Christ's church as a glorious church (though at present she appears to be anything but). In all these things (and many others besides) faith looks into the future and is persuaded that these things are real and these things are true. And so they shall prove to be.

## Faith's past

With what is to come as the chapter unfolds very much in mind, this opening section on the very nature of faith now declares: *'For by it* [that is, by faith] *the people of old* [literally, 'the elders', a number of whom are shortly to be mentioned] *received their commendation* [in the sense of divine approval]*'* (11:2). The roll-call will begin shortly, but the truth flagged up here is that faith—believing, persevering faith—is the great thing that all these people shared in common. Faith in the living God, faith in the covenant God, faith in the unchanging God, is the bond that unites them, even though many of them never knew one another. As verse 6 will teach us, 'without faith it is impossible to please (God)'. They spanned many centuries, they had many different experiences, they faced many trials and struggles, but their trust was in God and he never failed them. Just as he promised he would, God proved himself to be the God of the fathers, of their children, and of their children's children, through every generation.

One of the striking things about the men and women of faith who are mentioned personally by name in this chapter is that not only are the famous ones here, as we might expect (such as Noah, Abraham, Moses, David and Samuel), but so also are some of the lesser known, and often unsung, ones (like Abel, Enoch, Rahab, Jephthah, and—a special delight, this—Moses' parents). And for their faith (though not to their own glory) all of them *'received their commendation'*—that is to say, the divine approval (to God's own glory).

## Faith and creation (11:3)

Our writer has one further (and highly important) thing to say before getting down to his panoramic selection of Old Testament men and women of faith. He goes right back to the fundamental doctrine of creation, in order to relate this to the business of faith. *'By faith* [the key phrase which is used altogether eighteen times in this chapter] *we understand* [again he includes himself along with his readers in what is being written] *that the universe was created by the word of God, so that what is seen was not made out of things that are visible'* (11:3). This statement should in no way surprise us. We were not there when God created the world, and so believing the truth set forth in this verse also involves the realm of active faith.

The biblical doctrine of creation is mocked and under threat on many sides in our day—even sometimes from within 'the church'. There is much confusion, and the shout often frequently goes up that science has disproved it and that evolution is the thing that counts. Nothing could be further from the truth! And to prove it, 11:3 recalls us unashamedly to basics. It is helpful to put *four straight questions* to this verse, to which we shall find that it gives us *four straight answers*.

(1) *Question*: Who made the world? *Answer*: God did. The Bible knows and allows no other answer. God himself is the subject of the very first sentence of the Bible, and rightly so. 'In the beginning, God created the heavens and the earth' (Genesis 1:1). That is where the Bible starts, and so does our present verse, when it declares, *'the universe was created by ... God'*. The entire creation, from a planet to a flower, is God's own handiwork. And this truth, which should cause every child of God to rejoice in him, is also a solemn testimony to all

men, whether they believe in God or not. How so? 'For his invisible attributes, namely, his eternal power and divine nature, have been clearly perceived, ever since the creation of the world, in the things that have been made. So they are without excuse' (Romans 1:20).

(2) *Question*: How did God make the world? *Answer:* By his own word. The phrase used here is *'by the word of God'*, meaning by the word of his command. We only have to recall the repeated 'And God said' in the Genesis creation narrative. And the Psalms tell the same story. 'By the word of the LORD the heavens were made, and by the breath of his mouth all their host'; 'For he spoke, and it came to be; he commanded, and it stood firm' (Psalm 33:6, 9).

The emphasis is on the authoritative command of God, the expressing of his creative power, the working of his sovereign will. Here is the voice of the One who can do everything. And everything is to his own honour and praise—which is why, after having created the world in six days, 'God saw everything that he had made, and behold, it was very good' (Genesis 1:31). Of course it was—the perfect creation of the perfect Creator. And so 'God blessed the seventh day and made it holy, because on it God rested from all his work that he had done in creation' (Genesis 2:3). This was the rest of divine pleasure, repose and contentment.

(3) *Question*: Out of what did God make the world? *Answer:* Out of nothing. This is the import of the words, *'so that what is seen* (literally, 'what is being seen' or 'things appearing') *was not made* (literally, 'brought into being') *out of things that are visible* (or, 'being seen')'. This is what is often referred to with a Latin phrase, creation 'ex nihilo' (out of nothing). The point is clear. God made the world from nothing, not from other things which were already there. Nothing was already there! Moreover, the universe was created perfect, full of beauty, harmony, symmetry and design, with the first man and woman (Adam and Eve) created as full grown adults.

(4) *Question*: How do we know that what the Bible says about creation is true? *Answer:* By faith. This is precisely where 11:3 starts. *'By faith we understand'*. As was mentioned above, since we were not

present at the time of creation we are brought into the realm of faith, if we are to believe what the Bible says about it (though not forgetting those 'evidences' touched on in the Romans 1:20 quotation). We do not understand these things through human intellect or cleverness, but rather by humbling ourselves before God, knowing that God's 'word is truth' (John 17:17), and that it is the word of 'God, who never lies' (Titus 1:2). The Spirit of God, who is 'the Spirit of truth' who 'will guide (us) into all the truth' (John 16:13), enlightens 'the eyes of (our) hearts' (Ephesians 1:18) to perceive something altogether wonderful and glorious that has happened.

So, at the end of the day, the biblical doctrine of creation is not a difficult doctrine for a Christian to believe and accept (any more than is any other biblical doctrine, such as the Trinity, the virgin birth, the resurrection, the second coming, or the making one day of 'new heavens and a new earth', 2 Peter 3:13). For God is not man. God is God, 'from everlasting to everlasting' (Psalm 90:2), ever to be worshipped and adored. And in direct connection with our writer's insistence upon Jesus' pre-eminence, the testimony of John 1:3 to Jesus is highly significant: 'All things were made through him, and without him was not any thing made that was made'.

'Oh come, let us worship and bow down; let us kneel before the LORD, our Maker!' (Psalm 95:6).

## Faith illustrated (11:4–40)

Our writer now delves into the Old Testament in order to provide us with this rich selection of men and women of faith, those who are our brothers and sisters in the Kingdom of God.

### Abel: focused faith (11:4)

The focus of Abel's faith, as we shall see, is absolutely in tune with the theme and thrust of Hebrews. He was 'looking to Jesus' (12:2). *'By faith Abel offered to God a more acceptable sacrifice than Cain, through which he was commended as righteous, God commending him by accepting his gifts'* (11:4). God made a difference between them on the basis of their offerings.

There is something both tragic and poignant about the lives of Abel and Cain. They were brothers, the children of Adam and Eve. Significantly, both were born after the fall, and so were born with sinful natures, even from their mother's womb. The historical narrative is in Genesis 4, from which we learn that 'Abel was a keeper of sheep, and Cain a worker of the ground'. On a particular occasion, each of them brought an offering to the Lord. Cain's offering was 'an offering of the fruit of the ground', while Abel 'brought of the firstborn of his flock and of their fat portions'. These gifts, however, received very different responses from God. 'And the LORD had regard for Abel and his offering, but for Cain and his offering he had no regard'. Cain took a poor view of this; he 'was very angry, and his face fell'. Indeed, so angry was Cain, that he murdered his own brother as a result.

Why, in the language of our Hebrews verse, was Abel's *'a more acceptable sacrifice'* to God than Cain's? Why did God commend Abel *'as righteous'*, and do so *'by accepting his gifts'*, while Cain and his offering received no such commendation? The answer lies in their approach to God. They were bringing gifts, sacrifices, offerings. That is, they were approaching God in worship. Abel came before God on the basis of sacrifice, with a gift from his flock. Cain did not come before God on the basis of sacrifice, but brought something from the ground. As the old preachers used to say, there was no blood in Cain's potatoes!

Both brothers would have learned from their parents about the need to approach God on the basis of sacrifice—a lesson Adam and Eve would themselves have learned unforgettably from the skins God had provided for them to clothe them, skins which themselves came from a sacrifice (Genesis 3:21). Abel believed this, and came before God in God's way. Cain, it appears, did not. Abel came by the way of blood, while Cain did not. As a result, Abel was accepted and Cain rejected (although Scripture is silent as to how God made this known to the two men). No wonder we are warned in Scripture not to walk 'in the way of Cain' (Jude 11). Why not? 'Because his own deeds were evil and his brother's righteous' (1 John 3:12).

*'And through his* [Abel's] *faith, though he died, he still speaks'.* Abel
was the first martyr for the faith, and as such he continues to speak
to all who listen. We shall learn from 12:24 that Jesus' blood 'speaks a
better word than the blood of Abel', yet the very blood of Abel itself
still speaks, it still has its own voice. It is the voice which calls us to
faith in Christ, trust in his blood, and 'the new and living way that
he opened for us' (10:19). It is the voice which (looking on to verse
6) insists that 'without faith it is impossible to please (God)'. It is the
voice which recalls 10:38, where God declares 'but my righteous one
shall live by faith'. It is the voice which reminds us that, 'If we live, we
live to the Lord, and if we die, we die to the Lord. So then, whether
we live or whether we die, we are the Lord's. For to this end Christ
died and lived again, that he might be Lord both of the dead and of
the living' (Romans 14:8–9).

## Enoch: pleasing faith (11:5-6)

Enoch walks across the pages of Scripture in Genesis 5 in the manner
of 'enter stage left, exit stage right', and that is all. To read through
that chapter of Genesis is like taking a walk through a graveyard. Of
one person after another it is recorded, 'and he died'. Little more is
said of folk, apart from who their father was and how long they lived.
But when the record arrives at Enoch we are treated unexpectedly to
a brief cameo description of him, the nub of which is that 'Enoch
walked with God, and he was not, for God took him'. Interestingly,
Enoch (who died when he was 365 years old) was the father of
Methuselah, the man who lived until the age of 969. Enoch appears
in Luke's genealogy of Jesus (Luke 3:37), as well as in Jude 14–15,
where he is spoken of as 'the seventh from Adam', and it is mentioned
that he 'prophesied'.

The Hebrews reference to Enoch focuses not upon his life, but
upon his death. *'By faith Enoch was taken up* ('removed') *so that he
should not see* [that is, experience] *death, and he was not found, because
God had taken him'* (11:5). So, though we speak of his death, he did
not go through the actual experience of dying, but was rather (like
Elijah in 2 Kings 2) taken straight into heaven, bypassing death. There
is certainly something extremely appropriate in this with Enoch. We

noted the Genesis record that his entire life was a walk with God; that is, a life lived in fellowship with God, a life close to God. And God so appointed it that he passed from earth to heaven in the manner of a walk—he, as it were, just stepped into heaven, he walked right in. One moment he was walking with God on earth, the next moment he was walking with God in heaven! The statement that *'he was not found'* may imply that (as in Elijah's case) people went looking for him and could not find him anywhere. Or it might just mean that he was no longer among those present here below.

*'Now before he was taken he was commended as having pleased God'.* This must have arisen out of the character of his daily walk with God—in the midst of a sinful world, a family life, and (no doubt) a lonely experience. Yet he was God's companion, God's friend, God's confidant, God's witness, God's servant, to whom God gave this rich reward of not having to taste death. We cannot imagine quite what his experience must have been like, or what a surprise (a shock, even?) it must have been. It is worth remembering, however, that for those who are still alive when Jesus returns, their experience will be similar, for they (we?) 'will be caught up together with them ['the dead in Christ (who) will rise first'] in the clouds to meet the Lord in the air, and so we will always be with the Lord' (1 Thessalonians 4:16–17).

*'And without faith it is impossible* [a most forceful expression] *to please him* [God], *for whoever would draw near to God must* [note the strength of that word] *believe that he* [the one, true, living, eternal, covenant God of the Bible] *exists and that he rewards those who seek him'* (11:6). What a rich verse this is. Faith (the enduring, persevering, keeping going faith with which Hebrews is so concerned) is the only true way to live and the only true way to please God. It is the life of complete trust in and reliance upon God. For this faith to be a reality, there must, of course, be a firm belief that God exists (think back to 11:1 and 'the conviction of things not seen', for, as Jesus says in John 1:18, 'No one has ever seen God'). Then it is through faith that, believing he exists, we *'draw near to God'* and are given the reward (entirely of his grace, never of our merit) of being received and accepted by him. Indeed, God himself is the reward he gives to

all such, and he gives himself to us forever. It is more than enough reward to have such a God to be our God. Yet, as we learned from Abel, this drawing near to God through faith is with our eyes firmly fixed upon the Lord Jesus Christ and his sacrifice, looking always and looking only to him.

Here, in the fullness of this verse, is a gracious promise to the unconverted, to the backslider, and to the Christian. God's word through his prophet is pertinent here: 'Seek the LORD while he may be found; call upon him while he is near' (Isaiah 55:6). And the chief mark of this life of faith is that, like Enoch, we seek *'to please'* God in everything.

## Noah: conspicuous faith (11:7)

No less than six chapters of Genesis (the end of chapter 5 through to the beginning of chapter 10) are compressed here into one verse! *'By faith* [once again, as throughout the chapter, these words (translating only one in Greek) stand in the emphatic position in the sentence] *Noah, being warned by God concerning events as yet unseen* [recalling verse 1], *in reverent fear constructed an ark for the saving of his household'* (11:7).

For those of us who began to become familiar with the Bible from an early age, it is likely that the events surrounding Noah and the building of the ark prior to the flood that deluged over the whole earth, were among the first things that we learned. It is in no way surprising to discover Noah here in Hebrews 11. God spoke to Noah at a time of great wickedness in the world, when 'every intention of the thoughts of (man's) heart was only evil continually'. The effect of this wickedness was that 'the LORD was sorry that he had made man on the earth, and it grieved him to his heart'. So he determined to 'blot out man' from the entire globe. 'But Noah found favour in the eyes of the LORD'. Like Enoch, 'Noah walked with God', and is spoken of by God as 'a righteous man, blameless in his generation'.

Our writer draws attention to the *rock*, the *fruit* and the *proof* of Noah's faith. Its *rock* is that he believed every word that God spoke to him, and that he did so without question. He was *'warned by God concerning events as yet unseen*'—the coming of the deluge, the judgment upon mankind, and the salvation of his own family. Nothing further was required by Noah once this divine warning was given to him. He believed God in this, as in everything, knowing that God is absolutely trustworthy, and never owes us an explanation for whatever he asks us to do.

The *fruit* of Noah's faith is exhibited in that he, with only the bare word of God to go on, '*in reverent fear constructed an ark*'. Two notes are present here: his godly fear and his humble obedience. He had no precedent for such an event which God was about to perform. Neither was there sign of any rain. Yet in a manner of '*reverent fear*' he set about the task. The phrase used carries the sense of 'devoutness'. We noted above the way in which God regarded him, and it is completely in tune with this that Noah proceeded in a manner of holy and godly fear—not the fear which is frightened of God, but the fear which is in awe and wonder of God, which delights in him and seeks to honour him in all things and at all times, to do his pleasure. He had large thoughts of God and small thoughts of himself. What a stark contrast there was between Noah's faith and the multitude's unbelief.

This godly fear of God worked itself out in humble obedience to him. Noah '*constructed an ark*'. God gave him the precise design and dimensions of this huge 'sea going' vessel, and in the building of it Noah fulfilled all of this to the last detail. He did not adapt it or adjust it in a way which he felt might improve upon it or make it more suitable. He did exactly as God commanded him. God's word was enough for him, and so he set to work. It would no doubt have been costly. Costly in the labour it involved (for everything was to be done from scratch). Costly in the time it took (this was no rushed Saturday afternoon job, but went on for no less than 120 years—this is implied in Genesis 6:3). Costly, no doubt, in the reaction it will have produced from those who observed him going about his work. In passing, we would note how the patience of God is beautifully on view here. It is this to which 1 Peter 3:20 draws attention: 'when

God's patience waited in the days of Noah, while the ark was being prepared'.

And the *proof* of his faith is evidenced in the two things recorded in our Hebrews verse. Noah *'constructed an ark for the saving of his household. By this he condemned the world'*. Even as his family was saved (eight in all—Noah, his wife, their three sons, and their wives), the entire rest of mankind perished in the global deluge. And *'he condemned the world'*. He did this not only in the clear example he gave of godliness, holy fear, and obedience, but also in that as he worked he preached. Noah was a preacher! 2 Peter 2:5 calls him 'a herald of righteousness'. His preaching incorporated two things. There was a solemn warning 'to flee from the wrath to come' (Luke 3:7), which would be visited in the flood. And there was a heartfelt invitation to salvation by God's grace through faith, which was vividly pictured by the ark. In this connection (although our writer does not touch on this explicitly), the ark—as well as being just that, a boat— is a remarkable 'type' of the Lord Jesus Christ, the sinner's only safe refuge from the divine judgment, as well as his only solid hope and lasting joy.

His godly life condemned them, his obedient work condemned them, and his faithful preaching condemned them—left them without excuse, for they had had the testimony (visual and verbal) before them for a very long time. In all of this, Noah is an outstanding example, encouragement and rebuke to us, as he was to the Hebrews.

The verse concludes: *'and became an heir of the righteousness that comes by faith'*. Noah, believing God and his word, and acting by faith upon it, stood before God justified and approved, both a son and *'an heir'*. Back in 1:14, believers as a whole are called 'those who are to inherit salvation'—the heirs of salvation, the righteous ones who live by faith. All the riches of God's inheritance for his people belonged to Noah. He was a true possessor as a righteous one.

## Abraham (1): venturing faith (11:8–10)

We come now to a major section of the chapter which chronicles

something of the patriarchs (Abraham, Isaac and Jacob), beginning
with Abraham. His wife, Sarah, will also be singled out for mention
shortly, but for now we focus upon the husband. More of him is said
in this chapter than of any other individual.

*'By faith Abraham obeyed when he was called to go out to a place that
he was to receive as an inheritance. And he went out, not knowing where
he was going'* (11:8). It is in the nature of the Christian life that we
are on a pilgrim path, travellers from one place to another, heading
ultimately for heaven itself. God came to Abraham (when he was still
called Abram) in Genesis 12, and said to him, 'Go from your country
and your kindred and your father's house to the land that I will show
you'. God gave him great promises and prospects, saying, 'And I will
make of you a great nation, and I will bless you and make your name
great, so that you will be a blessing'.

Abraham did not need to be told twice. 'So Abram went, as the
LORD had told him'. The divine command was sufficient for him
(just as it was with Noah). He *obeyed when he was called'*. The most
important thing stated about Abraham anywhere in the Bible must
surely be Genesis 15:6: 'And he believed the LORD, and he counted it
to him as righteousness'. He is given the accolade in Romans 4:11 of
being 'the father of all who believe … so that righteousness would be
counted to them as well'. There is also the rich statement of Galatians
3:9, which declares, 'So then, those who are of faith are blessed
along with Abraham, the man of faith'. There can be no mistaking
the fundamental and living association between Abraham and faith.
Think of one, and you think of the other. He was a man of faith, for
whom that faith led him directly to be a man of action. His was faith
with works, not without them.

With the divine call came the divine promise: *'to go out to a place
that he was to receive as an inheritance'*. The theme of *'inheritance'*
is to the fore again. Yet—and here is where faith sprang into play,
bringing another recollection of 11:1, where this detailed treatment of
faith started—when he set off, he did so *'not knowing where he was
going'*. He was given no location, and had neither map nor compass.
In commencing his journey, however, he did not entertain any doubts

over what God was doing with him, or whether or not God would direct his steps. He committed himself to the LORD, and off he went, taking his family with him. It all sounds very simple and everyday, but it was no such thing. He ventured on the Lord, with a daring and boldness of faith, a faith which was not confounded or put to shame. He learned from deep experience what is involved when we both trust and obey. That is what faith requires. 'Let him who walks in darkness and has no light trust in the name of the LORD, and rely on his God' (Isaiah 50:10).

*'By faith he went to live in the land of promise* [the land of Canaan, Genesis 12:5]*, as in a foreign land, living in tents* [a classic image of not being rooted in a settled place] *with Isaac and Jacob* [his son and grandson]*, heirs with him of the same promise'* (11:9). Notwithstanding this being *'the land of promise'*, the martyr Stephen proclaimed that God 'gave him no inheritance in it, not even a foot's length, but promised to give it to him as a possession and to his offspring after him, though he had no child' (Acts 7:5). It was literally like living *'in a foreign land'*, someone passing through rather than there to stay, a visitor rather than a resident—the very thing that is true of the Christian, by definition, so long as we remain here on earth.

Everything might have appeared to be against Abraham exercising faith, yet faith was given to him and it triumphed over all obstacles and all temptations to unbelief. He faced one trial of faith after another—never more so than in the event which will be considered in 11:17–19. Even when offspring was given to him, in his and his wife's old age, it was still a case of *'living in tents'*—trusting the Lord and waiting upon him. The mention of Isaac and Jacob here is a demonstration and reminder of the precious truth of God undertaking to be the God not only of the 'fathers' but of their 'children' and their 'children's children'—the God who is God of one generation after another. Isaac and Jacob were *'heirs with him* [Abraham] *of the same promise'*.

What, in particular, assisted Abraham in this trusting and waiting? We are given the answer immediately. *'For he was looking forward* [an expression of confidence in a certainty, a waiting expectantly, not some blind hope that would come to nothing] *to the city that has foundations, whose designer and builder is God'* (11:10). The tents of Abraham's present experience, as he lived the life of faith, are here exchanged for *'the city'* to which he looked forward. The tent pegs are replaced by the *'foundations'*. The temporary and vulnerable gives way to the permanent and imperishable. And what a lesson this should have been to the Hebrews and should be to us. The danger is always present and pressing to put down roots here, to make ourselves at home where we are. Yet that is a great mistake. It is too limiting. It quenches faith. It dims hope. Abraham's was—and ours, as Christians, is—*'the city that has foundations* [strictly, 'the foundations'], *whose designer and builder is God'*. And where is it to be found? Heaven, and only heaven. That is the land of promise. That is the heavenly home. That is where, even now, our Lord Jesus Christ dwells, and where he awaits our arrival. In this respect, things were no different at all for Old Testament believers from how they are for those, the Hebrews and ourselves included, who follow them.

There is only one destination for the people of God, and that is 'with Christ, for that is far better' (Philippians 1:23). To long to be there is not a negative or escapist way of thinking, but is where the true child of God daily sets his gaze. The words used of God as the heavenly city's *'designer* (or, 'craftsman') *and builder'* make here their only New Testament appearances. It was *'by faith'* that Abraham persevered, having first ventured, and so it must always be. Here, we move from place to place. There, we shall settle down permanently. This is faith's constant and sure horizon. Ours, as was his, is the life and walk of faith, and one day it will be the triumph of faith as well.

### Sarah: expectant faith (11:11–12)

We move now from the focus on the faith of the husband (Abraham) to that of the wife (Sarah), although their lives and their faith were very much intertwined, as the lives of believing husbands and wives are. It is always a precious sight, and is highlighted by the way 11:11 actually begins, *'By faith also herself'*, although the 'also' is not translated in our version. *'By faith Sarah herself received power to conceive* [literally, 'for conception of seed'], *even when she was past* the age, since she considered him faithful who had promised' (11:11). The narratives of Genesis 18 and 21 record, respectively, the announcement to Sarah that she will have a child, and the birth of Isaac. At the time of Isaac's birth, Abraham was 100 and Sarah was 90.

When first Sarah heard the news of what was going to happen, she laughed and did not believe it. Our verse here, however, majors upon this fact: *'since she considered him* [God] *faithful who had promised'*. Clearly, ultimate faith triumphed over initial unbelief. She was enabled to believe that God would do what he had said he would do—and what he alone *could* do for her, considering the ages of the married couple. Hence, she *'received power to conceive'*, for she had no power of herself to do so. She was barren as well as past child-bearing age, whereas after her death Abraham (despite his age) fathered more children following his remarriage.

No small part of living by faith is to be assured of the truth of what God says of himself: 'Behold, I am the LORD, the God of all flesh. Is anything too hard for me?' (Jeremiah 32:27). Jesus says something directly similar: 'with God all things are possible' (Matthew 19:26). The things that are totally *im*possible with man are most gloriously possible with God. Sarah's experience here is a joyful illustration of this. He is truly the God of the impossible. This comes through further when we remember that not only was this seed (offspring) the one individual who was named Isaac, but an entire seed in the sense of a lasting posterity—the very thing which God had promised to Abraham as a covenant promise, and which will be recalled in the very next verse. Abraham and Sarah are mentioned together very beautifully in this connection in Isaiah 51:2, in the words, 'Look to Abraham your father and to Sarah who bore you; for he was but one when I called him, that I might bless him and multiply him'.

*'Therefore from one man* [Abraham]*, and him as good as dead* [a comment repeated by Paul in Romans 4:19]*, were born descendants as many as the stars of heaven and as many as the innumerable grains of sand by the seashore' (11:12)*. A striking contrast stands out between *'from one man'* and countless *'descendants'*. There are two strands of truth here. First of all, in immediate connection with God's covenant

with Abraham, God had made this promise to him: "'Look toward heaven, and number the stars, if you are able to number them'. Then he said to him, "So shall your offspring be'" (Genesis 15:5). Later on, at the time of the sacrifice of Isaac, God said to Abraham: 'I will surely bless you, and I will surely multiply your offspring as the stars of heaven and as the sand that is on the seashore' (Genesis 22:17). This aspect of the promise was fulfilled in the literal physical abundance of offspring given to Abraham.

There is a second, and deeper, strand here, however, and it concerns the one who is right at the centre of Hebrews—the Lord Jesus Christ. This has to do with his spiritual offspring. It is the apostle Paul who takes this up, where he refers to Jesus as the seed (offspring) of Abraham, and then writes: 'And if you are Christ's, then you are Abraham's offspring, heirs according to promise' (Galatians 3:16, 29). So that is to say that, in the fullest sense, Abraham's offspring are all those who belong through faith to the Lord Jesus Christ.

## The faithful so far: vindicated faith (11:13–16)

There comes at this point a gathering together of all those who have been named thus far in the chapter, with particular reference to the patriarchs. *'These all died in faith'* (11:13). They lived in faith, they walked by faith, and they *'died in faith'*—each and every one of them. Of course, you can only die in faith if you have lived in faith. To die in faith is to die believing upon the Lord, but it is something more than this as well, as a recollection of 11:1–2 should be enough to teach us. They all had this in common with one another: they died looking to the divine promises, waiting for the divine promises, but in vital respects not having inherited all the divine promises. Part of the reason why this had to be so will be revealed in 11:39–40 at the end of the chapter. 'And all these, though commended through their faith, did not receive what was promised, since God had provided something better for us, that apart from us they should not be made perfect'. In other words, they had to wait for the rest of us, so that all the faithful would inherit the fullness of the promised divine blessings together.

These dear people (our own brethren in the faith), although they died without receiving every dimension of God's promises to them, were very much promise driven, promise orientated, promise upheld, just as (once again) the Hebrews needed to be—and so do we. It is in the nature of being a Christian, of living by faith, that we give full and constant weight to God's 'precious and very great promises' (2 Peter 1:4), and live in the light (and the love) of them. Not one of them either can or will fail. Consequently the Hebrews 11 brigade, and their like from all those who do not get a mention here, are an example to us.

*'These all died in faith, not having received* (or, 'obtained') *the things promised, but having seen them and greeted* (or, 'welcomed') *them from afar'.* In a sense, their deaths were the finest hour of their lives of faith. The things that they had not *'received'*, they had *'seen'* and *'greeted'*. The fact that this seeing and greeting was *'from afar'* does not diminish the liveliness and reality of it one jot. Are we not in exactly the same position? Were not the Hebrews so? The call of this book of Scripture remains, as much as ever, the call to endurance, to perseverance, to keep going until the end.

The inheritance of these Old Testament saints was no mere earthly one, but heavenly. If it had been earthly, they would have forfeited it all at death, for they could not have taken it with them. Rather, they were enabled—by faith, for there is no other way—to 'look not to the things that are seen but to the things that are unseen', the 'eternal' things and not the 'transient' ones (2 Corinthians 4:18). And their greeting of them is a delightful expression, bringing to the fore, as it does, their enthusiasm for and anticipation of the heavenly joys and abiding delights that await the children of God. When Paul speaks of 'what God has prepared for those who love him', he immediately remarks that 'these things God has revealed to us through the Spirit' (1 Corinthians 1:9–10). It is not that we do not know about them, or that our possession of them is in any doubt. But there are some things (some of the best things) that we have to wait for patiently.

The verse continues: *'and having acknowledged that they were strangers and exiles on the earth'.* This recalls the 'living in tents' motif back in 11:9. Note our comments there. It will have been plain from the way they lived and the priorities they had that this was so of them. They were not secret believers. *'For people who speak thus make it clear that they are seeking a homeland'* (11:14). Heaven is rightly to be regarded as our 'home'—our true home, in contrast to any earthly home we dwell in. It is *'a homeland'*, one of which already we have 'citizenship' (Philippians 3:20), one to which we already belong.

*'If they had been thinking of that land from which they had gone out, they would have had opportunity to return. But as it is, they desire a better country, that is, a heavenly one'* (11:15–16). There is always the danger facing believers that we become too much at home in this present world and in our present environment. Everything feels familiar, and we readily are more at ease with the familiar. But our Hebrews 11 friends were not thinking like that. Abraham, to take one example, could have returned to the land he had come from originally, but it never crossed his mind to do so. They were all more 'ready to go' than 'ready to stay'. They wished to 'go on' rather than 'stay put' or 'go back'. This was no doubt the very note which needed to be sounded from the trumpet in the ears of the Hebrews. Their spirit, it appears, was the 'going back' sort, and our writer is continuing to do all that he can to dissuade them from such a course. Rather, he would have them cleave to Jesus and look forward to things to come by virtue of belonging to him. Such is the continual call to the church of Christ, needed with great urgency once again in our day. Jesus was never one to 'go back', as 12:2 will remind us very movingly. We are to be imitators of him.

That which they desired, and so should we, is *'a better country'*, and that is precisely because it is *'a heavenly one'*. There, we shall enjoy the immediate presence and sight of our Lord Jesus. There, we shall experience the 'no mores'—'and death shall be no more, neither shall there be mourning nor crying nor pain anymore, for the former things have passed away' (Revelation 21:4). There, we shall be free from sin, from trial and from hindrance. There, 'the city has no need of sun or moon to shine on it, for the glory of God gives it light, and its lamp is the Lamb' (Revelation 21:23). There, faith will be vindicated, for it will have vanished into sight (think of 2 Corinthians 5:7).

'*Therefore God is not ashamed to be called their God, for he has prepared for them a city*'. It is a remarkable thing to realise that God '*is not ashamed to be called* (our) *God*', considering all that we know we have to be ashamed of. Our great desire, surely, is never to bring shame upon him. Yet here is the assurance of God owning us for himself. We noted earlier how, among his other names, he is 'the God of Abraham, the God of Isaac, and the God of Jacob' (Exodus 3:6), and we may each put our own name in there along with them. Our God is the covenant God of his covenant people. That is no small part of his glory. He '*is not ashamed to be called their* [our] *God*' now, neither will he be so on the day of judgment, when we all stand before him, or throughout all the endless ages of eternity. We may compare what is said in 2:11–12 about Jesus and his own (especially, 'he is not ashamed to call them brothers'); and also in 2:13, quoting from Isaiah, 'Behold, I and the children God has given me'.

And this God who is not ashamed of us has himself '*prepared for them* [and for us] *a city*'. The word '*city*' captures the sense of something fixed, stable, established and enduring. No more tents! This mirrors the statement in 11:10, 'the city that has foundations, whose designer and builder is God'. This is the 'homeland' (verse 14). This is the 'better country', the 'heavenly one' (verse 16). This is the 'Father's house' where there 'are many rooms', and where Jesus has gone 'to prepare a place for (us)' (John 14:2). This is 'the heavenly Jerusalem' (Hebrews 12:22).

## Abraham (2): tested faith (11:17–19)

Throughout his entire long life of faith, Abraham must never have faced a sterner test of faith than when God spoke to him the words recorded in Genesis 22:2. 'Take your son, your only son Isaac, whom you love, and go to the land of Moriah, and offer him there as a burnt offering on one of the mountains of which I shall tell you'. This is the event which forms the backdrop to this further focus upon Abraham here in Hebrews 11.

'*By faith Abraham, when he was tested, offered up Isaac* [that is, he had full intent to do so, and would have done so, even though in the event the offering of Isaac never actually happened]' (11:17). The immediate and willing obedience of the patriarch to God's heart-rending command is very marked. The Genesis account tells us that 'he rose early in the morning, saddled his donkey, and took two of his young men with him, and his son Isaac'. It would be helpful if, at this point in reading the commentary, you (dear reader) took a moment to read the complete Genesis 22 narrative, for all the details of it cannot be rehearsed here. Suffice to say, Abraham showed a humble readiness to see the divine command all the way through, with no questioning of God or requiring an explanation, and came even to the point (having 'built the altar … laid the wood … bound Isaac'—just feel the emotion in those brief statements) of '(reaching) out his hand and (taking) the knife to slaughter his son'. It was at this point that God intervened.

Hebrews continues: '*and he who had received the promises was in the act of offering up his only son*'. The deed was as good as done. Yet remember who it was whom Abraham was about to sacrifice. This is not only a father with his son (as if that is not poignant enough). This is the aged patriarch about to sacrifice the offspring in whom all God's covenant promises resided. The divine command and the divine promise seem to contradict each other completely (though the patriarch, in a striking illustration of his faith, was entirely content to leave the reconciliation of these two things to God, who, after all, had given Isaac to him and Sarah in the first place). This is brought out by our writer concerning Isaac: '*of whom it was said, "Through Isaac shall your offspring be named"*' (11:18). This quotation from Genesis 21:12 underscores that if there was no Isaac, there would be no offspring. That is to say, even more seriously, if there was no Isaac, there would be no promise. The promise of God would have come to naught. Recall the words of God to Abraham in Genesis 17:21, 'But I will establish my covenant with Isaac'. We cannot begin to imagine how Abraham must have grappled with this in his thoughts, even though (as we have noted) he did not hesitate for a moment to set about fulfilling the divine command. Remember, also, what came out in our remarks upon verse 12 about Jesus himself being the seed (offspring) of Abraham. So, even more seriously still, if there was no Isaac, there would have been no messianic line and no Saviour. It is as solemn as that.

Yet this is where Abraham's faith was enabled to triumph. Rather than it being shattered, it was strengthened. *'He considered* [that is, reckoned, believed, was persuaded] *that God was able even to raise him from the dead, from which, figuratively speaking, he did receive him back'* (11:19). Take a look back to 6:13–15. He trusted God implicitly to keep and perform all his promises. So, Abraham argued to himself, if that requires God *'to raise him* [Isaac] *from the dead'*, then he is well able to do that. There is more than an implication of this persuasion in Abraham's remark to his servants in Genesis 22:5. 'Stay here with the donkey. I and the boy will go over there and worship and ['we', understood, not 'I'] come again to you'. God's word must be true. His promise must stand. And so, however perplexing everything might have seemed to Abraham, that really was the end of the matter. He waited patiently and expectantly to see what God would do. And that is exactly what God did do—*'figuratively speaking'* God did raise Isaac from the dead. True—the patriarch did not, in the event, actually have to kill his son. But Isaac was as good as sacrificed, when, at the last moment, God called to Abraham, 'Do not lay your hand upon the boy or do anything to him, for now I know that you fear God, seeing you have not withheld your son, your only son, from me'.

Faith rose to the occasion in a most remarkable way, to the glory of God. Abraham passed the test and received the blessing. And what ultimately happened to him (the best blessing of all) was that which Jesus said of him in John 8:56, when speaking to a gathering of questioning Jews. 'Your father Abraham rejoiced that he would see my day. He saw it and was glad'. The patriarch was granted to see *the day of Jesus' solemn humiliation* (for Jesus was far, far more the Son of the Father's love than ever Isaac could be of Abraham's—yet God 'did not spare his own Son but gave him up for us all', Romans 8:32); *the day of Jesus' total obedience* (seen in Isaac not questioning what his father was doing, but submitting to it without a murmur—just as Jesus, on a different plane altogether, 'humbled himself by becoming obedient to the point of death', Philippians 2:8); *the day of Jesus' utter loneliness* (what was transacted on Moriah was for none to see but Abraham and Isaac—while on Calvary, in those three hours of complete darkness, even the Son cried out, 'My God, my God, why have you forsaken me?', Matthew 27:46); *the day of Jesus' substitutionary death* (the 'ram, caught in a thicket by his horns', which Abraham took and 'offered it up as a burnt offering instead of his son', is a precious 'type' of Jesus, who 'himself bore our sins in his own body on the tree', 1 Peter 2:24); and *the day of Jesus' glorious resurrection* (for God raising Isaac from the dead, *'figuratively speaking'*, is a marvellous type of him literally raising his crucified and buried Son from the dead—Jesus, who said of himself, 'I died, and behold I am alive for evermore', Revelation 1:18).

## Isaac: visionary faith (11:20)

Three brief notices now appear, one after the other, covering between them three complete generations (from Isaac, through Jacob, to Joseph)—thirty chapters of Scripture reduced to three crisp verses. Each selected reference has to do with the end of their lives. Isaac himself is the next in line. Interestingly, the one event singled out here for mention comes from the end of his life of faith, rather than earlier on. *'By faith Isaac invoked future* ['things to come', or, 'coming things'—compare 11:1 again] *blessings on Jacob and Esau'* (11:20). We find Isaac in faith resting in the assurance that God does all things well. Here is an old man (blind, vulnerable, and on the receiving end of deceit and trickery from his son Esau) looking forward to the next generation of God's covenant grace and blessing.

The event being recollected here is narrated in Genesis 27. Although, of the twin sons, Esau was born first, with Jacob quickly following, they are named here in the order *'Jacob and Esau'*. The reason for this? Esau and Jacob was the order of nature, while *'Jacob and Esau'* was the order of grace. Esau despised both his birthright (the rights of inheritance of the firstborn in the family) and his blessing (again, the special blessings belonging to the firstborn). He did so, famously, for 'bread and lentil stew' (Genesis 25:34), and then blamed his brother for it ('He took away my birthright, and behold, now he has taken away my blessing', Genesis 27:36). When it came to the moment of Isaac (the one, remember, who had been on Mount Moriah with his father Abraham) passing on his paternal blessing to his sons, Esau received the very solemn blessing (if he felt it was a blessing at all) of Genesis 27:39–40, while Jacob (himself by no means altogether virtuous) received the full and rich blessing of Genesis 27:27–29. Please take a moment to read those verses now, so that they are freshly before you.

All this being so however, historically, why is this episode brought up in Hebrews 11, rather than (say) the moving incident in Genesis 24 concerning Isaac and Rebekah, or God's promise to Isaac in Genesis 26:1–5 with respect to God's presence with him and blessing upon him? The answer ultimately, of course, is that this is how the Holy Spirit chose that it should be in the writing of Scripture. Beyond that, all we can really say is this. The particular focus of Isaac's faith brought into view (*'Isaac invoked future blessings'*) is that—at the end of a life both long and difficult, with much against him and many obstacles faced—he was still confident in the covenant purposes of God, still looking to God to keep his promises, still keeping an eye on the offspring to come, and so still (like dear old Simeon in Luke 2:25) 'waiting for the consolation of Israel'. And who is that? None other than the Lord Jesus Christ, the glorious focus of the whole of Scripture and (not least) of Hebrews.

## Jacob: dying faith (11:21)

*'By faith Jacob, when dying, blessed each of the sons of Joseph, bowing in worship over the head of his staff'* (11:21). Having just recalled Isaac's blessing of his two sons, our writer now moves on to consider, from the next generation, Jacob (the previously blessed one) blessing the two sons of his own son Joseph (Ephraim and Manasseh). In another reminder of the circumstances behind 11:20, Jacob put his right hand (signifying the chief blessing) upon the head of Ephraim (the younger son) and his left hand upon the head of Manasseh, thereby putting the younger before the older.

The occasion is recorded in Genesis 48 (note especially the

beautiful verses 15–16 of that chapter, as well as verse 20), although no details are given here in Hebrews of the names of the sons or the nature of their blessings. The focus, rather, is upon the connection between *'dying'* and *'bowing in worship'*. As Jacob died, he worshipped. As he worshipped, he died. His death is recorded, simply and movingly, after he had gone on to bless all twelve of his sons and given them instructions concerning his burial. 'When Jacob finished commanding his sons, he drew up his feet into the bed and breathed his last and was gathered to his people' (Genesis 49:33).

Immediately there is an urgent lesson for the Hebrews (in danger, remember, of backing away from Jesus), and for us. Life is to be worship, and so is death. In many different ways, despite his many frailties, Jacob worshipped God while he lived by faith. In like manner, he worshipped God when the time came for him to die by faith. As he died, Jacob was able to testify to God's goodness and mercy having been his continual companions; and he desired the same, and no less, to be the portion of his children and grandchildren. So should we all desire and pray for God's choicest spiritual blessings (of salvation and all that accompanies it) for our families. It is a mark of the man and woman of faith that they do so. This is our most important legacy to leave to them—of far more value than anything material that might come to them from us.

How important—and how much to the glory of God—it is to leave behind us a fragrant testimony to the Lord's covenant faithfulness; a holy life which continues to 'speak' long after we cannot; and a golden casket of earnest, faithful and believing prayer that God would save them, bless them, keep them, use them, and bring them safe to glory.

And one other thing as well—indeed, that given special mention in our verse here: a memorable priority of reverent, humble worship of God. This is what is intended by the fact of Jacob *'when dying ... bowing in worship over the head of his staff'*. This detail is picked up from Genesis 47:31 (where 'staff' may also be translated 'bed', depending upon what we call the 'pointing' of the consonants of the word in Hebrew—in our present Hebrews context, it does not matter which). In truth, the *'bowing in worship'* preceded the blessing of Joseph's sons and Jacob's actual death. This need present no problem for us, however, for they all pertain directly to the end of Jacob's life. Again, the worship of God is the way to live, and the worship of God is the way to die. This, surely, is at the very heart of the Christian living well and dying well. How much we need the grace of God, the grace that was granted to these our brethren in Hebrews 11, to do so—'the fruit of lips [and of lives and of deaths] that acknowledge his name' (13:15).

### Joseph: realistic faith (11:22)

The Bible's account of Joseph, spanning as it does chapters 37–50 of Genesis, is exceedingly rich in the providence of God, and abounds in glorious 'types' of the Lord Jesus Christ. Here, however, as with Isaac and Jacob, all of Joseph's life is passed over, and our writer brings us straight to his death.

*'By faith Joseph, at the end of his life, made mention of the exodus of the Israelites and gave directions concerning his bones'* (11:22). We find here faith enabling the believer to die hopefully, and thereby (as with Jacob, above) to die well. The death of Joseph is recorded for us at the very end of Genesis, at the age of 110. In particular he makes mention of his hopefulness for the people of God (*'made mention of the exodus of the Israelites'*). Notwithstanding the fact that God had raised his servant Joseph to a position in Egypt second only to Pharaoh himself, Exodus will begin on the solemn note that, after Joseph had died, 'there arose a new king over Egypt, who did not know Joseph' (Exodus 1:8). From then on things got worse and worse for God's people, until eventually he led them out (*'the exodus'*) under Moses (who will be the next man of faith we meet here in Hebrews 11).

It is all too easy, when living in heavy days for the church of God, to imagine that things will always be like that, and so to settle for things as they are. That is wrong. It is to forget the history of the church in the Bible, Old and New Testaments alike, which went through great highs and great lows. Equally, it is to forget the history of the church down the centuries since Bible days, when there have been appalling days of dearth and glorious days of revival. In this matter (many other matters as well, but this is the one our writer highlights) Joseph is our teacher. He believed the promises of God, and even when he could not see them (or would not even live to see them) being realised, he still went on believing them.

In the bleakest of days for the church, what was he thinking about? Its demise? Its end? It remaining frozen in a state of bondage? Far from it! He was looking ahead, thinking optimistically, trusting robustly. The very last thing we have recorded that Joseph said to his brothers (indeed, he said it twice) is, 'God will visit you'. He was in no doubt about it. And this was in the midst of the very practical matter of giving *'directions concerning his bones'*—we might say, making practical arrangements for his funeral, burial, and so on, for when he had gone (have you done that—made your will, arranged your affairs in order, given thought and instruction concerning any service that might be held, and so on?).

And be sure to note the connection between *'the exodus'* and *'his bones'*—the connection being that his brothers were not to bury him in Egypt, but in the promised land. And that, of course, could only happen after *'the exodus'* had taken place, and it did (look up Exodus 13:19 and Joshua 24:32). 'God will surely visit you, and you shall carry up my bones from here' (Genesis 50:25). So speaks faith!

Joseph is not set before us as an example of a believer who did not want to die, was afraid of dying, would not speak of death, or longed to be able to put it off. No! He faced it realistically, hopefully, preparedly and reverently—and, most of all, he faced it believingly, in faith. Such is the believer's way.

Before leaving this section, it is significant for us to weigh carefully the emphasis we have noted upon dying in faith, and not just living in faith, and the necessary and intimate connection between the two. The applications of these verses are many in this connection, and it is worth tabulating the chief ones.

- Be absolutely convinced that heaven is your only sure treasure and happiness

- Be absolutely convinced that you have a personal interest in heaven and a personal title to it through faith in the Lord Jesus Christ

- Seek not to live in any known sin or any other impediment to a heavenly life

- Be careful to choose your company carefully, namely those who will most assist and encourage you in your journey to heaven

- Think frequently upon the nearness of death, for, as David recognised, 'there is but a step between me and death' (1 Samuel 20:3)

- Make sure that your practical affairs are in order, and not left in a muddle for others to have to sort out after you have gone

- Be much engaged now on earth in the activities of heaven, and, not least, the reverent and joyful worship of God, enjoying and serving him, and continually seeking to know him more closely.

## Moses' parents: courageous faith (11:23)

Along with Abraham, who has featured strongly in this chapter so far, Moses is one of the true giants of faith in the Old Testament. We are not in the least surprised to meet him at this point. We have, of course, already met him earlier in Hebrews. In 3:5 he was described as being 'faithful in all God's house as a servant'. He made an appearance in 8:5 in connection with the erection of the tabernacle, and in 9:19–21 in respect of declaring 'every commandment of the law' and the sprinkling with blood. And he is mentioned in 10:28 in the solemn context of the consequences of setting 'aside the law the law of Moses'. Now he is set before us again in 11:23 and some of the verses following.

The particular thing which strikes us, however, is that while this new section of the chapter begins with the words, *'By faith Moses'* (11:23), this verse itself focuses rather upon his parents. We shall comment upon this below. Their names, we learn from Exodus 6:20 (compare Numbers 26:59), were Amram and Jochebed, and they are without doubt two of the unsung heroes of Scripture. Miriam and Aaron were Moses' older sister and brother.

*'By faith Moses, when he was born, was hidden for three months by his parents, because they saw that the child was beautiful, and they were not afraid of the king's edict'.* As we noted above in respect of Joseph, things changed very radically for the people of God once the Genesis narrative gives way to that in Exodus. Once not only Joseph, but 'all his brothers and all that generation', had died, we learn that 'the people of Israel were fruitful and increased greatly; they multiplied and grew exceedingly strong, so that the land was filled with them' (Exodus 1:6–7). Yet this nearly proved to be their undoing. The new king not only 'did not know Joseph', but he did not know Joseph's God either. Very quickly he saw the Israelites as a threat, and 'said to his people, "Behold, the people of Israel are too many and too mighty for us"' (Exodus 1:8–9). Fearing, as a result, that the Egyptians would be overrun by them, he gave orders for them to be dealt with brutally as slaves, and issued a decree that all baby boys born among the people of Israel should be killed immediately. It is not melodramatic to assert that God's people looked to be in danger of extermination.

Yet (not for the only time in the history of his people), God, who watches over his own in faithfulness to his covenant, preserved them. Faith prospered in dark days. Faith discerned the Lord's hand in all that was happening. And faith triumphed over fear. The Lord raised up godly Hebrew midwives, Shiphrah and Puah (two more unsung heroes), who feared God rather than the king. And Moses' parents were of similar stamp. The very beautiful account of Moses' preservation is given in the first two chapters of Exodus, and it would be good to read it now in order to savour its many details. Moses was hidden by his parents until that no longer continued to be viable, and there then followed the famous event of him being placed in 'a basket made of bulrushes' and his mother placing 'it among the reeds by the river bank'. It was Pharaoh's daughter who found him, and adopted him as her own son. In between the discovery of the crying baby and Moses' being brought up in the palace, was the delightful providence of Miriam's intervention.

Two things stand out for special mention in this brief cameo of Moses' parents. The first is that although it is the parents' faith which is in view (it was they who hid the child, they who *'were not afraid of the king's edict'*), yet 11:23 begins not with 'By faith Moses' parents' (which is what we might expect), but with *'By faith Moses'*. The sentence continues, however, in such a way as to demonstrate plainly that it is the parents' faith that is being spoken of; the phrase, *'when he was born, was hidden for three months by his parents'* leaves that in no doubt. They were the ones, at this point, who were exercising faith, not Moses; and it was faith of the most courageous and demanding kind, in every way pleasing to God (recall the beginning of verse 6). The way in which the present verse opens is also a statement of the significance of Moses in the purposes of God, as well as of the vital part this event of his hiding and preservation played to that end.

The second thing for particular note is the reason given for Moses' parents hiding him. It was *'because they saw the child was beautiful'*. The adjective is an interesting one. It can signify 'proper, fair, special' or that he was 'no ordinary' child. No doubt every parent regards their own son or daughter as beautiful and special, but in the present case more than any mere outward appearance or sentimental emotion is intended. These parents clearly discerned something altogether unusual about their son Moses, and this contributed in no small measure to their determination (whatever the cost or danger to themselves) to keep him safe. Maybe they would not have been able to put into words exactly what it was about him, but we may take it that there was impressed upon them (surely by God himself) that Moses was to be in some special sense the object of God's grace, and that God intended to do something special with him and through him, to the divine glory. And how right they were! This is confirmed by Stephen, who, in his sermon before his martyrdom, speaks of Moses as 'beautiful in God's sight (or, 'to God')' (Acts 7:20). We must not underestimate the amazing quality of the faith of these two dear people (husband and wife, father and mother).

## Moses (1): considered faith (11:24–26)

The preservation of Moses in safety for the work of God cannot but make us think of the preservation of Jesus for the even greater work of God. Jesus, like Moses before him, was in danger of his life, because of a murderous decree from a wicked king; as a result, there was what we refer to as the flight into Egypt (Matthew 2:13–15). Moses having been kept safe and sound through those three 'hidden' months, was then looked after by his own mother in readiness for his transfer to the royal palace as the 'son' of Pharaoh's daughter. And so: 'When the child grew up, she [Jochebed] brought him [Moses] to Pharaoh's daughter, and he became her son. She named him Moses, "Because", she said, "I drew him out of the water"' (Exodus 2:10). The name Moses is reminiscent of the Hebrew verb 'to draw out'.

*'By faith Moses, when he was grown up, refused to be called the son of Pharaoh's daughter'* (11:24). The *'grown up'* here refers to a later stage in his life than the 'grew up' of the Exodus verse above. He is now in his manhood, and is before us here as a dissenter, a man of conviction, someone capable of making choices. Life could have been very easy for him if he had continued to spend it in the royal palace, with riches, rank and all manner of worldly things. This, however, was not the life for which God had preserved him, neither was it the life that this servant of God desired for himself. He would have known of his origins, his background, and his identity, and he had no wish to deny or abandon them, no thought of being ashamed of them. Although he 'was instructed in all the wisdom of the Egyptians, and he was mighty in his words and deeds' (Acts 7:22), this had in no way obliterated the work of God which must have been going on deep within him.

We are told that he *'refused to be called the son of Pharaoh's daughter'*. The verb *'refused'* indicates a settled persuasion that he was not to (and would not) continue as he was or continue where he was. Acts 7:23 refers to 'When he was forty years old, it came into his heart to visit his brothers, the children of Israel'. This is hugely significant in the light of what we have just said. He turned his back entirely on everything that was on offer from a lifetime in the palace, and willingly threw in his lot with the people of God, knowing that to be the place where he truly belonged.

In this, he showed himself to be in no way a negative man. Having made this costly (and, even, dramatic) refusal, what did he have in view? The answer is to hand: *'choosing* [a deliberate, considered, reflected upon course] *rather to be mistreated* [suffer] *with the people of God* [and there would be much of that, with the addition, sometimes, of being mistreated actually *by* the people of God, with their misunderstandings and jealousies] *than to enjoy the fleeting pleasures of sin'* (11:25). This is another branch of his faith being a considered faith. He was a man with a mind made up, the very opposite of 'a double-minded man', who is 'unstable in all his ways' (James 1:8). He had no relish for all the fancies of the court (where there was no place for God), and preferred the company of his own despised and burdened people (where God was pleased to dwell).

What a challenge to us as God's people in our own day, whether we are younger or older. It is a call to keep from worldliness, with its pleasures and pursuits, its godless company and earthbound priorities, and a resounding call instead to 'Set (our) minds on things that are above, not on things that are on the earth'. Why? 'For (we) have died, and (our) life is hidden with Christ in God' (Colossians 3:2–3). That sin has pleasures, goes without saying, otherwise sin would hold no appeal. As Moses discovered, however, they are *'fleeting pleasures'*. They soon fly away, and leave many a bitter taste of mornings after nights before, of one sort and another. They may seem to beckon us to *'enjoy'* them, but it is a deceitful claim on sin's part, and any enjoyment along the way soon proves false. Moses desired the things that last—the things of God, rather than the things that fail—the things of the world. So should the Hebrews (remember their neglect in 10:25), and so should we.

*'He considered* [that is, regarded, esteemed] *the reproach* (or, 'disgrace, abuse, reviling') *of Christ greater wealth than the treasures of Egypt'* (11:26). There is an immediate affinity here with the testimony of the apostle Paul in Philippians 3:7–8, 'But whatever gain I had, I counted as loss for the sake of Christ. Indeed, I count everything as loss because of the surpassing worth of knowing Christ Jesus my Lord'. As we have already remarked, the possessions and prospects for

Moses, having been brought up as the son of Pharaoh's daughter were immense. Well are they termed here *'the treasures of Egypt'*. Even today, so much later on from Moses' day, the pyramids, obelisks, statues and relics tell the story of such treasures, and many items in museums witness to them. Yet he was not the first, neither was he the last, to give up all for the sake of Christ. It is Jesus himself who speaks so clearly of denying ourselves in following him (see, for example, Luke 9:23–26).

How striking that it is the name *'Christ'* that is mentioned in this connection, the name indicating the Messiah, the promised and anointed one, rather than, say, the name 'God' or 'Lord'. Moses pinned his colours plainly and publicly to the mast of the Messiah, and the Messiah's people (for just as 'Messiah' means 'anointed one', so the Lord's people are called his 'anointed ones', as in Psalm 105:15). The connection between Christ and his people is very intimate (as, for example, in Isaiah 63:9: 'In all their [God's people's] affliction, he [Christ] was afflicted'). Just as Abraham saw Jesus' day and was glad (see the comments above on verses 17–19), so Moses also was given a sight of the Saviour. These two instances on their own (Abraham and Moses) should be sufficient to scupper comprehensively the view of some that the servants of God in the Old Testament somehow functioned apart from Jesus and the gospel. They did nothing of the sort.

If you ask, 'what did Jesus have to do with Moses?', remember that Moses, like every other Old Testament believer, looked to Jesus for salvation. They were saved on exactly the same basis that you and I were saved, if we are Christians—namely, by grace alone, through faith alone, in Christ alone. That is why there is only one church, one faith and one Lord, wherever and whenever anyone lived or lives.

That it is specifically *'the reproach of Christ'* that figured with Moses as being *'of greater wealth than the treasures of Egypt'* is very marked, and indicates that Moses understood something very deep—that it is an honourable thing to be despised, afflicted and to suffer dishonour for Christ's sake. Peter affirms this: 'If you are insulted for the name of Christ, you are blessed, because the Spirit of glory and of God rests upon you' (1 Peter 4:14).

There is a further detail. Why did Moses stand where he stood? It was for this reason: *'for he was looking* [this was his constant attitude] *to the reward'*. And what was that? Again, Peter can help us. 'But rejoice insofar as you share Christ's sufferings, that you may also rejoice and be glad when his glory is revealed' (1 Peter 4:13). This certainly sheds light at least on the long term reason for Moses' stance. He had caught a glimpse of the eternal reward (forever) with Christ, as opposed to the passing pleasures (for now) without him, and he knew which of the two was of true value. As we shall discover in the next verse, 'he endured as seeing him who is invisible' (11:27). Or as 12:2 expresses it, in the tightest language, he was 'looking to Jesus'. And, of course, it takes us back yet again to 11:1–2. All of which was very much a word in season to the Hebrews, who instead of looking forwards and pressing on were taking too many dangerous glances backwards, and have already had to be exhorted, in the strongest terms, 'Therefore do not throw away your confidence, which has a great reward' (10:35).

## Moses (2): fearless faith (11:27)

Of all the mighty works of God recorded in Scripture, the Exodus from Egypt must rank as one of the mightiest. It is recorded that God delivered his people from their long years of bondage in that alien country ('The time that the people of Israel lived in Egypt was 430 years', Exodus 12:40) and brought them out 'with a mighty hand and an outstretched arm' (Deuteronomy 26:8)—a wonderfully fitting phrase, to which then is added, 'with great deeds of terror, with signs and wonders'. It is this event which is now before us.

*'By faith he* [Moses] *left Egypt, not being afraid of the anger of the king* [just like his parents in verse 23], *for he endured* [our writer's continual theme of perseverance and steadfastness] *as seeing him* [that is, 'as if seeing him'] *who is invisible'* (11:27). He left Egypt's court, he left Egypt's society, he left everything to do with Egypt, including (literally) the land of Egypt itself, having been called by God to be

leader of the people of Israel. His call is recorded in Exodus 3–4, beginning with the amazing sight of the bush that was aflame but not burned. The exodus event follows in Exodus 12, following the ten plagues upon the land of Egypt, its king and its people. Moses was well aware of those to whom he really belonged. This the Hebrews needed to be reminded of, and it is a necessary reminder to all who truly name the name of Jesus. Where Christ is acknowledged as the sole head of the church, where the Scriptures are received as the sole rule of faith (everything we believe) and practice (everything we do), where the glorious doctrines of the grace of God in the gospel are clearly preached and unashamedly upheld, and where the Lord Jesus Christ in all things has the pre-eminence—that is where Christians belong, and we have no need to be afraid of any or all who may be against us.

It has been suggested that the leaving Egypt mentioned by our writer refers not to the exodus but rather to Moses' hasty flight to Midian after his killing of an Egyptian, in Exodus 2:11–15. On balance, however, the event of the exodus is to be preferred as the occasion here in 11:27. In everything that led up to that actually happening, Moses showed great boldness in all his dealings with Pharaoh, and a complete absence of fear. And while during the forty years which elapsed between the Midian flight and the burning bush (Acts 7:30) Moses most certainly *endured as seeing him who is invisible*, that was true of his entire life. Constant endurance is one of its leading marks, as year followed year in the wilderness wanderings, as he faced grumbling from the people whom he led, as he experienced solemn events like (on the one hand) the giving of the law (Exodus 20) and (on the other) the golden calf (Exodus 32), and as he then accepted the word of the Lord to him that he would not himself lead the people into the promised land (Joshua would do that, as his successor) but would have to be satisfied with beholding it from afar.

In everything, Moses kept his gaze upon *him who is invisible*—a classic mark of walking and living by faith. It incorporates absolute trust, humble dependence, heartfelt devotion, godly fear, patient

waiting, and much more besides. It is the only blessed way to live and
the only blessed way to die. God may indeed be *'invisible'*, and so he
is; that, however, does not make him any less real to those who know
him. Indeed, the *'invisible'* God was far more real to Moses than was
the very highly visible king of Egypt! He 'saw' the one who cannot
be seen. He was both focused and fearless, and the first enabled the
second.

## Moses (3): obedient faith (11:28)

Although strictly the institution of the Passover preceded the exodus
from Egypt, they are closely intertwined. Exodus 12 records that
'The Egyptians were urgent with the people to send them out of the
land in haste', and that 'the people of Israel journeyed from Rameses
to Succoth'. The Passover was then celebrated (Exodus 12:39–50),
and the chapter closes in this way: 'And on that very day the LORD
brought the people of Israel out of the land of Egypt by their hosts'. It
is the Passover which is now mentioned in Hebrews 11, very much in
connection still with Moses.

*'By faith he kept the Passover and sprinkled the blood, so that the
Destroyer of the firstborn might not touch them'* (11:28). The Passover was
brand new; it had never been celebrated before. This was the occasion
of its institution by God, and it was to be one of the most significant
of all the annual Old Testament festival times.

The final plague of the ten was peculiarly solemn. Moses had been
given very clear instructions from God as to what to do in preparation
for both it and the Passover, for 'It is the LORD's Passover' (Exodus
12:11). He was to prepare the lambs for the Passover meal, which
would be taken in the various Israelite families. He was to put some
of the blood of the slain lambs upon the doorpost and lintel of each
house where the meal would be eaten. No one was to go out of their
houses until the morning. Then this happened: 'At midnight the
LORD struck down all the firstborn in the land of Egypt, from the
firstborn of Pharaoh who sat on his throne to the firstborn of the
captive who was in the dungeon, and all the firstborn of the livestock'.
It was a horrendous night for the Egyptians. 'And there was a great

cry in Egypt, for there was not a house where someone was not dead'. Yet, in accordance with the divine promise given to Moses, God performed a glorious intervention for his people: 'The blood shall be a sign for you, on the houses where you are. And when I see the blood I will pass over [notice that: pass over], and no plague will befall you to destroy you, when I strike the land of Egypt'.

Hence the thread which runs through 11:28: the keeping of the Passover, the sprinkling of the blood, *'so that the Destroyer of the firstborn might not touch them'*. Israel was safe. God saw to it. And, as mentioned above, the Passover became one of the annual feasts in the calendar of feasts, fasts and festivals in the lives of the people of Israel thereafter. With this in mind, God told Moses to tell the people: 'And when you come to the land that the LORD will give you, as he has promised, you shall keep this service. And when your children say to you, "What do you mean by this service?" you shall say, "It is the sacrifice of the LORD's Passover, for he passed over the houses of the people of Israel in Egypt, when he struck the Egyptians but spared our houses". And the people bowed their heads and worshipped' (Exodus 12:25–27).

The Passover is full of gospel types, not the least of which is the fact that the Passover lamb which was sacrificed and whose blood was shed had to be unblemished, speaking to us of 'the precious blood of Christ, like that of a lamb without blemish or spot' (1 Peter 1:19), of Jesus, 'the Lamb of God, who takes away the sin of the world!' (John 1:29), and that 'Christ, our Passover lamb, has been sacrificed' (1 Corinthians 5:7). Moses looked forward to all of this by faith. And there is great significance in the fact that when Jesus announced that he would 'keep the Passover' with his disciples (Matthew 26:18), that very occasion was the time when he instituted the Lord's Supper, the regular remembrance in his church of 'the Lord's death until he comes' (1 Corinthians 11:26).

## The Israelites (1): dependent faith (11:29)

Although Moses receives no further mention in this chapter, he is still very much among those present in this latest verse, for he is the one who led God's people in the dramatic event of the crossing of the Red Sea, here recalled. Again, it was a tremendous activity of faith, on both his and their parts.

*'By faith the people crossed the Red Sea as if on dry land'* (11:29). How do you cross a waterway like the Red Sea without drowning—particularly when such a vast company of people as the Israelites are involved? The answer is: only by the miraculous intervention of God on their behalf. And that is exactly what happened. The occasion is recorded in Exodus 14, followed by an outburst of praise and thanksgiving to God for it in the following chapter.

Israel has finally left Egypt, after the years of increasingly hard labour and brutal treatment. We are told that 'God led the people around by the way of the wilderness toward the Red Sea' and that 'the LORD went before them by day in a pillar of cloud to lead them along the way, and by night in a pillar of fire to give them light, that they might travel by day and by night'. But when they arrived at the Red Sea, they seemed surrounded by insuperable obstacles. The Sea stretched out in front of them, the wilderness beckoned unwelcomingly around them, and when they looked back they saw Pharaoh and his army 'marching after them', Pharaoh having changed his mind about letting them go. They were hemmed in on every side. There appeared to be no way out for them in any direction. No way out, that is, until God came to their aid.

Moses, now facing increasing grumbling from the people who were beginning to think they might have been better off staying in Egypt after all, was enabled to speak to them the language of true faith. 'Fear not, stand firm, and see the salvation of the LORD, which he will work for you today. For the Egyptians whom you see today, you shall never see again. The LORD will fight for you, and you have only to be silent'. And what the Lord did for them that day would have been ever memorable. He divided the flowing waters of the Red Sea. 'Then Moses [in obedience to God's precise instruction] stretched out his hand over the sea, and the LORD drove the sea back by a strong east wind all night and made the sea dry land, and the waters were divided. And the people of Israel went into the midst of the sea on dry ground, the waters being a wall to them on their right hand and on their left'.

Yet even such a mighty divine intervention required faith to be in vigorous exercise as the people actually stepped into the 'corridor' between the walls of water. What if the walls of water did not hold? What if, what if, what if? When Moses told them 'to go forward', however, that is what they did. They were all enabled to step out and walk through by faith, and all reached the land on the far side of the sea safely.

Even that, however, was not the end to the events of that day. Our verse continues, *'but the Egyptians, when they attempted to do the same, were drowned* [the force of the verb means 'swallowed up, totally engulfed, utterly overwhelmed']'. Pharaoh and his armies ploughed on after the Israelites, but when Moses (again in obedience to God) 'stretched out his hand over the sea' once again, 'the sea returned to its normal course'; as a result, 'of all the host of Pharaoh that had followed them into the sea, not one of them remained'. The summary of the whole, to the glory of God and the blessing of faith? 'Thus the Lord saved Israel that day from the hand of the Egyptians, and Israel saw the Egyptians dead on the seashore'. They 'saw the great power that the Lord used against the Egyptians'; they 'feared the Lord'; and 'they believed in the Lord and in his servant Moses'.

Here, then, is a solemn and powerful illustration of the radical distinction between the way of the believer (the path of dependent faith, seen in Moses and Israel) and the way of the unbeliever (the path of reckless folly, seen in Pharaoh and the Egyptians). It would have been utter folly for the Hebrews to abandon Jesus and the gospel and go back to their old ways. And it would be utter folly for us to do so also. As has been remarked, faith walks dry-shod, while presumption drowns. So it does.

## The Israelites (2): battling faith (11:30)

Moses has now died, and under Joshua as their leader the people of Israel have now reached Canaan, the promised land. The Lord worked another great 'Red Sea style' deliverance for them, this time so that they could pass across the River Jordan. It was one thing, though, to be in Canaan, but another thing altogether to take possession of it, from not only the Canaanites themselves but other peoples besides. A fundamental early challenge to this end involved the need to capture Jericho. Yet 'Jericho was shut up inside and outside because of the people of Israel' (Joshua 6:1)—that is, to prevent them taking it.

God had other plans, however, and his word to Joshua was, 'See, I have given Jericho into your hand, with its king and mighty men of valour'. Yet, once again, there needed to be a substantial exercise of faith. It was not wanting. *'By faith the walls of Jericho fell down after they had been encircled for seven days'* (11:30). It was not the walls that had faith, of course; it was the people, including Joshua himself. After the strange strategy (no doubt strange both to the people of God who did it and to any from inside Jericho who were watching and wondering what could possibly be going on)—the strategy of marching right around the city once a day for six days behind the ark of the covenant, with the priests blowing trumpets, and then marching around it seven times on the seventh day with more blowing of trumpets, 'a long blast with the ram's horn', and then 'all the people (shouting) with a great shout'—a remarkable thing happened. They had battled on in faith, persevering in the face of nothing appearing to happen; yet our writer is able to recall how *'the walls of Jericho fell down'*, the Joshua account adding the detail that they 'fell down flat'. After this, it was the work of a moment for the Israelites to spring into action. They 'went up into the city, every man straight before him, and they captured the city. Then they devoted all in the city to destruction, both men and women, young and old, oxen, sheep, and donkeys, with the edge of the sword'.

The faith experiences of the men and women of God in the Old Testament that we are being reminded of in Hebrews 11 are nothing if not thrilling. The present instance is a vivid example of that. Battling faith, requiring great daring and much patience, yet triumphing in the end, is something for which there is tremendous need in our day. These are not times for the church of God to sit down and rest, but rather to be up and doing. Jericho was not defeated by cowardice and ease, but by divine aid and holy consecration.

## Rahab: hospitable faith (11:31)

The life of Rahab is intricately bound up with what happened at Jericho. It was where she and her family lived. Joshua 2 informs us that when Joshua 'sent two men secretly from Shittim as spies, saying, "Go, view the land, especially Jericho"', that they 'came into the house of a prostitute whose name was Rahab and lodged there'. When the king of Jericho's men came searching for them she hid them, kept them safe and enabled them to escape. In return, the two spies promised her that when the Israelites captured Jericho she and her family would be safe ('when the LORD gives us the land we will deal kindly and faithfully with you'), so long as she did precisely what they told her. What was that? This was their command: 'Behold, when we come into the land, you shall tie this scarlet cord in the window through which you let us down, and you shall gather into your house your father and mother, your brothers, and all your father's household'. Rahab agreed to these terms, understanding quite clearly from them that they could not be responsible for her or any of her family who left the house. It is this hospitality that Rahab showed to the spies which is recalled now.

*'By faith Rahab the prostitute did not perish with those who were disobedient, because she had given a friendly welcome to the spies* [literally, 'having received the spies 'in/with peace' or 'peaceably']' (11:31). Rahab had laid herself on the line in what she had done. Yet, very significantly, she told the spies at the time that she and her people had heard about the Red Sea incident and victories that God had given the Israelites over the two Amorite kings, Sihon and Og. 'And as soon as we heard it, our hearts melted, and there was no spirit left in any man because of you, for the LORD your God, he is God in the heavens above and on the earth beneath'. This is a most remarkable testimony from this woman.

At the time of the fall of Jericho, Rahab kept her part of the bargain, and so did the Israelites. It is recorded in Joshua 6 that

Joshua himself commanded the spies, 'Go into the prostitute's house and bring out from there the woman and all who belong to her, as you swore to her'. And so they did, and from that time onwards she (originally a foreigner) lived among the people of Israel—a lovely instance, as is that of Ruth and others, of the inclusion of the Gentiles among the worldwide people of God.

How graciously God first gave Rahab faith, and then rewarded her faith. It reminds us of what our writer said in 6:10 (see that verse and our comment), and of her mention at the end of James 2, in the teaching there about the relationship between faith and works. She is one of only three women mentioned in this chapter of Hebrews (Sarah and Moses' mother being the other two). The fact that she is referred to here as *'Rahab the prostitute'* is not intended to leave her past as a constant noose around her neck whenever she was spoken of (think, for example, of Matthew (Levi, as he was originally called) being termed 'Matthew the tax collector' in Matthew 10:3, or Simon being referred to as 'Simon the leper' in Mark 14:3). It stands, rather, as a continual testimony to the grace of God in her life, the life of a true trophy of grace.

What is even more gracious, however, is that she also appears in 'the genealogy of Jesus Christ' with which Matthew's gospel (and so the entire New Testament) begins. There she is in Matthew 1:5, and observe carefully her immediate company and relations there: 'and Salmon the father of Boaz by Rahab, and Boaz the father of Obed by Ruth, and Obed the father of Jesse, and Jesse the father of David the king'. Is that not absolutely wonderful? We can only say, with Paul, 'Oh, the depth of the riches and wisdom and knowledge of God! How unsearchable are his judgments and how inscrutable his ways!' (Romans 11:33).

## The generations: costly faith (11:32–38)

The writer to the Hebrews proceeds on a slightly different track from this point in the chapter. Having given a whole series of examples of different individuals (beginning with Abel, back in verse 4, and ending just now with Rahab in verse 31), he now takes a broad sweep involving some of the giants of the Old Testament. We remarked in our introduction to the chapter that his examples of faith are selective, not comprehensive. In the present section a final set of examples is given, though with those mentioned all grouped together.

*'And what more shall I say?'* (11:32). This question seems to have the dual sense of 'where do I go from here?'—that is to say, firstly, all these previous names have been mentioned, and there still remain so many names worthy of mention, so which ones should be chosen; and, secondly, the argument has been proved so thoroughly, what more needs to be said? It is as if he is running out of time and space. As a result, names are given, and experiences are recounted, the experiences going far beyond the lives of those who are actually named.

*'For time would fail me to tell of Gideon, Barak, Samson, Jephthah, of David and Samuel and the prophets'.* The list (not provided in strict chronological order) comprises three judges, one military leader associated with a judge, one king, and one named plus other unnamed prophets. We shall confine ourselves to a brief comment on each, considering both them, and the verses that follow, as demonstrations of costly faith. None of them were without blemishes and failures, but what they share in common is their faith and trust in God and his word—they all, when at their best, operated 'by faith', faith that was both costly and persistent.

First in line is *Gideon*. He belonged to the days of the judges, that period between the death of Joshua and the establishment of the kingship under Saul. They were bad days generally for God's people—days of covenant unfaithfulness on their part, days of turmoil and unrest, days when the people were vulnerable to repeated attacks from other nations. A clear pattern emerges in the book of Judges. God would deliver his people into the hand of their enemies because of their faithlessness and disobedience, they would cry to him for mercy and deliverance, and he would raise 'up judges, who saved them out of the hand of those who plundered them'.

The account of Gideon, who delivered Israel from the hand of the Midianites, is given in Judges 6–8. He was called to service by a visitation from an 'angel of the LORD', and his exploits include his destroying of the altar of the false god Baal; his fleece, as he sought assurance from God concerning the divine will; and God's reducing of his army from 32,000 fighting men to just 300 in order to ensure that God and not man got the glory.

Second to be mentioned is *Barak*. He is usually remembered in connection with Deborah (Judges 4–5). The enemy in their day was the Canaanites, and God gave his people a celebrated victory over the Canaanite armies under the command of Sisera, the general of the king of Canaan's army. Sisera came to an unpleasant end through the courageous act of Jael, wife of Heber the Kenite, who hammered a tent peg into his temple while he was asleep.

Next comes *Samson*. How thankful we are to have him mentioned here, for if he had not been we might have been very unsure as to what to do with him, or to know where he stood. Read all about him in Judges 13–16, where we learn of his activities (some of them very peculiar) against the Philistines. He was born to a mother who had been barren, and was set apart to 'be a Nazirite to God from the womb'—something which involved special consecration to God.

His exploits were certainly colourful, and include getting friends to work out a riddle; tying 300 foxes 'tail to tail' and putting a lighted 'torch between each pair of tails'; taking 'hold of the doors of the gate of the city and the two posts' of Gaza at midnight, pulling 'them up, bar and all', and carrying them on his shoulders 'to the top of the hill that is in front of Hebron'; his liaison with Delilah, which proved something of his downfall; his capture and blinding by the Philistines; and his final victory over them when he brought the temple crashing down on a great company of them, dying himself in the process, with this obituary: 'So the dead whom he killed at his death were more than those whom he had killed during his life'.

Fourth is *Jephthah* (Judges 11–12). He is described as 'a mighty warrior', and was raised up by God to deliver his people from the

Ammonites, concerning which he was careful to ascribe the victories over them to the Lord.

Mention Jephthah, and those who are familiar with the Bible narrative concerning him will very likely think immediately of the solemn vow he made to the Lord, prior to setting out against the enemy. 'If you will give the Ammonites into my hand, then whatever comes out from the doors of my house to meet me when I return in peace from the Ammonites shall be the LORD's, and I will offer it up for a burnt offering'. The trouble was that, in the event, it was his daughter who was first out of the house 'to meet him with tambourines and with dances. She was his only child'. So what did he do? Did he sacrifice his daughter as a burnt offering, or did he not? Interpreters have been divided down the years, and certainly upon a close reading of the Judges narrative there do seem to be cogent reasons for answering that question either way—yes he did, or no he didn't. Our writer of Hebrews does not comment, either one way or the other. But he does include Jephthah in this line-up of God's faithful ones.

On we go to *David*. He was 'the son of Jesse, … the man who was raised on high, the anointed of the God of Jacob, the sweet psalmist of Israel' (2 Samuel 23:1). Described as 'a man after (God's) own heart' (1 Samuel 13:14), he first appears in 1 Samuel 16, where Samuel anointed him as the future king of Israel, and his death is recorded in 1 Kings 2:10–11, after a reign of forty years altogether (seven in Hebron, and thirty-three in Jerusalem). His life and reign was pivotal in the history of God's people.

One of the most remarkable illustrations of his absolute and unflinching faith in God came before he was on the throne at all—the occasion of his slaying of the Philistine giant, Goliath of Gath, with a stone from his shepherd's sling. This gave Israel a magnificent victory over their enemy.

*Samuel* comes next, although his ministry preceded David's kingship, though was crucially involved with it. Called to the Lord's service as a young boy, he served the Lord faithfully throughout his life. Whether our writer had any particular instances of his life in mind in mentioning him here by name, we cannot know. But like the others singled out for representative mention, he believed God and his word and sought to act accordingly.

In company with Moses and Aaron, he is given honourable mention in Psalm 99:6 ('Samuel also was among those who called upon (God's) name. They called to the LORD, and he answered them'). This is a reminder, maybe, of his role as an intercessor in prayer. On one memorable occasion he said to the people, 'Moreover, as for me, far be it from me that I should sin against the LORD by ceasing to pray for you, and I will instruct you in the good and the right way' (1 Samuel 12:24). In this same connection, very likely, we read of him in Jeremiah 15:1 as standing before the Lord. His living and serving by faith was especially marked, it appears, by faithful, persevering prayer. This is noteworthy in that he was himself very much an answer to prayer, being God's special gift to his mother, Hannah, as recorded in 1 Samuel 1.

There then follows *'and the prophets'*. None are mentioned by name, but a whole vast company is gathered up in this simple reference. So many come to mind, including Nathan, Elijah and Elisha, Ezekiel, Jonah and Malachi, to name but a few. They were all men of faith. They received the word of the Lord, believed it, proclaimed it faithfully, and bore the consequences from the people. Their mutual slogan was, 'Thus says the Lord'.

What our writer now does is to give a sweeping set of works and endurances of faith, without attaching any personal names to them (although, at different points, some names come readily to mind). He does this, no doubt, in order to press home to the slackening-off Hebrews, in danger of apostasy, that if anything is to be attained in the spiritual life it must be by faith. Just as we learned in 11:6 that 'without faith it is impossible to please' God, so the companion lesson being enforced now is that it is equally impossible, without faith, to accomplish anything for God. In this sparkling array, we find faith continuously standing its ground—after the manner of Daniel 11:32, 'the people who know their God shall stand firm and take action (or, 'do exploits')'.

So off he goes: *who through faith conquered kingdoms* [such as Joshua taking possession of the promised land, and David subduing enemies on various sides], *enforced justice* [men like Samuel, Phinehas and Elijah, who sought to ensure that God's righteous laws were put into practice and that the people lived righteously; and compare David, who 'administered justice and equity to all his people', 2 Samuel 8:15], *obtained promises* [the people listed in verse 32, for example, were all men who believed the promises of God to them, and saw them fulfilled in different ways; and remember the fine testimony, to the glory of God, that 'Not one word of all the good promises that the LORD had made to the house of Israel had failed; all came to pass', Joshua 21:45], *stopped the mouths of lions* [we think immediately of Daniel in the den of lions, and God's wonderful protection of him there and subsequent deliverance], *quenched the power of fire* [referring, very likely, to Daniel's three friends—Shadrach, Meshach, and Abednego—in the fiery furnace, and their magnificent statement of faith recorded in Daniel 3:16–18], *escaped the edge of the sword* [this may be a more general reference to deliverances from extreme danger—think, for example, of the many times when God delivered David from the murderous attempts of Saul against him, or Elijah's escape from Jezebel], *were made strong out of weakness* [Gideon felt keenly his inadequacy for the task the Lord gave him, but was enabled to fulfil it; Hezekiah was restored to health from being at the point of death], *became mighty in war* [something very widely illustrated throughout the Old Testament], *put foreign armies to flight* [again, something testified to many times in the course of the history of God's people which our writer is surveying]' (11:33–34).

And there is more, as our writer turns his attention from those who triumphed by faith to those who suffered by faith: '*Women received back their dead by resurrection* [like the mothers in Zarephath and Shunem, in the ministries of Elijah and Elisha respectively, recorded in 1 Kings 17 and 2 Kings 4]. *Some were tortured* [indicating brutal and agonizing deaths], *refusing to accept release, so that they might rise*

*again to a better life* [the same spirit which motivated Abraham and
the other patriarchs, mentioned earlier in the chapter—keeping a
keen eye on what is yet to come, and which is altogether *'better'*, a
characteristic word in Hebrews]. *Others suffered mocking and flogging,
and even chains and imprisonment* [Jeremiah is one who suffered in
this way, and he was by no means the only one]. *They were stoned*
[this happened to Zechariah 'in the court of the house of the LORD',
as recorded in 2 Chronicles 24], *they were sawn in two* [there is a
tradition—only a tradition—that this was the manner of death
inflicted upon Isaiah by Manasseh], *they were killed with the sword*
[whether in battle or martyrdom]. *They went about in skins of sheep
and goats, destitute, afflicted, mistreated—of whom the world was not
worthy—wandering about in deserts and mountains, and in dens and
caves of the earth* [covering a whole range of trials and distresses
common to so many]' (11:35–38).

The phrase *'of whom the world was not worthy'* stands out here. The
world did not count them worthy of any notice, any honour; neither
(much of the time) did it pay any attention to them. Yet, ironically,
the real truth is that it was the world that *'was not worthy'* of *them*. As
in our own day, God's word (and so his people, his messengers) were
either patronisingly disregarded, or callously mocked and humiliated.
It need not trouble us, however, just as it certainly did not trouble the
likes of those of whom Hebrews 11 is full. Faith in God overcomes
such treatment from the world, and would be suspicious of the
world's applause anyway. What did Jesus say? 'Woe to you, when all
people speak well of you, for so their fathers did to the false prophets'
(Luke 6:26). Moreover, God's estimate of his people is altogether
different from that of the world. 'Blessed are you when others revile
you and persecute you and utter all kinds of evil against you falsely on
my account. Rejoice and be glad, for your reward is great in heaven,
for so they persecuted the prophets who were before you' (Matthew
5:11–12).

The Hebrews needed to be brought up short with this truth, that it
might be a fresh spur to them to cleave tightly to the Lord, and prize
Jesus and the gospel above everything and everyone else. Our need is

no different. The words of Jesus ring as true now as ever. 'If the world hates you, know that it has hated me before it hated you. If you were of the world, the world would love you as its own; but because you are not of the world, but I chose you out of the world, therefore the world hates you' (John 15:18–19). And again: 'In the world you will have tribulation. But take heart; I have overcome the world' (John 16:33).

## All the faithful together: perfected faith (11:39–40)

*'And all these* [all the above, and all the unmentioned ones as well], *though commended* [well attested, gaining a good report] *through their faith, did not receive what was promised* [compare verse 13]' (11:39). This galaxy of faith has drawn to a close, yet our writer now makes a most important point. He makes clear first of all what they were all *'commended'* for—namely, *'their faith'*. Of that fact we can be in no doubt. We have seen very vividly both the achievements of faith (what faith can do) and the sufferings of faith (what faith can bear). Their faith honoured God and enabled them to endure through thick and thin. And their faith prized the Lord Jesus Christ, as they believed and relished the Messianic promises.

However, he goes on to tell us that, notwithstanding their commendable faith (and not forgetting that they did, of course, receive many fulfilments of specific promises during their lives), they *'did not receive what was promised'*. What is meant by this? The answer is chiefly in connection with Jesus himself, the one who is the sum and substance of all the divine promises, the one in whom 'all the promises of God find their Yes' (2 Corinthians 1:20). Theirs was ultimately a Christ-focused and a Christ-expecting faith, yet despite this they did not literally live to see the day of his coming. They were continually being pointed forward, by all the types and shadows of the ceremonial law which have been dealt with in such detail in the preceding chapters, to the Calvary sacrifice, the mediatorial work of Jesus, Saviour, King and Great High Priest. They *'did not receive what was promised'*, in the sense that Jesus was not even incarnate, still less crucified and risen, in their lifetimes. So much still remained of the fullness of the promises by the time they all departed this life. Not that this left their salvation incomplete in any way, neither is their heaven incomplete. Rather, so much of what, during their days on earth, they lived to see and longed to see, they did not see.

So why was this? Our writer gives us the very reason: *'since God had provided something better* [that Hebrews word again] *for us* [Christian believers], *that apart from us they should not be made perfect'* (11:40). Something was left in store for them, and it was so left in order that they can share it with us and we can share it with them—in other words, so that we can all share it together. Not them without us, not us without them, but all the faithful together. This is the great and glorious Scripture principle of one church, one faith and one Lord, for all the faithful in every age and generation. Such is the communion and fellowship of the saints, who comprise together (them and us) the 'many sons' whom God will bring safe 'to glory' (2:10).

This closing verse of chapter 11 leaps all the way across the centuries to the return of Jesus at the end of this present age, the general resurrection of all mankind at the last day, and to the final judgment itself with Christ upon the throne, prior to which we must *all* both live and die in faith. Then—together—all true believers, the entire church of God chosen from eternity, will *'be made perfect'*. This is God's 'plan for the fullness of time' (Ephesians 1:10). For this is the time when 'the marriage of the Lamb has come, and his Bride has made herself ready' (Revelation 19:7). This is the time for which 'the whole creation has been groaning together in the pains of childbirth until now', and, indeed, 'not only the creation, but we ourselves, who have the firstfruits of the Spirit, groan inwardly as we wait eagerly for adoption as sons, the redemption of our bodies. For in this hope we were saved' (Romans 8:22–24). This is 'the salvation that is in Christ Jesus with eternal glory' (2 Timothy 2:10). This will be the time of 'new heavens and a new earth in which righteousness dwells' (2 Peter 3:13).

This, then, is when we shall all be *'made perfect'* together. If the Old Testament believers persevered with all of this in view, so should the Hebrews (no going back) and so, how much more, should we.

# Chapter 12
# Running the race

The very first word of this new chapter (*'Therefore'*) leaves us in no doubt that, despite our move from chapter 11 to chapter 12, there is complete continuity with what has just preceded. It is a word speaking of consequences, deductions, applications, things that follow on. And there is plenty to fulfil that brief. Not surprisingly, our writer makes no change of theme. It remains the absolute and incomparable pre-eminence and sufficiency of the Lord Jesus Christ, and, linked with that, the supreme need for all who truly belong to him of cleaving to him, following him faithfully, persevering in the faith, enduring to the end. Jesus himself is the ultimate vista of faith, hence the famous phrase in 12:2, 'looking to Jesus', which provides us with the central focus of the Christian life. The chapter falls naturally into two parts—verses 1–17 and verses 18–29.

## Four motives to persevere (12:1-17)

### (1) The cloud of witnesses (12:1)

The magnificent array of Old Testament believers that we have just met are still very much in view. *'Therefore, since we are surrounded by so great a cloud of witnesses'* (12:1). The word *'cloud'* is interesting, reminding us that the people of God in the days before the coming of Jesus into the world comprised not just the occasional one or two, here and there, but a vast company—or, in the light of the word used, not just a few little clouds dotted around in an otherwise vast expanse of blue sky, but a huge number of clouds embracing the entire sky and eliciting the cry, 'look at all those clouds!'. Indeed, together they formed one *'cloud'*, described as *'so great a cloud'*.

But a cloud of what? The answer is, *'a cloud of witnesses'*, heroes and champions of faith from across the generations, each and all of them faithful to God in their own day, and familiar with the ups and downs, smiles and tears, successes and failures of living for the Lord. Real men and women, young and old, whose priority in life it was to worship and serve the Lord. And remember yet again, that those mentioned in the previous chapter are only samples taken from the whole, not themselves the entire company. They themselves witnessed by life and lip, they bore the burden and heat of the day, they lived and died as the Lord's. He was glorified in them and through them, and again and again the savour they left behind them was a pleasing one. In the best sense, once their time came to leave this present world, they were missed.

Also, in a related application of the word, they are *'witnesses'* of us (notice how our writer includes himself again with those to whom he wrote, *'we are surrounded'*). They watch us, they observe how we are doing, they cheer us on, like spectators in an athletics stadium, all around us (*'we are surrounded'*). They have finished their course, and they are taking a keen interest in how we are faring in ours. This is stated for our encouragement and to spur us on to finish our Christian course faithfully ourselves. It must be remembered, of course, that this is pictorial language in the present Hebrews context, and we do not draw from it a general principle that departed saints are looking down to earth—rather, they are gazing at the Saviour.

The mention of an athletics stadium, spectators and so competitors prepares us for our writer's use of the imagery of a race (*'and let us run with endurance the race that is set before us'*). The Christian life is being likened to a race—not a fast sprint, over almost as soon as it has started, but more of a marathon, one which needs endurance if the runner is to complete it rather than drop out along the way. If we are Christians then we are runners in a race, albeit that we may go at different speeds. Like all races, it has a starting point, a course and a goal. The point here is that the race is to be completed. Paul could say, approaching the end of his earthly pilgrimage, 'I have finished the race' (2 Timothy 4:8). The danger was, so it appeared, that some of the Hebrews were showing signs of slowing down in the race, to the point where they might soon stop and give up altogether and never finish. The very same danger can threaten us. That's why endurance, perseverance, is always the need of the hour, whatever may be the temptations to stop, the discouragements to continuing, or the loneliness of the race. It is 'the one who endures to the end (who) will be saved' (Matthew 24:13).

If endurance in the race is to be maintained successfully, so that we actually cross the finishing line at the end of it, then certain things need to be paid constant attention to. These our writer speaks of as *'let us also* [as they did who went before us] *lay aside every weight, and sin which clings so closely'*. This brings in the sense of this race being an obstacle race, that is to say, a race with many and various potential obstacles in the way, to trip us up, cause us harm, knock us over and (one way or another) prevent us reaching the end. Just as runners take part in races wearing as little clothing as is appropriate (in some of the ancient games the competitors actually ran naked), so we are to do the same, spiritually speaking. We are to *'lay aside'* [do without, dispense with, leave alone, discard] *every weight* [anything which would slow us down, hold us up, prevent our progress]', and this is further explained by the phrase *'and sin which clings so closely'*. Sin, if allowed to be, is very much a clinging thing, just like the ivy on the old garden wall.

People talk sometimes of 'besetting sins' (or as they are sometimes termed, 'darling sins', 'bosom sins' or 'secret sins'), by which is usually meant that different ones of us have different sins which present particular problems to us—they 'beset' us. One person's besetting sin may not be the same as another's. While there is truth in this (and we each need to know our own weak points, the places where we are especially vulnerable to temptation, and keep clear of anything which panders to those things), the teaching here about weights and sins goes much wider than that. It really means sin itself, sin of any sort, sin however it displays, sin however it attacks. This can include not only that which is obviously sinful (because the Bible says it is and condemns it), but also anything which has the appearance of sin or which is incompatible with our retaining a good conscience (think of Romans 14:23, 'For whatever does not proceed from faith is sin'). The 'laying aside' speaks, in the Christian context, of self-discipline, training, keeping fit, being alert—some of those very things which are so vitally important to an athlete in the sporting sense. With it may be connected Jesus' vigorous call to us (metaphorically speaking) concerning hands, feet or eyes that cause us to sin (see Mark 9:43–48).

Making a fast start is all very well, but if your pace slows down, and slows down, and slows down, this is not a good sign at all. As for the Hebrews, they endured well to begin with ('recall the former days', 10:32), but they were in danger of drifting (2:1) and being overtaken by 'an evil, unbelieving heart, leading (them) to fall away from the living God' (3:12), causing them to be slack in holding 'fast the confession of (their) hope without wavering' (10:23). They needed to hear alarm bells ringing, before it was too late.

How about us? This concerns us, every bit as much as it concerned them. How well are we running the race? What are we doing with weights and sins—clinging on to them, or getting rid of them? We can tend to go slowly enough at the best of times, and just cannot afford to allow room for any impediments or any encumbrances whatsoever (the word for *weight* can mean 'swelling'). Running is not an activity which needs any excess weight or baggage. Even 'innocent' things and pastimes must be laid aside if they are impeding our spiritual progress. The surrounding *'so great a cloud of witnesses'* should be a challenge to us to keep on running, so that we may finish our race just as they finished theirs. And the central key to doing this is what our writer touches upon next.

## (2) The example of Jesus (12:2-4)

All the time we are to be *'looking to Jesus'*, and doing so for this particular reason—*'looking to Jesus, the founder and perfecter of our faith, who for the joy that was set before him endured the cross, despising the shame, and is seated at the right hand of the throne of God'* (12:2). Not only have the Old Testament witnesses run and completed the race before us, but, far more importantly so far as we are concerned, our Lord and Saviour Jesus Christ has run and completed his race. It is only insofar as we keep *'looking to Jesus'* that we shall make real progress and maintain steady endurance as we run the race. We must only have eyes for him. The verb here for 'look' carries the sense of looking away from other things and fixing our gaze upon one thing exclusively. It reminds us of what is said concerning Moses back in 11:26.

The significance of this call to be *'looking to Jesus'* must never be overlooked. We have been reminded of 'so great a cloud of witnesses', and realise all that we have to learn from them as we seek to live the life of faith. For instance, let us learn from Abel the necessity of approaching God in the right way; let us learn from Noah the costliness of serving God in a faithless generation; let us learn from Abraham the blessedness of keeping our eyes fixed on our heavenly goal; and let us learn from Moses the worthiness of the Lord Jesus. None of these our brethren, however, can even begin to compare with Jesus. So, here in chapter 12, Jesus stands alone as the one to whom supremely we are to look. He is not on the same level as any of the others whom we met in the preceding chapter. He is to be looked to and to be learned from in a completely different manner. He it is upon whom ultimately our hearts are fixed, not them. In that sense, we look to the one, rather than to the many.

There is much in this verse. For a start, what is meant by Jesus being *'the founder and perfecter of our* (literally, 'the') *faith'*? First of all, that Jesus is *'the founder'* (the word can be rendered 'author' or 'pioneer') reminds us that the very beginning, the very starting point, for us in running the Christian race involved looking to Jesus by faith, for how else could we have been saved? Compare Jesus as 'founder' (or 'pioneer') of our salvation in 2:10. The answer to the question, 'what must I do to be saved?', can only ever be, 'Believe on the Lord Jesus, and you will be saved' (Acts 16:30–31). This is *'looking to Jesus'*, the one in, through and by whom God provides salvation for us. It is to trust in all that Jesus has accomplished for us on the cross in order to reconcile us sinners to God. And that spirit in which we commenced the race is to be the very same spirit in which we continue it and, ultimately, conclude it. It is something we never go beyond or grow out of. That's the sequence: commence, continue, conclude.

What about Jesus being the *'perfecter of our faith'*? What does that mean? It includes the sense both of him being the one who prays for us so that our faith will not fail ('I have prayed for you [the 'you' is singular, assuring us that he prays for each one of us—we might say, individually or by name] that your faith may not fail', Luke 22:32)—and his great prayer in John 17 brings this truth out at various points; and of his being the one who is the great reward and goal of faith. Not only are our eyes fixed upon him, by faith, as we press on here below through what is often a 'vale of tears', but the day will come when, faith giving way to sight, we shall actually see him. Our 'eyes will behold the king in his beauty' (Isaiah 33:17); 'we shall see him as he is' (1 John 3:2). He in whom faith is begun is he in whom faith is perfected and brought thereby to a successful and blessed conclusion.

There is something more, however, to Jesus being *'the founder and perfecter of our faith'*, and this is really the best thing of all about it. Jesus is himself the leader and pattern of faith. Speaking carefully, we may say that he is the one who really exemplifies faith for us, as we observe his absolute and unwavering trust in and reliance upon the Father. He said as much himself, when taking upon himself the words quoted in 2:13, 'I will put my trust in him' (taken from the end of Isaiah 8:17). Would we know what faith is? Look *at* Jesus, even as you look *to* him. This is the way to ensure that we run well. He, supremely, is the one who has gone before us in the way of faith, the one who leads us on in the way of faith, the one who is the chief example of faith for us to follow.

This is what our writer now develops as the verse continues. What was it which, more than anything else, spurred Jesus on during his earthly life and ministry? It was this: *'who for the joy that was set before him'*. This it was, in the light of which he *'endured the cross, despising the shame, and is seated at the right hand of the throne of God'*. This requires some careful unpacking.

He *'endured the cross'*, *'endure'* being a key verb and theme in this epistle of endurance. This refers not merely to the event of the cross, the fact of it, but gathers up all the sufferings, all the humiliations, agonies, heartbreaks, abandonments and darkness of the cross—where 'it was the will of the Lord [the particular reference here is to God the Father] to crush (or, 'bruise') him' and 'put him to grief' (Isaiah 53:10)—as 'he poured out his soul to death and was numbered with the transgressors' and 'bore the sin of many' (Isaiah 53:12).

The phrase *'despising* [disregarding, scorning, not being put off by, caring nothing for] *the shame'* is a reminder that death by crucifixion was considered the most shameful of all deaths, as well as the most appalling in terms of what it involved for those who were crucified. It was reserved for the very worst of offenders. It has been argued that the shame of the cross was worse even than the pain of it. Certainly we may be allowed to think in these terms where Jesus is concerned, for in his case the shame was far heightened beyond any shame that others being crucified ever experienced (including the two crucified with him)—for, in Jesus' case, it was the one 'who knew no sin' who was being made 'to be sin' (2 Corinthians 5:21).

How, then, could Jesus so bear all that was involved with *'the cross'* and *'the shame'*? We are told here that it was *'for the joy that was set before him'*. So what was this *'joy'*, and how was it *'set before him'*? It was far more than just being 'the other side' of the Calvary experience, in the sense of getting it all over with, getting through it. It gathers up several things. Surely it was, at least, *'the joy'* of doing the Father's will (10:7), and of accomplishing all the work that the Father gave him to do (John 17:4); *'the joy'* of saving his people, those given to him by God in the divine counsels of eternity (2:13b); *'the joy'* of 'going to him who sent me' (John 16:5), and of being glorified 'in your [the Father's] own presence with the glory that (he) [Jesus] had with him [the Father] before the world existed' (John 17:5); *'the joy'* of his coming exaltation, which is referred to at the end of 12:2, *'and is seated at the right hand of the throne of God'* (see our comments on 1:3)— his ascension (John 20:17), coronation (Psalm 24:7–10), heavenly intercession (Hebrews 7:25), and exaltation (Philippians 2:10–11); and, beyond all of this, *'the joy'* of showing his people his glory (John 17:24) and 'the marriage of the Lamb' (Revelation 19:7).

This is *'the joy that was set before him'*—'set before him' in that he was assured of it, it was the promise of the Father to him, it was the prospect always in view for him, he kept his eyes firmly upon it, and was continually stirred up to press on to the possession of it. And where is he now? He *'is seated at the right hand of the throne of God'.* And he awaits us there, in the place of honour and of victory, so that when we each arrive in heaven at the end of the race he may welcome us home and say to us (though none of us deserve it), 'Well done, good and faithful servant … Enter into the joy of your master' (Matthew 25:21). Remember Paul's encouraging word to Timothy (and so to all of us who are following after Jesus): 'if we endure with him, we will also reign with him' (2 Timothy 2:12).

The exhortation to keep *'looking to Jesus'* (the Jesus who has been so beautifully spoken of in verse 2 as *'the founder and perfecter of our faith'*, to which we could add his own words concerning himself, 'I am the Alpha and the Omega, the first and the last, the beginning and the end', Revelation 22:13,) is continued in the next two verses by way of further encouragement to the Hebrews to hold fast to him and abandon without delay any foolish thought of departing from him and returning to Old Testament ways. It is a word to us, to the same end, that they and we would be those who endure to the end, not those who abandon on the way.

'Consider him [literally, 'the one', but clearly referring to Jesus] *who endured from sinners such hostility against himself, so that you may not grow weary or fainthearted'* (12:3). It is all too easy to *'grow weary or fainthearted'* in the course of running the Christian race, and only maintaining this firm gaze upon Jesus can keep us going. This is not the first time that we have been exhorted to *'Consider him'*. In 3:1 the call was to 'consider Jesus, the apostle and high priest of our confession', although a different verb was used there for 'consider'.

There are so many obstacles, hindrances and discouragements which we can face as Christians, and these can have the effect of sapping our strength, reducing our determination and clouding our joy. Yet none of these can match the obstacles, hindrances and discouragements which faced the Lord Jesus throughout the course of his earthly life and ministry. They were intense on all sides. The way this is expressed in our verse is that he *'endured from sinners such hostility against himself'*. Day after day he faced *'hostility against himself'*, whether verbally from those who disputed his claims or rejected his teaching (like the scribes, Pharisees and Sadducees), or physically from those who sought to kill him. It came *'from sinners'*, those who had no desire to believe upon him or 'take up (their) cross and follow (him)' (Matthew 16:24). And all of this reached a climax at Calvary itself when they 'denied the Holy and Righteous One' and 'killed the Author of life' (Acts 3:14).

In the light of this, the particular force of our being told to *'Consider him'* is that we are to weigh up, to think through, all that we know concerning him, and to realise that, in comparison with all that he faced and all that he bore (for us), all that we face and bear is little enough. This should help keep us from the ever present danger of weariness and faintheartedness, speaking between them of an exhaustion which is both physical and spiritual. Positively, it should be a powerful stimulant to energise us as his disciples—in mind, body, soul and strength.

*'In your struggle against sin you have not yet resisted to the point of shedding your blood'* (10:4). This presses home the point further. The presence and power of sin in us and against us involves a consistent and energetic effort from us to keep struggling and battling against it. It is a most hostile enemy, seeking our complete downfall. The words *'struggle'* and *'resisted'* indicate a strenuous fight. The Hebrews had endured a great deal, as we learned in 10:32–34, though there is no mention there of them having had to shed their blood. That is, they had not thus far been required to die for their faith in Jesus Christ. Some in the panoramic sweep of chapter 11 had done so (11:37), some in the days of the early church were required to do so (Stephen in Acts 7 and Antipas in Revelation 2 are a couple of obvious examples), and many Christians have been required to do so since, including in our own day. Maybe some of the Hebrews were beginning to get nervous about persecution and martyrdom reaching them, in which case this might have provided a further reason (as they saw it) for easing up in their allegiance to Jesus, at least publicly.

The intent of this verse, however, is to give added thrust to what was written in the previous verse—namely, that the sufferings, hardships and endurance of Jesus were of a different order altogether from anything that (thus far, at least) had come the way of the Hebrews. The entire purpose of *his* coming into the world was *not* to resist *'to the point of shedding (his) blood'* but to shed it upon the cross, for it is (he himself says) 'the new covenant in my blood' (Luke 22:20). It is 'the blood of his cross' (Colossians 1:20), 'the blood of Jesus (God's) Son' which 'cleanses us from all sin' (1 John 1:7), and 'without the shedding of blood there is no forgiveness of sins' (9:22). Had there been any resistance on Jesus' part, there would be no salvation, and we would all be still in our sins. As it is, 'There is therefore now no condemnation for those who are in Christ Jesus' (Romans 8:1). So, as Jesus suffered so much *more* in order to save us, cannot we be content to suffer what (in comparison) is bound to be so much *less* in order to serve him?

## (3) The benefit of discipline (12:5–11)

We proceed now to the third of the four motives supplied by our writer to assist us in the great business of endurance. No earthly athletics race can be seriously engaged in without rigid discipline. It is no use a runner just turning up at the track one day, with neither training nor discipline, and then expect to get anywhere in the race. Even so, in the Christian race, it is not something we just sail through at our leisure, as if it is the easiest thing in the world to make spiritual progress. The old adage of no gains without pains holds true for every generation of the Lord's people. That is what our writer now brings to the fore. We need to heed carefully all that is said to us here.

### The principle of discipline (12:5–7a)

The passage begins with a reminder of the danger of forgetting something of key importance. *'And have you forgotten the exhortation that addresses you as sons?'* (12:5a). Who is addressing who here? It is God our heavenly Father addressing us. And in what terms does he address us? As his children (*'sons'* here having the wider sense of 'children'). This is a family matter. One of the richest blessings of salvation is the truth of adoption. Paul provides this quotation from the Old Testament, where God says 'and I will be a father to you, and you shall be sons and daughters to me, says the LORD Almighty' (2 Corinthians 6:18). John announces in sheer wonderment, 'See what kind of love the Father has given to us, that we should be called the children of God; and so we are' (1 John 3:1). And the Lord Jesus provides us with this foundational teaching concerning how we approach God in prayer: 'Our Father in heaven [literally, 'the one in the heavens']' (Matthew 6:9). Is there a choicer privilege than this? God's entire dealings with us as we run the Christian race are on the basis of his adoption of us as his own children, a glorious truth which has a vital application to the case being dealt with here.

What, then is this word of *'exhortation'* [the same word is used in 13:22 of Hebrews as a whole] that we can so easily forget? It comes in a quotation from Proverbs 3:11–12. *'My son, do not regard lightly the discipline of the Lord, nor be weary* [grow faint, become discouraged] *when reproved by him. For the Lord disciplines the one he loves, and chastises every son whom he receives'* (12:5b-6). Notice here how Scripture itself is regarded as God speaking, for these are the very words uttered from the mouth of God. So '*the exhortation that addresses*' is as if to say 'God himself addresses'. He it is 'who is speaking' and he must not be refused (12:25).

The very affectionate way in which God regards his children is immediately apparent. The '*My*' indicates his covenant possession of us, while the '*son*' (singular) assures us of his attention to each individual within his family. We are not lost in the crowd. And this word concerning '*the discipline of the Lord*' is always to be understood and received in that context. Who does the Lord discipline? He '*disciplines the one he loves*'—that is, those who belong to him, those whose father he has become, those whom he loves with everlasting love (Jeremiah 31:3). This truth is enforced further in the words '*and chastises every son whom he receives*'. It is not all and sundry whom God '*disciplines*' or '*chastises*' (notwithstanding common grace), but his own loved and received ones. It is his training of his children. It is the way he brings us up. It is part of family life. Sonship and discipline make a pair. Furthermore, there may be times when we see more of God's love, care and tenderness in the course of a 'dark' providence than we do when in the midst of enjoying a 'bright' one.

This is very important, for it is all too easy to imagine (quite wrongly) that the Lord's disciplines and chastisements are indications of his *lack* of love for us, rather than (as they truly are) assurances of the *reality* of his love for us. That is why he takes such trouble over us, bears patiently with so much that is amiss with us, and has promised to complete the work he has begun in us (remind yourself of Philippians 1:6). For this reason, not least, we are not to '*regard lightly*' these experiences (since they are exceedingly necessary and valuable), nor to become '*weary*' on account of them (since they are intended for our blessing and strengthening).

Should the question be asked as to what form these dealings of God with us might take, the answer is that they include such things as these (in no order of significance): disappointments, when things we had set our hearts upon do not happen; sorrows and losses, which remind us of the vanity and passing nature of all earthly things; poorliness, when we are laid aside for a season from our regular service and have to learn to wait quietly and contentedly upon the Lord; troubles, misrepresentations and even persecution, as we learn what it is to suffer for Jesus and 'for righteousness' sake' (Matthew 5:10); and times of spiritual dryness, when the Lord appears to have withdrawn from us, in order that we learn to prize him all the more upon his drawing nearer to us again. The whole purpose of such divine dealings with his children is that God would grant to us an ever closer walk with himself. His plans for us are always and only to do us good, and never ever to do us harm; they are 'to give (us) a future and a hope' (Jeremiah 29:11). As we noted in 2:10 (see on that verse), even 'the founder of (our) salvation' was made 'perfect through suffering'.

*'It is for discipline that you have to endure. God is treating you as sons'* (12:7a). It is a proof of our being his true children. Surely we cannot still miss the point. However heavy upon us at any time may be his disciplines, however severe his chastisings, God is revealing the abundance of his heart of grace and tenderness towards us. He loves his children in a way that he loves no one else on earth. If only we could see that, for to see it is to go a good distance along the way towards benefitting from these things. They are always intended by God to draw us closer to him, and never to drive us further away from him. Our hearts sometimes attempt to tell us otherwise, and the devil will certainly seek to persuade us otherwise. In such cases we do not believe our hearts, and we certainly do not believe the devil. What do we do? We take God at his word and, humbly and thankfully, believe him.

This verse 7a brings out also the intimate connection between discipline and endurance. Discipline is a help to endurance, not a hindrance to it. Paul brings this out in Romans 5:3–4: 'we rejoice in our sufferings, knowing that suffering produces endurance, and endurance produces character, and character produces hope'—then adding, in the next verse, 'and hope does not put us to shame, because God's love has been poured into our hearts through the Holy Spirit who has been given to us'.

### The parallel of discipline (12:7b-9)

Still our writer is enforcing the message. The Hebrews hopefully will not have missed it, and neither must we. The parallel he draws is from the human family, and the place right discipline should play there as children are brought up and trained in the family home. *'For what son is there whom his father does not discipline?'* (12:7b). In our own day, sadly, there are all too many fathers who do not discipline their children. If, in a former day, parental discipline might at times have been too strict, a mark of the present day is that all too often it is too lax, or even absent altogether. This can even be the case in some Christian homes, accounted for sometimes, maybe, by fear of sanctions from the governing authorities, with whom biblical family discipline is very far from being in favour.

*'If you are left without discipline, in which all have participated, then you are illegitimate children and not sons'* (12:8). God's way for parents and children in families is that discipline which incorporates such things as training in the right way to live and warning not to live in wrong ways—parents, especially fathers, bringing children 'up in the discipline and instruction of the Lord' (Ephesians 6:4—that is, according to the Scriptures), and children obeying their 'parents in the Lord' (Ephesians 6:1). This should be exercised with a godly combination of firmness and affection. Parents are responsible to God for maintaining the discipline, children are responsible to God for accepting the discipline. All is to be done to the glory of God. Where parents abandon this important work, then (far from loving God and loving their children) they are treating their offspring as *'illegitimate children and not sons'*. To neglect discipline is to 'hate' your children, whereas to be 'diligent to discipline' them is truly to love them (Proverbs 13:24). This should be very sobering to us.

The parallel continues to be worked out between earthly discipline and heavenly discipline. *'Besides this* (or, 'Furthermore'), *we have had earthly fathers who disciplined us and we respected them. Shall we not much more be subject to the Father of spirits and live?'* (12:9). This is a classic argument from the lesser (our earthly father) to the greater (our heavenly Father). If we were disciplined by the former (as we should have been), and respected them for it (as we should have done), then how much more, when God disciplines us, should we respect him (which, in God's case, includes honour and worship due to him)? God is referred to here by the unusual name of '*the Father of spirits*'. It tallies with the description of him as 'the God of the spirits of all flesh' in Numbers 16:22, and his self-revelation, 'Behold, I am the LORD, the God of all flesh' in Jeremiah 32:27. The meaning is that he is the one who gives life to all mankind, as well as new spiritual life to all those who come to him for salvation through his Son. We are all '*subject*' to him. We submit to his ways with us and seek not to rebel or murmur against him, or foolishly charge him with not loving us after all.

### The purpose of discipline (12:10)

What is this divine discipline for? What is its intended aim and goal? The answer is here to hand. '*For they* [our parents] *disciplined us for a short time* [while we were under their roof, in their care, growing up in the family] *as it seemed best to them* [in their fallible humanity, with all the shortfalls of it], *but he* [God] *disciplines us for our good* (or, 'profit'), *that we may share his holiness*' (12:10). How striking to be told that '*our good*' [that is, our best good, the very best thing for us] is '*that* [purpose clause] *we may share his holiness*'. How completely 'upside down' this is from the world's assessment of priorities. Yet it is God's way which is actually the 'right way up'!

The phrase '*for our good*' points us to some of the key reasons *why* God disciplines his children whom he loves so much. We may say that these disciplines are: (1) to cause us to be more careful in our walk with God, so as not to displease him in any way; (2) to wean us off the world with all its seductions and beckonings; (3) to establish us more firmly in the way of obedience to his commandments; (4) to create in us a deeper and more consistent dependence upon God and his promises in all things; (5) to enable us to prove, again and again, the absolute sufficiency of divine and heavenly grace; (6) to stir up our affections and desires after Jesus more fervently and that he be more roundly formed is us (Christlikeness); (7) to enable us to 'know him and the power of his resurrection, (that we) may share in his sufferings' (Philippians 3:10); and (8) to instil in us a stronger longing for heaven. The psalmist knew the purpose of discipline very well, and rejoiced in God for it. Twice in Psalm 119 (at verses 67 and 71) he has a testimony to what we might call 'blessed discipline'. 'Before I was afflicted I went astray, but now I keep your word'. 'It is good for me that I was afflicted, that I might learn your statutes'. Could the Hebrews say the same? Can we?

### The produce of discipline (12:11)

This verse takes the long view, and in doing so expresses a keenly felt truth of Christian experience. *'For the moment all discipline seems painful rather than pleasant* [that can be how it feels at the time], *but later* [the aspect we often forget in our impatience] *it yields the peaceful fruit of righteousness* [worth waiting for] *to those who have been trained* [who have received the discipline well, have been well schooled, have learned the necessary lessons] *by it'* (12:11).

It is in the nature of *'all discipline'* that it is not fun. The word *'painful'* is more appropriate for it than *'pleasant'* while it is being gone through. And that is how it should be. Verse 11 said that God 'disciplines us for our good', not for our enjoyment, and related that 'good' to our sharing 'his holiness'. That's why this long view, as we called it, is so important. If it gets forgotten, the danger is that we can be overwhelmed by the difficult and uncomfortable experiences we face, and (thinking of the Hebrews) we could easily allow this to become an argument for turning our back on Jesus and the gospel, thinking that things were better back in the old days.

The *'For the moment'* covers the entire length of our earthly lives, whether that be shorter for some or longer for others, as God sovereignly and graciously appoints. Yet the thought of, one day, the painfulness giving way to the pleasantness should help us to see how worthwhile all God's dealings with us are—not least since, as he 'fulfils his purpose for' each one of us (Psalm 57:2), we know that he does so wisely, kindly and faithfully, for that is how our God is. In every sense the outcome of a Christian life of discipline is worth waiting for. Paul knew this, and (as with scales on a set of balances) could contrast confidently our 'slight momentary affliction' with the 'eternal weight of glory' it prepares us for (2 Corinthians 4:17). The word *'later'* is key.

With regard to the ultimate yield from the discipline, it is spoken of as *'the peaceful fruit of righteousness'*. The idea is of a rich and abundant harvest. The adjective *'peaceful'* maintains the theme of this chapter of running the race. Once the race is completed and the runner has crossed the finishing line, the struggle is past, the expending of energy ceases, the body rests and there is a sense of thankfulness and relief that it is all over. All the training, all the self-denial, all the hardships, all the discipline was worth it. How glad the contestant is that he did not abandon everything part way round the course. Transferring this to the Christian race, with all *its* training, self-denial, hardships and discipline, what a relief and joy beyond words it will be to cross the line and enter heaven, and there be with our Saviour to whom we have been looking all the way through the race. There will be no more trials, no more disturbances and no more conflict. All will be calm, all will be at rest, all will be *'peaceful'*.

The full phrase, though, is *'the peaceful fruit of righteousness'*. This links in with what verse 10 had to say about holiness. The harvest in view is when grace has done its final and glorious work, and the sinner who trusted in Christ for righteousness enters into the fullness of that righteousness, having at last been made perfectly holy. The process that is moving forward throughout our lives (as the present race is being run) will be completed at the end of the race. Then 'we shall be like him [Jesus]' (1 John 3:2). The sure prospect of this *then* should contribute to our keeping on going *'now'*, for 'everyone who thus hopes in him purifies himself as he is pure' (1 John 3:3).

## (4) The necessity of vigour (12:12–17)

The picture of running the race has not disappeared. Self-discipline and training have already been considered as absolutely necessary for such an activity; so also is vigour. Running races is an intense and demanding business, and vigour (a combination of such characteristics as strength, good health, effort, energy and enthusiasm) is of the essence. Once again, the same holds good for the Christian race. We shall never persevere or make progress if we are anything less than fully awake. Even being just half asleep is dangerous. What athlete can run a race, keep going, and cross the finishing line in that state?

'*Therefore* [following on directly from the previous verses] *lift your drooping hands and strengthen your weak knees* [many a hand can droop and many a knee can grow weak in a race—imagine a cross country race, full of obstacles and snares], *and make straight paths for your feet* [it becomes increasingly difficult to keep running a straight course, as the body begins to want to go all over the place], *so that what is lame may not be put out of joint* [the danger of injuries, which would cause a spiritual limping and hinder or prevent carrying on] *but rather be healed*' (12:12–13).

The picture is of weariness setting in. When this happens in a race, what might the runner begin to think to himself as he seeks to struggle on? Maybe something like this: 'Is it really worth finishing? What is to be gained? I've got this far, isn't that enough? There's still such a long way to go. I'm sure I'll never make it'. And that sort of thinking takes the runner well on the way to dropping out of the race. No doubt many of those whom we met in chapter 11 had moments when they felt like this; but they were enabled—divinely enabled—to press on with fresh vigour as they cast themselves upon the Lord. It reminds us of the precious promise stored up for us in Isaiah 40:31, that 'they who wait for the LORD shall renew their strength; they shall mount up with wings like eagles; they shall run and not be weary; they shall walk and not faint' (read the whole passage there from verse 25 through to the end of the chapter).

There is a richness of Old Testament allusion to what our writer says here. Behind the imagery of the '*drooping hands*' and '*weak knees*' lies Isaiah 35:3, while the exhortation to '*make straight paths for your feet*' finds its root in Proverbs 4:26–7. These are Scriptures with which the Hebrews will have been familiar, and so Scriptures intended to strike home to them with urgency. In the Christian race it is not some temporary and fading crown which is at stake, but rather 'the crown of righteousness, which the Lord, the righteous judge [writes the apostle], will award to me on that Day, and not only to me but also to all who have loved his appearing' (2 Timothy 4:8). Everything imaginable for the security of our eternal souls is in view. Hence there must be no straying out of the way, no putting ourselves in the way of injury, no playing games with serious matters, for when the Lord's true way is abandoned, apostasy beckons.

'*Strive for* (or, 'pursue, follow, make every effort to go after') *peace with everyone*' (12:14). Where does this fit, in the context of running the race? A race is not a solitary activity. If it was just a private runner out on his own it would not be a race. A race requires more than one runner, at the very least. So we are to have regard to our fellow runners. We are not to run selfishly, merrily tripping others up, pushing them out of the way, mocking them if they are making slow progress at the back of the field, or taking pride in our own performance. We are to be helpers and not hinderers of our brethren in the race. We are to be encouragers and not discouragers of one another as we run. By '*peace*' here, we imagine our writer is thinking along the lines of 'how good and pleasant it is when brothers dwell in unity' in Psalm 133:1; of the apostle's picture of the church as one body comprising many members, with Christ as the sole head (as set out in 1 Corinthians 12); and of 'the one hope that belongs to your call' of Ephesians 4:4.

This same verse continues with a most important call to every believer. Still under the verb with which the verse begins ('*Strive*'), we come to this: '*and for the holiness without which no one will see the Lord*'. The two things—'*peace*' and '*holiness*'—are joined vitally together. Both are brought together by Jesus in the Beatitudes with which the Sermon on the Mount commences. Who are the blessed ones? They are '*the pure in heart*'. Why are they blessed? It is '*for they shall see God*'. Who else are blessed? Those who '*are the peacemakers*'. Why are they blessed? It is '*for they shall be called sons of God*' (Matthew 5:8–9).

The false idea still surfaces sometimes that it is an easy thing, all in a day's work, to get to heaven. Anyone can do it, no matter how they live in the meantime. Yet such a view is entirely false, and the pursuit of it will likely have led many tragic souls to hell instead. Our writer exposes its lie here in insisting on the need for *'the holiness without which no one will see the Lord'*. It is the constant truth that if there is no holiness in us now, there will be no heaven for us later. Holiness and heaven go together. You cannot have one without the other.

The reason for this is not hard to find. God is holy and heaven is holy. That God is holy is asserted throughout the Bible. God says so of himself in both testaments—'be holy, for I am holy' (Leviticus 11:44, taken up in 1 Peter 1:15–16). In Isaiah 6:3 we learn that 'Holy, holy, holy is the LORD of hosts' (a Hebrew way of expressing superlatives by using repetition). That heaven is holy is true since of it the Lord declares, 'Heaven is my throne' (Isaiah 66:1); 'nothing unclean will ever enter it' (Revelation 21:27).

This is tremendously important in the overall context of Hebrews, for it keeps before everyone who claims to be a Christian the need for self-examination, that we may be as sure as it is possible to be that we have both the root and the fruit of the matter in us. Let 12:14b serve three very practical ends, therefore. It serves, first, as *a mirror to examine ourselves with* (as I know my heart and observe my life, are things in accord with the character and mind of God? do I hate what he hates and love what he loves? do I measure everything according to the gold standard of his word? does my life, both in private and in public, declare me to be a true child of God, or am I deceiving both myself and others?). It serves, second, as *a stick to prod ourselves with* (can I look back on past sin without deep and heartfelt sorrow? when contemplating present sin, can I do so without a smiting conscience? am I able to make provision for future sin without utter horror and disgust?). It serves, third, as *a promise to encourage ourselves with* (for it holds before us the beatific vision, the sight of God, the enjoying of God in his very presence throughout that eternal 'Sabbath rest for the people of God' which we read of in 4:9).

This first of the two major sections of Hebrews 12 rounds off with the sustained argument now presented in verses 15–17. It begins with an arresting exhortation. *'See to it that no one fails to obtain the grace of*

*God'* (12:15). With the call to holiness and heaven still ringing in the ears of all who read what has just been considered, here is the solemn warning of missing out on both. *'See to it'* is a forceful way a stating this. The first word of this verse is actually a participle, carrying on from the previous verse with a comma rather than a full stop. It could be rendered 'observing (or, 'looking, watching continually') lest'. To fail *'to obtain the grace of God'* here in Hebrews speaks of the danger of the apostasy which has loomed large in earlier passages. The verb translated here *'fail to obtain'* carries the note of missing out on something through your own fault, a falling back from something. In the present chapter (for the background still remains that of running the race) that can be illustrated by dropping out of the race, giving up part way through, and so losing the heavenly reward and blessing. This is not a 'blip' in the Christian life, an 'off moment'. It is a complete crash and consequent derailment.

The warning continues, with no let up in its seriousness: *'that no 'root of bitterness' springs up and causes trouble* [compare Deuteronomy 29:18–19, where Moses had the task of warning God's people in those days of the danger of apostasy—times do not change], *and by it many become defiled'*. The *'root of bitterness'* is an attitude directed against God, his covenant and his commandments. Indeed, it is more than an attitude, for a careful check on that Deuteronomy passage shows that it is personified—the 'root' there is 'one who', the person who says 'I shall be safe, though I walk in the stubbornness of my heart'. A person like that can 'lead to the sweeping away of moist and dry alike' (what an amazing phrase). Such a position is spiritually deadly. Back with our Hebrews verse, this makes complete sense of the connection with the *'many'* of *'and by it many become defiled'*. It only takes one to lead many astray. Someone starts the ball rolling, and in no time at all a whole company can have followed. Example—both for good and for ill—is a most influential thing among those who say they follow after Jesus. We can so easily take others with us, whether in pressing on in the race or in abandoning the race altogether.

At this point, our writer brings in the Old Testament example of Esau. He received a significant passing mention in 11:20, in connection with his brother Jacob. We might wonder exactly what Esau has to do with things. The answer is, he has a very great deal to do with them. He is a sad and classic example of such a 'root of bitterness'. With him, therefore, as the salutary warning, the argument proceeds: *'that no one is sexually immoral or unholy like Esau, who sold his birthright for a single meal. For you know that afterward, when he desired to inherit the blessing, he was rejected, for he found no chance to repent, thought he sought it with tears'* (12:16–17).

This episode is bad news. Two terms are used to describe Esau— *'sexually immoral'* and *'unholy'*. The first (a single word in Greek) must refer to his marrying foreign (non-Israelite) wives, an action which 'made life bitter' for his parents (Genesis 26:34–35). The strict meaning of the word here in Hebrews is 'fornicator'. In the light of 13:4, still to come, this will likely have struck home to the Hebrews with extra punch, for it appears that some among them were playing fast and loose in the area of sexual purity and marital faithfulness. This itself, all too often, can be a rung on the downward spiral into apostasy—a failure to heed Galatians 5:24, 'And those who belong to Christ Jesus have crucified the flesh with its passions and desires'. The citing of immorality here may also carry (as it often does in Scripture) the fundamental sense of turning away from God— spiritual immorality, idolatry, adultery, which is certainly appropriate to the case of Esau. This leads to what now follows.

The second word, *'unholy'*, may also be translated 'irreligious' or 'profane'. It describes someone who regards lightly spiritual things, who despises what is sacred, who wilfully casts aside the precious and holy things of God. Esau did this in the familiar event (see our comments on 11:20) of selling *'his birthright for* [that is, in exchange for] *a single meal'*. All that belonged to him as the firstborn son was recklessly given up for food. The material took precedence for him over the spiritual. The 'here and now' was more important to him than the things to come. With his *'birthright'* went the inheritance of his *'blessing'*, and he lost them both in a cavalier fashion. There was an unexpected problem for him, however. When (*'afterward'*) he came to his senses, realised what he had done, and wished to repossess what he had lost, it was too late. It could not be done. Even though '*he sought it with tears*' (the verb signifies the exerting of tremendous effort and urgency), it was no use. There was no way back. The implication is that his 'repentance' was not genuine. It was far removed from that 'godly grief' or 'godly sorrow' which is the mark of true repentance; instead it was 'worldly grief' or 'worldly sorrow' (2 Corinthians 7:10).

'*For you know* [what happened to Esau would be very familiar to the original readers] *that afterward, when he desired to inherit the blessing* [he wanted the blessing back, though not necessarily the covenant responsibilities that went with it—see Genesis 27:36], *he was rejected* [by his father Isaac, who would not be moved by his pleadings, but, more importantly, by God], *for he found no chance to repent*'. There is a strong recollection here of 6:4, with its solemn opening remark, 'For it is impossible to restore again to repentance those who have once been enlightened'. This keeps to the fore that our writer is not dealing with some theoretical situation that is never likely to happen, but rather one which *has already* happened—and which, in the case of the Hebrews themselves, is in real danger of happening all over again. The point is this: if they should turn away from Jesus and the gospel, so that they finish the race early before reaching the line, they will be committing an even greater folly than Esau did.

So the writer pleads with them, just as God, by his Holy Spirit, in bringing the word to bear, pleads with us also. Do not be like Esau, do not slight the favours of the gospel, do not prefer the temporal to the eternal or the material to the spiritual, do not choose the things of the body over the things of the soul, do not turn away from 'the truth of Christ' (2 Corinthians 11:10), 'the faith that was once for all delivered to the saints' (Jude 3), for 'how shall we escape if we neglect such a great salvation?' (Hebrews 2:3). Rather, 'seek first the kingdom of God and his righteousness' (Matthew 6:33); 'seek the things that are above, where Christ is, seated at the right hand of God' (Colossians 3:1); keep 'looking to Jesus' and keep striving 'for the holiness without which no one will see the Lord' (Hebrews 12:2, 14). This alone is 'the good way'; 'walk in it, and find rest for your souls' (Jeremiah 6:16).

## The two mountains (12:18–29)

Mountains figure on a number of significant occasions in Scripture, though without question two of the most significant are Sinai and Zion. These two mountains are now brought to the fore as our writer proceeds with his urgent argument to the Hebrews. Sinai (while it is not named as such, there is no doubting its identity here) features in verses 18–21, with Zion following in verses 22–24. The remainder of the chapter (verses 25–29) draws applications from the two. Before plunging into the text here, it might be helpful to give one summary sentence concerning each of these mountains, in terms which explain their appearance here.

- *Sinai* reminds us that the terrors of God's majesty kept the people at a distance from him

- *Zion* reminds us that the wonders of God's grace draw the people near to him.

### (1) A reminder of Sinai (12:18–21)

The two mountains are placed in direct contrast to one another, each of them representing in turn the old and new covenants (think back to chapter 8). This is clear from the language used. So 12:18 begins, 'For you have not come to', while 12:22 begins, 'But you have come to'. The danger with the Hebrews, as we have seen in different ways, is that they were showing a mistaken partiality for Sinai, and were becoming less and less enamoured with Zion. Their preference was increasingly for returning to Judaism, in favour of pressing on with the gospel. They were retreating to the shadows of night, instead of basking in the light of day. They were leaving the superior for the inferior. What sort of exchange is that?

'*For you have not come to what may be touched*' (12:18). This speaks of things tangible, things material. The illustration of Sinai is a reference to the giving of the law in the time of Moses. The Old Testament background is found in Exodus 19 (compare Deuteronomy 4). The people themselves were only allowed as far as the foot of the mountain. Then this happened: 'The Lord came down on Mount

Sinai, to the top of the mountain. And the LORD called Moses to the top of the mountain, and Moses went up'. It was all very solemn, and that solemnity is brought out very vividly in what is recalled here in Hebrews of that momentous occasion. It was predominantly one of terror and awe.

Our writer lists several features (it is striking that in each case, Sinai and Zion, seven things are noted). There was *'a blazing fire and darkness and gloom and a tempest and the sound of a trumpet and a voice whose words made the hearers beg that no further messages be spoken to them'* (12:18–19). These details are documented precisely in the course of the Exodus and Deuteronomy passages indicated above. Things reached the point where the people dared not see or hear any more. *'For they could not endure the order that was given, "If even a beast touches the mountain, it shall be stoned"'* (12:20). Moses, too, was deeply affected—and he was the one who was having to go up this blazing and tempestuous mountain. *'Indeed, so terrifying was the sight* [or, 'spectacle', a word occurring only here in the New Testament, and indicating an appearance of a startling nature] *that Moses said, "I tremble with fear"'* (12:21). This response of Moses does not appear in the Pentateuch accounts, though is given to our writer to record here, under the inspiration (as he, like all other 'Bible writers', was) of the Holy Spirit.

What is it that accounts for this response, both from the people and from Moses? It is surely this: their deep conviction of their sinfulness in the felt presence of God in his holiness. As this chapter of Hebrews will conclude by affirming, 'for our God is a consuming fire' (12:29). Recall, also, 10:31, 'It is a fearful thing to fall into the hands of the living God'. And why is this so? It is because 'God is light [that is, his holiness and purity], and in him is no darkness [that is, no sinfulness or impurity] at all' (1 John 1:5). As a result, '(our) iniquities have made a separation between (us) and (our) God, and (our) sins have hidden his face from (us)' (Isaiah 59:2). Sin separates. Sin ruins. Sin comes between. Sin brings us under judgment. And the clearer our understanding of God's law given at Sinai in these memorable circumstances, the clearer will be our realisation that we are under his condemnation and his judgment for having broken his law and sinned against his holiness. For that, the penalty is death, and the prospect is hell. And so things would remain, were it not for God's intervention and provision. To that the argument here now turns.

## (2) A welcome to Zion (12:22–24)

Why would the Hebrews (or anyone else) wish to return to what has just been described—the terrors, the fears, the pleadings that God would cease speaking to them, the desirings (in a sense) to run away? What is the attraction in that? Yet somehow this is the direction in which their hearts (and their steps) appear to be turning. But, insists our writer, this is not what you have come to. This is not where God has brought you, through his grace in the gospel. This is not the ultimate terminus of the law, for the very law itself (as the apostle Paul declares) 'was our guardian until Christ came, in order that we might be justified by faith. But now that faith has come, we are no longer under a guardian' (Galatians 3:24—25)—'justified by faith', that is, rather than by performing the works the law requires and bringing ourselves back to God through some merit or achievement of our own.

So the contrast is now presented. It is the contrast between the 'physicals' of Sinai and the law, and the 'spirituals' of Zion and the Saviour. It expresses the reality of the joys and horizons of freedom in Christ, in comparison with the fears and restrictions of bondage under the law. *'But* [a strong contrast] *you have come* [the same verb as in verse 18, which may also be translated 'approached'] *to Mount Zion'* (12:22). Zion was a specific location, the mount upon which the Jerusalem temple stood, the place of which the psalmist testified when affirming, 'I was glad when they said to me, "Let us go to the house of the LORD!". Our feet have been standing within your gates, O Jerusalem!' (Psalm 122:1–2). It stands here, however, not as a geographical place, but as symbolic of all the blessings of the gospel, those blessings provided through the Lord Jesus Christ, the 'great high priest' (4:14), 'the mediator of a new covenant' (9:15). The fact that our writer says to and of the Hebrews that it is to Zion (in this spiritual sense of Zion) *'you have come'*, suggests that—despite all the pastoral concern they were giving him—he still entertained a genuine hope that it was well with their souls, and would remain so. This confirms what he wrote in 6:9 and 10:39.

We remarked above that in both cases (Sinai and Zion) seven things are said. What are the seven things said here of their coming to Zion?

First, *'the city of the living God, the heavenly Jerusalem'*. It is best to keep these two phrases together as one. The reference is to that same prospect towards which Abraham and the others in chapter 11 looked—'the city that has foundations, whose designer and builder is God' (11:10), as well as that which will be spoken of in 13:14, 'the city that is to come'. There is a dual sense here, so far as Christian experience is concerned. We have already come to the spiritual Zion, the spiritual Jerusalem, through having been 'born again to a living hope' (1 Peter 1:3). At the same time, we are yet to come there, when we arrive (literally) at *'the heavenly Jerusalem'* in glory. We are both there and not there! We have both arrived and are still on the way! And if this seems something of a riddle, Paul explains it in Philippians 3:20, when asserting that 'our citizenship is in heaven' (right now, already, as we speak), even while 'from it we await a Saviour, the Lord Jesus Christ'. Zion is where the new covenant people of God should have their heart, for there our blessed and lovely Saviour is.

That we *'have come to Mount Zion, the city of the living God'* provides an assurance of the truth of God's self-revealing (and highly comforting) word in Psalm 132:13–14, 'For the LORD has chosen Zion; he has desired it for his dwelling place. "This is my resting place forever; here I will dwell, for I have desired it"'. Look it up, and read on to the end of the psalm. God dwells spiritually in the midst of his people, and in the hearts of his people. Where his people are, there God is, for he has taken us as his own in the eternal covenant of grace.

Second, *'and to innumerable* ['myriads of', indicating tens of thousands] *angels in festal gathering'*. To these also the Hebrews have come. In what sense? We met the angels early on, indeed in the very first chapter, as 'ministering spirits sent out to serve for the sake of those who are to inherit salvation' (1:14). The angels are intensely interested in the things of Jesus and the gospel, as 1 Peter 1:12 tells us—they 'long to look' into them. They were present at Sinai for the giving of the law (see Deuteronomy 33:2). Here at Zion, however, they are pictured *'in festal gathering'*, which has also been translated 'in joyful assembly'. The one word in Greek, making here its solitary New Testament appearance, signifies a gathering of celebration in connection with a festival of some sort. The point of it in 12:22 would seem to be to inform us that the angels gather continually around the throne of God, engaging in worship and praise. And it is to this company, as a real and true part of it, that Christians have come. It is in this eternal worshipping of God that we share. It is an exalted statement, which highlights not only the priority for every believer of the worship of God (it is for this, more than anything else, that we have been created—which is why the sinner's robbing God of the worship due to him is at the very heart of the sin of which he is guilty before God), but provides also this added dimension to God's worship and glory (namely that we join in it with the heavenly angels).

This angelic involvement in the worship of God is to the fore in the book of Revelation. Note, for example, Revelation 5:11–12, where, along with others whom John heard around God's throne, was 'the voice of many angels, numbering myriads of myriads and thousands of thousands, saying with a loud voice, 'Worthy is the Lamb who was slain, to receive power and wealth and wisdom and might and honour and glory and blessing'. To this *'festal'*, joyful, worshipful company in heaven itself (in contrast to the dark and threatening setting at Sinai), the Hebrews have been brought. Can they now contemplate leaving it? Can we?

Third, *'and to the assembly of the firstborn who are enrolled in heaven'* (12:23). The word *'assembly'* is the regular New Testament word for 'church', and may be rendered so here. It indicates not only a great number but the full, the complete, one. (The question has been raised by some interpreters as to whether the *festal gathering'* of 12:22

should be linked with *'the assembly of the firstborn'* of 12:23, rather than with the *'innumerable angels'*. There are pros and cons, but no overwhelming reasons to change things from how we have them translated in the ESV. The position of the repeated *'and'* is significant in establishing the matter. In the present instance, it follows the word translated *'festal gathering'* and precedes that translated *'assembly'* or *'church'*, indicating that the fresh thought commences with the latter).

The contrast between Sinai and Zion continues. On the former Exodus occasion the *'assembly'* of God's people gathered at the foot of Sinai (and note the expression 'the assembly of Israel' in Deuteronomy 31:30). In 4:10 of Deuteronomy, in the context of Sinai (Horeb is an alternative name for Sinai), the people who 'stood before the LORD' constituted an assembly ('Gather' = 'Assemble'); in 9:10 and 18:16 the occasion is called 'the day of the assembly'. The description reaches its fullest flowering, however, in the New Testament, where both Jesus (in the gospels) and the apostles (in the letters) speak of the whole company of the redeemed as 'the church' (see, for example, Matthew 16:18, where Jesus says, 'I will build my church'; and Ephesians 5:25, where Paul teaches how 'Christ loved the church and gave himself up for her'). To this chosen and blessed *'assembly'*, Christians, through grace, belong.

It is designated specifically *'the assembly of the firstborn who are enrolled in heaven'*. Both the title *'firstborn'* and the image of being *'enrolled'* occur in connection with the Egypt-wilderness-Sinai company, as verses like Exodus 4:22–23 and 32:32–33 indicate clearly. Here in Hebrews, the same descriptions are used in new covenant terms of the entire church of God, Old and New Testament members together as one, all those who belong to the Lord Jesus Christ and so who 'through him [Christ] … both have access in one Spirit to the Father' (Ephesians 2:18). Jesus himself is *the* 'firstborn', but not only this. He is 'the firstborn among many brothers' (Romans 8:29). Esau, we learned in 12:16–17, rashly sold his birthright and blessing as Isaac's firstborn son. Our writer is urging the Hebrews not to do the same, particularly because they are the *'firstborn'* in a higher and richer sense, having been redeemed with Jesus' precious blood, the true 'blood of the covenant' (9:20).

To this *'assembly of the firstborn'* we who are Christians 'have come'. We described it a couple of paragraphs ago as a chosen and blessed assembly, and the chosen aspect comes through in the words *'who are enrolled in heaven'*. No doubt our names are *'enrolled'* in various registers here on earth. The electoral register (so that we can vote) and the medical register (so that we can receive treatment) are two obvious examples. The register here in 12:23 is a different one altogether, however, for it is not an enrolment written on earth, but one written *'in heaven'*, written by God himself. This is 'the book of life of the Lamb who was slain', in which is 'everyone whose name has … been written before the foundation of the world' (Revelation 13:8). In a beautiful passage (Luke 10:20), Jesus encouraged his disciples with these words. 'Nevertheless, do not rejoice in this, that the spirits are subject to you, but rejoice that your names are written in heaven'. What a cause for rejoicing, indeed! In this heavenly register, our names are written, as it were, in indelible ink. The very tense of the verb *'enrolled'* conveys the sense of permanence. The Hebrews needed to stop back-pedalling where Jesus was concerned and start rejoicing in him again. And so must we, at all times.

Fourth, *'and to God, the judge of all'*. As far back as the instance in Abraham's life when he was interceding before God for Sodom, the patriarch affirmed, 'Shall not the Judge of all the earth do what is just?' (Genesis 18:25). The truth of God being *'the judge of all'* is testified to throughout the Bible, including in Hebrews itself. To him 'we must give account' (4:13). After death, for everyone, 'comes judgment' (9:27). 'The LORD will judge his people' (10:30). 'It is a fearful thing to fall into the hands of the living God' (10:31). 'God will judge the sexually immoral and adulterous' (13:4).

Any consideration of God's judgment is very serious and solemn. His judgment throne is part and parcel of what follows from the 'you have come to Mount Zion' of 12:22. That being so—linked with the statement now under discussion coming in association with the 'innumerable angels in festal gathering', 'the assembly of the firstborn who are enrolled in heaven', and (coming next) 'the spirits of righteous men made perfect' and 'Jesus, the mediator of a new covenant'—suggests that it is not the fearsome aspect of the divine judgment that is in view here, but, rather, the sweet assurance in the gospel that this throne is now become to us 'the throne of grace' (4:16). The condemnation of Sinai has given way to the justification of Zion, for all those who are in Christ. As Paul expresses it, 'since you are not under law but under grace' (Romans 6:14).

Fifth, *'and to the spirits of the righteous made perfect'*. This major sentence (begun in verse 22, and extending right through to the end of verse 24) continues with what must surely link up with 11:39–40. We learned there that, while the representative men and women of faith brought before us in that great chapter were 'commended through their faith', they 'did not receive that was promised' (that is, the fullness of all of that to which they looked by faith). And why is that? It is 'since God had provided something better for us, that apart from us they should not be made perfect'. So what precisely is this connection between these two verses from the end of chapter 11 and the particular phrase before us in 12:23? How do the two tie in?

The answer is clear to see. It speaks of the oneness or unity of the Hebrews (and all Christians who follow them, ourselves included) with those (including, though not restricted to, those mentioned in Hebrews 11 and their like) who have already entered into their heavenly rest. All those, in every generation, for whom it can truly be said that 'Christ is all, and in all' (Colossians 3:11), are one together. In the present context, we have 'come' to them (are one with them), having 'come' to the heavenly (as opposed to the literal) Zion. The value of the Hebrews being faced with this further shot across their bows is to insist to them upon the folly of looking backwards, *away from Jesus*, when all the Old Testament believers were looking forwards, *on to Jesus*. In distancing (and ultimately separating) themselves from the New Testament, they are, to all practical intents and purposes, distancing (and ultimately separating) themselves from the Old Testament as well! Then, where will they have left to go?

One detail does remain for comment. How is it that in 11:40 those who went before had not been 'made perfect', while in 12:23 they have been *'made perfect'*? The resolution of what on the face of it could look like a contradiction is found in the phrase *'the spirits of the righteous'*. We are best to understand *'spirits'* of those who have already died 'in the Lord', thinking of the statement in Revelation 14:13 that, 'Blessed are the dead who die in the Lord'. They are termed the *'spirits of the righteous'* because it is only of those who have been made righteous before God (under both the old and the new covenants) through the once for all and sufficient sacrifice of the Lord Jesus Christ of whom it can be declared that they died 'in the Lord'. It is not a description that can ever be applied to any others. So in that sense they have indeed (and joyfully) been *'made perfect'* (12:23, and compare 10:14), whereas at the time when they actually died they had not lived to see the fulfilment of their messianic hopes and promises (11:40). So, as always with Scripture, there is no contradiction whatsoever.

Sixth, *'and to Jesus, the mediator of a new covenant'* (12:24). Here, and in what follows immediately, we have arrived at the high point. This is the centrepiece of the entire purpose and theme of Hebrews. This is why our author has been given the book to write. It is to exalt the Lord Jesus Christ as the one who alone is high over all.

The description of Jesus as 'the mediator of a new covenant' ('mediator' being the character in which he has saved us from our sins and by which the favours of God are bestowed upon us) appeared in 9:15 (see on that verse), but this is no needless repetition. The *'new covenant'* of which he is *'the mediator'* is the 'better covenant' of 7:22 (see on that verse, and compare 8:6). It is both striking and beautiful that the name *'Jesus'* is used here on its own. This is the most precious and personal name of all belonging to the Saviour, and takes us straight to the very heart of both his person and his work: 'you shall call his name Jesus, for he will save his people from their sins' (Matthew 1:21). Were it not for him, we could never 'have come to Mount Zion', 'the heavenly Jerusalem', at all.

Seventh, *'and to the sprinkled blood that speaks* [a participle, 'speaking'] *a better* (or, 'superior') *word than the blood of Abel* [literally, 'speaking a better thing than Abel', though clearly it is Abel's blood which is signified, in contrast to Jesus' blood]'. This is closely linked with the sixth statement, just considered, for *'the sprinkled blood'* is the blood of Jesus, 'the blood of the eternal covenant' (13:20), the blood without which 'there is no forgiveness of sins' (9:22). Central to the old covenant itself and to its many and varied sacrifices was the shedding and sprinkling of blood (the 'sprinkling' indicates the application of the benefits of the blood to those on whose behalf the sacrifice has been made). The blood mentioned here, however, is *'the blood of Abel'*—that which was shed when he was murdered by his brother Cain (see on 11:4). The reference to it being 'speaking' blood arises from the words of God to Cain in Genesis 4:10, 'The voice of your brother's blood is crying to me from the ground'. Jesus' blood as well is referred to here in 12:24 as 'speaking' blood. In the light of what is said by way of comparison between the two, however, we must ask the question, 'in what ways does the blood of Jesus speak "*a better word than the blood of Abel*"? Here are seven ways in which it does so.

- Abel's blood cries for revenge, while Jesus' blood cries for pardon

- Abel's blood speaks against the guilty, while Jesus' blood speaks for the guilty

- Abel's blood drove Cain away from God, while Jesus' blood draws sinners near to God

- Abel's blood was the blood of one of his flock shed in sacrifice, while Jesus' blood is the blood of one who shed his own blood in sacrifice

- Abel's blood brought a censuring word from God, while Jesus' blood brings a delighting word from God

- Abel's blood was that of a man (albeit a man of faith), while Jesus' blood is that of the God-Man, the eternal Son of God

- Abel's blood speaks of a mark put upon Cain (a mark of punishment), while Jesus' blood speaks of a very different mark God puts upon the saved sinner (a mark of grace).

It is this 'precious blood' (1 Peter 1:19) to which we have come, and from which neither we nor the Hebrews must ever depart. It is the regular case in Scripture teaching that the life is in the blood. Where the blood of Jesus is concerned, never was there a truer word. We can never either get or make too much of the blood.

## (3) An assurance concerning God's kingdom (12:25–29)

This final paragraph of the chapter stands in direct continuity with what we have just been considering of the contrast between Judaism and Christianity. In the light of all to which 'you have come' (12:22), our writer continues, '*See* ('take heed') *that you do not refuse him who is speaking* ('the one speaking')' (12:25). It is God '*who is speaking*', and he it is who must not be refused. To '*refuse him*' in this context means to turn a deaf ear to him, to fail to heed his word, to cease to follow him. It is to become a rebel, to be overtaken by 'an evil, unbelieving heart, leading you to fall away from the living God', which was warned against in 3:12. God speaks, not least, through the blood of his Son (12:24), and does so very powerfully. He reveals himself therein to be the God who is holy (so cannot have anything to do with sin), the God who is just (so must punish sin), and the God who is gracious (who 'does not deal with us according to our sins, nor repay us according to our iniquities', Psalm 103:10). He *must* be listened to. Considering all that we 'have not come to' (pictured in Mount Sinai) and all that we 'have come to' (pictured in Mount Zion), he *must* be listened to, and listened to continually.

To enforce this further, the verse proceeds as follows. '*For if they did not escape when they refused him who warned* ('the one warning') *them on earth* [despite their extensive privileges], *much less will we escape if we reject* ('turn away from') *him who warns* [literally, just 'the one', with 'warning' understood, so making a parallel expression] *from heaven*'. There is a contrast between '*they*' and '*we*'. By '*they*' is meant the people of Israel at Sinai who, we noted earlier, desired God to stop speaking to them. What they actually said (to Moses) was, 'You speak to us, and we will listen; but do not let God speak to us, lest we die' (Exodus 20:19). They were afraid, and they were rebellious. Don't be like them, warns our writer. By '*we*' (again, with a pastor's heart, he includes himself) is meant the Hebrews, who are being addressed very directly by God in this portion of the New Testament. In each case (*'on earth'* and *'from heaven'*) it is God himself who is issuing the warnings. He warned *'on earth'* in the giving of the law at Sinai, and he warns *'from heaven'* in the proclamation of the gospel in Jesus.

The position is absolutely clear. The people of old *'did not escape'* divine judgment upon their refusing God's warnings, with the result (as 3:19 records) 'that they were unable to enter [Canaan, the land of promise] because of unbelief'. Even so (the classic 'how much more' argument), those who pay no attention to the warnings built in to the gospel (for example, to 'flee from the wrath to come' (Luke 3:7), to 'abide in' Jesus (1 John 2:28), and to 'endure to the end' (Matthew 24:13)) cannot expect to *'escape'* his warnings now. The former refusal was bad enough, under the old covenant; the latter is unspeakably worse, under the new. God having manifested himself so much more fully in the realities rather than in the shadows, much greater attendance needs to be given to his revelation, and a much fuller response is required. The danger of apostasy is being highlighted again. Never let it be thought that the danger is less now than it was of old. For all those who succumb, it will be discovered that their 'last state has become worse for them than the first' (2 Peter 2:20). This is a word to each and a word to all.

*'At that time* [another reference to the Sinai experience] *his voice* [there is a magnificent statement showing the effects of God's voice in Psalm 29:3–9] *shook the earth, but now he has promised* [we could render it, 'promises'], *"Yet once more I will shake not only the earth but also the heavens"'* (12:26). Exodus 19:18 records how 'the whole mountain trembled greatly' as 'the Lord had descended on it in fire'. Yet that shaking, that trembling, fearsome though it was, is a small thing when put alongside the shaking and trembling which will accompany the last judgment at the end of the world. The prophet Haggai spoke of this, and it is 2:6 of his prophecy which our writer quotes here—yet another example of our writer referring the Hebrews to the Old Testament in order to enforce his argument. It was *'the earth'* which shook at Sinai, whereas it will be *'not only the earth but*

*also the heavens'* (in other words, the entire created universe) which will shake when God 'comes to judge the earth. He will judge the world in righteousness, and the peoples in his faithfulness' (Psalm 96:13). There will have been nothing like it ever before. On that day, in utter terror, people will hide 'themselves in the caves and among the rocks of the mountains, calling to the mountains and rocks, "Fall on us and hide us from the face of him who is seated on the throne, and from the wrath of the Lamb, for the great day of their wrath has come, and who can stand?"' (Revelation 6:15–17).

The relevance of the Haggai quotation continues to be brought out in what now follows. *'This phrase, 'Yet once more', indicates the removal of things that are shaken—that is, the things that have been made—in order that the things that cannot be shaken may remain'* (12:27). This is not a new thought in Hebrews. In the opening chapter, by way of the quotation from Psalm 102 which extends through 1:10–12 and forms part of the asserting of the deity of the Lord Jesus Christ, it is stated that the Lord who created the earth and the heavens ('You, Lord, laid the foundation of the earth in the beginning, and the heavens are the work of your hands') is the one who will bring created things to an end ('like a robe you will roll them up, like a garment they will be changed'). The key thing, however, is that although 'they will perish', God 'will remain'. How so? Because 'you are the same, and your years will have no end'.

The obvious distinction is between what is temporary and what is permanent, what will go and what will stay. It is *'the things that have been made'* which will disappear in this shaking, *'in order that the things that cannot be shaken may remain'*. The timing of all this is at the second coming of the Lord Jesus Christ (compare 9:28). This should cause great disquiet to 'those who do not know God and … those who do not obey the gospel of our Lord Jesus' (2 Thessalonians 2:8), which company will include apostates as well as those who never made any profession of faith in Christ at all. The same event, however, should cause no disquiet at all to those who truly belong to Jesus, for 'he comes on that day to be glorified in his saints, and to be marvelled at among all who have believed' (2 Thessalonians 2:10).

It is the contrast (as has already been observed in this commentary) between 'the things that are seen (which) are transient, but the things that are unseen are eternal' (2 Corinthians 4:18). It is noteworthy that immediately before the verse in Haggai which is quoted here in Hebrews 12, God's word to his true people is 'My Spirit remains in your midst. Fear not' (Haggai 2:5), while the verses of the prophecy which follow Haggai 2:6 speak in encouraging terms of the covenant God's blessings and glories.

In the particular context of our writer's pastoral concerns over the Hebrews who (originally) are being addressed here, among the shaken things are included all the business of the Old Testament priesthood, sacrificial system, festivals, and so on—the things the Hebrews seem so keen to return to, and which (in the life, death and resurrection of Jesus) have already gone anyway. In broader terms, it will cover all those outward things in which people put their trust—including ornate cathedrals, great buildings, royal palaces, stately homes, elected governments, ancient universities, banks and building societies, football clubs, star celebrities, and on the list goes. There will be successive shakings along the way, and the final shaking at the end.

The chapter is nearing its grand climax. *'Therefore let us* [our writer, the Hebrews, and all the children of God] *be grateful* [or, 'thankful'; literally, 'have grace', though gratitude is what is intended] *for receiving* [in the gospel of God's grace, by which we participate in all its privileges and blessings] *a kingdom that cannot be shaken* [the kingdom of God, the kingdom of heaven, that set forth in 12:22–24, a kingdom of grace and of glory, of a completely different order from every other kingdom, a kingdom in which we are in total and willing subjection to the reign and rule of Jesus]*'* (12:28). At the end of this present age, when Jesus has appeared in glory, the mighty cry will he heard, 'The kingdom of the world has become the kingdom of our Lord and of his Christ, and he shall reign forever and ever' (Revelation 11:15). What a glorious moment that will be for the glory of Christ, as well as for all 'those who are eagerly waiting for him' (9:28). All the kingdoms, empires, governments and regimes of the earth, from the length and breadth of history, will be shaken to their foundations and collapse in a heap together (as so many have done already). Their arrogance and pride will be shattered, their claims and schemes will be ruined, their sins and iniquities will be exposed, 'that at the name of Jesus every knee should bow' (Philippians 2:10).

In contrast, the *'kingdom that cannot be shaken'*, God's own eternal kingdom of grace and peace, a spiritual and glorious kingdom, will stand unchallenged, and all who belong to it ('a great multitude that no one could number, from every nation, from all tribes and peoples and languages', Revelation 7:9), will stand unchallenged too, safe at Jesus' right hand (Matthew 25:33–34). Every last foe of the Lord and his kingdom will finally be vanquished, every last trace of sin and defilement will finally be removed, every last tear and sorrow of the Lord's people will finally be gone, 'that God may be all in all' (1 Corinthians 15:28).

The only appropriate response to this can be gratitude. *'Therefore let us be grateful'*. In view of all God's mercies, upon recollection of all God's promises, in the light of all God's providences, which will have brought us safely all the way from the city of destruction to the celestial city, how can any saved sinner be anything less than *'grateful'*? Gratitude should mark our daily walk with God, as 'all the days of' our lives he follows us with his 'goodness and mercy' (Psalm 23:6). But at the end of the journey, our gratitude should know no bounds. Sadly, were the Hebrews to walk away from Jesus, this would be the height of ingratitude. It would be the same if we were to do so.

Gratitude, however, is not the total response. There is more: *'and thus let us offer to God acceptable worship, with reverence and awe'*. As well as gratitude (itself an expression of worship), there is to be *'reverence and awe'*. The three together comprise an essential trio in offering *'to God acceptable worship'*. Note that—not just *'worship'*, but *'acceptable worship'*; *'acceptable'*, that is, to God himself. There is a great danger (much in evidence in our present day) of imagining that the worship which is pleasing to God is the worship which *we think* will be pleasing to him. This is a great mistake. The worship which truly is pleasing to God is the worship which *he declares* will be pleasing to him. He will be the judge of it, not us.

So there is, not least, this choice threefold combination, if we are to '*offer to God acceptable worship*'. There is gratitude ('*grateful*'), which is a due sense of thankfulness for all God's kindness and love towards us, not one jot of which have we deserved. There is '*reverence*', which is a due sense of the holiness and majesty of God, leading us to bow before him in adoration. There is '*awe*', which is a due sense of wonder and amazement in the presence of God, both because of who he is in himself and what he has done for us. He is 'a God greatly to be feared … and awesome above all who are around him' (Psalm 89:7).

The mention of '*reverence*' and '*awe*' prepares well for what comes next, for the chapter ends with a most telling statement, '*for our God* [the triune God of the covenant] *is a consuming* (or, 'devouring') *fire*' (12:29). This is essentially a quotation from Deuteronomy 4:24, 'For the LORD your God is a consuming fire', to which is then added there, 'a jealous God'. Fire featured significantly at Sinai. 'Now Mount Sinai was wrapped in smoke because the LORD had descended on it in fire. The smoke of it went up like the smoke of a kiln' (Exodus 19:18). Yet God does not change. He was '*a consuming fire*' then, in Moses' day. He was '*a consuming fire*' in the day when Hebrews was being written. He is '*a consuming fire*' now, as this part of Scripture comes home to us in our own Christian experience. And he will be '*a consuming fire*' on that day when he judges the world, and 'each of us will give an account of himself to God' (Romans 14:12).

God never changes. He tells us so himself. 'For I the LORD do not change' (Malachi 3:6). He is God 'from everlasting to everlasting' (Psalm 90:2). His attributes are unalterable, and this includes his anger just as much as his love. To provoke the former will always produce his judgment, just as to enjoy the latter will always be the path of blessing. Why, then, would any who have professed to belong to him and follow him ever turn aside from him? It is the most reckless action imaginable. Let us all 'cling to the LORD (our) God' and 'Be very careful, therefore, to love the LORD (our) God' (Joshua 23:8, 11). There can never be any serious alternative.

Hebrews 12 began with running the race, it continued with running the race, and now it ends, still with running the race. The race is never over until it is over. The Christian life is never finished until it is finished. This is not the time for giving up or dropping out, but of pressing on to God.

# Chapter 13
# Pressing the matter home

We might not have been very surprised if the letter had finished at the end of the previous chapter. At that point, a significant climax had been reached. 12:29 would have been a very powerful close. Things do not end there, however, as our coming to chapter 13 now demonstrates. There is a great danger of regarding this final chapter as a kind of 'ragbag' of various practical 'odds and ends', strung together in no particular sequence. Nothing could be further from the truth. For all the potentially climactic nature of chapter 12, this closing chapter provides the true climax to everything that has gone before. In no way is it an afterthought or mere appendix, but rather a very rich conclusion. Here, everything is pressed home one more time, as it were. We are still running the race.

A key importance attaching to this chapter has to do with the intensely practical and demanding nature of the Christian life.

To 'keep on keeping on', as the saying goes—to persevere in the Christian life—consistently 'to live a godly life in Christ Jesus' (2 Timothy 3:12)—to make sure work of abiding in Jesus, 'so that when he appears we may have confidence and not shrink from him in shame at his coming' (1 John 2:28)—requires close attention to detail. Clearly the Hebrews, if they were on the verge of leaving Jesus behind, were not going to give such attention. So, having set out much exalted doctrine throughout the epistle (interspersed with appropriate and direct application along the way), our writer brings further application of a similar character, so that all his recipients are well aware of the challenge they face (and the precipice they are in danger of going over).

In this chapter, then, the writer sets out a rich sequence of exhortations bearing upon living the Christian life, interwoven among which are several 'final flourishes' to do with his abiding and unflinching theme right from the start—the incomparable Jesus. It all arises very naturally from the call to 'offer to God acceptable worship' (12:28), for worship, if it is to be genuine, will always lead to service, and service looms large in chapter 13.

## Living the Christian life consistently (13:1–19)

### (1) Brotherly love (13:1)

He begins with a familiar New Testament theme, and one very close to the heart of Jesus and his teaching in the gospels. *'Let brotherly love continue'* (13:1). The fact that the writer exhorts them to a continuance of *'brotherly love'* implies that they are already exercising this virtue, and is a further indication (in line with 3:1, 6:9 and 10:39) that he has not abandoned a good hope that those to whom he writes are truly converted, and that this will prove to be so once any present crisis has passed. The one Greek word which it translates (as opposed to other words for 'love') is distinctively Christian in its biblical use. It is certainly the case that true *'brotherly love'* must flow from the good spring and the gracious principle of God's first love to us.

The words of Jesus in the upper room provide very relevant

background to this verse in Hebrews. 'A new commandment I give to you, that you love one another: just as I have loved you, you also are to love one another'. He then adds words which signify that such love among brethren in Christ is to be a fundamental and visible mark or badge of true Christians, and so of the true church. 'By all this people will know that you are my disciples, if you have love for one other' (John 13:34–35).

This is a recurring theme, not surprisingly, of the apostle Paul as well. 'Love one another with brotherly affection' (Romans 12:10) is a typical example. It is the same with the apostle John. Again let one example suffice. 'Beloved, if God so loved us [note the previous verse for the explanation of this: 'he loved us and sent his Son to be the propitiation for our sins'], we also ought to love one another' (1 John 4:11). With God as our Father, Jesus as our Saviour, and the Holy Spirit as the one who indwells us, Christians (by definition) belong together in a family sense as brothers and sisters, and are not given the choice of whether to love one another or not. It is a matter of commandment, though (hopefully) a commandment which is obeyed from the heart, for together we comprise the mutual company who are being brought to glory (look back to 2:10–12).

Mutual love among Christians, to which all believers are here exhorted, will be evidence of a sincere desire for their good and spiritual happiness, and will be pursued with a willingness to overlook their failures and infirmities, to love them in an impartial way (not having favourites, even if we may be drawn more to some fellow believers than to others), and a readiness to go on loving them whatever their circumstances or however much they disappoint us. Peter makes an important connection when, in writing upon supplementing our faith with various spiritual virtues, he says, 'and godliness with brotherly affection, and brotherly affection with love' (2 Peter 1:7).

Our writer's use of the verb *'continue'* [or, 'remain'—in other words, keep on doing it, keep it up] is a reminder that commencement is not sufficient in this matter; there must be continuance, perseverance, however unlovable or difficult to love any Christians might sometimes appear. It also alerts us to the reality that this continuance does not always happen—in which case, care should be taken to see how this has arisen, to discover where the problem lies, and to seek grace to put things right, being ready where necessary to take the humbler part and admit to our own failings and shortcomings. It cannot be gainsaid that this *'brotherly love'* is a necessary and visible fruit of new life in Jesus. For it not to be demonstrated should give great cause for concern.

## (2) Hospitality to strangers (13:2)

This is an extension and outflowing of the above matter, for if Christians do not properly love one another, they are unlikely to be bothered about anyone outside their number or fellowship. *'Do not neglect* (or, 'do not be unmindful') *to show hospitality to strangers'* (13:2). In the previous verse the word for 'brotherly love' is made up of two parts in the original. We may express it as 'phil-adelphia'. The word now before us for *'hospitality to strangers'* is also made up of two parts in the original. We may express it as 'philo-xenia'. The connection is unmissable.

There is an echo here of Galatians 6:10, which charges believers in this way: 'So then, as we have opportunity, let us do good to everyone, and especially to those who are of the household of faith'. Hospitality is a natural part of this doing 'good to everyone', and if it is to have that wider reach (as indeed it should) then it needs to start in the church, 'those who are of the household of faith'.

It can be a very blessed outworking of Christian fellowship to offer and to receive hospitality in one another's homes. The Lord's Day itself is a prime opportunity for this, between the morning and evening services. It is not necessary to provide a banquet, involving extensive (or expensive) labour on that day itself, or even beforehand. Simplicity has its own beauty. Let our engaging in hospitality extend also (and this is the point of 13:2) *'to strangers'*, whether (for example), visitors to the church, newcomers to the area where you live, or people you meet in the regular things of life.

To encourage Christians (the Hebrews and us included) in this, a remarkable (and surprising?) incentive is given: *'for thereby some have entertained angels unawares'*. That is to say, such hospitality can lead to some pleasant surprises! There is a delightful play on words here. The phrase *'to show hospitality'* is literally 'love of strangers' (only one word in the original), but part of that one word is the same as the verb which is then translated *'entertained'*. So there is really a double appearance of the thought of entertaining. What our writer is saying is really, 'entertain strangers—and you may discover that you're entertaining angels!' The amazing truth that God has entertained us in his grace, drawing us to himself, should exhibit itself automatically in our readiness to entertain our brethren in Christ, and others also.

The immediate occasion that comes to our minds when contemplating the entertainment of angels is surely that recorded in Genesis 18 in the life of Abraham, when 'the LORD appeared to him by the oaks of Mamre, as he sat at the door of his tent in the heat of the day'. As he looked up, the patriarch saw that 'three men were standing in front of him', so he invited them to receive hospitality. Two of these were clearly angels, while the one whom Abraham addressed as 'Lord' (Genesis 18:3, and note carefully 'The LORD said' in 18:17) indicates that this one of the three was the Lord Jesus Christ, making this what we call a Christophany (that is, a pre-incarnation appearance of the second person of the Godhead, of which there are several in the Old Testament). Other instances of the Lord's people entertaining angels included Lot (Genesis 19), Gideon (Judges 6), Samson's parents (Judges 13), and—in very different circumstances— Daniel's three friends (Daniel 3).

For ourselves, the exercise of Christian *'hospitality to strangers'* may turn out to be that we *'have entertained angels unawares'* in the blessing that they and their fellowship are to us. Little did we know what grace awaited us when we invited them home with us, and how thankful we may end up being that God was pleased to send them to us. And in this connection we are reminded of the emphasis in Jesus' teaching that, rather than majoring in our hospitality upon those who will be in a position to invite us back, we should be ready and willing to invite those who will not be in that position (Luke 14:12–14). In other words, we do not do this in order to get something from people in return; we do it rather in obedience to the Lord's command and as an expression of Christ-like behaviour. Yet in one way or another, the Lord's blessings will rest upon us, for he himself is so very gracious and generous towards his own.

## (3) Compassion for the needy (13:3)

Two illustrations are provided here: '*those who are in prison*' and '*those who are mistreated*'. As above, these may potentially be both Christians and unbelievers. In each case the people spoken of are in situations of need, which require our attention in appropriate ways. First to be mentioned are the prisoners. '*Remember those who are in prison*' (13:3).

In Jesus' parable of the sheep and the goats in Matthew 25, he makes the very memorable statement that at the final judgment he will say to those whom he receives to himself (the sheep on his right hand), 'I was a stranger and you welcomed me …, I was in prison and you came to me'. When the righteous ask him when they did this, Jesus replies, 'Truly, I say to you, as you did it to one of the least of these my brothers, you did it to me'. This sets the hospitality we commented upon in 13:2 and the matter presently before us in 13:3 in the precise context of serving and honouring Jesus as we minister both among his people and more widely.

The call not to neglect '*those who are in prison*' is enforced with the remark, '*as though in prison with them*'. How are we to understand this? In different practical ways, is the answer. We can remember them in faithful prayer, bearing them up before the Lord and seeking his upholding grace for them; by actually visiting them, seeking to offer a ministry of encouragement—especially as, being in prison, they are not in any position to receive hospitality in Christian homes; and by corresponding with them, sharing choice Scriptures and assuring them of our love and concern. The Hebrews were commended in 10:34 for fulfilling this very ministry ('For you had compassion on those in prison'), and are now being exhorted to continue in the same manner. It remains a form of service which is very appropriate as churches and Christians have opportunity.

This verse continues, *'and those who are mistreated, since you also are in the body'*. The nature of the mistreatment is not stated, but it is a suitably broad word to allow for a variety of possibilities. The context would at least imply that those who are experiencing it are doing so on account of being Christians, and remaining faithful and true to the Lord. They also are to be remembered—maybe in prayer, in practical support, in financial provision, in sharing with them suitable encouragement from the Scriptures, and in reminding them that their and our heavenly home and rest is still to come. 'For here we have no lasting city, but we seek the city that is to come' (13:14). There will be no mistreatment there!

The remark, *'since you also are in the body'*, is not here a reference to the church as the body of Christ (and so all those who are members of it belonging to one another and rejoicing and suffering together), very true though that is; but rather that all of us, being bodily people, may suffer in similar ways, and that what one person is facing at the moment another might face the next. Mutual identification is the key.

Both matters touched upon here—imprisonment and ill-treatment—remain highly relevant for our own times. In different parts of the world even now there are many Christians who suffer 'on account of the word of God and the testimony of Jesus' (Revelation 1:9). Some of these will be in prison, some will not. But it is very much the business of Christians as a whole to be ever mindful of them, to be as well acquainted with their circumstances as is possible, and to be ready and willing to perform whatever service on their behalf is open to us—and especially prayer, which is open to us all. Persecution, abuse, false accusation, physical danger, marginalisation, and much else is very present. Even in our own country (the United Kingdom, for all its rich Christian heritage), current and pending legislation puts Christians increasingly on the spot and in the firing line, and we have no idea what a day or a year may bring forth in terms of what may be required of us, if we would remain faithful to

Jesus, and to the cause of God and truth. May the Lord himself be our helper in the midst of an evil day.

## (4) Marriage (13:4)

Our writer now proceeds to another example of living the Christian life consistently—one which, once again, is so very relevant to our own times. *'Let marriage be held in honour among all'* (13:4).

Marriage is one of the richest and most blessed of all God's gifts—not only to his people, but to all mankind. It is what we call a creation ordinance, which is to say that God established it at the time of creation. The Genesis 1 and 2 account records how, as soon as God made Adam (the first man) and Eve (the first woman), he became (as it were) their minister, who joined them together in marriage as man and wife. Eve was provided to be 'a helper fit for' Adam, and that fitness is wide-ranging—physically, spiritually, emotionally, in every way. God ordered it this way: 'Therefore a man shall leave his father and his mother and hold fast to his wife, and they shall become one flesh' (Genesis 2:24). The Lord Jesus reinforced this absolutely in his own teaching on marriage (Matthew 19:5), immediately adding very significantly, 'What therefore God has joined together, let not man separate'.

In the light of this, it is certainly the case that *'marriage* (should) *be held in honour among all'*. The implication is that this was not always happening, hence the need for this reminder of something basic. In New Testament days, there were some who advocated the single life as being superior to and purer than the married life, some who were unfaithful to their marriage commitment and played fast and loose with its bonds, and some who pursued an immoral lifestyle as they pleased. Not much changes.

The phrase *'held in honour'* carries the sense of honourable, valued, highly prized, and the words *'among all'* do not allow any room for people to take their own course as to how they view marriage. As well as it being honourable for the reason stated above (it being a creation ordinance), there are other strong reasons and arguments as well. One is that it is a covenant relationship, involving solemn vows and promises made before both God and men; not to be entered into lightly, but (when it is entered into) to be upheld and cherished both to the glory of God and the blessing of the couple. Another is that it is a beautiful picture of the marriage relationship between the Christian (the church) and the Lord Jesus Christ—he the heavenly bridegroom, she the purchased bride. The Song of Songs in the Old Testament is taken up with this, but so is much else of the Bible as well. In his great Ephesians 5 treatment of marriage, Paul declares, 'This mystery is profound, and I am saying that it refers to Christ and the church' (Ephesians 5:32).

The exhortation continues, *'and let the marriage bed be undefiled'.* The defiling in view would be through unfaithful or promiscuous behaviour, the breaking of the marriage covenant, or the engaging in sexual relationships outside of marriage altogether. All such is an assault upon the holiness of God and the holiness of marriage. Scripture (the word of God) could not be plainer in its insistence upon purity, holiness and faithfulness in marriage between a husband and his wife, a wife and her husband. That very insistence carries with it the unchanging truth that marriage only has been, only can be, and only ever will be between one man and one woman. The thought of marriage being 'redefined', when it is God who gave it and defined it from the beginning, is blasphemous, and those who propose such a thing set themselves up directly against God, and will have to answer for it at the judgment. Husbands cannot have husbands, and wives cannot have wives. A husband has a wife and a wife has a husband. The truth stands: 'male and female he [the sovereign God] created them' (Genesis 1:27).

What is in view, then, for those who do not hold marriage *'in honour'* or who defile *'the marriage bed'*? Our writer does not beat about the bush, when he writes, *'for God will judge the sexually immoral and adulterous'.* The two words do not have identical meanings. The first refers more generally to those who engage in sexual relationships outside of marriage, whether heterosexual or homosexual (fornication). The second refers to those who are unfaithful to their marriage (adultery). Both are sinful, and abhorrent to God. As a result, they will bring upon those who commit them the holy judgment of God (*'for God will judge'*). To commit fornication or adultery is to play with fire—and no ordinary fire, 'for our God is a consuming fire' (12:29).

A further indication of how seriously God regards these things is to be observed in the solemn argument of the apostle in Romans 1. There, in the context of 'the wrath of God' being 'revealed from heaven against all the ungodliness and unrighteousness of men, who by their unrighteousness suppress the truth', it is (not least) sexual sin which is the cause of the visitation of that wrath. God's word to the Hebrews (and so his word to us) is crystal clear: 'For God has not called us for impurity, but in holiness. Therefore whoever disregards this, disregards not man but God, who gives his Holy Spirit to you (1 Thessalonians 4:7–8).

## (5) Contentment (13:5–6)

Contentment as a spiritual grace has well been called a rare jewel. We can testify to that being so, knowing our own hearts. It is the latest application our writer comes to in his very practical treatment of living the Christian life (the persevering Christian life) consistently. To be a discontented Christian is to be an inconsistent Christian, for it implies dissatisfaction with God himself, in his being, works and ways. This virtue of contentment is set here in contrast with covetousness, something which has discontent at its root.

*'Keep your life free from love of money, and be content with what you have'* (13:5). Without wishing to slur them, we may take it that our writer had concerns over the Hebrews in this matter of lack of contentment, and, as an evidence of that, were showing too much partiality for material things (not least, money itself). The potential connection between covetousness and losing a firm grip upon Jesus (the 'one thing leads to another' scenario), is touched upon very directly by Paul, when writing these words to Timothy: 'Now there is great gain in godliness with contentment … But those who desire to be rich fall into temptation, into a snare, into many senseless and harmful desires that plunge people into ruin and destruction. For the

love of money is a root of all kinds of evils. It is through this craving that some have wandered away from the faith and pierced themselves with many pangs' (1 Timothy 6:6, 8–10).

Hence the importance of so keeping '(our) *life free from love of money*' and being '*content with what* (we) *have*'. These two exhortations belong intimately together. The less we are taken up with the things of the world, the more we shall realise the greatness of all the divine mercies we have. The less we are murmuring and fretting for things that wax and wane, the more we shall be satisfied with the things that abide for ever. The less our hearts are in turmoil over the riches that others possess, the more will our hearts be possessed by a gracious frame which delights in God for himself. In truth, we have everything we could ever possibly require or desire in God and the gospel of his grace—he 'who has blessed us with every spiritual blessing in the heavenly places' (Ephesians 1:3). God is our 'portion' (Lamentations 3:24), an all-embracing picture of him being everything to us and us possessing everything in him.

Our treasure is not on earth but in heaven, and so 'where (our) treasure is, their (our) heart will be also' (Matthew 6:21). Certainly that is where our heart should be, and it is one of our key duties in the Christian life to 'Keep (our) heart with all vigilance, for from it flow the springs of life' (Proverbs 4:23), to ensure that this is so. We cannot both love money and be content in God (note Jesus' words in Matthew 6:24, 'You cannot serve God and money ['mammon', a word which covers more than just money and includes possessions and such like]').

The apostle Paul, whom we quoted above, has penned the classic statement so far as contentment is concerned: 'for I have learned in whatever state I am to be content. I know how to be brought low, and I know how to abound' (Philippians 4:11–12). Later in that same chapter he assures those to whom he writes (and every other believer), 'And my God will supply every need of yours according to his riches in glory in Christ Jesus' (Philippians 4:19). Such a truth accords precisely with what the writer to the Hebrews is saying at the present point in Hebrews.

He underscores his exhortation to live lives *free from love of money*
and to *'be content with what you have'*, with a glorious affirmation,
reminding them of something which God first said to Joshua, as a
promise both given to him and proved by him: *'for he has said* [and,
of course, continues to say], *"I* [the divine 'I'] *will never* [a double
negative, 'by no means'] *leave you nor* [a triple negative, 'nor by no
means'] *forsake you"'*. This, surely, is all that any Christian could ever
wish—this secure promise of the covenant God's continual presence
with us, through thick and thin. If we doubt this, then in a sense we
doubt everything, for every 'word of the LORD proves true' (Psalm
18:30) and every promise of the Lord is 'precious and very great'
(2 Peter 1:4). God's honour is attached to the fulfilling of his word and
the keeping of his promises, and this we do well to remember.

*'So we can confidently* [this is the fifth occurrence of the concept
of confidence in Hebrews, and speaks of absolute well-grounded
certainty] *say, "The Lord is my helper; I will not fear; what can man
do to me?"'* (13:6). With this quotation from Psalm 118:6, our writer
bolsters his argument further, and presents his final citation of
Old Testament Scripture in this letter. Fear of man is a great and
abiding snare for all who love the Lord. It ought not to be, but all
too often it is. At the end of the day, what people think of us or
what people do to us is of little consequence. The overarching truth
is that 'Our help is in the name of the LORD, who made heaven and
earth' (Psalm 124:8). He it is who is our *'helper'*, which speaks of
him in a comprehensive way as, in David's very personal testimony,
'a shield about me, my glory, and the lifter of my head' (Psalm 3:3).
Interestingly, in the verse following this psalm quote in 13:6, the
psalmist certainly adds *'confidently'*, 'The LORD is on my side as my
helper; I shall look in triumph on those who hate me' (Psalm 118:7).

Men may wreak all manner of havoc with us (recall what the
Hebrews themselves had suffered, 10:32–34). Yet, as the writer sought
to encourage them there, they bore it all 'joyfully'; and why? It was
'since you knew that you yourselves had a better possession and an
abiding one' (10:34). This provides us, at one and the same time, with
both motivation to persevere and motivation to live as consistent

Christians. Jesus himself spoke powerfully to this point when he said, 'And do not fear those who kill the body but cannot kill the soul' (Matthew 10:28). No one and no thing can tear the true believer from the Saviour—ever!

## (6) Imitation (13:7)

No one of us is the only Christian there has ever been. We have many fellow Christians alive now, and countless ones who have been and gone before us. Here it is the latter who are in view, whereas in verses 17 and 24 the focus will be on the former. This becomes a further and potentially very fruitful line that our writer pursues as he continues.

*'Remember your leaders, those who spoke to you the word of God'* (13:7). The call to remembrance is concerned with *'your leaders'*—those, that is, who in days past exercised leadership over them. In particular, it is those who also ministered the word of God among them, *'those who spoke to you the word of God'*. The Hebrews are being encouraged to do something which we should all benefit from. Take a moment to recall those who in the past have cared for your soul, taught you, taken time over you. Such people can include both those whom we actually knew and were blessed under when they were alive and those whom we know and have been blessed under who lived in former days to our own (through their abiding publications, maybe). In remembering them, praise God for them—that ever he was pleased to bring them into your life and to do you good by means of their ministry. Perhaps they were even blessed of God to your salvation.

The exhortation here, however, is to do more than only praise God for them, unless we view this as part of praising God for them. We are to *'Consider the outcome of their way of life* ('conduct'), *and imitate their faith'*. There is a right and a wrong imitation. That commended here is the best and wisest sort. Being thankful for their ministry, recall also the godly life and example that accompanied it, reinforced it, authenticated it. Learn well from 'the truth' they made known to you—'the truth, which accords with godliness' (Titus 1:1). Reflect on how their behaviour was an adornment of their doctrine (Titus 2:10). In some cases, maybe, their ministries may have proved immensely costly—so learn from that also concerning the demands of true and faithful discipleship. Be careful never to become so proud as to imagine that we can never learn anything from anyone. Remember how they lived, and remember how they died. As they pressed on, so must you. Let your affectionate memory of them encourage you, stir you, inspire you. Let it persuade you of the importance of pressing on and not giving up. Did they abandon the Lord Jesus? No—and neither must you!

## (7) The unchanging Jesus (13:8)

Here before us is what is very likely the best known (and most cherished) verse in all of Hebrews, and even in the entire New Testament. Keep in mind the present context of living the Christian life consistently, for we do not have here a comment which stands in isolation from all around it. The surest way to do that is to be 'looking to Jesus' (12:2), so now—in the midst of his wealth of application in this final chapter—our writer gives this magnificent statement of the Jesus upon whom our gaze is to be fixed. *'Jesus Christ is the same yesterday and today and forever'* (13:8).

The emphasis, which is clear immediately, is upon the great fact that he is unchanging. He never changes, he never alters, in any way whatsoever. Whether in the past (*'yesterday'*), in the present (*'today'*), or in the future (*'forever'*), Jesus always remains the same! His 'origin is from of old, from ancient days' (Micah 5:2). All that he was, for example, to the men and women whom we met in chapter 11, he is to his people to whom Hebrews was originally written, and he will continue to be to all who follow after them down the generations until his glorious promised return.

This is a many splendoured truth which, like an expensive diamond, needs to be viewed from many angles. Jesus is unchanging in his person (the God-Man, having two perfect and complete natures in his one glorious person); in his work (which in some ways is finished—his making atonement for sin on the cross—and in some ways is continued—not least in the Hebrews emphasis upon his priestly character in heaven); in his three great offices (prophet, priest and king); in his relationships (such as shepherd, bridegroom, advocate and teacher); in his very names (such as Saviour, Master, Lord and Lamb); in his love towards men's souls as the friend of sinners, in his power and willingness to save all who come to him, in his grace to restore those of his own who stumble and fall, in his strength and determination to preserve to the end all for whom he died and rose again, in his pouring out of his Spirit upon his church and his defending of her against all comers; in his enthusiasm to welcome us into his presence in heaven that we may see his glory— and on the list goes, for the Jesus who is unchanging is uncontainable as well.

There really is nothing which should thrill and encourage the people of God more as we press on along our pilgrim path, than to know this unchanging Jesus. The *'and forever'* with which the verse concludes is literally 'to the ages'. He does not grow old or weary, he is not subject to any of the maladies that affect us here on earth, he never forgets who we are and is never unaware of our various names and needs, he never proves false or goes away. Our names are engraved upon his heart. What a Saviour the Hebrews had. What a Saviour we have. He is all-sufficient in every way imaginable. Shall the Hebrews, shall we, abandon him, turn against him, grow tired of him, think meanly of him, doubt him or set out to dishonour him in any way? Never! Perish the very thought.

However much the 'leaders' of the previous verse may come and go, the ultimate leader, the one head of the church, abides for all time and for all eternity. Their eyes were fixed upon the unchanging Jesus, and so must the eyes be of all believers at all times.

## (8) Steadfastness (13:9)

There is never a day when false doctrine is not making itself heard in some way or another. This presents a constant peril for the church of God, and for each individual believer within it. The need of the hour continually is steadfastness, which will combine watchfulness (so as not to be taken in by what is false) and faithfulness (so as to hold firm to what is true). This is the latest matter to be addressed in these practical and pastoral exhortations to the Hebrews.

'*Do not be led away by diverse and strange teachings*' (13:9). The phrase '*diverse and strange teachings*' is a potent and pertinent reminder that false teaching can and does come in a huge variety of forms, and can cover every aspect of doctrine. It has so often been the case, however, that false doctrine relates most of all to errors concerning the person and work of the Lord Jesus Christ. That is to say, more often than not people first go wrong in their understanding of Christ, and then, arising from that, proceed to go wrong elsewhere. It is not at all surprising, therefore, that having urged the Hebrews to remember their leaders, and then having followed that with the call to maintain (or, where necessary, recover) their central focus on Jesus, our writer should now utter this warning about false doctrine.

The verb '*led away*' can be rendered 'carried away', in the sense of going off course, off the straight and narrow, or 'flow away', like a river sweeping everything away with it. Its tense can imply that this was already happening to a degree. There is an echo of the apostle Paul's warnings about being 'tossed to and fro by the waves and carried about by every wind of doctrine' (Ephesians 4:14), and those 'who have swerved from the truth' (2 Timothy 2:18).

The Hebrews no doubt needed this warning in various directions (as we all do), though a particular example is presented, that of foods; '*not by foods, which have not benefited those devoted to them*'. What these '*foods*' are is not stated here, though verse 11 will refer to 'the bodies of those animals whose blood is brought into the holy places by the high priest as a sacrifice for sin'—in other words, sacrificial foods. What our writer likely has in mind in 13:9, is all part and parcel of the dangerous tendency the Hebrews were evidencing of wandering back into Old Testament ways, away from fullness and finality in Jesus. It must stop! It will not benefit them in any way; indeed, it will do the opposite of benefiting them. Nothing must be added to Jesus, or even brought alongside him. This is key to all that is being taught the recipients of this letter. Everything is found in Jesus, and there must be no looking elsewhere.

This is enforced in the words '*for it is good for the heart to be strengthened by grace*'. What good will foods do to the heart? The writer is not speaking here of diet, and things good or bad for our heart in that sense—he is not giving advice on nutrition. His concern is with spiritual health and growth. In that vital sense the great need of every Christian heart is *'to be strengthened by grace'*—that grace which (remember verse 8) is 'the grace of our Lord Jesus Christ' (2 Corinthians 8:9). For constant and refreshing supplies of this grace we are 'with confidence (to) draw near to the throne of grace', and for this compelling reason: 'that we may receive mercy and find grace to help in time of need' (4:16). Such has been the writer's insistence all along. It was the hardening of their hearts which led the people astray in the wilderness (3:8); it was 'an evil, unbelieving heart, leading you to fall away from the living God', which was highlighted in 3:12; and now it is the priority of the right spiritual feeding and maintenance of the heart which is in view in 13:9.

## (9) Bearing reproach for Jesus (13:10-13)

Following on directly from the warning about false teaching and the importance of grace in the heart, there comes a section which, overall, is concerned with bearing reproach for Jesus, the unchanging and unchangeable Jesus of verse 8. He is altogether worth it. Things begin with a mention of the old days once again.

*'We have an altar from which those who serve the tent have no right to eat'* (13:10). There was an abundance of altars in the old sacrificial system of priests and offerings. They were being built right, left and centre. Altars, however, are now a thing of the past. They do not exist anymore. No church building is to have one. No Christian is to desire one. Yet our writer declares that we do have one: *'We have an altar'*. So what is the position? Is there an altar, or is there not? The point is this: 'no', we have no Old Testament style altar, for Jesus, by his sacrifice of himself at Calvary, has fulfilled all the ceremonial law— but 'yes', we do *'have an altar'*, in that we look to that very place, Calvary, and to the cross where Jesus died, and place all our trust and confidence in him for salvation and eternal life. To that extent, it is proper to say that Jesus himself is our altar.

In order to grasp the argument here, it is necessary to scroll back to those Old Testament days for a moment. When sacrifices were offered upon the altars, there was a distinction God made between those where the priests were allowed to eat of the sacrificial offerings, and those where they were not. In particular, the latter was the case with the sin offering of Leviticus 4 and with the sacrifices of the annual Day of Atonement in Leviticus 16. Of these it was a case of *from which those who serve the tent* [the Levitical priests] *have no right to eat*. So what happened to these sacrifices, if they were not to be eaten? *'For the bodies of those animals whose blood is brought into the holy places* [the holy of holies] *by the high priest as a sacrifice for sin are burned outside the camp'* (13:11).

We have no more sacrifices and no more altars and no more priests. But we have more than all of these, because we have Jesus and his sacrifice, Jesus and his offering, Jesus and his shed blood, Jesus and his altar (the cross). So, again, why would the Hebrews be hankering after that which was *gone* when they possess so very much more in that which has *come*—where everything, to use a favourite word of our writer, is *better*? Why would any Christian ever even dream of looking to anyone but Jesus? All those priests who offered the sacrifices could not eat them. Yet we, who have believed upon the Lord Jesus Christ for the eternal salvation of our souls, continually 'eat' of him—which means, we partake spiritually day by day of all the benefits of his sacrifice, all the blessings that flow from Calvary, all the glories that are wrapped up in him, as those who, through grace alone, have been blessed 'in Christ with every spiritual blessing in the heavenly places' (Ephesians 1:3). It is this 'feeding' upon Jesus which explains how our hearts are 'strengthened by grace' (13:9). What more could we possibly desire?

Full as ever of passion for Jesus, our writer pursues his theme, arising from this contrast of Old Testament sacrifices (plural) and New Testament sacrifice (singular). *'So Jesus also suffered outside the gate* [thereby setting aside all the rituals still going on within those gates] *in order to sanctify the people through his own* [note the '*his own*'] *blood'* (13:12). Jesus did not die in Jerusalem itself, but *'outside the gate'* (Jerusalem was a walled city, with gates at different points in the walls). John records that 'the place where Jesus was crucified was near the city' (John 19:20). This is highly significant. The area 'outside the camp' where the bodies of the animals were burned (verse 11) was unsanctified ground. The area outside Jerusalem where Jesus was crucified corresponded to this, and reminds us of the central gospel truth that God 'made him to be sin who knew no sin, so that in him we might become the righteousness of God' (2 Corinthians 5:21). The sacrificial blood shed at Calvary is both pardoning and sanctifying blood. By it, we are 'reconciled to God' (2 Corinthians 5:20). By it, God 'has blessed us in the Beloved' (Ephesians 1:6). By it, 'by a single offering he [Jesus] has perfected for all time those who are being sanctified' (9:14).

'*Therefore let us* [note the writer's identification with those to whom he writes—in no way does he set himself apart from them or above them] *go to him outside the camp and bear the reproach he endured*' (13:13). We have here a magnificent call to unqualified and wholehearted discipleship, arising from our union with Christ. He was crucified for us 'outside the camp' (compare verses 11 and 12, and the recollection of the scapegoat who 'shall bear all their iniquities on itself to a remote area', Leviticus 16:22—a picture which points us directly to Jesus). So it is completely appropriate that we who owe everything to him should '*go to him outside the camp*'. It is the only proper response that we can give.

And what will be involved for us in doing this? We shall find that we are often called upon to '*bear the reproach he endured*'. Living the Christian life consistently must involve readiness for this, for we can be sure it will come our way. Jesus spoke of this himself to his disciples, when he said, 'If anyone would come after me, let him deny himself and take up his cross daily and follow me' (Luke 9:23). The word '*reproach*' in this context covers shame, disgrace, abuse, ill treatment, and such things. There is a stigma which attaches to us once we are Christians. It is the way of the cross. It was so, uniquely, for the Lord Jesus (12:2), and it is so, in a companion though not identical way, for his disciples. Remember Moses (11:26), who 'considered the reproach [same word as here in 13:13] of Christ greater wealth than the treasures of Egypt'.

Would the going to Jesus *'outside the camp'* have carried any particular reference for the Hebrews themselves? Certainly it fits precisely with the concern the writer has had for them all the way through the letter (and, not least, which caused him to write it in the first place). They had been converted from Judaism, and so, no doubt in a costly way, had nailed their colours to the mast and taken a new stand for Jesus. They had gone *'to him outside the camp'*. This will have been a momentous thing for them, in terms of all that they had left behind, with its history and associations. The danger now, however, is that they are going into reverse gear and going back inside the camp, back to the pre-Calvary situation. Maybe they were imagining (wrongly) that things would be easier there. Their responsibility (and privilege) is now to 'share (Christ's) sufferings' or 'the fellowship of his sufferings' (Philippians 3:10)—and so is ours.

It may be as well that our writer intended to set bells ringing in the minds of the Hebrews regarding something that is recorded in Exodus 33, and of which they would have been fully aware. Following the sad episode of the golden calf in the previous chapter of Exodus, and the rejection of God by the people within the Israelite camp, Moses set up the 'tent of meeting' outside the camp. As a result, the people had to go outside the camp whenever they wished to enquire of the Lord. Even so, in the Jerusalem and Calvary situation, God has been rejected again by his people inside the camp, and so it is *'outside the camp'* that he must be sought, in and through the Lord Jesus Christ.

In the fullness of Scripture there is a glorious encouragement. It is recorded in Acts 1:12 that Jesus, having died outside the city confines of Jerusalem, also ascended into heaven from outside those confines (in this latter case, from 'the mount called Olivet, which is near Jerusalem, a Sabbath day's journey away'). The encouragement is to be found in linking this with the promise that 'If we have died with him, we will also live with him; if we endure, we will also reign with him' (2 Timothy 2:11–12), and in remembering that as well as being called to fellowship with Jesus in 'his sufferings', we are also called to 'know him and the power of his resurrection' (Philippians 3:10). For Jesus, 'the cross' and 'the shame' was followed by his enthronement (12:2). The order is no different for his own dear people.

## (10) Heavenly mindedness (13:14)

The strong emphasis upon Christians going to Jesus 'outside the camp' leads very naturally into the comment here concerning where our true belonging and stability is found. It is in heaven, not on earth. *'For here we have no lasting* ('enduring, abiding, continuing') *city, but we seek the city that is to come'* (13:14).

This perspective has already come through strongly in connection with the patriarchs in Hebrews 11. When Abraham was 'living in tents', this was an evidence that 'he was looking forward to the city that has foundations, whose designer and builder is God'. He, and others of like faith, 'acknowledged that they were strangers and exiles on the earth', 'seeking a homeland', desiring 'a better country, that is, a heavenly one'. That section concluded with the lovely words, 'Therefore God is not ashamed to be called their God, for he has prepared for them a city'.

The subject is now brought up again at a very telling point in our writer's detailed examples of living the Christian life consistently. Being 'outside the camp' with Jesus and for Jesus reminds us that there is much here on earth which is alien to us. Part of 'the conviction of things not seen' (11:1) is the sure prospect of our heavenly home. It is always appropriate to speak of Christians, when they die, as having 'gone home'. The cities of history come and go. Some ancient ones are no more, and some new ones arise. Only one city abides, and that is the city of God, heaven itself. That is where we have our true 'citizenship' (Philippians 3:20). That is where our names are written. That is where we are awaited.

It is possible to live as a Christian while taking little (or no) thought of heaven. If we do that, we rob ourselves of the grandest future prospect we could have. We have mentioned before in this commentary the crisp contrast Paul draws between 'the things that are seen' and 'the things that are unseen', and how the former 'are transient' while the latter 'are eternal' (2 Corinthians 4:18). The life that will count most effectively, the testimony which will have the most impact, the priority which will make most impression for the Lord, is that which is most heavenly minded. In response to the miserable jibe about those who are most heavenly minded being of least earthly use, the opposite is true, and the history and usefulness of many a Christian proves that beyond argument or doubt. Our heavenly habitation is 'a better possession and an abiding one' (10:34). Seek to meditate often from Scripture upon what it will be like to be there. Best of all, 'the Lamb in the midst of the throne will be (our) shepherd, and he will guide (us) to springs of living water, and God will wipe away every tear from (our) eyes' (Revelation 7:17).

## (11) Praise (13:15)

Central to the entire argument of Hebrews has been the once for all sacrifice of the Lord Jesus Christ upon the cross. However, in this latest verse applying things to the Christian life, we come now to the first of two sacrifices which Christians are to offer. They are, of course, of a very different nature from Jesus' sacrifice. The one drawn attention to in the present verse is *'a sacrifice of praise to God'*, while the one which follows in the next verse has to do with not neglecting 'to do good and to share what you have'.

*'Through him* [Jesus] *then let us continually offer up a sacrifice of praise to God'* (13:15). All those who are identified with Jesus 'outside the camp' and who 'bear the reproach he endured' are to respond in appropriate ways to such marvels of divine grace. It is reminiscent of the psalmist's great question, 'What shall I render to the LORD for all his benefits to me?' (Psalm 116:12). The answer given to that question here in Hebrews is that, approaching God through Jesus, 'the new and living way that he opened for us' (10:20), we are (our writer uses the inclusive *'let us'* again) to *'offer up* [heavenwards] *a sacrifice of praise to God'*, and we are to do this *'continually'* [not occasionally or spasmodically, but as a matter of constant habit and regular worship]. It is a matter of Christian duty, and not optional. This *'sacrifice of praise'* is a spiritual sacrifice and not one involving altars and blood— all those sacrifices, Hebrews has insisted, are well and truly finished

with. The apostle Peter speaks of it in 1 Peter 2:5, where he describes Christians as 'a holy priesthood, to offer spiritual sacrifices acceptable to God through Jesus Christ'.

This spiritual *'sacrifice of praise'* is defined here: *'that is, the fruit of lips that acknowledge* ('confessing, professing') *his name'*. This will involve sung praise (encompassing public worship, family worship and when on our own in the secret place), but will not be limited to this, as 13:16 will demonstrate. Both lips of praise and lives of praise are embraced. It is the lips of praise in view here, and the lives of praise which follow in the next verse. Jesus taught in the Sermon on the Mount that 'where your treasure is, there your heart will be also' (Matthew 6:21). If the Lord Jesus Christ is your treasure (and our writer is concerned lest he is becoming less so to the Hebrews), then your heart will be full of him. And, says Jesus, 'out of the abundance of the heart the mouth speaks' (Matthew 12:34).

The Psalms teem with one *'sacrifice of praise'* after another, with glorious statements such as 'Great is the Lord and greatly to be praised' (Psalm 48:1), 'Oh sing to the Lord a new song' (Psalm 96:1), 'Praise, O servants of the Lord, praise the name of the Lord' (Psalm 113:1), and 'I will give thanks, O Lord, with my whole heart' (Psalm 138:1). There is also David's beautiful testimony, which should find an echo from every Christian's heart and upon every Christian's lips, 'He put a new song in my mouth, a song of praise to our God' (Psalm 40:3). Heaven itself (our 'lasting city', 13:14) is, and ever will be, a world of praise.

## (12) Generosity (13:16)

This is the second of the two sacrifices mentioned here. Following the lips of praise (13:15), there comes now the lives of praise. Lips and lives are never to be separated from one another if our Christian life and testimony is to be truly consistent. *'Do not neglect to do good and to share what you have, for such sacrifices are pleasing to God'* (13:16).

It may strike us as unexpected to have doing good and sharing the things we have as a sacrifice. This is not in any way inappropriate, however, for all that we have comes from God and all that we are depends upon him. As we considered earlier when commenting upon the opening verses of this chapter, all who are members through grace of the church, the body of Christ, have both a solemn and cheerful responsibility for the mutual care of one another, and this is to spill over into a concern for those who do not belong to the family of God. In such a light, the language of our present verse should not be surprising at all.

The twinned call '*to do good and to share what you have*' is capable of as wide an application as can be put upon it. It may include, for example, spiritual encouragement, practical help, financial assistance, acts of kindness, and other such expressions of love and care. Some may involve considerable self-denial, but that is the way the Master went, and, as Jesus stated, 'A servant is not greater than his master' (John 15:20). The emphasis is laid by our writer upon Christian obligation; hence, '*Do not neglect*'.

Both the presentation of lips of praise and lives of praise are gathered together in the statement, '*for such sacrifices are pleasing to God*'. This is one of our highest motivations, to be '*pleasing to God*'. Romans 12:1 is relevant here. 'I appeal to you therefore, brothers, by the mercies of God, to present your bodies [representing our entire being, everything that we are and have] as a living sacrifice, holy and acceptable to God, which is your spiritual worship'. While worship is a specific activity (on the Lord's Day being the chief example), at the same time all of life is to be regarded as worship, on the basis of the fundamental principle, 'whatever you do, do all to the glory of God' (1 Corinthians 10:31).

## (13) Submission (13:17)

In 13:7 the Hebrews were exhorted to remember their leaders from past days, 'those who spoke to (them) the word of God'. They were to 'Consider the outcome of their way of life' (how their faith and preaching actually worked out in practice), and to 'imitate their faith'. We noted in our comments at that point that in verses 17 and 24 it would be their current leaders who would be spoken of. So it is, then, here.

'*Obey your leaders and submit to them*' (13:17). There are two particular dangers relating to this subject in the present times. One is for the whole New Testament concept of leadership in the church to be abandoned, on the basis that the exercise of authority is unhealthy or open to abuse, or that everyone can be a leader in their own way. The other is that leadership can be exercised in such a stifling way, that no one dares move without permission, thus allowing resentment to build up and fester. In the first instance, church discipline is an unknown feature of church life. In the second, discipline can be wrongly understood and incorrectly or insensitively applied. Both dangers need to be avoided. Whether or not our writer sensed that the Hebrews were in difficulty in this area, he is careful to address the matter in the present context of 13:1–19, and he does so in a way which, if heeded properly, should lead to the avoidance of both dangers touched upon above. He does so especially by making a careful distinction between the duties of pastors and people. Each of these duties is intended for the mutual benefit of all, both those who are called by God to lead and those who are called by him to be led.

Leaders are to lead and to be obeyed. The word translated here '*leaders*' is a participle, 'the ones leading'. They will be the ministers (pastors) and elders in the local church. They are, in leading, to do so as those who are themselves led—led by God through his word—and not as those who are 'doing their own thing'. They are themselves men under authority (and only men are allowed to lead in the church of God). It is a solemn thing to be called to lead, and no one must accept or exercise the role lightly.

Their particular task focused upon here is pastoral: '*for they are keeping watch over your souls, as those who will have to give an account*'. Interestingly, the phrase about '*keeping watch*' takes us back to that matchless and glorious occasion when the angels appeared to the shepherds when they were 'out in the field, keeping watch over their flock by night' (Luke 2:8). It speaks of heartfelt, tireless, affectionate, dutiful, earnest (and, when required, sleepless, for the verb '*keeping watch*' means 'to pass sleepless nights' or 'to go sleepless') concern for and care of the flock of God. Think of someone sitting up all night nursing a person requiring special care. Paul speaks of it most movingly in Acts 20:28. 'Pay careful attention to yourselves and all the flock, in which the Holy Spirit has made you overseers, to care for the church of God, which he obtained with his own blood'. Its model, without question, is Jesus the good shepherd, as set out in John 10.

This *'keeping watch over your souls'* has both an internal and an external aspect. From the outside, watch must be kept lest 'fierce wolves will come in among you, not sparing the flock' (Acts 20:29)—false doctrines, carnal influences, worldly pressures. From the inside, watch must be kept on how those of the flock are running the race (recall the great theme throughout chapter 12), their ups and downs, healths and weaknesses. And this must all be done in light of the momentous consequences of the work: *'as those who will have to give an account'.* The giving of account will take place at the last judgment, 'For we must all appear before the judgment seat of Christ, so that each one may receive what is due for what he has done in the body, whether good or evil' (2 Corinthians 5:10). This is a sobering prospect, intended to stir up and keep to the mark all to whom God gives authority in his church. Their responsibility is for the flock, but their answerability is to God.

This same truth should be equally sobering for those who are led. Those to whom God gives rule in the church are not those who have taken it upon themselves (or it certainly should not be such—recall the detailed argument of 5:4–5), but those who have been called and set apart to it by God. They are *his* men. Hence the call to *'Obey'* and *'submit'.* The two verbs complement each other. Together they convey the sense of responding trustingly, confidently and yieldingly. Yet this is not to be performed in a grudging manner, through clenched teeth, with a cold heart. Rather, *'Let them do this with joy and not with groaning, for that would be of no advantage* ('without profit') *to you'.* It would be profitless because a *'groaning'* and unresponsive congregation is no encouragement to those who lead it, and consequently will not issue in benefit to those who are cared for by them. So let them demonstrate love and prayerful concern for those who shepherd them, a thankfulness to God for them, and a readiness to receive from them all the good things of the word of God. Just as ministers and elders *'have to give an account'*, so do the people among whom they serve. As Paul puts it to the Thessalonians, 'For what is our hope or joy or crown of boasting before our Lord Jesus Christ at his coming? Is it not you? For you are our glory and joy' (1 Thessalonians 2:19–20).

The happiest relationship between those who lead in the church and those who are led is when both responsibilities are being engaged in with joy—joyful shepherds and joyful sheep, joyful pastoring and joyful being pastored. Where this is not the case, the Lord Jesus Christ, the head of the church, will not be honoured, and where the Lord Jesus is not honoured in his church, blessing will not be enjoyed.

## (14) Prayerfulness (13:18–19)

This major applied section dealing with living the Christian life consistently rounds off with an important word upon prayer. It follows on naturally from the previous verse on pastors and people, and includes a personal reference from our writer to himself.

*'Pray for us, for we are sure that we have a clear conscience, desiring to act honourably in all things'* (13:18). Notice the *'us'* and the *'we'*. Who is the writer associating with himself here? We cannot give any names, for none are supplied, but it is a fair assumption to take the reference as being to the folk mentioned in verse 24 who send their greetings from Italy. It is not the first time that he has used the plural (compare, 'About this we have much to say', 5:11; 'Though we speak in this way', 6:9; 'And we desire each one of you', 6:11). The fact that prayer is desired and requested from the Hebrews is another indication that he who writes to them has not abandoned hope of their genuineness as Christians, but continues to hope that they will prove to be 'of those who have faith and preserve their souls' (10:39).

Similar requests for prayer are familiar from the apostle Paul. Examples are found towards the end of several of his epistles. In the light of the teaching we have just considered in 13:17, this demonstrates how one of the best and most spiritual ways to oil the wheels of pastor-people relationships in the local church is by a deep mutual concern for one another expressed practically in prayer. If the pastor does not pray for the people, or the people do not pray for the pastor, things are very far from well. We all need to pray, and we all need to be prayed for.

The mention of having *'a clear conscience'* indicates that in all his dealings with them the author has the assurance of such 'toward both God and man' (Acts 24:16). Whatever anyone either says of him or thinks of him, his conscience is clear concerning the truth and sincerity of all that he has written and the spirit in which he has written it. It is interesting to compare this with Paul's statement to Timothy: 'The aim of our charge is love that issues from a pure heart and a good conscience and a sincere faith' (1 Timothy 1:5).

The further remark, *'desiring to act honourably in all things'*, bears directly upon the matter of the *'clear conscience'*. In all that he has written, he has exemplified the principle of Proverbs 27:6, 'Faithful are the wounds of a friend; profuse are the kisses of an enemy', for he is very much their friend, desiring their spiritual wellbeing (that is, their growth in grace and progress in the faith). This being so, he has not held back from saying all that is needful. Our writer is no false shepherd, but rather one who 'will seek the lost, ... bring back the strayed, ... bind up the injured, and ... strengthen the weak' (Ezekiel 34:16). He desires that he and those mentioned along with him would themselves be like the leaders of old (13:7), whose 'way of life' and 'faith' was worth considering and imitating.

He then reverts to the personal *'I'* in his next exhortation. *'I urge you the more earnestly to do this in order that I may be restored to you the sooner'* (13:19). Not only does he desire them to pray for him, but he is keen to be reunited with them as soon as possible as well. This establishes beyond question the close relationship that existed between the writer of Hebrews and the recipients of it, and underscores the pastoral tone that has been present throughout. Had he been one of their leaders at some point? If so, we do not know what accounts for him not still being so and led him to be writing to them from elsewhere. The verb *'restored'* suggests a real closeness between them. His heart is very much towards them, and the desire of that heart is very much to be with them and to see them again.

## The closing benediction (13:20–21)

Things are rapidly drawing to the close of this magnificent New Testament book, yet even these final verses are full of riches. As we approach them, it is delightful to note that, having just sought the prayers of the Hebrews on his own and others' behalf, our writer now brings them before the Lord himself. Here is an excellent illustration of the matter commented upon above—both pastor and people praying for one another. Surely the Lord is pleased to hear such prayers, and to answer them to his own glory.

'*Now may the God of peace who brought again from the dead our Lord Jesus*' (13:20). The name ascribed here to God is very revealing. It is a divine name which appears in a number of magnificent statements at or towards the end of several of Paul's epistles, as well as here in Hebrews. That on its own is not sufficient to assert that Paul must have written Hebrews, even if it may justifiably be included among the arguments put forward by those who are persuaded that he did. What it does do is play a part in demonstrating the unity of Scripture's portrayal of the doctrine of God.

God is '*the God of peace*' in a manifold sense. He is the holy God who, though offended with our sins, has in divine mercy and amazing grace made for us with himself 'peace by the blood of his [Jesus'] cross' (Colossians 1:20). In the gospel, 'since we have been justified by faith, we have peace with God through our Lord Jesus Christ' (Romans 5:1). In the comforting language of Philippians 4:7, 'the peace of God which surpasses all understanding, will guard (our) hearts and (our) minds in Christ Jesus'.

This name of God is one of the finest examples of relating who he is to what he has done for us. As for what that is that God has done for us his people, sinners saved by grace, our writer immediately cites the resurrection—'*who brought again from the dead our Lord Jesus*'. The words '*our Lord Jesus*' come at the end of the sentence in the original, as a kind of climactic emphasis. He it is, of course, who is the one whom the Father has *'brought again from the dead'*. If it be asked as to why Jesus' resurrection is chosen for mention rather than his death, Romans 4:25 provides the answer: 'who was delivered up for our trespasses and raised for our justification'. Although they were separate and distinct events, they belong inextricably together. In that sense, either one may be drawn attention to, yet stand for them both. On the cross, Jesus effected our reconciliation with the Father. By his resurrection, the Father expressed his complete approval of Jesus' finished and all-sufficient sacrifice. Had Jesus not died, he could not have risen. Had he not risen, he would still be dead, death would have had dominion over him, and he would not have ascended into heaven and 'sat down at the right hand of the Majesty on high' (1:3).

Yet the verse goes deeper still. Firstly, Jesus is spoken of as *'the great shepherd of the sheep'*. The shepherd imagery is found across Scripture in connection with God, and, not least, in connection with Jesus, the second person of the Godhead. In John 10:11 he is, in his own words, 'the good shepherd' who 'lays down his life for the sheep'. In 1 Peter 5:4 he is 'the chief shepherd' who, when he appears, will give 'the unfading crown of glory' to faithful elders who in his name 'shepherd the flock of God' (1 Peter 5:2). Here in 13:20 he is *'the great shepherd'*, the one who stands alone, the one beyond compare. Here we are again, still at the very heart of the central theme of Hebrews, namely, the absolute and complete superiority and supremacy of the Lord Jesus Christ. Our writer has not budged on this all the way through, and he is not going to do so now.

Secondly, his blood which he shed at Calvary and which was so pleasing to the Father for his satisfaction and for our salvation is spoken of as *'by the blood of the eternal covenant'*. This immediately strikes us as classic Hebrews language. It has chapters like 9 and 10 written all over it. 9:15 presented Jesus as 'the mediator of a new covenant', and that covenant is *'the eternal covenant'* by which is secured to us 'the promised eternal inheritance'. It was not made in time but in eternity by the everlasting God, and its blessings last to all eternity. 'Eternal' is one of the big words in Hebrews. We have read of our 'eternal salvation' (5:9), 'eternal judgment' (6:2), 'eternal redemption' (9:12), 'the eternal Spirit' (9:14) and (just mentioned) 'the promised eternal inheritance' (9:15). There is a strong sense of all these being gathered in together now as part and parcel of *the eternal covenant*.

So, seeking this benediction upon the people in the name of the God of verse 20, our writer now proceeds to describe the blessings sought. They pertain to the Lord fulfilling his purpose for them and working his pleasure in them. He desires for them that God would *equip you with everything good that you may do his will, working in us that which is pleasing in his sight'* (13:21). The relationship between the two verses is that in verse 20 our writer focuses upon God's work through Jesus for us, while in verse 21 his companion focus is upon God's work in us as believers, as a result of our reconciliation through the Lord Jesus.

The equipping of the Hebrews *'with everything good'* in order to do God's will means the perfecting of them, in terms of their increasing conformity to that will, so that nothing remains which is out of joint with it or opposed to it. The accompanying petition on the Hebrews' behalf that God would be *'working in us that which is pleasing in his sight'* confirms this and takes it a little further. We might express it in this way: the more we are made like Jesus, then the more we shall do God's will, and the more will God be pleased with what he sees in us. It has to do, ultimately, with holiness, Christ-likeness, and echoes the call to pursue 'the holiness without which no one will see the Lord' (12:14). We must pursue it, but only God can produce it, *'working in us'*.

We are reminded of Philippians 2:12–13, 'work out your own salvation with fear and trembling, for it is God who works in you, both to will and to work for his good pleasure'. When himself in the world, Jesus declared, 'for I always do the things that are pleasing to him [God the Father]' (John 8:29). We do well to learn from this that God's will is always what *'is pleasing in his sight'*, and cannot possibly ever be anything which is not. Scripture teaches us precisely what pleases him and what does not, and it is our business to discover what God says there to us, the Holy Spirit being our divine teacher.

How does God perform this work? The answer is, just like everything else in respect of 'such a great salvation' (2:3)—'*through Jesus Christ, to whom* [the reference here is very likely to God the Father, in the light of verse 15 and the beginning of verse 20—although glory belongs to Jesus as God the Son, and so it may be addressed to them jointly] *be glory forever and ever. Amen*'. These words form a very fitting doxology to end this fulsome benediction.

## Parting words and greetings (13:22-25)

We remarked when embarking upon this final chapter that we would not have been surprised if Hebrews had finished at the end of chapter 12. In the event, it does not. We may now go on to say that we would not have been surprised if it had finished with 13:21, at the end of the benediction and doxology. Once again, it does not. Yet the final few verses that remain are in no sense 'add ons'. They bring a further personal note to Hebrews (whether we call it a letter or a book, and it can properly be termed either), and round things off very appropriately and warmly. We shall see that the way the writer does eventually close the letter could not possibly be improved upon.

'*I appeal to you, brothers, bear with my word of exhortation, for I have written to you briefly*' (13:22). The word '*briefly*' (literally, 'through few words') has come in for some comment down the days, not least along the lines of if Hebrews is to be considered brief, what might an extended version have been like? Yet considering the weight of the subject matter, the depth of the doctrine, the fullness of the application, the author has written '*briefly*'. Volumes could have been penned, whereas in the event everything has been compacted into what, for us, is thirteen chapters and what, for the Hebrews themselves, could be read out to them at a sitting.

We have just remarked above over whether Hebrews is best considered as a letter or a book. It really does not matter at all, though the '*I have written*' suits well the concept of a personal letter, from 'him' to 'them'. The writer himself calls it *'my word of exhortation* [the word incorporates both challenge and comfort, both warning and encouragement]*'*. That is how he sees it. That is the motive with which he writes. He desires to exhort the recipients—to exhort them to hold fast to Jesus, to cleave to the gospel, to endure to the end, and not to step back in time into the old regulations, sacrifices and ways, not to commit apostasy. And he does so in an affectionate pastoral manner: *'I appeal to you, brothers, bear with'* me in this, give me a fair hearing, take notice of what I write, be sure to take it to heart, for there is nothing more serious or more needful that I could write than this. The verse could be rendered along the lines of 'I urge you, brothers, to bear with my urging', or 'I beseech you, brothers, to bear with my beseeching'. Hebrews has a passion about it, and rightly so, and is written very much from a brother to brothers (and sisters) in Christ.

*'You should know that our brother Timothy has been released, with whom I shall see you if he comes soon'* (13:23). We know Timothy from elsewhere in the New Testament, and especially in connection with the apostle Paul. There is no reason to assume that the Timothy mentioned here in Hebrews is a different man. Clearly he was known to both writer and recipients, hence *'our brother Timothy'*. They will no doubt be delighted to hear the news of his release from prison. We cannot determine at what point this being in custody happened in Timothy's life, but the reason for it will very likely have been his faithful profession of Jesus and adherence to the gospel. The hope is held out here by our writer that both he and the newly released Timothy will be able to visit the Hebrews together *'soon'*. This prospect of a pending visit from the writer of Hebrews might itself be a further incentive to them to give serious attention to all that he has taken time to write to them.

*'Greet all your leaders and all the saints'* (13:24). In other words, our writer sends Christian greetings to the entire company of those to whom this letter is written, the whole church as a family—*'all your leaders'* (those mentioned in verse 17) and *'all the saints'* (every one of you, no one omitted). The description of Christians as *'saints'* is very

appropriate, and provides a challenging reminder to all believers that we are to be separated ones (belonging to Jesus) and sanctified ones (becoming like Jesus). When writing to the Christians in Rome, Paul addresses them as 'To all those in Rome who are loved by God and called to be saints' (Romans 1:7). Talking of Rome makes us think of Italy, which is mentioned next.

*'Those who come from Italy send you greetings'.* We have no way of knowing who these Italian brethren were, or whether they were actually in Italy at the time of writing or had some former association with that country. Neither does it shed any conclusive light upon where Hebrews was written from. What we do see is that these warm greetings form a choice description of what it is like to be united in gospel bonds. Noteworthy also is the likelihood that many (though not necessarily all) of these Italian brethren will have been Gentiles; and here they are, sending their greetings to the Hebrews who, we understand, had come to Christ out of Judaism. A lovely example of Ephesians 2:16, with its teaching in the context there of Jesus, by his death, reconciling 'both [Jew and Gentile alike] to God in one body'.

*'Grace be with all of you'* (13:25). There could be no finer way of concluding this great book than this. It is very similar to the way the entire New Testament (and, thereby, the whole Bible) concludes (Revelation 22:21). Divine grace encompasses everything for us. It is by grace that we are saved. It is by grace that we are kept. It is by grace that we are sanctified. It is by grace that we endure. It is by grace that we shall be glorified. There are no limits to what divine grace may do. This is the divine grace by which Jesus tasted 'death for everyone' (2:9). This is the divine grace spoken of so magnificently in 4:16, 'Let us then with confidence draw near to the throne of grace, that we may receive mercy and find grace to help in time of need'. This is the divine grace concerning which the Hebrews are urged, 'See to it that no one fails to obtain the grace of God' (12:15). This is the divine grace of which our writer says, 'for it is good for the heart to be strengthened by grace' (13:9).

*'Grace'* always comes through the Lord Jesus Christ. He is its channel. And it is the Lord Jesus Christ who, from the very beginning

of Hebrews, has been central to all that has been written. The focus, as we have seen time and time again, is upon his supremacy, his superiority, his pre-eminence, his all-sufficiency. Our writer ends as he began, with Jesus, the one whose name truly (and everlastingly) is the name high over all.